SECURED TRANSACTIONS

TEACHING MATERIALS

Second Edition

By

James J. White

Professor of Law
University of Michigan Law School

AMERICAN CASEBOOK SERIES®

THOMSON

WEST

American Casebook Series, and West Group
are registered trademarks used herein under license.

COPYRIGHT © 2000 WEST GROUP
COPYRIGHT © 2002 By WEST GROUP
            610 Opperman Drive
            P.O. Box 64526
            St. Paul, MN 55164–0526
            1–800–328–9352

ISBN 0–314–14403–X

TEXT IS PRINTED ON 10% POST
CONSUMER RECYCLED PAPER

FOREWORD

Teaching the rules of Article 9 is only one of the purposes of this book. The student should regard this book and any course in which it is used as an opportunity to examine the economic and commercial reasons for many of the practices that underlie Article 9. This is also an opportunity to learn the nomenclature of secured credit and commercial law. At the end of this course the student should understand the terms "nonrecourse loans", "securitization", "cramdown" and a variety of others that are the everyday fare of commercial lawyers. The student should also have an idea why one might make a recourse as opposed to a nonrecourse loan. Finally, the book introduces the student to some of the forms that are used in secured transactions.

The book focuses on 1999 Article 9. It does so in the belief that the student can learn only a limited amount in a course of this kind and that new law is more important than old. Since all the cases were decided prior to the adoption of 1999 Article 9, some exposure to former Article 9 is inevitable, but the materials deal with that Article only to the extent necessary to explain 1999 Article 9. When students are confronted with intricate questions in practice, it will be soon enough to dig deeply into pre-1999 law.

The book is organized by transactions (Security in Equipment, Security in Inventory, etc.) not by Article 9 events (scope, attachment, perfection). I believe this facilitates learning about the underlying transactions. It also enables the teacher to lead the student into the shallow end of the pool by first dealing with a relatively simple transaction—the security interest in equipment. This book is sparse (much is omitted) but it deals with some highly sophisticated transactions, such as securitization and repo transactions.

Chapter 7 deals with bankruptcy. One can take as little or as much as one wishes from the bankruptcy chapter. It can serve as a mere tincture of avoidance power or as a full immersion into some of the most complex provisions in Chapter 11.

Good Luck.

James J. White
Ann Arbor, 2002

*

ACKNOWLEDGEMENTS

I wish to thank Jeffrey Kayes '00, Christopher Liro '00, Manjari (Kiki) Purkayastha '01, Robert Waldner '00 and Jon-Micheal Wheat '04 for their research assistance and Janis Proctor for her secretarial support.

*

Summary of Contents

*

Table of Contents

*

Table of Cases

The principal cases are in bold type. Cases cited or discussed in the text are roman type. References are to pages. Cases cited in principal cases and within other quoted materials are not included.

SECURED TRANSACTIONS

TEACHING MATERIALS

Second Edition

*

Chapter One

SECURITY IN BUSINESS EQUIPMENT

§ 1. INTRODUCTION

In this chapter, we study the simplest and most straightforward of all security interests in personal property: a security interest taken by a seller or a financial institution in the equipment of a business. This equipment might be construction equipment, automobiles, business machines, or a variety of other personal property, such as office furniture, and the like.

The loan against business equipment is different from a typical inventory loan. The inventory loan is often a "line of credit" on which the debtor draws and pays down. The inventory loan will be outstanding for an indefinite period, rising and falling with the debtor's need for new inventory. In a classic equipment loan, the loan is paid down over a period of time; it gradually and continually decreases to zero. In the typical equipment loan, the debtor and creditor will sign a written security agreement. This agreement must meet the conditions in section 9–203, but those are easy to meet, and even a banker or lawyer with limited understanding of Article 9 can easily draft an adequate security agreement. Almost always, perfection occurs by the filing of a financing statement that complies with 9–502, et seq.

To see a financing statement form, look at section 9–521; note how skeletal this document is. It need only identify the debtor, the creditor, and the collateral. It is not signed by anyone. And while it is possible to do it wrong (especially to get the debtor's name wrong), it is simple and usually easy to complete, particularly in a basic transaction like a business equipment loan.

Having lent money to the debtor, having had the debtor sign a security agreement, and having filed a financing statement, the creditor is a perfected secured creditor entitled to priority over lien creditors, particularly the trustee in bankruptcy, and in general over later secured creditors, and even over buyers in good faith.

1

First, we consider attachment requirements of 9–203, perfection requirements of 9–502 et. seq., and errors one may commit in fulfilling each. We will then consider the legal rights enjoyed by the perfected secured creditor and look at the particular sections that grant priority. In addition, we will consider several practical and economic alternatives to a security interest in business equipment. These include finance leases, governed by Section 2A of the Uniform Commercial Code, leases that are not finance leases but are nevertheless covered by Article 2A, and, finally, documents titled "leases," that under section 1–201(37) are security agreements. To consider those questions, we will deal with a complicated problem, and a complicated case, Lykes Brothers.

Also, we consider alternatives to the security agreement, such as the "negative pledge clause." A negative pledge clause is a promise by the debtor not to grant security to any other person and has some of the practical consequences of a security interest. Finally, we consider the secured creditor's rights upon the debtor's default.

§ 2. MAKING AN ENFORCEABLE SECURITY INTEREST

How does a secured party create an enforceable Article 9 security interest? Section 9–203 requires only a few steps: (1) the creditor must give value, (2) the debtor must have rights in the collateral, (3) there must be a security agreement, (4) the security agreement must describe the collateral, and (5) either the security agreement must be in a writing signed by the debtor or there must be some other "authenticating" event, as described in 9–203(b)(3), to provide grounds for concluding that the parties have entered into a security agreement. There might, for example, be an authenticated security agreement that was not in writing. Under 9–102(a)(7)(b) one might authenticate security by putting it in a "record" and adopting a symbol, or there might be some other substitute for a writing such as the creditor's taking possession under 9–313, the creditor's taking "delivery" of certificated securities under 8–301, or the creditor's achieving "control" over certain kinds of collateral.

Nine times out of ten an enforceable security interest will arise from a loan or extension of credit by the creditor to the debtor (value), the debtor's ownership of the collateral (rights in the collateral), and a written agreement that describes the collateral and is signed by the debtor (9–203(b)(3)(A)). The remaining cases involve no signed writing but only possession by the creditor, an electronic record or control. Consider how little suffices to bind the debtor. For example, it is enough for the debtor to write on the back of an envelope, "I hereby grant bank a security interest in my cattle, John Jones". If the bank makes a loan and the debtor owns the cattle, the parties have created a valid security interest despite its informality.

Section 9–203 reads in part as follows:

(a) [Attachment.] A security interest attaches to collateral when it becomes enforceable against the debtor with respect to the collateral, unless an agreement expressly postpones the time of attachment.

(b) [Enforceability.] Except as otherwise provided in subsections (c) through (i), a security interest is enforceable against the debtor and third parties with respect to the collateral only if :

(1) value has been given;

(2) the debtor has rights in the collateral or the power to transfer rights in the collateral to a secured party; and

(3) one of the following conditions is met:

(A) the debtor has authenticated a security agreement that provides a description of the collateral and, if the security interest covers timber to be cut, a description of the land concerned;

(B) the collateral is not a certificated security and is in the possession of the secured party under section 9–313 pursuant to the debtor's security agreement;

(C) the collateral is a certificated security in registered form and the security certificate has been delivered to the secured party under section 8–301 pursuant to the debtor's security agreement; or

(D) the collateral is deposit accounts, electronic chattel paper, investment property, or letter-of-credit rights, and the secured party has control under section 9–104, 9–105, 9–106 and 9–107 pursuant to the debtor's security agreement.

* * *

(f) [Proceeds and supporting obligations.] The attachment of a security interest in collateral gives the secured party the rights to proceeds provided by section 9–315 and is also attachment of a security interest in a supporting obligation for the collateral.

(g) [Lien securing right to payment.] The attachment of a security interest in a right to payment or performance secured by a security interest or other lien on personal or real property is also attachment of a security interest in the security interest, mortgage, or other lien.

No secured creditor willingly enters into a commercial security arrangement without a written security agreement (or electronic record). Nevertheless, occasional creditors find themselves unable to put their hands on a signed agreement when trouble comes, months or years after the agreement was concluded. These creditors have to argue that various scraps of paper, some signed by the debtor and some not, together constitute a security agreement that satisfies 9–203. The two cases that follow deal with these issues.

IN THE MATTER OF A–1 PAVING AND CONTRACTING, INC., APPEAL OF THE PEOPLES STATE BANK

United States Court of Appeals, Seventh Circuit, 1997.
116 F.3d 242.

KANNE, CIRCUIT JUDGE:

A–1 Paving and Contracting Inc. filed for Chapter 11 bankruptcy. Port Royal Aggregates Inc., claiming a security interest in specific equipment and vehicles of A–1, sought termination of the automatic stay order and asked for abandonment of those assets from the bankruptcy estate. Peoples State Bank, asserting a security interest in the same assets, intervened and objected to Port Royal's request.

The bankruptcy court determined that Port Royal had a valid purchase money security interest in the assets in question. The court, therefore, terminated the automatic stay order and abandoned the specified assets from the bankruptcy estate. On appeal the district court affirmed the bankruptcy court's grant of relief from the stay and order of abandonment.

As did the courts below, we find that the Indiana Supreme Court case of Gibson County Farm Bureau Co-op. Ass'n, Inc. v. Greer, 643 N.E.2d 313 (Ind.1994), controls and that Port Royal held a valid purchase money security interest in equipment and vehicles sold to A–1 by way of a Conditional Sales Contract. We thus affirm.

I. HISTORY

In late August 1992, Port Royal entered into a Conditional Sales Contract with A–1 for the sale of equipment and motor vehicles. These assets were purchased by A–1 for use with its asphalt and aggregate businesses. The purchase price of these assets was to be paid by A–1 in monthly installments to Port Royal. Paragraph 23 of the Conditional Sales Contract reserved to Port Royal "all rights and remedies under the Indiana Uniform Commercial Code relating to the foreclosure of mortgages."

Following the formation of the Conditional Sales Contract, Port Royal filed a UCC–1 financing statement with the Indiana Secretary of State and with the Morgan County and Johnson County Recorders. The financing statement lists A–1 as the "debtor" and Port Royal as the "secured party." This financing statement reveals the existence of a separate document, identified as "Exhibit B," which provides a description of the equipment and vehicles being transferred under the Conditional Sales Contract. Exhibit B was attached to the financing statement. Port Royal maintained title to all the collateral transferred under the Conditional Sales Contract while A–1 gained physical possession of the collateral.

A–1 defaulted on the payments due Port Royal under the Conditional Sales Contract and subsequently filed for Chapter 11 bankruptcy on September 13, 1994. Later that month, another of A–1's creditors, State Bank, intervened in A–1's bankruptcy proceeding. On December 1, Port Royal sought to gain access to the assets in which it claimed title and interest by filing with the bankruptcy court an "Application for Order Terminating the Automatic Stay, for Abandonment of the Automatic Stay and for Adequate Protection." The bankruptcy court held a hearing on February 24, 1995. At that time, A–1 announced its intent to convert from Chapter 11 to Chapter 7, thus eliminating the issue of reorganization. The bankruptcy court then heard evidence on Port Royal's request. On March 16, the bankruptcy court issued its findings of fact and conclusions of law. The court determined that Port Royal had a valid security interest concerning the collateral identified in the UCC–1 financing statement and that it therefore was entitled to relief from the automatic stay and abandonment of the relevant assets from A–1's bankruptcy estate. The district court affirmed the decision of the bankruptcy court and the State Bank appealed to this court.

II. ANALYSIS

In an appeal from a bankruptcy court's decision, we use the same standard of review used by the district court below: the bankruptcy court's findings of fact are upheld unless clearly erroneous and the legal conclusions are reviewed de novo. In re Marrs–Winn Co., 103 F.3d 584, 589 (7th Cir.1996).

We consider a single issue in this case—whether, under Indiana law, Port Royal and A–1 created a valid security interest in the assets that Port Royal contracted to sell to A–1. We must decide this case using principles of Indiana law because "Congress has generally left the determination of property rights in the assets of a bankrupt's estate to state law." Butner v. United States, 440 U.S. 48, 54, 99 S.Ct. 914, 918, 59 L.Ed.2d 136 (1979). Our task is made easier because in Gibson County, the Indiana Supreme Court was presented with a case that is quite similar to the facts and issue presented here. In Gibson County, Indiana's highest court held that a properly-filed UCC–1 financing statement may create an effective security interest under Article 9 of Indiana's Uniform Commercial Code if that financing statement meets the formal writing requirements under § 9–203(1) and the finder of fact determines that the parties intended the financing statement to serve as a security interest. 643 N.E.2d at 320.

In Gibson County, a farm products supplier extended credit to a farmer upon a promise to repay and the execution of a financing statement by the farmer. The financing statement 1) was signed by the debtor, 2) identified the farm products supplier as the secured party, and 3) identified the collateral. Id. at 314–15. When the farm products supplier sought to recover proceeds from the sale of the same collateral, a judgment creditor (Gibson County Farm Bureau) claimed an interest superior to the farm products supplier. The trial court determined that the farm products supplier held a valid security interest in the collateral and was entitled to the proceeds. Id. at 315.

The Indiana Court of Appeals reversed, but the Indiana Supreme Court affirmed the trial court. The Indiana Supreme Court indicated that the sole issue was whether the supplier held a valid security interest in the collateral; and that the resolution of that issue depended on whether the UCC–1 financing statement, properly filed with the county recorder, also served effectively as a security agreement. Id. at 315–16.

In resolving this issue, the court held that "[a]lthough we are not willing to go so far as to hold that a standard-form UCC–1 financing statement alone is, as a matter of law, sufficient evidence that the parties intended to create a security interest, we do hold that once the Writing Requirement of § 9–203(1) is satisfied, whether the parties intended the writing to create a security interest is a question of fact for the trier of fact to determine." Id. at 320.

In reaching this decision, the Indiana Supreme Court explicitly adopted the approach recommended by White & Summers, which provides:

> Ordinarily, the writing which satisfies the objective statute of frauds requirement above [section 9–203(1)(a)] will also be sufficient proof of an actual intention to create such an interest in the first place. But in problem cases, the writing may barely meet the objective test and no more, leaving for further factual inquiry the question whether the parties also actually intended to create a security interest. Parol evidence is admissible to inform this second inquiry, but not the first. Id. (citing White & Summers, Uniform Commercial Code § 24–5 at 300 (2d ed.1988)).

Gibson County set forth a test requiring both a legal and a factual inquiry to determine if the parties intended a particular writing to create a security interest. In the present case, neither party disputes that the UCC–1 financing statement filed by Port Royal, as a matter of law, satisfies the writing requirement of § 9–203. We therefore may proceed directly to the factual inquiry: Did A–1 and Port Royal actually intend the financing statement to create a security interest? Typically, such an issue of fact is resolved by the bankruptcy court's finding. See In re Krause, 114 B.R. 582, 593–94 (Bankr.N.D.Ind.1988) ("Whether * * * the agreement satisfies the threshold statute of frauds requirement * * * is a question of law for the court. The factual issue of whether * * * there was an underlying contractual intent to create a security agreement is a question of fact.").

State Bank argues that "no finding was made, and no evidence was offered, which shows that [Port Royal] and A–1 intended to create [a] security interest in the financing statement." A review of the bankruptcy court's opinion, however, squarely contradicts State Bank's assertion. First, within the "Findings of Fact" section of the opinion, the bankruptcy court stated that "[t]he Conditional Sales Contract, at paragraph 23 * * * reserved to the seller all rights and remedies under the Indiana

Uniform Commercial Code relating to foreclosures of mortgages. In addition, the Conditional Sales Contract speaks to liens upon motor vehicles transferred under the contract." In Re: A–1 Paving & Contracting, Inc., No. 94–06792–FJO–11, at 2 (S.D.Ind. March 16, 1995) (Judge Otte). The Conditional Sales Contract served as strong evidence suggesting that the parties intended their agreement to be governed by the security interest regulations of the UCC.

Another of the court's factual findings explained that "[a] UCC Financing Statement was filed with the Indiana Secretary of State and with the Morgan County Recorder and Johnson County Recorder. A certified copy of the Financing Statement filed with the Indiana Secretary of State was introduced into evidence without objection. The Financing Statement refers to Port Royal as a secured party and A–1 as a Debtor and refers to the equipment and vehicles being transferred under the Conditional Sales Contract as collateral." Id. Finally, the court concluded that "[a]fter review of the Conditional Sales Contract, the Financing Statement executed by the Debtor and the conduct of the parties both during and following the transaction, this [c]ourt finds * * * that the parties intended the transaction to be a secured transaction, with Port Royal maintaining a purchase money security interest in all equipment and vehicles transferred under the Conditional Sales Contract as collateral for payments called for under the Conditional Sales Contract." Id. at 3.

Thus, contrary to State Bank's claim, the bankruptcy court unquestionably found that A–1 and Port Royal intended the financing statement to create a security interest. The factual findings of the bankruptcy court are based on parol evidence as well as the UCC–1 financing statement itself—both of which are permissible sources of evidence to determine that the parties intended to create a security interest. Consequently, not only were there findings made, but those findings were not in error.

Because we have concluded that the bankruptcy court made the appropriate legal and factual determinations consistent with Gibson County, it should therefore come as no surprise that we also agree with the bankruptcy and district courts that the UCC–1 financing statement filed by Port Royal and A–1 created a valid secured interest and the relief sought by Port Royal was properly granted.

Accordingly, the opinion of the district court is hereby AFFIRMED.

IN RE VIC SUPPLY CO., INC.

United States Court of Appeals, Seventh Circuit, 2000.
227 F.3d 928.

POSNER, CIRCUIT JUDGE:

This case involves a dispute between two creditors of the bankrupt Vic Supply Company. Bank One had a security agreement with Vic, covering all of Vic's assets. Falconbridge sold Vic nickel for resale, acquiring a purchase money security interest covering the proceeds of the resale. The bankruptcy court, seconded by the district court, to which Falconbridge had appealed, ruled that Bank One's security interest was prior to Falconbridge's under Article 9 of the Uniform Commercial Code (codified in Illinois as 810 ILCS 5/9). Falconbridge argues that its interest is prior because the security agreement between the bank and Vic was never accepted by the bank. The argument turns on whether a secured lender's failure to sign such an agreement, when the agreement provides that it is effective only when signed by the lender, allows a subsequent secured lender to take priority over the earlier one.

The bank began lending money to Vic in 1980, and that year it filed a UCC financing statement with the Secretary of State of Illinois covering all of Vic's inventory, accounts receivable, and equipment. The statement implied that the parties had or intended soon to make an agreement granting the bank a security interest in these assets, the purpose of filing such a statement being to perfect such an interest. The UCC does not require, for a security interest to be perfected, that the security agreement precede the filing of the financing statement, § 9–402, let alone that it be attached to the statement (the statement "indicates merely that the secured party who has filed may have a security interest in the collateral described," § 9–402, official comment 2; see In re Varney Wood Products, Inc., 458 F.2d 435 (4th Cir.1972)), although that is often done; and we do not know the agreement's terms.

Ten years later, with the bank continuing to extend credit to Vic, Vic signed another agreement, granting the bank a continuing security interest in all Vic's assets. The agreement expressly covered—what was anyway implicit, § 9–306(2)—the proceeds of sales from inventory. A few months earlier the bank had filed with the Illinois Secretary of State a continuation financing statement materially identical to the one filed back in 1980.

Years passed, and Falconbridge, having obtained a purchase money security interest in the nickel that it was selling to Vic, filed a financing statement, just as Bank One had done. This security interest, like Bank One's, automatically extended to the proceeds of Vic's resale of the nickel. When Vic later defaulted, Bank One's security interest, having been recorded before Falconbridge's, would normally have had priority, § 9–312(5)(a); Falconbridge was not entitled to the superpriority that is accorded to a purchase money security interest when the debtor receives cash proceeds in a sale of the collateral, § 9–312(3), because the proceeds that Vic received were in the form of accounts receivable rather than cash.

But Bank One had failed to sign the 1990 security agreement, and Falconbridge argues that this failure means that the agreement did not become effective. The agreement provides that "the terms and provisions of this agreement shall not become effective and Bank shall have no duties hereunder unless and until this agreement is accepted by Bank as provided below"—and below is a blank for a signature that was never filled in. Falconbridge reminds us that "a security agreement is effective according to its terms between the parties, against purchasers of the collateral and against creditors." UCC § 9–201. "According to its terms," Falconbridge argues, the agreement never came into effect. Although the agreement authorizes the bank to fill in any blanks in it, the bank had not done that; and according to Falconbridge, it was too late for the bank to do so once Falconbridge perfected its own security interest by filing a UCC financing statement. In short, Falconbridge argues, the bank had no security interest when Falconbridge acquired its own security interest.

Ordinarily, only a party (actual or alleged) to a contract can challenge its validity, e.g., Williams v. Eggleston, 170 U.S. 304, 309, 18 S.Ct. 617, 42 L.Ed. 1047 (1898); IDS Life Insurance Co. v. SunAmerica, Inc., 103 F.3d 524, 529 (7th Cir.1996); Ope Shipping Ltd. v. Allstate Ins. Co., 687 F.2d 639, 643 (2d Cir.1982); Tri–Star Pictures, Inc. v. Leisure Time Productions, B.V., 749 F.Supp. 1243, 1250 (S.D.N.Y.1990), and neither party to the security agreement that is at issue in this case—neither Bank One nor Vic—challenges the validity of the agreement. Of course there are illegal contracts that the government, or persons injured by the contract, can challenge, such as a contract in restraint of trade, but there is no suggestion of that here. Obviously the fact that a third party would be better off if a contract were unenforceable does not give him standing to sue to void the contract. A contract that while not unenforceable by either party, or within the class of contracts deemed illegal, might, intentionally or negligently, deceive a third party, who in that event might have a tort remedy. But there is no suggestion that the defect in the bank's security agreement with Vic—the absence of the bank's signature—harmed Falconbridge. So far as appears, Falconbridge was unaware of the defect or of anything else about the agreement. It knew, or at least thought, there was an agreement, because before extending credit to Vic it checked the UCC registry and read the bank's financing statement, which notified Falconbridge that the bank had a security interest, implying, as we said, that it had a security agreement with Vic. Falconbridge even wrote Bank One that it was planning to obtain a purchase money security interest in the nickel it was selling Vic and in any proceeds of resales of the nickel. The bank cannot be accused of having misled Falconbridge. National Bank v. Haupricht Bros., Inc., 55 Ohio App.3d 249, 564 N.E.2d 101, 114 (1988) (per curiam); cf. Elhard v. Prairie Distributors, Inc., 366 N.W.2d 465, 468 (N.D.1985).

So Falconbridge cannot appeal to any general legal or equitable principle that might enable it to challenge the validity of the bank's agreement with Vic. But we must consider the bearing of UCC § 9–203(1)(a), which provides that a security interest is not "enforceable against the debtor or third parties with respect to the collateral" unless (the collateral not being in the creditor's possession or control) "the debtor has signed a security agreement which contains a description of the collateral." Some courts have permitted a subsequent creditor to use this provision to knock out the priority of an earlier creditor without requiring proof that he was actually misled or otherwise prejudiced by any defect in the security agreement. World Wide Tracers, Inc. v. Metropolitan Protection, Inc., 384 N.W.2d 442 (Minn.1986); In re Middle Atlantic Stud Welding Co., 503 F.2d 1133, 1136 (3d Cir.1974). This result, which is contrary to the Haupricht case cited earlier, strikes us as questionable despite its conformity to the literal language of section 9–203; it gives the later creditor a windfall by enabling him to knock out a priority on the basis of a defect on which he did not rely. No matter. The debtor signed the security agreement in this case and the agreement describes the collateral. The fact that section 9–203 requires the debtor to sign and does not mention signature by the creditor helps to show that the draftsmen did not think that a priority should be lost merely because the creditor's signature was missing.

A complicating factor in some cases, though not in this one, is that a trustee in bankruptcy (or debtor in possession) has the status of a hypothetical lien creditor "without regard to any knowledge of the trustee or of any creditor," 11 U.S.C. § 544(a), entitling him to void a security interest because of defects that need not have misled, or even have been capable of misleading, anyone. Pearson v. Salina Coffee House, Inc., 831 F.2d 1531 (10th Cir.1987); In re Sandy Ridge Oil Co., 807 F.2d 1332 (7th Cir.1986); Sommers v. International Business Machines, 640 F.2d 686, 688–89 (5th Cir.1981). The trustee did not assert this right here, probably because the only benefit would have been to another secured creditor, Falconbridge, and the trustee's duty is to maximize the recovery of the unsecured creditors.

For completeness we further note that while the provision requiring an adequate description of the collateral is intended in part for the protection of subsequent creditors, In re Martin Grinding & Machine Works, Inc., 793 F.2d 592, 596–97 (7th Cir.1986); In re Laminated Veneers Co., 471 F.2d 1124, 1125 (2d Cir.1973), and so may be enforced by them, at least when they can show they were misled by an inadequate description, the provision requiring the debtor's signature is not intended for their protection. It is a statute of frauds provision intended to make it easier for courts to resolve disputes over the meaning of the agreement. 2 James J. White & Robert S. Summers, Uniform Commercial Code § 24–4 at 305 (1988). Falconbridge had no standing to enforce it. See UCC § 2–201, official comment 4; cf. BDS, Inc. v. Gillis, 477 A.2d 1121, 1123 (D.C.App.1984) (per curiam); 2 E. Allan Farnsworth, Farnsworth on Contracts § 6.10, p. 168 (1990).

The real significance of section 9–203 in this case is in helping to explain section 9–201. In providing that a security agreement is effective only according to its terms, the draftsmen meant to state the general rule to which section 9–203 creates an exception. See UCC § 9–201, official comment. An agreement that violates section 9–203 may not be effective according to its terms. But explaining what happens if section 9–203 is not applicable is not the only function of section 9–201. For the fact that Falconbridge is not permitted to question that the bank had a security interest does not automatically extinguish Falconbridge's security interest. That depends on the relative priority of the contestants' security interests, and this is where section 9–201 could bite in this case: the bank can enforce a security agreement against a subsequent creditor of its debtor, that is, can retain its priority, only insofar as the agreement gives it a security interest. Had the agreement granted the bank a security interest only in inventory by expressly disclaiming any grant of a security interest in proceeds as well, the bank could not claim the proceeds in derogation of Falconbridge's later-perfected security interest in them. But there is nothing like that here. There is no discrepancy between the bank's financing statement and its security interest. Both cover all the assets of Vic, leaving nothing for Falconbridge until the bank's claim has been satisfied.

Although unnecessary to add, the security agreement was valid; that is, Vic would have had no defense against enforcement of the agreement by the bank, or vice versa. For one thing, it is apparent from the wording of the signature requirement and the fact that the bank was authorized to fill in any blank in the agreement that the requirement was intended solely for the bank's protection, and was not intended to confer any right on Vic; it was a defect of which no one could complain. For another thing (but it is actually closely related), after the agreement was not signed the bank lent money to Vic against its inventory nonetheless, and the parties assumed that this extension of credit was pursuant to the terms of the security agreement. Acceptance can be effectuated by performance as well as by a signature. Restatement (Second) of Contracts § 30(2) (1981); 1 Farnsworth, supra, § 3.12, p. 222; see also UCC § 2–206(1)(a); 1 White & Summers, supra, § 1–5, p. 55. And while parties can specify that performance shall not be effective as acceptance, Golden Dipt Co. v. Systems Engineering & Mfg. Co., 465 F.2d 215 (7th Cir.1972); In re Newport Plaza Associates, L.P., 985 F.2d 640, 645 (1st Cir.1993); Restatement, supra, § 30, comment a, this would be an implausible interpretation of the acceptance clause that we quoted earlier. It would amount to saying that if the parties had been asked, "if the bank fails to sign the agreement, will the agreement be void even if the parties behave in a way that shows they thought it was in effect?" they would have said "yes." Or that if they had been asked, "does the bank's failure to sign mean that the debtor could repudiate the agreement at any time?" they would have said "yes." What they really would have said would have been, "don't be silly; it was just an oversight, of no significance—and anyway the requirement of the bank's signature was for the protection of the bank, not of the debtor."

Falconbridge's argument that the bank's effort to show acceptance by performance violates the parol evidence rule (which both parties call the "parole evidence" rule) is frivolous. The rule bars evidence oral or written concerning negotiations leading up to an integrated contract, not evidence of events subsequent to the writing that is claimed to be the statement of the parties' contract. Fischer v. First Chicago Capital Markets, 195 F.3d 279, 282 (7th Cir.1999); Williams v. Jader Fuel Co., 944 F.2d 1388, 1394 (7th Cir.1991); 2 Farnsworth, supra, § 7.6 p. 228.

Anyway, to repeat a theme of this opinion, the parol evidence rule, like other contract defenses, is intended for the protection of parties or alleged parties to contracts; it is not intended to enable a stranger to break up a contractual relation. Northern Assurance Co. v. Chicago Mutual Building Ass'n, 198 Ill. 474, 64 N.E. 979 (1902); Quality Lighting, Inc. v. Benjamin, 227 Ill.App.3d 880, 169 Ill.Dec. 890, 592 N.E.2d 377, 382 (1992); Rittenhouse v. Tabor Grain Co., 203 Ill.App.3d 639, 148 Ill.Dec. 958, 561 N.E.2d 264, 271 (1990). So there was acceptance; but if there hadn't been, yet the parties agreed they had a contract, that would be enough to defeat Falconbridge's effort to invalidate a contract on which (or on the defect in which) it did not rely in extending credit to Vic.

AFFIRMED.

WILLIAMS, CIRCUIT JUDGE, concurring:

I agree with my colleagues that Falconbridge cannot challenge the validity of the security agreement between Bank One and Vic Supply. I write separately to voice my concern regarding the majority's further determination that the security agreement is, in any event, valid. While I am sympathetic to the majority's intuition that Bank One and Vic Supply could not have intended the signature provision to mean what it says, I am not persuaded that such an intuition justifies reading the provision out of the agreement.

Under the signature provision, the security agreement becomes effective only if and when Bank One accepts the agreement by filling in the signature blank; something Bank One did not do. The signature provision is not at all ambiguous, nor is there any reason to believe it is merely surplusage. It is a cardinal principal of contract law that since the language of a contract is the best evidence of the parties' intent, every provision of a contract should be given content and effect, and unambiguous contractual language should be given its plain and natural meaning. See, e.g., Emergency Med. Care, Inc. v. Marion Mem'l Hosp., 94 F.3d 1059, 1061 (7th Cir.1996) (applying Illinois law); River Forest State Bank & Trust Co. v. Rosemary Joyce Enters. Inc., 294 Ill.App.3d 173, 228 Ill.Dec. 291, 689 N.E.2d 163, 167 (1997). It does not matter that in hindsight one or both parties (or a court) might have second thoughts about the wisdom of including a particular term. Our task is to enforce the terms the parties included in their contract.

To my mind, moreover, it is telling that the majority cites not a single case adopting the same pragmatic approach it employs in interpreting the signature provision of the security agreement. No rule of law of which I am aware allows us to disregard the unambiguous terms of a contract in favor of what we believe the parties must have intended. Again, our task is to enforce the terms the parties included in their contract. Accordingly, I cannot join in the majority's conclusion that the security agreement between Bank One and Vic Supply is valid.

Note

1. Judge Posner dismisses the "literal language" of 9–203 but suggests that his view might be different if a trustee in bankruptcy were challenging the Bank. Can you explain his position?

2. Note too the public embarrassment that awaits anyone who confuses getting out of jail (parole) with speaking out of turn (parol).

IN RE HARDAGE

United States Bankruptcy Court, N.D. Texas, Lubbock Division, 1989.
99 B.R. 738.

AKARD, BANKRUPTCY JUDGE:

The issue before the Court is: Do the sales slips denominated "credit billing copy," of Sears, Roebuck & Co. (Sears), constitute valid security agreements such that pursuant to Uniform Commercial Code (UCC) Article 9 Sears has perfected security interests in the consumer goods sold?

FACTS

The Debtors in this Chapter 7 proceeding, Jimmy Doyle Hardage and Danelle Hardage, are typical of the many financially overextended consumer debtors who appear before this Court to request relief. On June 14, 1986, and on November 8, 1987, the Debtors purchased a videocassette recorder for $315.36 and a guitar board for $181.89, respectively, from Sears by using their charge card. Mr. Hardage signed the sales slips at the time of purchase.

On December 17, 1987, thirty-nine days after the purchase of the guitar board, the Debtors filed for relief under Chapter 7 of the Bankruptcy Code.[1] Debtors listed Sears as an unsecured creditor without priority, disclosing a claim in the amount of $1,453.07. On February 19, 1988, notice of Debtors' Petition in Bankruptcy was mailed to all parties in interest, stating that no proofs of claims need be filed at that time as this was a no-asset case. On March 12, 1988, the Debtors filed a reaffirmation agreement, agreeing to pay Sears the amount of $402.64, but this reaffirmation agreement stated on its face that it may be rescinded at any time prior to discharge or within 60 days after the agreement is filed with the Court. On June 29, 1988, the Debtors filed a Motion to Deem this debt unsecured. This Motion stated that Sears had filed a proof of claim in the amount of $1,496.33, claiming a security interest in the goods for the sum of $402.64 based on the sales slips Mr. Hardage had signed, as well as an unsecured claim in the amount of $1,093.69. The motion further stated that Sears had provided no evidence of an executed agreement by Debtors granting Sears a security

---

1. The Bankruptcy Code is 11 U.S.C. § 101 et seq. References to section numbers   are to sections in the Bankruptcy Code.

interest. In an answer to the Debtors' motion, filed on July 8, 1988, Sears admitted that it had filed a Proof of Claim in the sum of $1,496.33, but denied that it had not provided any evidence of an executed security agreement which would grant it a security interest. Sears' answer prayed that the Court determine that its security interest was valid as evidenced by the sales slips signed by Mr. Hardage.

The sales slips at issue contain, among other things, the following information:

1. The Debtors' credit account number;

2. Mr. Hardage's name;

3. The date of purchase;

4. The amount of purchase;

5. A brief description of the goods sold;

6. An invoice number;

7. One sales slip contains the Debtors' address; the other does not;

8. Mr. Hardage's signature appears on both sales slips immediately below the legend:

This purchase is subject to the approval of the Sears Credit Sales Department and is made under my SearsCharge Account Security Agreement for my SearsCharge Modernizing Credit Plan Security Agreement which is incorporated herein by reference. I agree that Sears retains a security interest under the Uniform Commercial Code in the merchandise purchased until fully paid.

No SearsCharge Account Security Agreement or SearsCharge Modernizing Credit Plan Security Agreement were introduced, so a security agreement, if one exists, must be found in the last sentence of the quoted provisions of the sales slip. No evidence was introduced as to the terms of payment or remedies available to Sears upon default, as would be normally contained in a security agreement, nor was evidence introduced as to the definition or occurrence of default. At hearing, the Debtors alleged that the Sears sales slips do not constitute sufficient evidence of an agreement executed by Debtors granting Sears a security interest in the consumer goods they purchased. Sears insisted that the documents in question granted it a valid security interest in the goods it sold.

Discussion

The Texas version of the UCC sets forth the formal requisites a party must follow to create an Article 9 security interest enforceable against the buyer or third parties with respect to the collateral. In pertinent part, these steps are: 1) the debtor signs a security agreement which contains a description of the collateral; 2) value has been given; and 3) the debtor has rights in the collateral. Tex.Bus. & Com.Code Ann. § 9.203(a) (Vernon Supp.1989). A financing statement is not necessary to perfect a purchase money security interest in consumer goods. Id. at § 9.302(a)(4).

The writing requirement may be simply expressed as follows; it must: 1) contain sufficient language to embody a "security agreement"; 2) include an adequate description of the collateral; and 3) be signed by the debtor. J. White and R. Summers, 2 Uniform Commercial Code § 24–3 at 297 (West 3d. ed. 1988) (hereinafter White & Summers). Since items 2 and 3 are not in dispute, we turn to item one, the sufficiency of the language to embody a security agreement.

Section 9.105(a)(12) states a security agreement means "an agreement which creates or provides for a security interest." Tex.Bus. & Com.Code Ann. § 9.105(a)(12) (Vernon Supp.1989). Where the parties are in dispute on this issue, the court may have to resolve first, as a question of law, whether the language in the agreement objectively indicates the parties may have intended to create or provide for a security interest. White & Summers, supra at 299. See, e.g., In re Bossingham, 49 B.R. 345 (Bankr.S.D.Iowa 1985) aff'd, 794 F.2d 681 (8th Cir.1986) (opining where the "magic words" of "security agreement" and "collateral" are present, "the legal question is not even close" under the objective test of intent to create a security interest. Id. at 350).

Although some courts read "may have intended" to require more, other courts rely on Comment 5 to § 9.203, which states that the writing requirement is more in the nature of satisfaction of the statute of frauds. White & Summers, supra at 299 (citation omitted). The Fifth Circuit stated that ("there must be language in the instrument which leads to the logical conclusion that it was the intention of the parties that a security interest be created."); Sommers v. IBM, 640 F.2d 686, 689 (5th Cir.1981). Accord In re Bollinger Corp., 614 F.2d 924 (3d Cir.1980) ("writing should demonstrate an intent to create a security interest in the collateral." Id. at 928); In re Bossingham, supra at 350 ("specific 'words of grant' are not required").

A "security interest" is defined as "an interest in personal property or fixtures which secures payment or performance of an obligation." Tex.Bus. & Com.Code Ann. § 1.201(37) (Vernon Supp.1989). The Fifth Circuit in Looney v. Nuss (In re Miller), 545 F.2d 916 (5th Cir.) cert. denied, 430 U.S. 987, 97 S.Ct. 1687, 52 L.Ed.2d 382 (1977) outlined the principal test to be used in determining whether a transaction is to be treated as a security interest. The appellate court stated that where a transaction is intended to have the effect of creating a security interest, this creation requires no formal wording; rather the court is to examine the substance of the documents in light of the circumstances of the case, in view of the fact that:

> [t]he Code eliminated traditional formal distinctions among security devices and left room for new forms of secured financing to 'fit comfortably under its provisions' without the necessity of passing new statutes and amending existing ones. The principal test for determining whether a transaction is to be treated as a security interest is: '[I]s the transaction intended to have effect as security?' No formal wording is required; we are to examine the substance of

the documents, in light of the circumstances of the case (citations omitted) (emphasis in original). Id. at 918.

The UCC does not require special words or any special form to show a possible security interest. White & Summers, supra at 301. Further, the courts have recognized unorthodox documents containing certain words as adequate security agreements. Even when conventional words do not appear, some courts find security interests. Clark v. Vaughn, 504 S.W.2d 550, 553 (Tex.Civ.App.—Dallas 1973, writ ref'd n.r.e.). Or, where one document is not sufficient to create a valid security interest, creditors may show such creation by introducing multiple executed documents. Therefore, once the agreement meets the § 9.203 writing requirement, the court may or may not ask for other evidence of whether the parties actually intended to create a security interest, a question of fact. White & Summers, supra at 300.

Since § 1.201(3) (Vernon 1968) defines agreement as "the bargain of the parties in fact as found in their language or by implication from other circumstances ...," the writing which satisfies the statute of frauds will also serve as sufficient proof of an actual intent to create such an interest. Where this is the case, no further questions are necessary. However, in a problem case, where the writing barely meets the objective test, further facts may be necessary to show whether the parties also actually intended to create a security interest. See Semco Division, Delwood Furniture Co. v. Williams (In re Metzler), 405 F.Supp. 622 (N.D.Ala.1975).

The Metzler court found that the "fundamental requirement of meeting of the minds is inherent in such agreements, as it is in all contracts. Without a contract there can be no security interest." Id. at 625. "Some courts have focused on the debtor's intention at the time of contract formation. The burden is on the creditor to establish the intention.... The question is what did the debtor agree to?" White & Summers, supra at 300 n. 14. Parole evidence is admissible to inform the second inquiry, but not the first. Id. at 300 (citing In re Lockwood, 16 UCC 195, 200 (Bankr.D.Conn.1974)). This conclusion follows from the definition of "agreement" in § 1.201(5). See In re Lockwood, supra at 200 ("[p]arol evidence is admissible to reveal the actual negotiations of the parties in arranging the transaction and any supplemental oral discussions of the parties which demonstrate their true intentions and understanding of the transaction"). In the case Improved Mach. Inc. v. Delta Molded Products, Inc. (In re Delta Molded Products), 416 F.Supp. 938, 942 (N.D.Ala.1976), aff'd, 571 F.2d 957 (5th Cir.1978), the court noted that "[s]ection 9.203 being in the nature of a statute of frauds, parole evidence is not admissible [only where it is offered] to establish the statutory requirements" of a writing. (citation omitted)

Extensive research by the Court indicates many cases in which Sears seeks to assert its status as a secured creditor by virtue of a purchase money security interest in consumer goods. In all the cases in which Sears was involved as the creditor, as well as every other case researched for this opinion, the security agreement or the documents evidencing a security interest were introduced into evidence at trial. The significance of this fact can hardly be overstated, as proof of the default terms in the security agreement is necessary before the courts would allow creditors to proceed against the Debtor's property in accordance with state laws. See, e.g., In re Moody, 62 B.R. 282, 283 (Bankr. N.D.Miss.1986); In re Orecchio, 54 B.R., 685, 686 (Bankr.D.N.J.1985); Tucker v. Sears, Roebuck & Co. (In re Tucker), 36 B.R. 706, 707 (Bankr.S.D.Ill.1984); Sears, Roebuck & Co. v. Hamilton (In re Hamilton), 22 B.R. 560, 561 (Bankr.D.Del.1982).

CONCLUSION

The Court concludes that as a matter of law the sales slips retained a security interest in the items purchased. Clearly Sears intended for the sale slips to be a security agreement and the intention of Mr. Hardage for the sale slips to be a security agreement must be found from the fact that he signed the sales slips immediately below the language creating the security interest.

The debtor and the creditor contemplated a security agreement, and in the instant case the security interest actually arose in spite of the fact that important terms including the method of securing a release from the lien and the terms of payment were not agreed upon.[2] Presumably Sears expects to be paid for the items listed on the sales tickets, but in its pleadings and argument Sears offered no hint as to how it expected to be paid. In view of its failure to comply with applicable consumer creditor laws, it is doubtful that Sears could be paid in accordance with its "standard terms."

ORDER ACCORDINGLY.

Problem 1–1

If you represented Sears, how, for the future, would you remedy their inability to find the original credit card agreement (that was apparently executed by Mr. Hardage)?

Note

Because *Hardage* involved consumers' giving a security interest in consumer goods, it does not technically belong in this Chapter which deals only with security interests in equipment. It is here to illustrate how an informal and incomplete document may yet constitute a security agreement under Article 9. There are similar cases involving business collateral. In the business cases, the secured creditor has sometimes forgotten to get the signature of the debtor on the security agreement or, if it has done so, is

---

2. This Court cannot and should not speculate as to what the parties might have agreed to had they negotiated further, nor should this Court consider as the terms of the transaction Sears' "standard deal" because the parties never agreed to those terms.

unable to locate the security agreement at the time of the foreclosure. In those cases the secured creditor argues that section 9–203 is satisfied by a combination of documents such as the minutes of a meeting of the debtor's board of directors, a signed note that has a memorandum on it indicating that security has been given for the note and, of course, a financing statement. Under 1999 Article 9 the financing statement need not be signed by the debtor, and thus it alone cannot be an effective security agreement. In many of these cases the behavior of the parties after the documents were executed but before default will give strong reason to believe that security was granted, particularly since the creditor will have filed a financing statement.

Problem 1–2

Your client, First Bank, is trying to reduce its paper records. It would like to destroy its copies of financing statements and security agreements with various debtors, and store those in electronic format. What risk does it run and what suggestions would you make to ensure that its electronic copies will satisfy the requirements of 9–203 if litigation occurs?

Problem 1–3

Assume First Bank did not exactly follow your instructions. Instead of getting the debtor somehow to authenticate an electronic record of the written security agreement in each case, it simply took several security agreements, put them on diskettes, and then destroyed the written security agreements. Bank is now litigating with a particularly contentious trustee in bankruptcy, who argues that a $20 million loan to a large supplier who has gone bankrupt is an unsecured loan because there is no signed security agreement. She has argued that Bank cannot bring an electronic record into court to prove the presence of a security agreement that was destroyed. She notes correctly that Bank never got the permission of the debtor to record the agreement electronically and to destroy the paper document, therefore, there is no "authentication" as required by 9–203 and that Bank has no security interest and is unperfected. What do you think?

§ 3. PERFECTION

Perfection in Article 9 is a complex term of art. Sections 9–308 through 9–316 specify how one perfects in each of the various transactions under Article 9. The perfected secured creditor is nearly as far above the unperfected secured creditor in the priorities pecking order as the unperfected secured creditor is above the general creditor. Perfection also earns the secured party priority over a subsequent lien creditor. The lien creditor *par excellence* is the trustee in bankruptcy wielding rights under section 544(a) of the Bankruptcy Code. Thus a secured party who perfects prior to bankruptcy usually enjoys a solitary feast, but an unperfected secured party will invariably have to eat from the general creditors' trough in bankruptcy. Likewise, the date of the perfecting act is commonly the date from which priority is measured vis-à-vis other perfected secured creditors. Usually, though not invariably, a creditor who perfects, or does the perfecting act (filing) first, takes priority over secured creditors who perfect or file later, yet is subordinate to those who perfected or filed previously.

Security interests can be perfected in four ways. First, by far the most common and important method is the filing of a financing statement. This document contains only enough information to notify a reader that the creditor named may claim an interest in described collateral of the debtor. Only rarely is the financing statement also the operative document which creates the security interest between the parties; normally it is a publicly filed skeletal notice that tells a reader where to hunt for more information. A second method—one that *may* be used with respect to certain kinds of collateral and that *must* be used with respect to some—is creditor possession of the collateral. A third method, useable with some kinds of intangible collateral, is "control". A direct security interest in a deposit account or letter of credit may be perfected *only* by taking control; it is a permissible but not the exclusive mode of perfection for investment property and electronic chattel paper. "Control" is to intangibles as "possession" is to goods. Finally, some security interests are automatically perfected at the time of their creation without any additional act of the secured creditor. The most important of this last group are purchase money interests in consumer goods.

Perfection generally requires some action, such as filing or possession, which would put a diligent searcher on notice of the secured party's claim. The drafters also wished to increase the certainty that a good faith effort by the secured creditor at filing would successfully communicate all necessary information, and that a good faith search by later parties would reveal the presence of the earlier secured creditor's claim. As we will see, the drafters compromised some of these policies where the cost of providing public notice appeared to outweigh the benefits of that notice.

Article 9 does not state rules for perfection with respect to all security interests in all types of personalty. For example, security interests in aircraft are perfected according to a federal law by filing in Oklahoma City. Federal filings may also be required in certain cases for interests in patents, copyright and trademarks. As to collateral or transactions that are excluded from Article 9 under 9–109, taking and perfecting a secured interest may still be possible under the common law or under some other statute of a particular state.

Perfection By Filing, In General

Perfection by filing is by far the most common method of perfecting a security interest under Article 9. Section 9–310(a) identifies filing as the norm and, except when the accounts are proceeds, there is no other way to perfect a security interest in most accounts (as distinguished from deposit accounts) and general intangibles. Filing is a permissible but not the only method of perfection as to goods, chattel paper, documents and investment property. For the first time, in 1999 Article 9, filing is a permitted method of perfecting a security interest in instruments, see 9–312(a).

There are a few things at the other end of the spectrum too; filing is not a permissible method of perfection with respect to money (9–312(b)(3)), deposit accounts (9–312(b)(1)), or letter of credit rights (9–312(b)(2))—except when those assets are proceeds. Also a UCC filing is not adequate for goods covered by a certificate of title (as to these, the "filing" must be under the certificate of title legislation 9–311(a)(2) and (3)). Nor is a UCC filing adequate if federal law calls for a federal filing (9–311(a)(1)).

For most of the security universe, perfection occurs by some form of filing of a document which the UCC calls a "financing statement". This document is the bikini of Article 9; it barely covers the collateral and the parties. It omits almost all of the important terms of the parties' agreement. Filing of a financing statement as to personal property was revolutionized by the initial adoption of the UCC, and later by the widespread use of electronic data storage. Prior to the Code's filing system, filing was haphazard and non uniform; there were state-wide systems in some states for some kinds of collateral, while other states provided for recording of chattel mortgages in the local offices where real estate mortgages were recorded. The first revolutionary act of the UCC in this field was to provide for the "filing" of a separate skeletal document in place of the "recording" of the actual document executed by the parties with all of its terms, as in the case of a chattel mortgage. The second major innovation was to move a substantial part of filing out of local registries into a single state-wide registry.

The proposal for state-wide filing conflicted with local practices and traditional policies. It was generally thought that local creditors should be able to walk to the local courthouse and examine the files, and the local recorder of deeds should collect a fee with each filing. Nevertheless, the drafters of the 1962 Code (and the 1972 Code) proposed three alternative filing systems. These were designed to minimize the political objections of local filing officers who might lose fees from a state-wide system and also to meet the concerns of people who still wished to be able to determine a debtor's status from local files. Even at the outset, the drafters recognized the efficiency of a state-wide filing system; creditors could search at one place and filers could file at one place. Both would avoid the mistakes of searching and filing in the wrong location.

Under the first alternative (all alternatives appeared in 9–401), one filed locally only with respect to timber to be cut, oil and gas, and "fixture filings". All other filings were in one state-wide office, usually the office of the Secretary of State. The second alternative was the most widely adopted; it added consumer and farm collateral to local filing. The third alternative not only adopted all the local filing requirements of the second alternative, but also required a filing both state-wide and locally in cases where the debtor's place of business was in only one county in the state. As more state filing systems became computerized, it became possible to search by computer and ultimately, to file electronically. The convenience of being able to walk across the street to the courthouse therefore disappeared, and the cost associated with local filing could no longer be justified. In the 1999 revision, section 9–501 calls for state-wide filing, except for fixture filings, "as-extracted" collateral (oil, gas and minerals), and timber to be cut.

Of course, Article 9 does not contain the only filing system in each state or even the only one in most states. Section 9–311 must bow to federal filing systems that preempt Article 9. Clearly the federal filing system with respect to aircraft fits this definition. The extent to which the federal filing rules as to patents, copyrights, and trademarks preempt the UCC is unclear.

The certificate of title notation rules take the place of Article 9 filings with respect to goods covered by certificates of title. Thus, because of 9–311, a secured creditor perfects its security interest in an automobile for which a certificate of title has been issued, by complying with the state's certificate of title law (usually notation on the certificate). This *state* exception to Article 9 filing is subject to an exception for cases where cars or other goods subject to the certificate of title laws are held in inventory for sale, (9–311(d)). In that case the vehicles are treated like any other inventory and so must be the subject of an Article 9 filing for perfection.

Prior to 1999 Article 9, it was always possible to file both locally and at the state capital—where there was any question about the classification of the collateral (as with consumer goods calling for a local filing or equipment calling for a state-wide filing) or where there was a question whether a debtor was engaged in business in only one county in the state. But many secured creditors did not file in both places, and the courts were called upon to determine, for example, whether large broods of laying hens should be classified as inventory (calling for a filing in the state capital) or farm products (calling for a local filing); or whether a boat used for Coast Guard volunteer work was equipment as opposed to consumer goods; or whether a computer bought initially for home use became equipment when it was devoted to business use. Section 9–501 sweeps all these questions away. Whether the debtor's goods are consumer goods or business equipment, the filing is at the state capital (the filing for a debtor's computer is at the state capital whether the debtor uses it for personal or business purposes). And the searchers search in state-wide databases.

With the combination of a state-wide filing system and the substantial elimination of local filing, and given the advances in electronic filing, data storage and searching, further advances will surely revolutionize the states' filing systems. As state databases become available on the internet for searches by anyone with a computer connection, and as the software for searching becomes more sophisticated, the filing and search problems discussed below will diminish significantly. The possibility will decline that a creditor who has made a good faith attempt to perfect by filing will find itself unperfected because it filed in the wrong place or filed the wrong document, and the probability that a searcher will discover a prior filing will increase.

The Basics of Filing and the Effects of Imperfect Filing or Indexing

Section 9–502 states the minimum data that must be included on a financing statement for it to be effective. Section 9–516 states additional requirements and has rules on the extent of effectiveness of imperfect financing statements. Section 9–520 specifies the duties of the filing office with respect to certain defective financing statements and the legal effects of those statements if they are accepted.

Subsections 9–502(a) and (b) state what is necessary (if not in all cases sufficient) for a document to qualify as a financing statement:

(a) [Sufficiency of financing statement.] Subject to subsection (b), a financing statement is sufficient only if it:

(1) provides the name of the debtor;

(2) provides the name of the secured party or a representative of the secured party; and

(3) indicates the collateral covered by the financing statement.

(b) [Real-property-related financing statements.] Except as otherwise provided in section 9–501(b), to be sufficient, a financing statement that covers as-extracted collateral or timber to be cut, or which is filed as a fixture filing and covers goods that are or are to become fixtures, must satisfy subsection (a) and also:

(1) indicate that it covers this type of collateral;

(2) indicate that it is to be filed [for record] in the real property records;

(3) provide a description of the real property to which the collateral is related [sufficient to give constructive notice of a mortgage under the law of this State if the description were contained in a record of the mortgage of the real property]; and

(4) if the debtor does not have an interest of record in the real property, provide the name of a record owner.

Under the predecessor of 9–502 (9–402(1)) a financing statement had to include the addresses of the debtor and secured parties, and had to be signed by the debtor to be effective. The drafters of 1999 Article 9 apparently concluded that the debtor's signature was an unnecessary technicality and that the addresses of the parties were useful but not critical, for a searcher could find the address of any earlier secured creditor and presumably the searcher has the address of its debtor. (The requirement for addresses now appears in 9–516(b) where, as we will see, their omission has only limited adverse consequences for the secured creditor.) The section allows the use of a mortgage as a financing statement in certain real estate transactions and, like the former law, requires a financing statement that is to be filed for record in the real property records to contain a description of the real property and to state to the filing officer that it must be filed in those records. The troublesome requirement of a real estate description covering growing crops is gone; security interests in growing crops are now perfected by a plain vanilla financing statement without any mention of real estate.

Section 9–516(b) contains certain additional requirements, for example, a financing statement is to provide a "mailing address for the debtor". Section 9–520(a) directs the filing officer to refuse to accept a record that does not meet the additional requirements of 9–516(b). Yet, if the filing officer accepts a financing statement which meets the conditions of 9–502 but not the additional requirements of 9–516(b), the filing is effective for most purposes. So we now have two classifications of defective financing statements: defective and *really* defective. If a filing officer mistakenly accepts two defective financing statements, the first being defective because it omits the name of the secured party (so failing 9–502), and the second because it omits the address of the secured creditor (so failing 9–516(b) but not 9–502), the first creditor is not perfected, but the second one is.

The additional requirements stated in 9–516(b) are as follows:

(b) [Refusal to accept record; filing does not occur.] Filing does not occur with respect to a record a filing office refuses to accept because:

(1) the record is not communicated by a method or medium of communication authorized by the filing office;

(2) an amount equal to or greater than the applicable filing fee is not tendered;

(3) the filing office is unable to index the record because:

(A) in the case of an initial financing statement, the record does not provide a name for the debtor;

(B) in the case of an amendment or correction statement, the record:

(i) does not identify the initial financing statement as required by section 9–512 or 9–518, as applicable; or

(ii) identifies an initial financing statement whose effectiveness has lapsed under section 9–515;

(C) in the case of an initial financing statement that provides the name of a debtor identified as an individual or an amendment that provides a name of a debtor identified as an individual which was not previously provided in the financing statement to which the record relates, the record does not identify the debtor's last name; or

(D) in the case of a record filed [or recorded] in the filing office described in section 9–501(a)(1), the record does not provide a sufficient description of the real property to which it relates;

(4) in the case of an initial financing statement or an amendment that adds a secured party of record, the record does not provide a name and mailing address for the secured party of record;

(5) in the case of an initial financing statement or an amendment that provides a name of a debtor which was not previously provided in the financing statement to which the amendment relates, the record does not:

(A) provide a mailing address for the debtor;

(B) indicate whether the debtor is an individual or an organization; or

(C) if the financing statement indicates the debtor is an organization, provide:

(i) a type of organization for the debtor;

(ii) a jurisdiction of organization for the debtor; or

(iii) an organizational identification number for the debtor or indicate that the debtor has none;

(6) in the case of an assignment reflected in an initial financing statement under section 9–514(a) or an amendment filed under section 9–514(b), the record does not provide a name and mailing address for the assignee; or

(7) in the case of a continuation statement, the record is not filed within the six-month period prescribed by section 9–515(d).

If the filing officer refuses to accept the filing based upon reasons not identified in 9–516(b), then the attempted filing is effective under 9–516(d) (provided 9–502(a) and (b) are met), "except as against a purchaser of the collateral which gives value in reasonable reliance upon the absence of the record from the files". One has to make several rather far-fetched assumptions to raise the issues that are buried in section 9–516(d). First, one has to assume the secured creditor presents a financing statement which complies with 9–502. Second, one has to assume the filing officer refuses the filing based on reasons *other than* non-compliance with 9–516(b). Third, one must assume the filing officer either failed to tell the secured creditor of its refusal to accept the filing, or the secured creditor and the filing officer must get into an angry standoff. Finally, one must assume that a "purchaser" gives value in reasonable reliance on the absence of the filing. Among those who would qualify as "purchasers" would be buyers of the collateral and also other secured creditors who might take a security interest in the collateral in ignorance of the earlier and unrecorded security interest. If each of these improbable events comes to pass, the unindexed financing statement is valid against non-reliance creditors but not against those who acted in reliance upon the absence of the filed financing statement. Presumably the most likely set of events are those in which the filing officer refuses the filing but, by mistake, fails to notify the secured creditor. The debtor then goes bankrupt and the secured creditor of the bankruptcy case has to prove that it attempted to make a filing and that it qualifies for the protection of section 9–520(c).

If the filing office does the converse, accepts for filing a record it should refuse (only because of defects of the kind described in 9–516(b)), section 9–520(c) makes that filing effective but opens the possibility that certain subsequent parties would take free of the security interest if they were misled by the inaccuracies on the financing statement, see 9–338. Assume creditor one files a financing statement which indicates the debtor is an individual when debtor is a corporation; that financing statement is defective under 9–516(b)(5)(B). Assume further that a second creditor examines the filing and concludes that there is no filing against its debtor of the same name because that debtor is a corporation, not an individual. In that case the combination of 9–520(c) and 9–338(1) would subordinate the earlier secured creditor who had provided inaccurate information—at least if the later secured creditor could show it had given "value in reasonable reliance upon the incorrect information".

Notwithstanding 9–520(a)'s direction to decline financing statements that fail 9–516(b), filing officers will in practice have some discretion about the financing statements they will accept. If the filing officer refuses a financing statement because it fails one of the requirements in 9–516(b), there has never been a filing. If, on the other hand, the filing officer accepts the financing statement despite the failure, the secured creditor is properly filed (except against subsequent purchasers who reasonably rely on the incorrect information) if its financing statement contains the minimum requirements of 9–502. Conceivably the filing officers in some states will insist upon compliance with every part of 9–516(b); others may not do so. Some of the requirements are merely common sense obligations that must be fulfilled in order to get an understandable financing statement properly indexed. For example, if an electronic record is communicated by a "medium of communication" that is incompatible with the electronic communication system of the filing officer, presumably no filing is possible because the filing officer will be unable to get the communication out of its system in comprehensible form.

Section 9–520 states the limits of the filing officers' discretion:

(a) [Mandatory refusal to accept record.] A filing office shall refuse to accept a record for filing for a reason set forth in section 9–516(b) and may refuse to accept a record for filing only for a reason set forth in section 9–516(b).

(b) [Communication concerning refusal.] If a filing office refuses to accept a record for filing, it shall communicate to the person that presented the record the fact of and reason for the refusal and the date and time the record would have been filed had the filing office accepted it. The communication must be made at the time and in the manner prescribed by filing-office rule [,but in the case of a filing office described in section 9–501(a)(2),] in no event more than two business days after the filing office receives the record.

(c) [When filed financing statement effective.] A filed (i.e., accepted) financing statement satisfying section 9–502(a) and (b) is effective, even if the filing office is required to refuse to accept it for filing under subsection (a). However, section 9–338 applies to a filed financing statement providing information described in section 9–516(b)(5) which is incorrect at the time the financing statement is filed.

(d) [Separate application to multiple debtors.] If a record communicated to a filing office provides information that relates to more than one debtor, this part applies as to each debtor separately.

Section 9–520(a) is a legislative direction to the filing officer to refuse to accept filings which fail any of the tests in 9–516(b) although the phrasing of the sentence is awkward. More important, Comment 2 gives a stern warning to filing officers; it basically tells them to keep their fingers out of the pot in other respects: "under this section, the filing officer is not expected to make legal judgments and is not permitted to impose additional conditions or requirements".

And, according to Comment 3 to 9–516: "neither this section nor section 9–520 requires or authorizes the filing officer to determine, or even to consider, the accuracy of information provided in a record. For example, the State A filing office may not reject under subsection (b)(5)(C) an initial financing statement indicating the debtor is a State A corporation and providing a three-digit organizational identification number, even if all State A organizational identification numbers contain at least five digits and two letters".

It seems likely that most filing officers will insist upon most of the requirements in subsection 9–516(b) and such insistence will improve the quality of the filings and index. For example, (b)(3)(D) permits the filing officer to require a sufficient description of the real estate, and (b)(4) and (5)(A) authorize the requirement of the mailing address of the secured party and the debtor. Subsection (b)(5)(C) authorizes the filing officer to insist upon information on whether the debtor is an individual or an organization and if an organization, the type, its jurisdiction and an "organization identification number".

To reiterate: (1) if a financing statement fails to meet the conditions of 9–502, the filing is not effective, even if it is accepted and indexed, (2) if a financing statement satisfies 9–502 but not 9–516(b), and the filing officer refuses to accept it because of its failure, the filing is not effective, (3) if a financing statement satisfies 9–502 but not 9–516(b) and the filing officer accepts it, the filing is effective (for most purposes), and (4) if a financing statement satisfies section 9–502 and the filing officer refuses to accept it for reasons other than those stated in section 9–516(b) (we never take financing statements from red haired people), the filing is effective (for most purposes).

1999 Article 9 goes well beyond the former law. Among other things section 9–521 sets forth a uniform financing statement form which will likely be adopted by most states. The form was worked out in consultation with the filing officers of several states. The combination of the use of identical documents throughout the states and conformity to uniform requirements on numbering and indexing as specified in 9–522, should facilitate uniformity and minimize the cases in which filing is done improperly or where proper searches fail to find filed financing statements.

Problem 1–4

Your client is lending to Retondo Brothers, an Illinois corporation located in suburban Chicago.

How do you perfect an interest in its equipment (drill presses, grinders, and sophisticated machine tools and their operating software)?

Assume the person at the bank who filled out the financing statement made a couple of errors in the filing. First, the former, and not the current, address was used for the debtor and the address of the bank was entirely omitted. Also the box to indicate that the machine shop was a corporation was not checked and the person denies checking *any* of the boxes; however, the copy of the statement you retrieved has the box checked indicating the machine shop is a sole proprietorship. You are now interested in these issues because the debtor has gone into bankruptcy and the trustee in bankruptcy has claimed that the bank is unperfected. The trustee has pointed out the financing statement fails to meet several of the requirements in section 9–516. Also in the bankruptcy, a subsequent secured creditor has asserted priority over your client by claiming that it was injured by the failure of the financing statement to state the address of the bank and to indicate that the debtor was a corporation.

What do you make of these arguments?

Problem 1–5

Assume you represent Bank One, and that it proposes to lend $20 million to a large construction company that does business in Wisconsin, Minnesota, and the Dakotas. The construction company is a Delaware corporation, and it has three subsidiaries, two of which are Minnesota corporations, and one of them is a Wisconsin corporation. It also has an unincorporated joint venture with its principal office in western North Dakota, where it is constructing a dam. The equipment that is being offered as collateral consists mostly of conventional construction equipment, such as large off-road trucks, bulldozers, hoists, cranes, cement mixers, gravel dispensers, and other more elaborate equipment. The banker tells you the equipment is worth at least $30 million and is located at various places throughout the four state area where the debtor does business. It is, of course, possible that during the term of the loan some or much of the equipment will be moved to other places. What documents must you file, in which places, in order to perfect the Bank's security interests?

Assume that the parent debtor's name is Bisgard–Larson Construction Co., that the Wisconsin subsidiary name is Milwaukee Construction Co., the two Minnesota subsidiaries are called Minnesota 1 Co. and Minnesota 2 Co., and the joint venture is known colloquially as the Williston Dam Co., but in fact has a formal partnership name, which is Bisgard, Larson and Lempke. What should your financing statements say?

Problem 1–6

Assume a financing statement filed in North Dakota for the Joint Venture transposed the name Bisgard, Larson and Lempke so that it read "Lempke–Bisgard, Larson". The filing was indexed under the Ls, not the Bs. Assume, too, that out of an excess of caution the banker filed a second financing statement, listing the name of the debtor as "Williston Dam Co." The Joint Venture has now gone bankrupt, and the trustee claims that the financing statements are not adequate to perfect the bank's security.

What do you think?

Problem 1–7

In the third year of the loan, assume that Bank One changed its name to Bank of the Universe. Would that render the financing statements invalid?

§ 4.   PERFECTION IN MULTIPLE STATE TRANSACTIONS

Sections 9–301 through 9–307 deal with choice of law—transactions somehow associated with more than one jurisdiction. Although it is technically correct to regard these sections as full-fledged choice of law provisions on perfection and priority, their real function is to answer a single question: where to file? When 1999 Article 9 is adopted by all states, every state will have nearly identical statutory law on how one takes and perfects a security interest, on the rights of the creditor on default, and on rules of priority. If we are lucky, there will be no need for choice of law rules to determine, for example, whether the rules of priority in Illinois or those in Ohio govern a particular transaction, nor will we have to ask whether repossession was proper under the law of Illinois versus the law of Ohio. In these cases every state's law will be the same.

That is not true of the place of filing, however. When the law of Ohio controls, it will tell one to file a financing statement in Columbus, but when the law of Illinois controls, one must file in Springfield. Because most perfection is accomplished by filing, and because a filing in the wrong place is no filing at all, the "choice of law" on place of filing is as important as choice of law on other Article 9 questions is unimportant.

Pre 1999 Rules

Prior to 1999 Article 9, section 9–103 contained a comprehensive and complicated set of rules about place of perfection. These rules were built upon the premise that filing with respect to goods should normally be at the place where the goods are located and that filing with respect to intangibles should normally be at the place where the debtor is located. The drafters classified some goods as "mobile"; these they treated like intangibles. Filing for mobile goods was at the debtor's location, not at the location of the goods themselves. Former 9–103 also had a separate rule for purchase money security interests where goods purchased in one state were to be shipped to the debtor in another. In the prior Code, a debtor's location was at its chief place of business, usually the place of the chief executive office.

Each of these rules had a perfectly understandable, rational basis, and, in theory, the rules were easy to understand and apply. In practice, the pre–1999 rules presented considerable difficulty. First, one needed to understand whether the goods were mobile goods or not. If they were mobile, the filing was where the debtor was located; if they were not mobile, the filing was where the goods were located. Second, one needed a rule for the case where goods were moved from one state to another. Since the perfection depended upon the location of the goods in a particular state, a security interest perfected by filing at the original location would necessarily become unperfected at some point after the goods were moved from that state, for the person in the new state would expect to search in the new state. Thus, former 9–103 had a four month "grace period" in which perfection would continue in the new state despite the movement of the goods. If the creditor did not catch up with the goods before the end of the four months and file in the new state, generally it was rendered unperfected. Finally, determining the location of a debtor's "chief place of business" was not always easy. This was particularly true with respect to modern companies that have businesses in many states where the chief executive officer might be in one location part of the week, and in another location the other part of the week, and where the remaining members of the executive staff might be in yet a third place. Of all the problems in the pre–1999 Article 9, those presented by the multi-state rules in former 9–103 were the easiest to see and, we hope, the easiest to resolve.

General Rule—1999 Revision

With exceptions we will discuss elsewhere, section 9–301 directs that the law of the debtor's location "governs perfection". Section 9–301(2) excludes possessory security interests from that rule and 9–301(3) excludes fixture filings and security interests in timber to be cut, but the general rule applicable to 99% of all filing is that one perfects by filing at the debtor's location. This means the distinction that formerly had to be recognized between tangible and intangible collateral is gone; the distinction that had to be drawn between mobile and non-mobile goods is not necessary; and rules about continued perfection after goods are moved from one state to another are also not needed.

Section 9–307, on location of debtor, makes a second important change in the law. Subsection (b) adopts the conventional rules about the location of an individual (individual's principal residence), an organization with only one place of business (place of business), and an organization with more than one place of business (chief executive office). But the major change comes in 9–307(e) where corporations and other organizations that qualify as "registered organizations" are considered to be located in the state where they are organized. Thus a corporation incorporated under Illinois law is located in Illinois, even if its principal office and all of its business is in California, and a business incorporated in Ohio is located there, even if 90% of its business is in states other than Ohio and even if its chief executive office is located in Chicago. This means that for all corporate debtors and for certain other entities that qualify as "registered organizations" (such as limited liability companies and certain partnerships), all the ambiguity about location will be gone. The messy, practical question about where the CEO goes to work and whether that is the chief office will not be relevant. For this important insight, we thank Professor Lynn LoPucki and Los Angeles lawyer, Harry Sigman.

The choice of "debtor's location"—particularly in the case of corporate debtors, of their place of incorporation—brings a bonus. The movement of a corporation from one place to another by reincorporation in a new place is far less common than movement of goods from one state to another. Presumably the change of incorporation is also less frequent than the moving of a chief executive office or other indicia of business affairs. Thus, while the law still has to have a provision for change of the debtor's location, the particular indicia of "location" are less likely to change than the former indicia, and debtor's location is far less likely to change than is the location of the goods.

Here the drafters have done us a favor that is hard to exaggerate. Under 1999 Article 9, it will be far easier to determine where to file than under the pre–1998 law. It will also be less likely that a security interest, once perfected, will become unperfected because of a change in location of goods or the like, and it will be less likely that someone who does a diligent search will fail to find a properly filed financing statement.

To understand the rules we have just described, consider 9–301 which reads in full below:

> Law governing perfection and priority of security interests. Except as otherwise provided in sections 9–303 through 9–306, the following rules determine the law governing perfection, the effect of perfection or nonperfection, and the priority of a security interest in collateral:
>
> (1) Except as otherwise provided in this section, while a debtor is located in a jurisdiction, the local law of that jurisdiction governs perfection, the effect of perfection or nonperfection, and the priority of a security interest in collateral.
>
> (2) While collateral is located in a jurisdiction, the local law of that jurisdiction governs perfection, the effect of perfection or nonperfection, and the priority of a possessory security interest in that collateral.

(3) Except as otherwise provided in paragraph (4), while negotiable documents, goods, instruments, money, or tangible chattel paper is located in a jurisdiction, the local law of that jurisdiction governs:

(A) perfection of a security interest in the goods by filing a fixture filing;

(B) perfection of a security interest in timber to be cut; and

(C) the effect of perfection or nonperfection and the priority of a nonpossessory security interest in the collateral.

(4) The local law of the jurisdiction in which the wellhead or minehead is located governs perfection, the effect of perfection or nonperfection, and the priority of a security interest in as-extracted collateral.

Having read 9–301, you might doubt what is said above. Perfection by filing is at the debtor's location, yet subsection (2) adopts the law of the place where the collateral is located and (3)(C) applies the law where the goods are located on the "effect of perfection", not so? Section 9–301 requires careful, patient reading. First, 9–301(2) does choose the law where the goods are located but only in the case of a *possessory security* interest. Thus if perfection depends on filing or control or if the security interest attaches automatically, subsection (2) does not apply. Moreover, that subsection will presumably become irrelevant or nearly so once 1999 Article 9 has been adopted in every jurisdiction; what is sufficient to perfect by possession in one state will not be significantly different from what is sufficient to perfect in another state.

But what is the distinction between 9–301(1) that directs one to the debtor's location and 9–301(3)(C) that directs one to the location of the collateral? Compare the phrase in (1): "perfection, the effect of perfection or nonperfection and the priority * * *" with the phrase in (3): "the effect of perfection or nonperfection and the priority * * *." The distinction is between "perfection" on the one hand and "the *effect* of perfection" on the other.

Assume a court sitting in Ohio is determining the right of a secured creditor against goods located in Ohio belonging to a company doing business in Ohio but incorporated in Illinois. Assume further that both Ohio and Illinois have adopted 1999 Article 9. The Ohio court should look at 9–301(1) and 9–307; these two provisions of Ohio law will direct the court to look to Illinois law to see whether the secured creditor has filed the proper documents in the proper place, in this case, Springfield. If the secured creditor has properly filed in Illinois, 9–301(3)(C) instructs the Ohio Court to grant the secured creditor the rights and priority of a perfected secured creditor under Ohio law. If the secured creditor is being challenged by a second creditor or by a judicial lien holder in Ohio or by any other claimant, 9–301(3) directs the court to determine the *priority dispute* by reference to Ohio law. In most priority disputes and in most other cases, the "effect of perfection" will be the same under every state's law once every state has adopted the same version of Article 9.

Finally, observe that neither section 9–301 nor any of the other choice of law provisions in Article 9 purports to choose the law for questions such as attachment or characterization of the transaction (lease vs. security agreement). These issues are left to the choice of law rules in section 1–105. Comment 2 to 9–301 makes the point as follows:

> Scope of This Subpart. Part 3, Subpart 1 (sections 9–301 through 9–307) contains choice-of-law rules similar to those of former section 9–103. Former section 9–103 generally addresses which State's law governs "perfection and the effect of perfection or non-perfection of" security interests. See, e.g., former section 9–103(1)(b). This Article follows the broader and more precise formulation in former section 9–103(6)(b), which was revised in connection with the promulgation of Revised Article 8 in 1994: "perfection, the effect of perfection or non-perfection, and the priority of" security interests. Priority, in this context, subsumes all of the rules in Part 3, including "cut off" or "take free" rules such as sections 9–317(b), (c), and (d), 9–320(a), (b), and (d), and 9–332. This subpart does not address choice of law for other purposes. For example, the law applicable to issues such as attachment, validity, characterization (e.g., true lease or security interest), and enforcement is governed by the rules in section 1–105; that governing law typically is specified in the same agreement that contains the security agreement. And, another jurisdiction's law may govern other third-party matters addressed in this Article. See section 9–401, Comment 3.

But never fear; with uniform adoption of 1999 Article 9, these issues too will disappear.

Problem 1–8

Consider the following variation to problem 1–5.

Assume you represent Bank One, and that it proposes to lend $20 million to a large construction company that does business in Wisconsin, Minnesota, and the Dakotas. The construction company is a Delaware corporation, and it has three subsidiaries, two of which are Minnesota corporations, and one of them is a Wisconsin corporation. It also has an unincorporated joint venture with its principal office in western North Dakota, where it is constructing a dam. The equipment that is being offered as collateral consists mostly of conventional construction equipment, such as large off-road trucks, bulldozers, hoists, cranes, cement mixers, gravel dispensers, and other more elaborate equipment. The banker tells you the equipment is worth at least $30 million and is located at various places throughout the four state area where the debtor does business. It is, of course, possible that during the term of the loan, some or much of the equipment will be moved to other places.

Assume that the parent debtor's name is Bisgard–Larson Construction Co., that the Wisconsin subsidiary name is Milwaukee Construction Co., the two Minnesota subsidiaries are called Minnesota 1 Co. and Minnesota 2 Co., and the joint venture is known colloquially as the Williston Dam Co., but in fact has a formal partnership name, which is Bisgard, Larson and Lempke.

Where would you have filed under pre–1999 Article 9?

KONKEL v. GOLDEN PLAINS CREDIT UNION

Supreme Court of Colorado, 1989.
778 P.2d 660.

VOLLACK, JUSTICE:

Golden Plains Credit Union (Golden Plains) appeals the judgment of the court of appeals in *Golden Plains Credit Union v. Konkel,* 759 P.2d 788 (Colo.App.1988), holding that the trial court erred in concluding that Golden Plains lost its security interest in a farm combine purchased in Kansas and subsequently moved and sold in Colorado. We affirm in part and reverse in part and remand the case to the court of appeals with directions to remand for further hearings.

I.

Golden Plains is a Kansas credit union. On May 4, 1978, it financed the purchase of two 1978 John Deere combines[1] by Duane Lewis, a farmer[2] and custom cutter.[3] In May 1978, Golden Plains filed a financing statement for the combines with the registrar of deeds in Hamilton County, Kansas, the county in which Lewis resided.

In the latter half of October 1979, Lewis transported the combines from Hamilton County, Kansas, to a farm he had recently purchased in Baca County, Colorado. On February 7, 1980, Lewis sold one of the combines in Colorado to Bud Konkel (Konkel), doing business as Konkel Equipment Company. Konkel made no effort to determine whether a financing statement describing Golden Plains' security interest in the combine was filed, nor did he have actual knowledge of Golden Plains' security interest. Konkel later sold the combine to a Colorado farmer.

In April 1984, Golden Plains filed a complaint in the Baca County District Court against Konkel for conversion of the combine, seeking its return or damages.[4] Golden Plains moved for summary judgment against Konkel on the ground that Golden Plains held a security interest in the

---

1. Lewis bought two combines in 1977. He traded them in for two 1978 combines in May 1978.

2. In his deposition, Lewis stated that he farmed 920 acres of land in Hamilton County, Kansas, in 1978, 600 of which he owned and 320 of which he rented. He also stated that he purchased and maintained an 1120–acre farm in Baca County, Colorado, in 1979.

3. In his deposition, Lewis stated that he had been a custom cutter of crops since 1970. In 1977, 1978, and 1979, he would cut crops in Oklahoma during the early part of the season, move the operation to Kansas and Nebraska, and finish the season in Colorado. He would then store the combines in Colorado during the winter.

4. After Golden Plains filed its complaint against Konkel, Konkel filed a third-party complaint against Lewis, alleging false representation at the time of the 1980 purchase.

combine at the time Konkel bought the combine from Lewis. Konkel moved for summary judgment against Golden Plains on the ground that Golden Plains lost its security interest in the combine in 1980 when it failed to file a second financing statement in Colorado within four months of the date Lewis moved the combine to Baca County.

The trial court granted Konkel's motion for summary judgment. It made no attempt to classify the combine under the Kansas version of the Uniform Commercial Code (UCC or Code). Instead, it held that Golden Plains lost its security interest in the combine four months after Lewis moved the combine to Baca County, Colorado, pursuant to section 84–9–103(1)(d) of the law of Kansas.

The court of appeals reversed the judgment of the trial court. It first found that Golden Plains had perfected its security interest in the combine in May 1978 by filing its financing statement in Hamilton County, Kansas. The court of appeals relied on *Sequoia Machinery, Inc. v. Jarrett,* 410 F.2d 1116 (9th Cir.1969), in concluding the combine was properly classified as "equipment used in farming operations" under section 84–9–401(1)(a) (1983) of the law of Kansas because the combine was "specifically designed to be used for farming functions." *Golden Plains Credit Union v. Konkel,* 759 P.2d at 790. The court of appeals noted that the proper place for a creditor to file a financing statement and thereby perfect its security interest in a combine is the office of the registrar of deeds in the county in which the debtor resided, a procedure that was followed in this case.

The court of appeals then concluded that the trial court erred in concluding that Golden Plains lost its security interest in the combine under section 84–9–103(1)(d)(i) four months after the combine was "brought into" Colorado. Instead, the court of appeals found that the applicable Kansas statute was section 84–9–103(3) (1983 & 1988 Supp.), governing "mobile goods." It noted that section 84–9–103(3)(a) and the Code commentary listed "commercial harvesting machinery" as an "excellent example" of mobile goods. It concluded that Golden Plains retained its security interest in the combine under section 84–9–103(3)(e) until four months after "a change of the debtor's location to another jurisdiction." The court of appeals remanded the case to the trial court for a factual determination of whether Lewis had "changed his location" within the meaning of section 84–9–103(3)(d) when he moved the combine to Colorado in October 1979.

We granted certiorari to determine two issues: first, whether Golden Plains properly perfected its security interest in the combine in May 1978; and second, assuming that Golden Plains had properly perfected its security interest in May 1978, whether Golden Plains lost its security interest in 1980 by failing to file a new financing statement in Colorado within four months of the time the debtor moved the combine to Baca County, Colorado.

II.

A.

Resolution of the first issue requires us to examine the efficacy of the "normal use test" in classifying collateral under the Kansas equivalent of section 9–401(1)(a) of the Code. Konkel argues that Golden Plains never perfected its security interest in the combine in May 1978 because Golden Plains did not file its financing statement in the Office of the Kansas Secretary of State. Implicit in this is the argument that the combine is equipment other than "equipment used in farming operations" within the meaning of section 84–9–401(1)(a) of the law of Kansas.[5] Golden Plains contends that this argument should not be addressed because it was raised for the first time before the court of appeals. Golden Plains argues that its security interest was properly perfected in May 1978 because the combine is "equipment used in farming operations" within the meaning of section 84–9–401(1)(a) of the law of Kansas.

While the thrust of the arguments in the district court hearing of October 23, 1985, centered on whether Golden Plains' security interest remained in effect after Lewis brought the combine to Colorado in the latter half of October 1979, Konkel's attorney did raise the issue of whether Golden Plains' security interest was properly perfected in May 1978. The attorney noted that equipment such as a combine may alternately be classified as farm equipment, requiring filing in the county of the debtor's residence, or commercial equipment, requiring filing with the Kansas Secretary of State. He argued that by classifying the combine as commercial equipment requiring filing with the Kansas Secretary of State, Golden Plains' filing in Hamilton County was "an erroneous filing, and [Golden Plains] [hasn't] continued that. That would be by operational [sic] law in '78–'83, five years." The lawyer cited *Mountain Credit v. Michiana Lumber & Supply, Inc.*, 31 Colo.App. 112, 498 P.2d 967 (1972), to support this argument. *Mountain Credit* concerns whether a creditor failed to perfect its security interest by filing a financing statement in the wrong place. From this, we conclude that the issue of perfection of Golden Plains' security interest in May 1978 was properly raised before the district court. We therefore must consider the merits of this argument.

Under Kansas law, the proper place to file a financing statement and thereby perfect a security interest is generally in the office of the secretary of state. Kan.Stat.Ann. § 84–9–401(1)(c) (1983 & 1988 Supp.). The practice of filing with the secretary of state, known as "central filing," however, is subject to a number of exceptions.[6] When the debtor

---

5. Konkel and Golden Plains agree that the combine is "equipment" within the meaning of section 84–9–109(2), which includes goods that are "used or bought for use primarily in business (including farming or a profession) or by a debtor who is a nonprofit organization or a governmental subdivision or agency or if the goods are not included in the definitions of inventory, farm products or consumer goods."

6. At the time this dispute arose, central filing was not required in Kansas for "equipment used in farming operations,"

is a resident of the state, the proper place to file a financing statement for collateral properly classified as "equipment used in farming operations," for example, is "in the office of the registrar of deeds in the county of the debtor's residence."[7] The practice of filing in the county of the debtor's residence is known as "local filing." If the combine is properly classified as "equipment used in farming operations," then Golden Plains' local filing was sufficient to perfect its security interest in the combine. If the combine is properly classified as equipment other than equipment used in farming operations, however, then central filing would be required to perfect Golden Plains' security interest in the combine. In order to determine whether the court of appeals erred in concluding that central filing was not required to perfect Golden Plains' security interest, we must first classify the collateral. *In re Reier,* 53 B.R. 395, 396 (Bankr.S.D.Ohio 1985).

In jurisdictions such as Kansas that adopt the second alternative subsection (1) of section 9–401 of the UCC, the most difficult problem involving equipment not subject to a certificate of title law "is drawing the line between 'equipment used in farming operations,' which normally requires local filing, and commercial equipment, which normally requires central filing." B. Clark, *The Law of Secured Transactions Under the Uniform Commercial Code* § 8.3[1][a], at 8–8 (1980). The problem arises because the UCC does not define the phrase "equipment used in farming operations." *See* 1 P. Coogan, W. Hogan, D. Vogts & J. McDonnell, *Secured Transactions Under the Uniform Commercial Code* § 6.03[2][a], at 6–34 (1989) ("'[i]nartful drafting [of the phrase 'equipment used in farming operations'] has unintentionally produced a 'trap for the unwary' ").

As a result of this statutory ambiguity, courts have devised a number of tests to determine whether the collateral is properly classified as equipment used in farming operations. One such test is the "normal use test," which focuses on the inherent qualities of the collateral and the uses to which such collateral would normally be put. The leading case advocating the normal use test is *Sequoia Machinery, Inc. v. Jarrett,* 410 F.2d 1116 (9th Cir.1969). The normal use test has been adopted by a

"farm products," "accounts or general intangibles arising from or relating to the sale of farm products by the farmer," "consumer goods," or "crops." Kan.Stat.Ann. § 84–9–401(1)(a) (1983), repealed and reenacted (1984) (requiring central filing for "equipment used in farming operations," "farm products," and "crops"). In such cases the proper place to file a financing statement depended on whether the debtor was a Kansas resident. If the debtor was a Kansas resident, then the proper place to file was "in the office of the registrar of deeds in the county of the debtor's residence." If the debtor was not a Kansas resident, then the proper place to file was "in the office of the registrar of deeds in the county where the goods are kept." Id.

7. Although at the time this dispute arose a security interest in "equipment used in farming operations" could be perfected only by filing locally, the Kansas legislature amended section 84–9–401(1)(a) in 1984 by deleting the phrase "equipment used in farming operations" from the subsection relating to local filing. Ch. 345, sec. 1, § 84–9–401, 1983 Kan.Sess.Laws 1562, 1563. As a result, a security interest in such equipment is now perfected under Kansas law by filing centrally rather than locally. See Balloun, Survey of Kansas Law: Secured Transactions, 32 U.Kan.L.Rev. 351, 368 (1984).

minority of jurisdictions. *See, e.g., In re Burgess,* 30 B.R. 364, 366 (Bankr.W.D.Okla.1983).

A second test is the "intended use test," which focuses on the use the debtor intended to make of the collateral as contemplated by the parties at the time of the sale. *See In re Collins,* 3 B.R. 144, 146 (Bankr.D.S.C.1980). A third test is the "actual use test," which focuses on the use the debtor actually made of the collateral. *See In re Yeager Trucking,* 29 B.R. 131, 134 (Bankr.D.Colo.1983) ("it is the use by the debtor, not any intended use by the creditor, that is controlling as to classification of the collateral"); *In re Butler,* 3 B.R. 182, 183–84 (Bankr. E.D.Tenn.1980) ("the purpose for which the goods are bought and used determines the category in which goods should be placed"). Most courts follow either the intended use test or the actual use test. *See generally* T. Crandall, R. Hagedorn, F. Smith, *Debtor-Creditor Law Manual* § 7–06[3][d][i], at 7–87 (1985).

According to Professors White and Summers, the real debate in classifying "equipment used in farming operations" is between the actual use test and the intended use test rather than between those tests and the normal use test:

> How one resolves the intended use versus actual use dispute depends ultimately on whether he values more highly secured creditors' interests or third party creditors' interests. A secured creditor would like to rely upon the debtor's statement about his intended use at the time the loan is made. A careful creditor can procure the debtor's written statement about his intended use and can then file in the proper place according to that use. On the other hand, third party creditors will surely argue for the actual use test. J. White & R. Summers, *Uniform Commercial Code,* 24–15, at 362 (3d ed. 1988).

Although the normal use test, intended use test, and actual use test each has some logical appeal, the Kansas legislature has demonstrated its preference for the actual use test. The 1983 Kansas commentary to section 84–9–109 (1983 & 1988 Supp.)[8] states that the key in classifying the collateral "is the use to which the debtor puts the goods, not any inherent quality of the goods themselves." Given this choice by the Kansas legislature, we must conclude that the court of appeals erred in concluding that the normal use test employed in *Sequoia Machinery* was the proper test to determine whether the combine was "equipment used in farming operations" within the meaning of section 84–9–401(1)(a) of the law of Kansas.[9]

8. Section 84–9–109 governs the classification of collateral. It creates four such classifications: consumer goods; equipment; farm products; and inventory.

As the 1983 Kansas comments to section 84–9–109 recognizes: "The classification of goods is important in a number of situations, e.g., to answer questions of priority (84–9–312), in determining the proper place to file a financing statement (84–9–401), and in determining the rights of persons who buy from a debtor goods subject to a security interest (84–9–307)."

9. We need not decide and therefore express no opinion as to the appropriate test under Colorado law for determining wheth-

While the prudent creditor in close cases such as this should file a financing statement both locally and centrally as insurance against an adverse judicial determination of the proper classification of a particular piece of equipment, *In re Burgess,* 30 B.R. at 366; B. Clark, *The Law of Secured Transactions Under the Uniform Commercial Code,* 9.5, at 9–21 (1989); J. White & R. Summers, *Uniform Commercial Code,* 24–14, at 359 (3d ed. 1988), the Code does not demand dual filing. Where the financing statement must be filed to perfect a security interest depends on the proper classification of the collateral. The trial court did not classify the combine. On remand, it must decide whether Lewis in May 1978 actually used the combine as "equipment used in farming operations." If the answer to this question is "no," then Golden Plains failed to perfect its security interest and judgment must be entered for Konkel.

B.

If the trial court decides that Lewis' actual use of the combine in May 1978 was as "equipment used in farming operations," however, then the trial court must decide whether Golden Plains' security interest remained in effect after Konkel purchased the combine. Resolution of this issue requires a determination of whether the combine is an "ordinary good"[10] or a mobile good.

Konkel argues that Golden Plains' security interest lapsed under section 84–9–103(1)(d) when Golden Plains failed to file a financing statement in Colorado four months after Lewis brought the combine into Colorado. Golden Plains argues that its security interest remained in effect in February 1980 under section 84–9–103(3)(e) because Lewis did not "change" his "location" of Hamilton County, Kansas, when he moved the combine into Baca County, Colorado, in the latter half of October 1979.

Section 84–9–103(1), the Kansas equivalent of section 9–103(1) of the Code, resolves priority disputes among creditors from different states having an interest in "ordinary goods" moved from one state to another. A security interest in ordinary goods which is properly perfected in one state expires four months after it is brought into the second state "and is thereafter deemed to have been unperfected as against a person who became a purchaser" in the second state. Kan.Stat.Ann. § 84–9–103(1)(d)(i) (1983 & 1988 Supp.). This rule, known as the "carry-over perfection rule," gives secured creditors in one state a four-month grace period to relocate the ordinary goods and file a second financing statement. The grace period for ordinary goods begins to run from the time the collateral "is brought into" the second state. J. White & R. Summers, *Uniform Commercial Code* § 22–21, at 1057 n. 28 (1988). Failure to file a second financing statement during the four-month grace period,

---

er a particular piece of machinery is "equipment used in farming operations."

10. Under section 84–9–103(1)(a), what are colloquially known as "ordinary goods" are defined as "goods other than those cov-

ered by a certificate of title described in subsection (2), mobile goods described in subsection (3), and mineral described in subsection (5)."

however, will cause the secured creditor to lose his or her priority and be subordinated to the interest of a purchaser of the ordinary goods during the grace period. *Massey–Ferguson Credit Corp. v. Wells Motor Co.,* 374 So.2d 319, 322 (Ala.1979); *Rockwell Int'l Credit Corp. v. Valley Bank,* 109 Idaho 406, 408, 707 P.2d 517, 519 (Idaho App.1985); UCC § 9–103 comment 7. As one commentator describes the operation of section 9–103(1)(d):

> When ordinary goods are brought into another state subject to a perfected security interest, there is a carry over into the second state of the perfection obtained in the first state. This carry-over perfection is conditional, being conditioned upon the creditor's taking within the second state the steps required by that state to reperfect the security interest. If such steps are taken in the second state there is a perfection that continues according to the terms of the law of the second state. This perfection relates back to the initial acquisition of perfection in the first state.

> If the security interest is not perfected in the second state during the period of the carry-over perfection, it lapses retroactively and relative rights are determined as though such carry-over perfection had never existed. 8 R. Anderson, *Anderson on the Uniform Commercial Code* § 9–103:39, at 510 (1985) (footnotes omitted).

In contrast to section 84–9–103(1), section 84–9–103(3), the Kansas equivalent of section 9–103(3) of the Code, resolves priority disputes among creditors from more than one state having an interest in "mobile goods" moved from one state to another. Mobile goods are defined in section 9–103(3)(a) as "goods which are mobile and which are of a type normally used in more than one jurisdiction."[11] A security interest in mobile goods which is properly perfected in one state expires four months after "a change in the debtor's location to another jurisdiction." Kan.Stat.Ann. § 84–9–103(3)(e). Under section 84–9–103(3)(d), a debtor is deemed to be "located" at his "place of business if he has one, at his chief executive office if he has more than one place of business, otherwise at his residence." Therefore, if the combine is properly characterized as a mobile good and Lewis was deemed to be located in Hamilton County, Kansas, then his transporting of the combine to Colorado in October 1979 would have no effect on his perfected security interest in Kansas and Konkel would take the combine subject to Golden Plains' security interest. If the combine is properly characterized as an ordinary good, however, then Konkel would take free of Golden Plains' security interest.

We agree with the analysis of the court of appeals that the combine is properly characterized under Kansas law as a mobile good. The court of appeals correctly noted that the definition of mobile goods in section

---

11. The definition of mobile goods also requires that the goods are not covered by a certificate of title under § 9–103(2)(a) and that the goods are either debtor's equipment or his inventory that he leases to others. UCC § 9–103(3)(a); J. White & R. Summers, Uniform Commercial Code § 22–23, at 1063 (1988). Both parties agree that neither of these requirements is at issue.

84–9–103(3)(a) expressly included "commercial harvesting machinery and the like." The court of appeals also properly recognized that the 1983 Kansas commentary to section 84–9–103 describes precisely the problem presented in this case:

> An excellent example of mobile goods, and one which is set forth expressly in [§ 84–9–103(3)], is commercial harvesting machinery. For example, if the debtor is a custom cutter headquartered in Wichita, [then] Kansas would be the proper place to file the financing statement even though the harvesting machinery goes from Texas to North Dakota during the cutting season.

For these reasons, we conclude that the combine Konkel purchased was a mobile good within the meaning of section 84–9–103(3)(a). Because the combine was properly characterized as a mobile good, the trial court erred in concluding that Golden Plains lost its security interest in the combine solely because Golden Plains failed to reperfect its security interest within four months of bringing the combine into Baca County, Colorado. When the collateral was "brought into" the second state is a relevant inquiry for ordinary goods but is an irrelevant inquiry for mobile goods. The relevant inquiry for mobile goods under Kansas law is whether the debtor has "changed his location," see Kan.Stat.Ann. § 84–9–103(3)(e), which in this case requires a determination of the debtor's place of "residence," see Kan.Stat.Ann. § 84–9–103(3)(d). The court of appeals correctly noted that this issue was not decided by the trial court. We leave that determination for the trial court on remand.

III.

On remand, the trial court must use the actual use test to determine whether Golden Plains properly perfected its security interest in the combine under Kansas law in May 1978. If it determines that the actual use of the combine was as "equipment used in farm operations," then the trial court must also determine if Lewis had "changed his location" under section 84–9–103(3)(d) at the time Konkel purchased the combine.

The judgment of the court of appeals is affirmed with respect to its decision that the combine was a mobile good. The judgment of the court of appeals is reversed with respect to its decision to require application of the "inherent use test." The case is remanded to the court of appeals with directions to remand to the trial court for further hearings.

Problem 1–9

How does the *Konkel* case come out if both Kansas and Colorado have 1999 Article 9 at all relevant times? Most of the issues that troubled the court in *Konkel* are gone. Note particularly that the parties need not concern themselves with the question whether these combines are commercial equipment or farm equipment, nor whether they are mobile goods or only conventional goods, nor whether the combines moved from Kansas to Colorado. But under 1999 Article 9, it will remain important to know when and if Lewis ceased to reside in Kansas and commenced to reside in Colorado.

§ 5. THE LEGAL RIGHTS ACQUIRED BY ATTACHMENT AND THE GREATER LEGAL RIGHTS ACQUIRED BY PERFECTION

Even an unperfected security interest—one that complies with 9–203, but not with 9–309, et seq.,—gives the secured creditor all the rights it needs vis-à-vis the debtor and unsecured creditors of the debtor. But an unperfected secured creditor will lose to any other secured creditor who perfects—even those who perfect with knowledge of the preexisting unperfected security interests—and far more important, will lose to that trustee in bankruptcy if the debtor goes bankrupt. These conclusions follow from 9–203, 9–317, and 9–322, read them. Section 544(a) of the Bankruptcy Code gives the trustee in bankruptcy the rights of a lien creditor under state law on the date the petition is filed. Thus the trustee or the debtor in possession will enjoy the rights specified in 9–317 to defeat unperfected security interests. Most of the litigation on perfection occurs in the bankruptcy court to challenge security interests that are not properly perfected. By doing that, the trustee reduces the secured creditor to an unsecured creditor and forces him to share his asset pro rata with all of the unsecured creditors.

But what are the legal rights of the secured creditor, assuming that it cannot be defeated? First is the right to repossess and sell the asset, and thus turn the claim to money. It is a mistake, however, to assume that repossession is the best course of action for a secured creditor. Here as elsewhere, the threat of action may be more powerful than the action itself (the second right); and the threat to deprive the debtor of the collateral (or where the debtor is insolvent, to deprive other creditors of the collateral) may itself be more productive than the actual repossession and sale. Assume, for example, that a particular piece of equipment is critical to the operation of the debtor's business, and the piece of equipment, standing alone, has a very modest value but is difficult to reproduce. In that case, the power of the threat against the debtor is likely to have greater value than the value of the machine itself.

The third right is the right of the perfected secured creditor in bankruptcy. These are rights to be protected during the bankruptcy, to insist upon the return of the collateral (or payment in lieu of) and also to influence the bankruptcy in ways not available to the unsecured creditor.

Rights of Unperfected Secured Creditors v. Unsecured Creditors with and without Judicial Liens

Section 9–201 states the basic right of the secured creditor vs. other competitors. Subsection (a) reads as follows:

> Except as otherwise provided in the Uniform Commercial Code, a security agreement is effective according to its terms between the parties, against purchasers of the collateral, and against creditors.

The sentence means what it says; the secured creditor, even an unperfected secured creditor, has greater rights in its collateral than any other creditor unless the Code provides otherwise. Of course, a creditor without a security interest or a lien has no claim on any specific collateral and 9–201 gives an unperfected but *secured* creditor rights superior to the rights of that *unsecured* creditor.

Section 9–317 subordinates an unperfected secured creditor to a lien creditor and, by negative implication, says that a perfected secured creditor beats a lien creditor. The most important part of 9–317 is (a)(2) which renders an unperfected security interest subordinate to the rights of one who "becomes a lien creditor before the earlier of the time the security interest or agricultural lien is perfected and a financing statement covering the collateral is filed". Thus, if a bank takes a security interest in the debtor's equipment but fails to file a financing statement or to take possession, and an unsecured creditor levies against the property and so procures a judicial lien on it, this formerly unsecured creditor (now a "lien creditor") will defeat the prior unperfected secured creditor. Subsection (e) states an exception to this rule for purchase money claims; the holder of a purchase money security interest has 20 days in which to file. If that secured creditor files within 20 days "after the debtor receives delivery of the collateral", the security interest takes priority over the rights of a lien creditor that attaches to the collateral between the time the security interest arose and the time of the filing.

Subsections (b), (c), and (d) give priority over unperfected secured creditors to a variety of buyers and lessees. Under 1999 Article 9 these parties "take free" of the security interest. The rules in the various subsections are somewhat different but all require that the party who is to defeat the secured creditor must give "value" and, in the case of tangibles (or as to intangible collateral represented by an indispensable "res" like an instrument), "receive delivery", all "without knowledge of the security interest".

In section 9–317 the drafters have made several cosmetic and a few minor substantive changes from former 9–301. For example, they have chosen the language "takes free" in lieu of "is subordinate to". And the statute now provides that all buyers meeting the qualifications take free, not just "buyers not in ordinary course of business"; also the basic rule in (a)(2) no longer requires the victorious secured creditor be perfected before the lien becomes effective; it is now sufficient that a financing statement be filed before that time. In that sense 1999 Article 9 follows the basic rule always applied in competition between secured creditors— priority dates from the earlier of filing or perfection.

It may be useful to understand what is implicit in the drafters' decisions here. In some cases a "gap" creditor who lends money in the "gap" after another creditor's security interest attached, but before it was perfected, can make a plausible claim that he has been injured. Prior to the adoption of 1999 Article 9, a few states gave priority to gap creditors over unperfected secured creditors even though the gap creditors had no lien. By generally subordinating creditors without liens to unperfected security interests, 9–201 makes a conscious judgment that those "gap" creditors and others like them are not entitled to protection.

This decision means that section 544(b) of the Bankruptcy Code has much less significance than it would otherwise have.

In general the secured creditor has claims on the collateral superior to those of any unsecured creditor who has no lien. A secured but unperfected creditor will usually be subordinate to lien creditors and to all buyers who give value and take without knowledge.

Basic Priorities among Conflicting Security Interests: First in Time, First in Right

Section 9–322(a) states the basic priorities among secured creditors precisely:

[General priority rules.] Except as otherwise provided in this section, priority among conflicting security interests and agricultural liens in the same collateral is determined according to the following rules:

(1) Conflicting perfected security interests and agricultural liens rank according to priority in time of filing or perfection. Priority dates from the earlier of the time a filing covering the collateral is first made or the security interest or agricultural lien is first perfected, if there is no period thereafter when there is neither filing nor perfection.

(2) A perfected security interest or agricultural lien has priority over a conflicting unperfected security interest or agricultural lien.

(3) The first security interest or agricultural lien to attach or become effective has priority if conflicting security interests and agricultural liens are unperfected.

When section 9–312 (predecessor to section 9–322) was adopted, it replaced a multitude of unclear and inconsistent state laws. When section 9–322 becomes law in all 50 states, it will continue the certainty that the former section imposed and, like its predecessor, foreclose choice of law arguments over priority among secured creditors. First in time, first in right—that general rule runs like a thread through virtually all priority schemes and 9–322 is no exception. However the Code is uniquely precise. The drafters of the Code well appreciated the ambiguity inherent in "the first in time" slogan; namely, first what? Does the person who makes a first loan have priority? Or is it the first to file? Or the one who first procures the debtor's signature on a security agreement? Particularly where a creditor will make repeated advances (for example, lines of credit secured by inventory or accounts receivable where there might be repayments and new extensions of credit daily), pre-Code law was in conflict. Some rules gave the lender priority from the time it filed or did some other perfecting act; others measured the priority only from the time of the advance (the time the loan was actually made). The drafters of 9–322 and its predecessor chose the former approach and have stated all the rules with precision.

Observe first that subsection (a) is a "pure race" statute as opposed to a "notice-race" statute. That is, the one who wins the "race" to the courthouse to file is superior even if that one had "notice" or "knowledge" of an earlier claim. The section nowhere requires that the victor be without knowledge of its competitor's claim. Example 1 of Comment 4 illustrates both the unimportance of knowledge and the fact that one who is perfected second may be prior if first to file. One justification for the rule is certainty. Under 9–322 no disappointed secured creditor can assert trumped up (or true) facts from which a compassionate court might find sufficient knowledge to subordinate the winner of the race. If the competitor filed first or perfected first, as the case may be, that is the end of it; that party wins even if aware of the other party's prior but unperfected claim.

Because the drafters chose to permit perfection by possession and by certain other non-filing acts, they could not simply give priority to the first to file. However, they went as far as possible in that direction and 9–322(a) is the result: the first to file wins if both competitors perfect by filing. Since filing is a public act, the timing of which can be proved with accuracy from public record, it is the most certain and satisfactory of the measuring points for priority. The drafters meant "filing", not more and not less. Assume for example that an unscrupulous debtor simultaneously negotiates with two creditors. Creditor One files long before it makes a loan; later Creditor Two loans and files. At that point Creditor Two has a perfected security interest under 9–203 and 9–310, but Creditor One has no interest at all for One has neither made a loan nor agreed to do so and so has not yet given "value". But if Creditor One thereafter receives debtor's security agreement, lends and so becomes a perfected secured creditor, who wins and why? Although Creditor One was the last perfected (recall "perfection" requires "attachment" and attachment requires the creditor give "value"), it filed first and wins. Creditor Two has no meritorious complaint, for Two could have protected itself by checking the files (so finding Creditor One's earlier filing).

The justification for determining priority by order of filing here lies in the necessity of protecting the filing system—that is, allowing the first secured party who has filed to make subsequent advances without each time having to check for subsequent filings as a condition of protection. Both as to future advances and to after-acquired collateral, a lender's priority generally dates back to the time of filing.

The guiding principle of section 9–322(a) is that the secured party who either files or otherwise perfects before the other person, wins. If both parties perfect by filing, priority goes to the person who filed first. Likewise, if one or both parties perfect by means other than filing, priority goes to the one who first perfected or filed, whichever came first.

Problem 1–10

Debtor One has given a perfected security interest in a large and expensive piece of industrial machinery to Bank One. Debtor One then sold the machine to Debtor Two whose bill of sale explicitly provided that Debtor Two took subject to Bank One's security interest. Debtor Two then went to Bank Two, represented that he owned the machine free and clear and procured a $200,000 loan against it. Bank Two checked the files under Debtor Two's name and, finding nothing, perfected its security interest by a filing. When the scheme was discovered, both Bank One and Two claimed the asset.

Assume there was a defect in Bank One's financing statement that caused it to be unperfected. Bank Two argues that it is a perfected secured creditor and as such has priority over Bank One's interest because of sections 9–201 and 9–322.

Can you see an argument that you could make on behalf of Bank One? Who prevails?

Problem 1–11

In May 1989, Jeffery Sharp and Thurman Agee, individuals doing business as T & J Logging, approached Ms. Krystal Hill about a loan for their business. Ms. Hill lent $25,000 to Sharp and Agee in exchange for a note bearing 10% interest. Simultaneously, Sharp and Agee executed a security agreement granting Ms. Hill a security interest in specified collateral. The names appearing on the security agreement and the promissory note were "James Thurman Agee" and "Jeffery Keith Sharp." On June 8, 1989, Ms. Hill filed a financing statement under their full names with the Office of the Secretary of State describing the collateral and listing Ms. Hill as the secured party.

Three years later, Sharp and Agee borrowed from Fifth Bank and granted Bank a security interest in the same collateral that secured the note to Ms. Hill. The two signatures on the notes to the bank were "Jeff Sharp" and "Thurman Agee" as officers of "T & J Loggers." The Bank filed financing statements under the names "Jeff Sharp", "Thurman Agee" and "T & J Loggers" with the Office of the Secretary of State.

In October of 1992, Sharp and Agee defaulted on the loan to Ms. Hill, and she repossessed the collateral. When Fifth Bank learned of the repossession, it sent a letter to the Secretary of State's office requesting a list of all financing statements under the names "Jeff Sharp," "Thurman Agee," and "T & J Loggers." The Office of the Secretary of State responded that only the Bank had filed under those names.

Fifth Bank has brought an action seeking a declaratory judgment that Ms. Hill's security interest was not perfected by a properly filed financial statement. The Bank has emphasized that the Office of the Secretary of State did not find a copy of Ms. Hill's financing statement during its search. As a result, Fifth Bank argues that Ms. Hill's financing statement was never properly filed and, thus, her interest never perfected. In response Ms. Hill has introduced into evidence a copy of her financing statement, properly stamped by the Office of the Secretary of State and filed on June 8, 1989.

Does Fifth Bank win? What is the Bank's best argument?

Problem 1–12

Debtor, Smokee–Linc, Inc., a sausage manufacturer, executed a security interest in its accounts, equipment and inventory to secure a working capital loan from Centerville National Bank (CNB). CNB filed a financing statement covering the property at the Secretary of State's office. The UCC–1 filed by CNB listed "Smokee–Linc, Inc." as the debtor.

One month after CNB filed the UCC–1, Debtor filed for a corporate name change as required under the Corporation Code. The corporation name was changed to "Smokey Link, Inc." CNB was not notified of the change of corporate name. Six months after CNB filed its UCC–1, Debtor filed in Chapter 11.

Assume the Secretary of State files its UCC–1's in a central computing system. Whenever a filing search is requested, the computer searches for the debtor's name. Once this name is found, the computer prints out all filings under that name. The computer also prints out the filings under the three names alphabetically prior to and the three names alphabetically from the spot where the requested name should appear. On the date of the filing of the petition in bankruptcy, the trustee requested a filing search of "Smokey Link, Inc." and received the following names on the computer print out:

Smoker Heaven, Inc.

Smokers Anonymous, Inc.

Smoker's Nook, Inc.

Smokey Mountain Trails, Ltd.

Smoothee–Cream Ice Creams, Inc.

Smothers, Richard

Smothers, Thomas

The trustee argues that CNB is not perfected because the change in the debtor's name did not appear on the search and that the filing is therefore seriously misleading. Is she correct?

§ 6. SUBSTITUTES FOR SECURITY IN BUSINESS EQUIPMENT

Instead of buying equipment and giving the seller or bank a security interest to secure the debt, some businesses lease equipment. Short-term leases have quite different economic characteristics from purchases, but long-term leases—particularly long-term leases that have concluding options to buy for small amounts—are almost identical to purchases, and, as we will see, the law sometimes treats them so. Also there are particular kinds of leases described in Article 2A as "finance leases." These are explicitly recognized by Article 2A as true leases, even though they have some of the financing characteristics of a secured sale. Even though one might argue the lessor's interest in such a case should be made a part of the public record by filing, the drafters have not chosen to do so.

A quite different substitute for a security interest loan is an unsecured purchase together with a "negative pledge clause." The "negative pledge" clause is a promise by the debtor not to grant any other person a security interest in the asset purchased. If the debtor is true to his word this means that no person can get a security interest that would defeat the seller or lender's claim to the asset purchased. Of course, a negative pledge clause will not protect against claims of creditors that are asserted involuntarily, i.e., claims arising out of a judgement and a levy on the property, nor would it protect against the claims of a trustee in bankruptcy. A creditor with a negative pledge clause is treated in bankruptcy as no more than an unsecured creditor.

Problem 1–13

Assume four leases:

1.   United Airlines leases five airbus A–320s to Northwest Airlines for a two year term. At the end of the two year term, the airbuses will be returned to United and there is no option to purchase. This is a lease; it is covered by Article 2A of the Uniform Commercial Code, and it has none of the significant characteristics of a security interest. True?

2.   Citicorp agrees with Northwest Airlines to purchase five airbus A–320s for a total price of $300 million, and to enter into a lease with Northwest to use the airplanes for a lease rental for 20 years. There is no option to purchase; Northwest negotiates directly with Airbus for the seat configuration, the galleys, the engines, and the like. This, too, is a lease governed by Article 2A. Unlike the lease from United, this is a "finance lease." The consequences of a lease being a "finance lease," as opposed to a conventional lease is that the lessor, as a quasi-financier, gives more limited warranties to the lessee than a conventional lessor gives. Would this be a security agreement if the A–320s had a predicted life of only 20 years?

3.   Bank One takes back five A–320s from Eastern Airlines (bankrupt) and offers to "lease" them to Northwest Airlines for a total payment of $40 million for each of five years, and at the end of five years to give Northwest the right to buy each for a $100 option payment. These are nearly new A–320s. This transaction is a sale with a security interest attached, even though it is labeled as a lease; true? To confirm your instincts, consider 1–201(37). In reality, the repossessing bank has made a time-sale of the airplanes; we know that because it has no expectation of getting them back. In the words of the first year property course it has no "reversionary interest."

4.   Bank leases aircraft to Northwest Airlines at a total payment of $10 million a year for five years, with an option for Northwest to purchase the five airplanes at their fair market value at the end of the five year term. What do you think?

————

Section 1–201(37) defines "security interest" to mean *any* "interest in personal property or fixtures which secures payment or performance of an obligation," a definition broad enough to include *any* distinctive claim to assets of a debtor that a creditor might assert on default. That definition of security interest, however, cannot be taken at face value. For example, section 9–339 (like former 9–316) states that nothing in Article 9 prevents subordination agreements in which a superior creditor subordinates its interest to another. It might be argued that when one creditor of a debtor agrees to subordinate its claim to that of another creditor, the elevated creditor acquires a "security interest"; the Permanent Editorial Board was worried enough about this possibility to amend the 1962 Official Text in 1966 to add section 1–209 which provides that this subordination does not create a security interest.

Security Interest or Lease?

A fecund source of disputes that 1999 Article 9 does not resolve is the question whether a particular document labeled a "lease" is a true lease—and so outside of Article 9 and under Article 2A—or whether it is a security agreement that creates a security interest under the terms of section 1–201(37). We now address that problem.

The Problem

The rights of a true lessor in personal property do not qualify as an Article 9 security interest. If a levying creditor of the lessee or the lessee's trustee in bankruptcy claims leased goods as against the lessor, Article 9 does not determine the outcome, and the lessor generally prevails under Article 2A. That is so even though no filing or other public record shows the lessor's interest. The drafters could have required lessors to file financing statements so third parties dealing with the lessee could better learn of the lessor's interests, but they did not. Under 9–505, a nervous lessor is permitted, but not required, to file (Comment 2 to 9–505).

If, on the other hand, the transaction is indeed not a true lease but an installment sale, and the "lessor" is in reality retaining a security interest to secure the obligation of the "lessee" to buy and pay for the goods, Article 9 governs. Such a "lessor" who does not comply with section 9–203 will not be entitled to enforce its interest even as against the debtor. If it does not file a required financing statement, it loses to all parties who, under Article 9 and other law, take priority over an unperfected security interest. These include certain purchasers from the "lessee," certain lien creditors of the "lessee," the "lessee's" trustee in bankruptcy, and others. The "lease vs. security interest" issue will continue to be one of the most frequently litigated issues under the Uniform Commercial Code. But why do secured creditors persist in claiming to be lessors? There are many reasons. A lessor has different rights than a secured creditor on default, on lessee bankruptcy, under federal, state and local tax laws, under rules of accounting, and under state usury laws. Many transactions with financing attributes are true leases under 1–201(37).

The distinction between lessor and secured creditor takes on added importance when the debtor is in bankruptcy. If a true lessee goes into bankruptcy, normally the lessee or trustee must affirm the lease and make full payments, or reject the lease and return the leased goods. The true lessor's rights to these payments or to return of the goods do not depend upon the filing of a financing statement or the taking of any action to "perfect" the lessor's interest. One claiming to be a lessor but who is found to be a secured seller and has filed no financing statement loses to the trustee in bankruptcy as an unsecured creditor. Even a perfected secured creditor may fare worse in Chapter 11 of the bankruptcy laws than a lessor because the debtor may be able to keep the collateral in a "cramdown" by paying its fair market value, instead of the contracted liability. The distinction is important in other contexts as well. Assume a debtor has signed a covenant with a lender that it will not borrow money except with lender's approval. If a "lease" is not a "borrowing" and so outside that covenant, the debtor may do it without the lender's approval. These and other rules like them may lead the lessor (or secured party) to characterize the transaction one way for one purpose (e.g., Article 9 law) and another way for another purpose (e.g., tax law). The lessor's lawyer may also try to draft something that will be accepted as a lease for accounting purposes, yet confer the economic rights of a security agreement.

One without experience in commercial law might think it a simple thing to distinguish between a lease and a security agreement. In fact, distinguishing between leases and secured sales agreements has been troublesome and the trouble has not abated in the years since the Code's enactment. Section 1–201(37) is the road sign that directs one to Article 9 for transactions that are really security transactions, or to Article 2A or other law for transactions that are truly leases. It has been twice revised since its origin in the 1950s; by far the most significant revision came in 1987 (which was done at the same time Article 2A on leases was drafted and promulgated). In connection with 1999 Article 9, the drafters made cosmetic changes in the opening paragraph of 1–201(37) that do not bear on any of the following discussion. So be careful here: references to "Revised 1–201(37)" usually mean to the 1987 revision, not to the 1999 revision. As of January 1999 the 1987 revision was the law in 49 states and the District of Columbia.

True Leases

Consider the purest form of lease and contrast it with the purest form of security agreement. A classic lease would be the lease of a truck for one year. If the truck has a useful life of ten years, the lessor, not the lessee would stand to gain from appreciation in the truck's value or to lose from its depreciation. The lessor has the "entrepreneurial stake" in the truck, and a valuable "reversionary" interest. Compare that to the position of a bank which lends money to a trucker so he can purchase the truck. If the bank takes security in the truck, the bank, of course, has an interest that the truck's value not decline below the amount of the debt outstanding, but beyond that the bank has no interest in the truck itself. If the truck proves to be worth twice what was expected, this is a windfall to the debtor, and if the truck is destroyed or declines radically in value, that loss falls on the debtor (provided it is solvent) and not on the bank. The trucker, not the bank, has the entrepreneurial stake.

When the term of a lease gets longer and inches toward the full economic life of a commodity, when an option to purchase is granted to the lessee, and when the lessee assumes many of the risks of ownership (secures for itself most of the benefits or detriments of ownership) a lease looks more and more like a secured loan in which the attributes of ownership are held not by the lessor (creditor), but by the lessee (buyer-debtor). In a 1988 Article, Edward Huddleson, a serious student of personal property leases, suggested that the real issue here is whether there is truly a reversionary interest in the hands of the lessor after the agreement is signed. He made the point as follows:

> The central feature of a true lease is the reservation of an economi-cally meaningful interest to the lessor at the end of the lease term. Ordinarily this means two things: (1) at the outset of the lease the parties expect the goods to retain some significant residual value at the end of the lease term; and (2) the lessor retains some entrepre-neurial stake (either the possibility of gain or the risk of loss) in the value of the goods at the end of the lease term.

Section 103(1)(j) of Article 2A offers a somewhat less helpful defini-tion of a "lease":

> "Lease" means a transfer of the right to possession and use of goods for a term in return for consideration, but a sale, including a sale on approval or a sale or return, or retention or creation of security interest is not a lease. Unless the context clearly indicates otherwise, the term includes a sublease.

Section 2A–103(1)(j) directs one to section 1–201(37) for answers to the hard questions. As you will see, the drafters of 1–201(37) failed to focus on the existence of a reversionary interest. Rather than state a bold and explicit definition based on the reversionary interest, the drafters offered a list of factors that should or should not support an inference of lease.

Problem 1–14

To: Law Clerk

From: Judge Carlton, U.S. Bankruptcy Judge

Recently a case has come before me involving two of our state's corporations. As you know, our state has adopted the Uniform Commercial Code in its entirety. The pertinent facts regarding the matter, are as follows:

Manheim Packing Co., Inc. purchased one Sausage Stuffer under a conditional sale contract, under which Resin retained a security interest in the machine, which it perfected by filing a financing statement with the Secretary of State. Another stuffer was delivered to Manheim under a written "Lease Agreement."

The Lease Agreement provided for monthly payments of $600.00 over a term of 48 months. The last six months payments, totaling $3,600, were payable upon execution of the lease. Some of the other terms of the agreement are as follows:

1. The equipment shall at all times be located at: Manheim Packing Co., Inc., 500 Elmore Way.

2. The equipment will carry a ninety-day guarantee for workmanship and materials and shall be maintained and operated safely and carefully in conformity with the instructions issued by our operators and the maintenance manual. Service and repairs of the equipment after the ninety-day period will be subject to a reasonable and fair charge.

3. If, after due warning, our maintenance instructions are violated repeatedly, Resin will have the right to cancel the lease contract on seven days notice and remove the equipment. In that case, lease fees would be refunded pro rata.

4. If lessee, Manheim Packing Co., Inc., violates any of the above conditions, or defaults in the payment of any lease charge hereunder, or becomes bankrupt, makes any assignment or becomes party to any proceedings for the benefit of its creditors, Resin shall have the right at any time without trespass, to enter upon the premises and remove the aforesaid equipment, and if removed, lessee agrees to pay Resin the total lease fees, including all installments due or to become due for the full unexpired term of this lease agreement and including the cost for removal of the equipment and counsel fees incurred in collecting sums due hereunder.

5. The equipment shall remain personal property of Resin and retain its character as such no matter in what manner affixed or attached to the premises.

In a letter accompanying the lease, Resin added two option provisions to the agreement. The first provided that at the end of the four-year term, Manheim could purchase the stuffer for $8,500.00. In the alternative, it could elect to renew the lease for an additional four years at an annual rate of $2,000.00. At the conclusion of the second four-year term, Manheim would be allowed to purchase the stuffer for one dollar.

Manheim never exercised either option. About one year after the stuffer was delivered to its plant, it ceased all payments under the lease and shortly thereafter filed a voluntary petition in bankruptcy. The trustee applied to the Court for leave to sell the stuffer free and clear of all liens on the ground that the "Lease Agreement" was in fact a lease intended as security within the meaning of the Uniform Commercial Code ("Code") and that Resin's failure to perfect its interest as required by Article 9 of the Code rendered it subordinate to that of the trustee. Resin responded with an answer and counterclaim in which it alleged that the agreement was in fact a true lease, Manheim was in default under the lease, and its equipment should therefore be returned.

Is Resin really just an unperfected secured creditor?

IN RE LYKES BROS. STEAMSHIP CO., INC.

United States Bankruptcy Court, M.D. Florida, Tampa Division, 1996.
196 B.R. 574.

PASKAY, CHIEF JUDGE:

This is a Chapter 11 reorganization case and the matters under consideration are two Motions for Summary Judgment. One is filed by the Debtor, Lykes Bros. Steamship Co., Inc. (Lykes) and the other by Blue Water Associates, L.P., GATX Financial Services, Inc., GATX Capital Corp., and Gilman Financial Services, Inc. (Blue Water). Both Motions are addressed to Counts I and Count II of Lykes' Cross–Claim against Blue Water. Each side contends that there are no genuine issues of material fact concerning the two claims under consideration and they are entitled to the relief they seek in their respective favors as a matter of law.

The claim of Lykes in Count I of its Cross–Claim against Blue Water is based on the contention that the transaction between Lykes and Blue Water was, in fact, a financing transaction and not a true lease and the relief sought is a declaration by this Court that this contention is correct. The claim in Count II of the Cross–Claim seeks a decree to quiet the title in the four vessels further described below and deem them owned by Lykes.

In due course, Blue Water filed its own Motion for Partial Summary Judgment, of course, contending the opposite; that is, that the transaction between Blue Water and Lykes concerning the four vessels was a pure and true lease. Under that theory, the vessels were owned and still are owned by Blue Water and Lykes' interest is limited to rights of a charterer of vessels under the transaction as documented between the parties. As an aside, it should be noted that Blue Water also filed an "Objection to Lykes' Motion for Summary Judgment," a pleading unknown in federal practice.

In support of its Motion for Summary Judgment, Lykes filed four Affidavits: two by Allen G. Tomek (Tomek) and two by Carl J. Horn (Horn), both of whom are employees of Lykes. In support of its Motion for Summary Judgment, Blue Water filed two Affidavits: one by Thomas C. Nord (Nord) and the other by Mark P. Hirschhorn (Hirschhorn), both of whom were in-house attorneys of Blue Water at the time their Affidavits were filed. In addition, the Debtor and Blue Water rely on numerous and voluminous documents evidencing the transaction between the parties which will be discussed in greater detail below. As a preliminary matter, it should be noted that none of the facts surrounding the series of transactions are in serious dispute, but, of course, the parties offer widely different interpretations of those facts and suggest different conclusions from same. The relevant facts as they appear from the record are as follows:

I. Cast of Characters—The Major Players

American President Lines, Ltd. (APL) is a Delaware corporation and maintains its principal place of business in Oakland, California. At all relevant times, APL was the owner or charterer/operator of a merchant marine fleet of vessels.

Lykes, the Debtor–In–Possession, is a Louisiana corporation which maintains its principal place of business in Tampa, Florida. Lykes was, and still is, the owner and operator of a merchant fleet just as APL.

Blue Water Associates, L.P. is a partnership organized under the laws of Delaware.

Meridian Trust Co. is a trust company organized under the laws of Pennsylvania and is Trustee for Blue Water Parties.

Both Mitsui Engineering and Shipbuilding Co. (Mitsui) and Mitsubishi Heavy Industries, Ltd. (Mitsubishi) are corporations organized and existing under the laws of Japan.

Chase Manhattan Bank, N.A. is a national banking association organized and existing under the laws of the United States of America and is Trustee for Mitsui and Mitsubishi.

GATX Capital Corp. is a Delaware corporation with its principal place of business in San Francisco, California.

Gilman Financial Services, Inc. is also a Delaware corporation with its principal place of business in New York, New York.

InterOcean Steamship Corp. (InterOcean) is a Florida corporation with its principal place of business in Tampa, Florida. InterOcean is the parent company of Lykes.

Blue Water, GATX Capital, GATX Financial and Gilman are collectively referred to as the Blue Water group or Blue Water Partners and are all financing institutions, as is Meridian which serves as Trustee for the Blue Water Group.

II.　Events Leading Up to the Present Controversy

On December 17, 1986, APL and Lykes entered into reciprocal Bareboat Charter Agreements (Debtor's Exhibit B) under which Lykes chartered four vessels to APL named, respectively, M/V PRESIDENT ARTHUR, M/V PRESIDENT BUCHANAN, M/V PRESIDENT GARFIELD AND M/V PRESIDENT HARDING, referred to by the Parties as the "Pacific-class or L–9 Vessels". In turn, APL chartered four vessels to Lykes, three of which were Seamaster class ships and one of which was a C–5 class vessel. The initial terms of these Charter Agreements were three years with two successive three-year options exercisable by APL. Both options were exercised and, thus, the second option will expire shortly—that is, in 1996.

The Pacific-class or L–9 vessels Lykes chartered to APL were to be built by two Japanese shipyards, Mitsubishi and Mitsui, respectively. The construction contracts, which were executed in 1984, initially called for the construction of three Pacific-class vessels by Mitsubishi and three by Mitsui. However, because of the economic crisis it faced, Lykes decided to cancel its trans-Pacific operation. Thus, before construction was completed, Lykes entered into negotiations with Mitsubishi to cancel its construction contracts on two of the vessels. Those negotiations culminated with an agreement pursuant to which Lykes agreed to pay Mitsubishi approximately $19 million as termination damages. As the result of mitigation of certain damages, that amount was later reduced to $5 million. In order to avoid any additional penalties, and since Mitsui and Mitsubishi agreed to finance the purchase price of the remaining four vessels, Lykes agreed to take delivery of the those vessels upon completion.

Under the construction contract, Mitsubishi was required to build a vessel bearing Hull No. 11158 for Lykes. The construction price was $41 million U.S. dollars toward which Lykes was entitled to a $2 million rebate. Lykes made an initial deposit of $4 million toward the purchase price, which was to be credited to Lykes upon closing. The three construction contracts with Mitsui were for vessels bearing Hulls Nos. 1323, 1324, and 1325. The construction price in U.S. dollars was approximately $41 million per vessel. Again, Lykes was entitled to a $2 million rebate per vessel. Lykes deposited more than $16 million toward the purchase price which was to be credited to Lykes upon closing. Lykes' contract with Mitsui contained a provision designed to protect Lykes against currency fluctuation risks and upon termination of the contract with Mitsui, Lykes agreed to an adjustment of the purchase price to reflect the then prevailing exchange rate which added an additional $18 million to the purchase price.

The construction of the three Mitsui vessels was completed on March 30, 1987, April 6, 1987, and April 28, 1987, respectively. Upon delivery, Lykes became the fee title owner of the vessels which were registered as U.S. flag vessels under the names M/V President Arthur, M/V President Buchanan and M/V President Harding. As security for the purchase money promissory notes executed by Lykes, Mitsubishi and Mitsui executed preferred ships' mortgages in favor of Chase, acting as indenture Trustee for the Shipyards on the Mitsubishi and Mitsui vessels. Although not directly relevant to the matters under consideration at this time, it appears that Lykes also granted, as further security, additional preferred ships' mortgages to Chase on other vessels owned by Lykes.

III.   Owner Participation Agreements and Bareboat Charters

By 1986, the container shipping industry was in severe recession. The competition was particularly fierce in the US/Pacific rim area. Lykes had no choice but to discontinue its trans-Pacific trade and was faced with the dilemma of how to utilize the four L–9 Pacific-class vessels.

Lykes was faced with the possibility of being burdened with the Mitsui financing arrangement, under which Lykes was required to pay 28 billion Japanese yen over 15 years, equivalent to an obligation of $198 million in U.S. dollars, or $47 million per vessel, an amount that was $6 million per vessel higher than the actual construction price. Lykes was forced to find a use for the Pacific-class vessels and had two alternatives: (1) to sell them and remove itself from the transaction completely, or (2) to find an economically sound financing arrangement under which Lykes could retain its interest in the vessels, yet live with the terms of the financing arrangement. The first alternative was out of the question since all four vessels were burdened by preferred ships' mortgages in favor of Mitsui and Mitsubishi, which secured an indebtedness far in excess of the original construction price, and also, far in excess of the actual value of the vessels. Moreover, these vessels were already under charter with APL, as will be discussed later, who had an option to renew the original three-year term three times, for a total of nine years. Additionally, these vessels were U.S. flag vessels and had the benefit of an operating differential subsidy granted by the U.S. Maritime Administration. Only APL was qualified to obtain similar benefits. Further, APL had enough volume to fully utilize the shipping capacity of these vessels.

Lykes decided that the only sensible solution to this dilemma was to obtain financing. One of the entities Lykes approached in early 1987 was Drexel Burnham Lambert Incorporated (Drexel Burnham) which agreed to explore the possibility of financing the four L–9 vessels built by Mitsui and Mitsubishi. There is no question that at the time the Blue Water transaction started to be negotiated, Lykes already owned the Pacific-class vessels subject, of course, to the preferred ships' mortgages of Mitsui and Mitsubishi. There is evidence in this record to indicate that the parties were aware that Mitsui and Mitsubishi had to consent to the financing, and counsel for Drexel Burnham specifically advised Mitsui and Mitsubishi that in the event Lykes filed for bankruptcy protection, the Bankruptcy Court could view a possible sale-leaseback arrangement as a method of financing the construction of the vessels and Blue Water as a secured lender, citing as authority for that proposition In re PCH Associates, 804 F.2d 193 (2d Cir.1986).

The heart of the controversy is the interpretation of the documents evidencing the transaction between Lykes and Blue Water concerning the four Pacific-class vessels chartered by Lykes to APL. The basic Agreements, each of which covered a separate vessel, are entitled "Bareboat Charters," and were entered into by Lykes with Blue Water on July 30, 1987, after the Pacific-class vessels were already chartered to APL. The principal features of these Agreements are as follows:

(1) Lykes agreed to convey to the Trustee for the benefit of Blue Water record title to the Pacific-class vessels;

(2) Blue Water agreed to charter back those vessels under a long-term charter arrangement to Lykes;

(3) Lykes was granted an option to repurchase the vessels; and

(4) Blue Water agreed to assume without recourse the underlying mortgage debt owed to Mitsubishi and Mitsui and agreed to lend to Lykes approximately $14.2 million plus simple interest calculated at the rate of 7.59% per annum, which amount was to be paid by Blue Water to Lykes in five annual installments from 1987 to 1992. The purchase price

fixed in the Agreements for the Pacific-class vessels was established at approximately $205 million, for an average of more than $51 million per vessel including the assumption of the principal balance of the Mitsui and Mitsubishi purchase money notes of approximately $27 billion yen or more than $190 million U.S. dollars at the then prevailing exchange rate.

As part of the transaction, the parties also executed a number of additional documents including an "Owner Participation Agreement" dated June 30, 1987, between Meridian as Trustee, Blue Water, Lykes and InterOcean. This document was designed to effectuate transfer of ownership of the Pacific Class vessels to Meridian as trustee for the benefit of Blue Water. (Ex. A to Lykes' Counterclaim and Cross–Claim). The Agreement further provided that Lykes was required to make 178 monthly payments for each vessel to Blue Water which was calculated to match the precise amount of the underlying-yen denominated mortgage debt owed to Mitsui and Mitsubishi.

The Agreement further provided that beginning in the 179th month and continuing through the end of the charter period, Lykes had two options: (1) to continue making the $12,500 daily charter payment for each vessel until the end of the charter period, that is the year 2007, or $4,562,500 per year per vessel, for a total of $91 million in charter payments; or (2) to exercise the right to purchase, at the end of the initial 178th month of the charter by Meridian to Lykes and at stated annual intervals thereafter, including at the end of the 238th month, one or more of the Pacific-class vessels for a termination value of the greater of $44.4 million dollars or the fair market value of the vessels.

The Agreement also contained the following provisions: first, it provided that if any of the Pacific-class vessels was declared a total loss or if title to the vessels was requisitioned by the government, Blue Water had the right to reconvey ownership of the vessels to Lykes upon payment by Lykes of a stipulated loss amount which had two components: (1) full payment of the balance on the Mitsubishi and Mitsui notes; and (2) a payment by Lykes to Blue Water. The Agreements further provided that, absent a total loss of the vessels, or any one of them, or a requisition by the U.S. government of the title to the vessels, or any one of them, Lykes was obliged either to exercise its option to purchase the vessels or continue to make the charter payments for the remaining years under the Agreements. Lykes did not have the option to purchase the vessels during the first 178 months of the Agreements and Lykes had no right to terminate the Agreements during its first 178 months, nor thereafter, unless it exercised its option to purchase.

In addition, Lykes also entered into various other agreements under which Lykes was required to make 178 monthly payments to Blue Water in the precise amount of the underlying yen-denominated mortgage debt which was due and payable to Mitsui and Mitsubishi which, as noted earlier, was assumed without recourse by Blue Water through its trustee, Meridian. Lykes also agreed to indemnify Blue Water against any adverse tax consequences which might be visited upon Blue Water as the result of the Agreements. (Exh. B to Lykes' Counterclaim and Cross-Claim).

As part of the transaction with Blue Water, Lykes executed a "collateral mortgage note" in the amount of $61,747,414.00. This was a bearer note, payable at 4% per annum until paid. It was payable at the offices of Meridian, the Trustee for Blue Water's interest. Under the note, Lykes also obligated itself to pay attorneys' fees if it was necessary to engage the services of an attorney to collect the note at the fixed rate of 10% of the amount due and sued for. To secure this collateral mortgage note, Lykes also executed a "collateral ship mortgage" and a "collateral chattel mortgage." It should be noted that in order to secure the collateral mortgage note, Lykes mortgaged to the holder of the note the M/V PRESIDENT ARTHUR, one of the very vessels which was allegedly transferred to Blue Water as a result of which Blue Water became the owner of the vessel which was then "leased back" to Lykes, a legally incongruous proposition indeed because it is axiomatic that one cannot hold a mortgage on the very property that is owned.

At the time of the Blue Water transaction, Lykes was indebted to the Bank Group led by Chemical Bank, in the amount of approximately $25 million. As part of the Blue Water transaction, Chemical Bank agreed to partially subordinate its lien on the accounts receivables of Lykes in favor of Blue Water. Of course, subordination by its very nature involves a legal proposition whereby one agrees to subordinate its secured position to the secured position of another, and this Court is not aware of any transaction which involves subordination when a secured creditor subordinates its rights to an ownership interest.

Under the Owner Participation Agreement, Blue Water was to advance toward its "equity" in the vessels, the sum of $14,170,564.00. Out of this amount, a total of $1 million was paid at closing. There was an additional escrowed amount in excess of $1 million and the balance of the so-called purchase price was retained by Blue Water, secured through Blue Water's deferral and set-off rights of Lykes' obligations to Blue Water. The $1 million cash payment was used to pay professional fees; Lykes received nothing at closing. The balance of the payment consisting of $1,023,529.00 was placed in escrow and out of that, $200,000 was transferred to an additional escrow account so that ultimately Lykes ended up with a balance of $800,000.00. The total investment of Blue Water in 1987 in this transaction was $2 million, for which Blue Water claimed an investment tax credit of more than $12.8 million, which permitted Blue Water partners to deduct dollar-for-dollar the amount of $12.8 million to be paid as so-called purchase price for the vessels from their federal income tax returns.

As part of the transaction, the parties also entered into a "Tax Indemnity Agreement" under which Blue Water was guaranteed that it would realize a "net economic return" which was defined as its "after-tax rate of return" on its investment. The Tax Indemnity Agreement required Lykes to guarantee that it would pay Blue Water any amounts necessary for Blue Water to maintain its net economic return. Lykes even indemnified Blue Water for any increase in the federal income tax rates, an event over which Lykes obviously had no control.

Thus, under the Agreements, the total amount invested by Blue Water was $14.2 million paid over five years between 1987 and 1992. In turn, Blue Water was to receive at least $44.4 million by the year 2002 if Lykes exercised its option to purchase at that time. If Lykes did not exercise the option, Blue Water would receive, until the year 2007, some $12,500 per day per vessel or $4,562,500 per year per vessel for, under this scenario, a total of $91 million in charter payments.

Basically, these are the relevant facts which, according to Lykes, would support its contention that the Owner Participation Agreement and Bareboat Charters collectively created a financing transaction and not a true lease or charter; therefore, Lykes is still the owner of the four Pacific-class vessels currently under charter to APL. Based upon these facts, both Lykes and Blue Water contend they are entitled to a ruling on the issue, i.e., the legal nature of the transaction—lease v. purchase—in their respective favors as a matter of law.

IV. GOVERNING LAW

There are essentially three potential sources of non-bankruptcy law which may be applicable for a proper analysis and characterization of the Blue Water transaction. The first and most obvious would be federal maritime law; the second is the applicable law of the state, in this instance the State of New York, which the parties agreed applies and governs the interpretation of the documents relevant to the issues under consideration; and lastly, the law of the state where Lykes maintains its principal place of business, that is, in Florida. Based on the parties' agreement, as evidenced by paragraph 15 of the Owner Participation Agreement which is Lykes' Exhibit A, this Court is satisfied that the laws of the State of New York shall apply to construe the Blue Water transaction, especially since section 671.105 of the Florida Statutes (1995) recognizes the parties' right to determine the choice of law. See, e.g., Citi–Lease Co. v. Entertainment Family Style, Inc., 825 F.2d 1497 (11th Cir.1987).

V. CHARACTER AND CONTROLLING FEATURES OF TRUE LEASES

It should be noted at the outset that it is a well-accepted and established proposition that the record title itself is not conclusive as to ownership of a vessel. Interpool, Ltd. v. Char Yigh Marine (Panama) S.A., 890 F.2d 1453, 1460 (9th Cir.1989); see, e.g., Jones v. One Fifty Foot Gulfstar Motor Sailing Yacht, Hull Number 01, 625 F.2d 44 (5th Cir.1980); The Kitty C., 20 F.Supp. 173 (S.D.Fla.1937). The structuring of a financing arrangement in the shipping industry is not novel and the vehicle of a bareboat charter was frequently used as part of a financing transaction. As noted by the Ninth Circuit, such arrangement has been a common method of ship financing since World War II. Interpool supra.

While one must concede that the maritime adaptation of a tripartite agreement poses a great many questions, in the last analysis, one must view the transaction not only in a pure pragmatic and technical legal point of view but also by taking into account all the economic factors which drove the transaction and which were the prime impetus to the ultimate decision to enter into the transaction and the reasons for structuring the transaction as it was done. There is nothing in federal maritime law which provides a good answer to the question, but courts have taken the approach of the Uniform Commercial Code as indicative of the federal common law of admiralty and for this reason, frequently looked to state law to fill this admittedly existing gap in maritime law. E.g., Bank of America N.T. & S.A. v. Fogle, 637 F.Supp. 305 (N.D.Cal. 1985).

New York adopted the Uniform Commercial Code and the statutory provisions in effect at the time of the Blue Water transaction provided:

UCC § 1–201(37)

"Security interest" means an interest in personal property or fixtures which secures payment or performance of an obligation. The retention or reservation of title by a seller of goods notwithstanding shipment or delivery to the buyer (2–401) is limited in effect to a reservation of a security interest * * *. Whether a lease is intended as security is to be determined by the facts of each case; however, (a) the inclusion of an option to purchase does not of itself make the lease one intended for security, and (b) an agreement that upon compliance with the terms of the lease the lessee shall become or has the option to become the owner of the property for no additional consideration or for a nominal consideration does make the lease one intended for security. UCC 9–102(1)

Except as otherwise provided * * *, this chapter applies:

(a) To any transaction (regardless of its form) which is intended to create a security interest in personal property or fixtures including goods, documents, instruments, general intangibles, chattel paper, or accounts. UCC 9–102(2) This chapter applies to security interests created by contract including * * * lease * * * intended as security. UCC 9–202

Each provision of this chapter with regard to rights, obligations, and remedies applies whether title to collateral is in the secured party or in the debtor.

N.Y.UCC 1–201(37), 9–102(1), 9–102(2) and 9–202 (1993 and Supp. 1995). It is noteworthy that the statutory provisions quoted are virtually identical to the standards established by § 101(50) of the Bankruptcy Code itself concerning true leases. The legislative history of that section states:

Whether a "lease" is a true or bona fide lease or, in the alternative, a financing "lease" or a lease intended as security, depends upon the circumstances of each case. The distinction between a true lease and a financing transaction is based upon the economic substance of the transaction and not, for example, upon the locus of the title, the form of the transaction or the fact that the transaction is denominated as a "lease." S.Rep. No. 989, 95th Cong.2d Sess. 64 (1978) U.S.Code Cong. & Admin.News 1978, pp. 5787, 5850.

The courts utilizing New York law to resolve this question generally applied a two-fold test: first, if the so-called lessee has an option to become an owner for no additional consideration or for nominal consideration upon completing the lease terms, the so-called lease is conclusively deemed to be a financing transaction. If that has been established, the court's inquiry ends. National Equipment Rental, Ltd. v. Priority Electronics Corp., 435 F.Supp. 236, 238 (E.D.N.Y.1977). However, if a court finds that the price required to exercise the option is not nominal, the court would then consider other factors, and most importantly "the economic substance" of the transaction. Courts have adopted a number of tests to determine whether the option to purchase is nominal and if the option price meets any of these tests, it has been regarded as nominal:

(a) Token or No Additional Consideration. A one dollar option is nominal. E.g., In re Ram Mfg., Inc., 56 B.R. 769 (E.D.Pa.1985); In re All American Mfg. Corp., 172 B.R. 394, 398 (Bankr.S.D.Fla.1994).

(b) Nominal Compared to the Total of Rental Payments. Matthews v. CTI Container Transport Int'l., Inc., 871 F.2d 270 (2d Cir.1989).

(c) Nominal Compared to the Original Purchase Price or List Price. E.g., In re AAA Machine Co., 30 B.R. 323 (Bankr.S.D.Fla.1983).

(d) Nominal if the "Lessee" is left with "No Sensible Alternative But to Exercise the Option." E.g., In re Oak Mfg., Inc., 6 UCC (Callaghan) 1273, 1277 (Bankr.S.D.N.Y.1969); In re Vaillancourt, 7 UCC (Callaghan) 748, 761–762 (Bankr.D.Me.1970).

(e) Nominal Compared to Fair Market Value at the Time of Exercise. E.g., In re Beker Industries Corp., 69 B.R. 937, 940 (Bankr. S.D.N.Y.1987).

One must concede at first blush, that the option price fixed by the Blue Water Agreements was facially not nominal at all, in that in order to exercise the option, Lykes was required to pay Blue Water the greater of the fair market value of the vessels or $44.4 million dollars. If this provision is viewed in a vacuum and any other surrounding provisions are disregarded, one might conclude that this is a true lease with an option to purchase. It is without dispute that under the Agreements, Lykes was required to pay to Blue Water over the full term of the charter period the total amount of $430 million dollars, comprised of the following components: (1) rental payments of 42.8 billion yen during the first fifteen years of the charter, which equates to the approximate amount of $3.29 million U.S. dollars at the exchange rates which existed in July, 1987, and (2) the rental payments totaling $91 million in U.S. dollars that Lykes was required to pay for years fifteen and beyond to the end of the term, i.e., between 2002 and 2007. In comparison, Lykes had the right to purchase the Pacific-class vessels in the year 2002 for the greater of $44.4 million or the fair market value. The original construction price per vessel was $41 million.

While the evidence presented indicates several different values on different dates, it is clear that at the end of the lease term, the vessels had, in terms of economic residual value, at least 20% of their appraised value. After the use of these vessels for fifteen years, the vessels were valued at $11.1 million each for a total of $44.4 million. Clearly, Lykes had nothing but a Hobson's choice to either purchase the vessels by exercising the option and paying the greater of $44.4 million or the fair market value in the year 2002, thus relieving itself of the requirement to make charter payments for the remaining five years, or to continue making the charter payments up to the year 2007 which would total $91 million. The net effect of exercising the option in year 2002 is that by prepaying the rent and using that savings, Lykes in fact doesn't have to pay any additional consideration for the purchase of the vessels.

The situation under consideration here is very similar to the factual scenario in In re Vaillancourt, 7 UCCRep.Serv. (Callaghan) 748 (Bankr. D.Me.1970). where the debtor had the choice in December 1973 of paying $147.25 to become the owner of certain equipment or to lease it for an additional year by paying $204.80. As the court noted, "[t]he choice between the two alternatives does not seem difficult. In the event the equipment was worth leasing at all, it would seem only sensible to pay the lesser sum to become its owner rather than the larger sum merely for the privilege of using it for another year." Id. at 762. As a matter of common sense and sound economics, it would have made no sense for Lykes to pay $91 million in rent for the five years following the year 2002, when it could purchase the vessels in the year 2002 for the greater of their fair market value or $11.1 million each. The evidence of whether or not these vessels collectively had a market value greater than $44.4 million in the year 2002 is conflicting. According to the affidavits submitted by Lykes, the value of these vessels in the year 2002 would be low, especially in light of their age and because Lykes' operating differential subsidy, provided by the United States and the Maritime Subsidy Board pursuant to 46 U.S.C. § 1171, was scheduled to expire in 1997. Without this subsidy, U.S. flag vessels bore high operating costs due to the requirement, among others, that a U.S. crew be utilized. That fact no doubt would have caused a substantial negative impact on the ultimate success of Lykes' continuing operation in the trans-Pacific arena.

Assuming for purposes of discussion, without conceding, that the option price was more than nominal, this does not end the inquiry and the Court must still look to a number of other factors which are indicative of the true nature of the Blue Water transaction. Other courts faced with that issue generally consider the following:

> (1) Which party bore the risk of loss during the term of the lease. See, e.g., Orix Credit Alliance, Inc. v. Pappas, 946 F.2d 1258 (7th

Cir.1991); Credit Car Leasing Corp. v. DeCresenzo, 138 Misc.2d 726, 525 N.Y.S.2d 492 (N.Y.Civ.1988).

(2) Whether the so-called "lessor" had any input on the selection of the equipment and its purchase. Orix, supra; National Equipment Rental, Ltd. v. Priority Electronics Corp., 435 F.Supp. 236 (E.D.N.Y. 1977); International Paper Credit Corp. v. Columbia Wax Products Co., Inc., 102 Misc.2d 738, 424 N.Y.S.2d 827 (Sup.Ct.1980).

(3) Which party was required to pay taxes and to maintain the "leased" equipment. Orix, supra; Matthews v. CTI Container Transport International, Inc., 871 F.2d 270 (2d Cir.1989).

(4) Whether the agreement grants to the "lessor" the right to accelerate the rents due over the remainder of the lease term, to sell the collateral, and to hold the "lessee" liable for any deficiency. Matthews, and Credit Car, supra.

(5) Whether the "lessor" was in the business of leasing. Matthews, O.P.M., and International Paper, supra.

(6) Whether the "lessee" was required to be responsible for all liability related to the equipment and to indemnify the "lessor" against all losses. Matthews and Credit Car Leasing, supra.

(7) Whether the "lessee" was required to maintain insurance on the property. Orix, Credit Car Leasing and International Paper, supra.

(8) Whether the equipment was custom designed for the "lessee's" use. In re The Answer—The Elegant Large Size Discounter, Inc., 115 B.R. 465 (Bankr.S.D.N.Y.1990).

(9) Whether the equipment would have significant value to other users or, because of the peculiar nature of the equipment or because it was difficult to remove after installation, the equipment would have less value to a subsequent user. The Answer, supra.

(10) Whether the "lessee's" payments were not calculated to compensate for use but rather to insure a return on investment. In re PCH Associates, 804 F.2d 193 (2d Cir.1986).

(11) Whether the initial purchase price, in a sale/leaseback transaction, was related to the value of the assets. PCH Associates, supra.

(12) Whether the transaction was structured as a lease to secure tax advantages. PCH Associates, supra.

The Eleventh Circuit, construing the same UCC provisions which apply in New York, similarly considered the following as indicative of a financing transaction because the "lessee" was required to:

(1) insure against risk of loss;

(2) bear the risk of loss yet remain liable for the "rent;"

(3) to indemnify the "lessor" against all liability;

(4) to pay all charges and taxes;

(5) to pay an advance rental or security deposit;

(6) to pay the collection costs and attorneys' fees of the lessor;

(7) to pay all accelerated lease payments upon default.

Citi–Lease Co. v. Entertainment Family Style, Inc., 825 F.2d 1497, 1499–1500 (11th Cir.1987). In Citi–Lease, just like in the present instance, the so-called lessor "entered the transaction without any property to lease. Its sole concern was to finance the acquisition of the [equipment] at a profitable return and a minimum of risk." Id.

In the case of In re Tillery, 571 F.2d 1361 (5th Cir.1978), the Fifth Circuit construed the transaction to be a financing transaction even though there was no option to purchase the leased property in question. The court based its findings upon the "lessee's" obligations to insure, pay taxes, pay license and registration fees, indemnify the "lessor," place a security deposit, and bear all risk of loss. Id. New York courts have recognized that the existence of an option to purchase at the fair market value does not necessarily compel the conclusion that the agreement was a true lease, and having considered numerous other factors, have concluded that the arrangements were, in fact, financing transactions. For example, in the cases of Guardsman Lease Plan, Inc. v. Gibraltar Transmission Corp., 129 Misc.2d 887, 494 N.Y.S.2d 59 (N.Y.Sup.Ct.1985) and National Equipment Rental, supra, the option provisions were identical to the provision in the Blue Water transaction. In each case, the purported lessee was granted the option to purchase at the higher of a fixed price or the fair market value.

The proposition advanced by Blue Water, that Florida law might apply, of course flies in the face of the specific provision in the Blue Water Agreements, which as noted earlier, clearly specify that the Agreements shall be construed pursuant to the laws of the state of New York. Be that as it may, even if Florida law applies, the results would be the same. There is a plethora of authority to support the proposition that similar transactions have been construed to be financing transactions. See, e.g., In re All American Manufacturing Corp., 172 B.R. 394 (Bankr. S.D.Fla.1994); In re Howell, 161 B.R. 285 (Bankr.N.D.Fla.1993); In re Canaveral Seafoods, Inc., 79 B.R. 57 (Bankr.M.D.Fla.1987); In re Chisholm, 54 B.R. 52 (M.D.Fla.1985); In re Associated Air Services, Inc., 42 B.R. 768 (Bankr.S.D.Fla.1984); In re AAA Machine Co., 30 B.R. 323 (Bankr.S.D.Fla.1983); U.C. Leasing, Inc. v. Barnett Bank, 443 So.2d 384 (Fla. 1st DCA 1983). Although the majority of these cases were decided within the context of a bankruptcy case, nevertheless, the courts applied the applicable state law, in this instance, the laws of the state of Florida. In U.C. Leasing v. Barnett supra, the Court considered the following as indicative of a financing transaction:

(1) The lease gave the "lessee" an option to purchase the equipment for a price which was 10% to 15% of the initial price. The court found that this was nominal.

(2) The initial payments, the monthly payments, and the option price were the "equivalent of the making of a down payment, monthly installment payments, and balloon payments as would have

been the case in a financing transaction" and the resulting yield to the "lessor" was readily equated to a current rate of interest in amortization.

(3) The "lessor" was not regularly involved in the manufacture or sale of the equipment. Its business instead consisted of procuring equipment at the instruction of a buyer who had previously made arrangements for the purchase of such equipment at a specific price. The "lessor" did not negotiate the price nor procure the equipment.

(4) The "lessor" does not regularly have inventory available for lease nor facilities not personnel to handle such inventory.

(5) The "lessor" on occasion required a guaranty of payment from third parties, which reflects security anxiety indicative that the lease is actually intended for security.

(6) The remedies of the "lessor" in the event of default are basically the equivalent of the rights and remedies of a secured party under the provisions of Article 9.

(7) The "lessee" was required to pay taxes, procure insurance, maintain and repair the equipment, and bear responsibility for loss and damage.

None of these cases accepted the suggestion that the "fair market value purchase option" was determinative. In the case of In re KAR Development Associates, L.P., 180 B.R. 629 (D.Kan.1995), the district court, reviewing on appeal an unpublished opinion of the bankruptcy court, stated:

This court concludes that the legislative history of § 502(b)(6), read together with § 365, shows Congressional intent that an economic realities test be used to determine whether a real estate transaction should be characterized as a lease. This, coupled with the interest in fulfilling bankruptcy purposes and objectives, provides an adequate "federal interest" to justify using a federal rule rather than a state law to define this particular property interest. Id. at 638.

Blue Water also urged this Court to reject application of the governing principle as enunciated by some courts and referred to as the "pragmatic test," contending that the decisions in this Circuit recognizing this test did so only in dicta, and the test is contrary to well-established precedents. This is not quite a correct statement of the law. In the Eleventh Circuit, in the case of In re Martin Brothers Toolmakers, Inc., 796 F.2d 1435 (11th Cir.1986), the court considered a transaction within the context of the applicability of § 365 of the Bankruptcy Code, a section which deals with assumption and rejection of executory contracts. In Martin Brothers, the Eleventh Circuit indicated that if a particular agreement is not unduly burdensome or is especially advantageous, it should not be construed as an agreement that is subject to § 365. Id. at 1439. While it is true that the Eleventh Circuit did not utilize the pragmatic test, that court's recognition of this rule is indicative and should be accorded great weight although it is technically not binding. One would be less than candid not to concede that application of the pragmatic test was not designed to benefit lessors but designed to promote rehabilitation and benefit the debtor and all of the creditors involved in the case.

In support of its position, Blue Water urges and advances a number of different propositions, such as that the documents constantly refer to Blue Water's interest as one of "ownership;" next, that Blue Water received an "independent" appraisal; third, that the Agreements required that Blue Water be treated as the owner for tax purposes; fourth, subsequent "confirmation" of such tax treatment by the IRS; fifth, the fact that GATX and Gilman, two parties of Blue Water, are claimed to be in the leasing business, and have treated similar transactions like thousands of other leases; next, that Lykes admittedly did not treat itself as owner of the L–9 vessels for tax and accounting purposes; seventh, that Lykes never operated the L–9 vessels itself; eighth, the fact that Blue Water borrowed funds and obtained financing to enter into the transaction; and ninth, Lykes invested no equity into the L–9 vessels.

Without giving short shrift to these contentions, it will suffice to say that this Court is not only in disagreement with the factual premises asserted by Blue Water, but also the legal conclusions drawn from those facts. Without discussing them in detail, it is sufficient to point out that the characterization of the transaction by Blue Water is obviously not controlling and just as the label placed on the transaction is not controlling, and the fact that Blue Water obtained an independent appraisal is a total non sequitur. One would be naive to assume that a financier would enter into a transaction involving millions of dollars without obtaining an independent appraisal of its collateral. The tax provision relied on by Blue Water is equally non persuasive. The advisory committee note to UCC 9–202 states:

> [I]f a revenue law imposes a tax on the "legal" owner of goods * * * this Article does not attempt to define whether the secured party is a "legal" owner or whether the transaction "gives" a security interest for the purposes of such laws. Other rules of law or the agreement of the parties determine the location of "title" for such purposes.

UCC 9–202. The fact that the transaction transfers investment tax credits and depreciation rights to a third party under the tax code, does not automatically signify transfer of ownership for purposes of the UCC or the Bankruptcy Code. In re Chateaugay, 102 B.R. 335 (Bankr. S.D.N.Y.1989). Lastly, the fact that GATX and Gilman are allegedly leasing companies has clearly no bearing on the intent of the parties. This is especially true, because GATX and Gilman are actually johnny-come-latelys to this transaction, having replaced the original partners of Blue Water long after the transaction was already structured and effectuated. The original lenders were Drexel Burnham and GECC. Drexel Burnham was never in the leasing business, it is a brokerage firm which ultimately landed in Chapter 11 itself. GECC is a secured lender who was, in fact, then a secured creditor of Lykes. The lead party to the transaction, Blue Water, was a newly-formed entity with no financial resources, no other leases in its portfolio, and clearly had never been nor intended to engage in the shipping business. It is illuminating to note the comments of another bankruptcy court on the business of GATX:

> In his deposition, the vice president of GATX testified that "we are in the business of asset-based financing, and basically we seek security." It is not difficult to infer an attempt to create a security transaction based on this statement. In re Eureka Southern Railroad, Inc., 72 B.R. 813 (Bankr.N.D.Cal.1987).

The balance of the propositions urged by Blue Water, such as the allegation that Blue Water obtained financing for the purchase of the L–9 vessels, is not true. The purchase of the L–9 vessels was financed by Mitsui and Mitsubishi and not by Blue Water. The fact that the lessor used its own money or borrowed money is without significance. The allegation that Lykes invested no funds in the L–9 vessels is equally untrue. Lykes paid $22.7 million in deposits, made several monthly debt service payments and carried a $300,000 monthly shortfall in payments to Mitsui and Mitsubishi for years. Considering the totality of the picture, this Court is constrained to conclude that the transaction under scrutiny was, in fact, a financing transaction and not a bona fide sale by Lykes to Blue Water of the L–9 vessels.

In sum total, having considered all the factors relevant, which are recognized by courts generally in determining whether a particular transaction is a true lease or a financing agreement, and considering the facts which are really indeed without dispute in this case, including the relevant documentary evidence, this Court is satisfied that, in fact, there are no genuine issues of material facts and the Debtor, Lykes, is entitled to resolve this controversy in its favor as a matter of law. This determination is based on the conclusion that the Owner Participation Agreement and the Bareboat Charters were, as a matter of law, not leases at all but financing arrangements and, therefore, the ownership interest remained in Lykes and the four Pacific-class, L–9, vessels are still owned by Lykes. This conclusion has no bearing or relevance whatsoever on the rights of Mitsui or Mitsubishi and has no reflection or determination of anybody else's interest, if they have any, on the L–9 vessels.

Accordingly, it is: ORDERED, ADJUDGED AND DECREED that the Debtor's Motion for Summary Judgment as to Counts I and II of the Counterclaim and Cross–Claim is granted.

It is further ORDERED, ADJUDGED AND DECREED that the Blue Water Parties' Motion for Summary Judgment as to Counts I and II of the Counterclaim and Cross–Claim is denied.

It is further ORDERED, ADJUDGED AND DECREED that Lykes is the record title owner of the four Pacific-class, L–9 vessels known as the M/V PRESIDENT ARTHUR (Official No. 695901), M/V PRESIDENT BUCHANAN (Official No. 697633), M/V PRESIDENT GARFIELD (Official No. 905624), AND M/V PRESIDENT HARDING (Official No. 909326). A separate Partial Final Judgment will be entered in accordance with this Order.

DONE AND ORDERED.

Problem 1–15

1. Assume the present value of the charter payments, if made, would be $90 million.

2. Assume the four ships have a value of $6 million each ($24 million total). If the charters are treated as leases and governed by section 365 of the Bankruptcy Code, the lessors can expect to receive full payment with a present value of $90 million; do you see why? If on the other hand the charters are treated as security agreements and the lessees as debtors, the lessors will receive payments under section 1129 that are likely to have a present value of far less than $90 million. To see why, consider sections 1129(a)(7), (a)(8), 1129(b) and 506. You may also want to take a look at the discussion on page 315 et seq. and in section 8 of this chapter.

§ 7. FORECLOSURE

To understand how the secured creditor's rights differ from those of the unsecured creditor, consider the rights of a typical secured creditor. Upon default by the debtor, the secured creditor would have a right to possession of all the collateral under 9–609, and the right to take possession of it by self-help as long as there was no breach of the peace. Thus, in problem 1–5, Bank One could ask the debtor to bring all the equipment to the construction lot, and to allow the creditor to come and get it at a particular time. If the debtor complied with the request, there would be no difficulty.

The Bank also might hire someone to go out on the weekend and take possession of all the goods, and, as long as there was no angry confrontation or breaking and entering at the construction site, it probably would have a right to take possession under 9–609. Even if the debtor refuses to give possession, there would be a quick cause of action such as replevin or the like, that would likely get it possession shortly after the demand and far sooner than possession could be had on behalf of an unsecured creditor.

Once the secured creditor has possession, it is entitled to sell the property—after proper notice and with proper "commercially reasonable" efforts under section 9–610(b), and assuming it complies with the other provisions in 9–611 through 9–614. Then, under 9–615(d)(2), it could sue the debtor for the deficiency (the difference between the amount due and the amount recovered on the sale). In the deficiency suit, the debtor might claim many things. First, it might claim the notice of the sale was deficient. Second, it could claim that some element of the sale (timeliness, place it was held, mode of advertising or a variety of other terms) was not "commercially reasonable," and thus, the sale could not be used as a basis to establish the deficiency.

The secured creditor would also have significant rights if the debtor went into bankruptcy before the repossession. Under section 506 of the Bankruptcy Code, the secured creditor would be recognized as "secured" to the extent of the value of its collateral, and under 361 would be entitled to "adequate protection" to protect it against the decline in value of its collateral. When and if a plan was proposed in Chapter 11, section 1129 would further protect the rights of the secured creditor, and would ensure that the plan would give it an amount, in cash if necessary, equal to the value of its collateral. If, on the other hand, the creditor were not secured, it would have no rights under 361, and would have considerably fewer rights under 1129. Its principal right was simply to share equally with the other unwashed.

Outside of bankruptcy, the unsecured creditor's rights are equally meager. Its remedy is to sue the debtor, ultimately to recover a judgment, and then, if the debtor has not yet gone into bankruptcy, to realize on the judgment by causing the sheriff to seize and sell assets of the debtor. This lawsuit will not be a quick replevin lawsuit. It will be a suit on the debt which, if brought in a crowded jurisdiction, or brought against a debtor who is determined in its opposition, and who asks for a jury and presents defenses, may come only at the end of long delays and a long trial. Pending the outcome of this trial, the debtor will have possession of the assets and will be able to dissipate them.

Problem 1–16

Assume Bank One assembles a team of repossessors who, on a Sunday afternoon, go to the construction site in Williston where the dam is being built. By threatening the security guard, they get him to open the gates. With a caravan of flatbed trucks, the repossessors take away several millions of dollars worth of bulldozers, cranes, cement mixers, and other construction equipment. The next day Bank One sends an e-mail to the joint venture, debtor, stating they intend to sell, a week from the following Monday, the collateral they have seized. In the meantime, Bank One advertises the material in the local newspaper in Williston, and contacts several people who are in the construction business in Montana, South Dakota, North Dakota, and Minnesota. On the following Monday, it sells the equipment in a private sale to a Minneapolis construction company. It then commences suit against the joint venture, for the difference between the $10 million debt then due, and the $2.3 million it recovered in the foreclosure sale. It also commences suit against the parent, who has guaranteed Joint Venture's debt.

Assume you are counsel either for the Joint Venture (which is still outside of Chapter 11, and is struggling to continue in existence), or the parent (who is solvent, but is obviously not looking for the opportunity to pay a $7.7 million deficiency). What defenses could you raise on their behalf under Part 6 of Article 9?

Problem 1–17

In 1999, First Bank loaned Northern Airlines, Inc. $225M to finance the purchase of five new Boeing 737s to be used in Northern's general operations. Northern granted the Bank a security interest in the 737s; Bank perfected.

For a period of seven years, Northern's financial condition steadily worsened though it managed to meet all of its obligations to the Bank. On September 1, 2006, Northern defaulted. There was an outstanding balance of approximately $140M. On January 5, 2007, the Bank took possession of the 737s.

1. Assume that the Bank spent $10M refurbishing the repossessed aircraft and an additional million in storing and maintaining them prior to sale. On April 5, 2007 it sold two of the aircraft for $30M cash; in November, 2007 it sold the remaining three for $60M plus interest to be paid over 40 years. The Bank would like to recover its deficiency under 9–615. (You may assume that the Bank's behavior has been commercially reasonable and timely, and that it has given all the proper notices.) What can the bank recover?

2. If the Bank held additional security in the form of a $10M letter of credit from CitiCorp in part 1 above, how would that affect the outcome? What would the Bank be expected to do?

3. Assume alternatively that the Bank has proposed to take the 5 aircraft in full satisfaction of its debt under section 9–620. What must it do to comply with that section and what are the legal consequences of so proceeding? Incidentally, why would anyone use 9–620 instead of going for a deficiency?

4. Assume that the Bank could not sell the aircraft and has, instead, decided to lease the 737s to startup Jet Blue for a period of 2 years at an amount of $7.5M per annum ($15M over the life of the lease). At the time the lease commenced, the appraised value of the 737s was approximately $100M.

During the two year lease to Jet Blue, soaring gas prices and impending federal noise regulations cause the value of the noisy, gas-guzzling 737s to depreciate rapidly. As a result, when the lease expired and the Bank retook possession of the 737s, the aircraft were worth only $25M. After applying the proceeds of the lease, a balance of approximately $125M remained on the debt. The Bank then held a public sale of the aircraft. The Bank set the date of the sale as February 1, 2009 and sent a timely and proper letter to Northern notifying it of the time and place of the sale. At the sale, the aircraft sold for $20M.

The Bank wishes to collect a deficiency in the amount of $105M. Advise the debtor about any challenges it can make.

§ 8. INTRODUCTION TO BANKRUPTCY

In the first chapter of this book, you have already seen four bankruptcy cases. In *A–1 Paving,* a secured creditor seeks "termination of the automatic stay" and asks for "abandonment of [its] assets from the bankruptcy estate." *In re Vic* arises from a similar dispute between secured creditors. In *Hardage*, Sears asserts a security interest over the personal property of the debtor; and Sears attempts to get a "reaffirmation" from the debtor. Although the case does not say so, the two issues are probably related. The debtor may be willing to reaffirm the debt only if Sears has a perfected security interest that will permit Sears, in the absence of a reaffirmation, to repossess the goods that the debtor wishes to keep. Finally, in *Lykes Bros*, the court wrestles with a complex set of rules to determine whether certain agreements are leases or security agreements and whether the debtor should be treated as subject to a security agreement or a lease. Each of these cases is in this chapter to expose some aspect of secured credit under the Uniform Commercial Code. But the outcome in each is ultimately dependant upon bankruptcy law that looms mysteriously over each court's more forthright interpretation of Article 9.

Start first with bankruptcy vocabulary:

1. Trustee: In bankruptcy there are three quite different "trustees". First is the person called "The United States Trustee" who is a federal official who serves as part of the federal hierarchy in each of the federal circuits. In theory the 1978 Bankruptcy Code separated the judicial functions from the administrative functions in bankruptcy. The former were given to the bankruptcy judge (who before 1978 had had many administrative functions) and the latter were given to the "US Trustee". According to its mission statement: "The United States Trustee Program acts in the public interest to promote the efficiency and to protect and preserve the integrity of the bankruptcy system. It works to secure the just, speedy, and economical resolution of bankruptcy cases; monitors the conduct of parties and takes action to ensure compliance with applicable laws and procedures; identifies and investigates bankruptcy fraud and abuse; and oversees administrative functions in bankruptcy cases."

Among its most critical functions, the US Trustee appoints panels from which individual trustees are selected for Chapter 7 cases. In Chapter 11 cases, the US Trustee also appoints and oversees the members of the creditors' committee. If warranted, the US Trustee is also authorized to appoint one or more individuals to serve as a standing trustee in cases under Chapter 12 or 13.

A second "trustee" is the "standing Chapter 13 Trustee". This is a person appointed by the US Trustee who supervises and facilitates all of the Chapter 13 plans in a particular jurisdiction. When a debtor files in Chapter 13, he or she must propose and get approval of a plan for payment to his or her creditors over a 3–5 year period. Someone must examine those plans to determine whether they are feasible and whether they conform to the rules in Chapter 13. That is the responsibility of the Chapter 13 Trustee. He is critical in the operation of the Chapter 13 process.

The last and most important trustee is the trustee who is appointed in every Chapter 7 case. This is a private citizen who receives a percentage of the assets of the bankruptcy estate (up to 25% of the first $5,000; 10% between $5,000–$50,000; 5% up to $1,000,000 and up to 3% of amounts above $1 million). This trustee is a representative of the "estate"; his responsibility is to hold the debtor upside down, shake him and then retrieve the coins that fall from his pockets. It is also this trustee's responsibility—where it is appropriate—to avoid unperfected security interests under section 544(a) or to set aside those that are preferences under section 547 or are otherwise avoidable. To the extent that the trustee avoids a security interest, he is representing the unsecured creditors against a secured creditor. One of the incentives for pursuing such actions is that his contingent fee grows larger as the estate is swollen by assets that, but for the avoidance, would have gone directly to a secured creditor.

2. <u>Debtor in Possession</u>: A Debtor in Possession, sometimes called the "DIP", is the person who runs a company in Chapter 11. In rare circumstances a trustee will be appointed to operate a business in Chapter 11, but almost always it is the DIP. In most circumstances the "debtor in possession" is the manager who ran the debtor company before the bankruptcy petition was filed. In some circumstances the management in place prior to the petition will be removed and another person will be installed as the DIP. A cynic might say that the choice between a debtor in possession and a trustee is the choice between a knave and a fool. By hypothesis the management who led the debtor into bankruptcy was not able to steer the business well enough to stay out of the ditch, so why would these knaves stay in charge? Because the alternative may be a fool, a smart lawyer with no understanding of the particular business and nothing but his intelligence to commend him as an operator of a particular business in a particular industry. Based on experience under the law of 1898, the drafters of the Code of 1978 thought it better to go with the knaves than to proceed with the fools. The DIP has the same rights as the trustee and thus is empowered to avoid security interests that are not properly perfected and, of course, to make dozens or hundreds of decisions each day with respect to the operation of the business in Chapter 11.

3. Established in almost all Chapter 11 cases, the <u>Creditor's Committee</u>, is composed of representatives of the creditors holding the largest claims in the bankruptcy. Since these are the same people who have the power to vote a plan up or down under the provisions of section 1129, any DIP who hopes to get out of bankruptcy by an agreed plan of reorganization must listen carefully to the committee's wishes and must ultimately negotiate with them about the shape of any plan.

4. <u>Holders of Secured and Unsecured Claims</u>: Under section 506 a person who has a perfected security interest in an asset of the debtor or has a right of set-off against an asset of the debtor, is regarded as a secured creditor—but only to the extent of the value of the collateral. For the purposes of Article 9 we usually refer to anyone with a perfected

security interest as a secured creditor even if the value of the collateral is insignificant. The Bankruptcy Code draws a different line. If one is owed $20M by a debtor and that debt is secured by collateral with a value of $11M, in bankruptcy the creditor would be treated as though he held two claims: a secured claim for $11M and an unsecured claim for $9M. In a plan this creditor would be a member of two classes and would be entitled to vote its secured claim in one class (where in most circumstances it would be the only member of the class) and its unsecured claim in a second class (along with many others).

5.   Bankruptcy Court. It is perhaps too obvious to state that the federal law establishes a bankruptcy court with its own judges who hear nothing but bankruptcy cases. Unlike the typical state or federal judge, these judges are specialists. Day in and day out, like a cow chewing its cud, they grind away on Chapter 11s, 7s and 13s. Obviously they are the experts on the meaning and operation of the Bankruptcy Code; less obvious they are also the experts on the meaning and operation of Article 9, for it is in bankruptcy that security interests are truly tested. Appeals from these courts go usually to local Federal District Courts. In some districts, some cases go to Bankruptcy Appellate Panels (BAP) made up of bankruptcy judges.

Consider now the various forms of bankruptcy, what they do and how they behave. First, understand that the legal issues in a typical Chapter 7 bankruptcy diverge about as far from the legal issues in a Chapter 11 bankruptcy as the issues in a merger diverge from those in an automobile accident case. Chapter 7s produce hundreds of thousands of relatively straight forward consumer cases each year. For those cases the bankruptcy court is like a giant mill that takes predictable input day by day and gives predictable output day by day. On the other hand are large Chapter 11 cases where there are many complex legal issues and where the problems brought to the bankruptcy court and to the parties for negotiation and litigation are often idiosyncratic and complicated. Chapter 13s, while similar to Chapter 11s in that there is a plan and a periodic payout, are in fact more like Chapter 7s in the sense that their processing is routine and not idiosyncratic.

By number individual Chapter 7 cases outweigh all others. In 2002 more than 1.5 million individual Chapter 7 cases will be filed. In theory in each of these cases the trustee will collect the debtor's assets and after setting aside assets that are exempt from the claims of creditors and that therefore must go back to the debtor, will distribute the remaining assets among unsecured creditors pro rata or allow the secured creditor to take those in which there is a perfected security interest. This picture of Chapter 7 is wrong. Many, perhaps a majority, of the 1.5 million consumer bankruptcy cases will be what are known as "no asset" cases. These are cases where the available exemptions permit the debtor to keep all of his assets and to enjoy a Chapter 7 discharge without giving anything to his unsecured creditors. The debtor's goal in a Chapter 7 is to get the discharge so to free his assets from the state law claims of his creditors and to leave him free to begin his life anew.

To see what assets might be exempt and so retained by the debtor even after the bankruptcy, consider section 522(d) (e.g., $15,000 of real property, $2,400 worth of a motor vehicle, $1,000 of jewelry, etc.). State law exemptions in some states are much more generous than those listed in 522(d); use of state law exemptions will sometimes allow a debtor to keep several hundred thousand dollars of assets (as this is written, Congress is wrestling with a new Bankruptcy Code that, for the first time, will place some restrictions on the homestead exemption which in Florida and Texas is now unrestricted).

The holder of a perfected security interest in a debtor's asset in Chapter 7 will often get much better treatment than his unsecured brethren. In theory perfected security interests are respected and protected in bankruptcy. At the end of a Chapter 7 a creditor holding a perfected security interest in a debtor's automobile is not limited by any exemption and may insist upon the return of the automobile notwithstanding the debtor's discharge. One suspects that the presence of a security interest mostly gives the secured creditor rights which it will use in negotiation with the debtor. In *Hardage*, Sears probably does not want to get the VCR and guitar board back. It is unlikely to recover its outstanding balance on a resale after repossession; to the contrary, the most likely "purchaser" of these assets is the debtor himself. By buying and using particular goods, this debtor has already demonstrated his interest in owning them and may have developed an affection for them. Moreover, these assets are already in the debtor's house, operate in a way he understands, and perhaps enjoys, and there is a significant transaction cost to replace them. For that reason it is often in the interest both of the debtor and of the secured creditor for the debtor to "reaffirm".

Under section 524(c) a debtor (provided he and the creditor follow the procedures there set out) "reaffirms" and so binds himself to continue to pay in accordance with the reaffirmation agreement even after the discharge. When Sears says to the debtor, "do you wish to reaffirm or would you rather have us repossess the washing machine," it is initiating a negotiation that is likely to result in a reaffirmation for the benefit of both parties. The debtor is spared the cost and inconvenience of finding a new washing machine and Sears gets a larger payment than it probably would get if it had to repossess and resell.

So most, though not all, of the legal action in Chapter 7s involves reaffirmation, the discharge under section 524, exceptions to discharge under section 523 (certain debts, e.g., alimony, are not dischargeable) and the workings of the exemption law under section 522.

Turn now to Chapter 13s, sometimes called "wage earner plans". Use of Chapter 13 varies widely among federal districts for reasons that are hard to explain. In most places Chapter 13s are only a small percentage of Chapter 7s. There are several virtues to Chapter 13s for some debtors. Some debtors feel a moral obligation to pay as much of their debt as they can. Chapter 13 allows those debtors to make significant payments over 3–5 years within the structure established by Chapter 13. There are more selfish reasons for Chapter 13s too. Under Chapter 13 the debtor can keep his secured asset notwithstanding the objection of the secured creditor provided he makes appropriate payments. Except with respect to his home mortgage, the debtor can normally keep a secured asset by making payments over 3–5 years equal to the "value" of the asset even though that value may be less than the outstanding debt. Thus, for example, one might be permitted to redeem his automobile by making payments with a present value of $10,000 for a car worth $10,000 even though the secured debt outstanding is $20,000. In Chapter 7 the debtor could not redeem his car by making a series of payments with a value of $10,000 without the agreement of the creditor.

Only a small percentage of all bankruptcies are Chapter 11s (reorganizations), but this is where the sport is. Most, but not all, Chapter 11s are filed by corporations and many of those wind up as liquidations either back in Chapter 7 or as "liquidating Chapter 11 plans". Many of these will be small one horse operations (like T & J Loggers had they been incorporated); most of these small businesses never had a hope of reorganization. Filing in Chapter 11 in those cases is sometimes motivated by the debtor's wish to remain as the "debtor in possession" (and to keep earning a salary as such) and to avoid the sharp eye of a Chapter 7 "trustee."

In a Chapter 11 of a sizeable going concern (such as K–Mart, Fruit of the Loom or Owens Corning all residing in Chapter 11 as of this writing), the bankruptcy can be divided into several phases. The first phase arises out of the rights and obligations conferred by sections in chapter 3: 361 (adequate protection), 362 (automatic stay), 363 (use, sale or lease of property), 364 (obtaining credit; yes, as remarkable as it may seem, large companies in bankruptcy often borrow large amounts of money), and 365 (executory contracts and leases; this section probably underlies the Lykes case). In such a case the DIP will propose a "first day order" for the court's approval. This order will conform to idiosyncrasies of the court where the bankruptcy is filed and its terms may have been negotiated, even prior to the filing, with some of the important creditors. It will allow the DIP to use cash to meet its current expenses and will give certain protections to creditors against losses that might result from the use of that cash. Depending on the case and the court, there will be many other terms in this order about payment of fees and the like.

Shortly skirmishes may develop between the DIP and various secured and unsecured creditors. Because of the automatic stay under section 362, no secured creditor can repossess its collateral, nor any unsecured creditor try to collect without having the stay lifted. Some secured creditors may come to court and ask that the stay be lifted, usually by claiming that their assets are declining in value or will be used up and thus they will be left without sufficient funds at the end of the Chapter 11. These claims will be met by counter assertions (the assets are increasing, not decreasing, in value) and by offers of adequate protection under section 361 (i.e., of substitute collateral or current payments). There may also be skirmishes over section 365 where the debtor may choose to reject certain leases or executory contracts (as this is written, K–Mart has said that it is using section 365 to cancel more than 100 of its leases).

It is important to understand the straight jacket into which a Chapter 11 puts even a fully secured creditor. First, section 362 bars repossession and nearly all other acts to collect. Second, there will be no lifting of the automatic stay of 362 if the DIP can make a plausible case for adequate protection under 361 (that will protect the secured creditor against the declining value of the collateral). Third, the creditor collects no interest on its secured debt because of section 506, except to the extent that the value of the collateral exceeds the amount of the debt. Thus if a secured creditor contemplates a Chapter 11 that would last for 3 years and holds a $30M loan that is secured by only $25M of assets, it can look forward to 3 years without a meal. Because there is a lot of play in the joints on what is "adequate" under section 361, a nervous secured creditor may foresee and fear the possibility not only that he will not be paid interest for the period of the bankruptcy but also that his collateral may be used up or sold by the DIP (see section 363) and replaced by some asset of undetermined value found to be "adequate" by the bankruptcy court. This is one of the fears of the holders of rights in accounts receivable in the LTV case below. A creditor secured by good accounts receivable owed by financially responsible purchasers from LTV might fear the possibility that the bankruptcy judge would substitute a mortgage on a rusty steel plant as adequate protection in return for the DIP's use of the payments that are coming in on those accounts receivable.

A second phase in many Chapter 11 cases might involve the DIP's attempt to avoid certain security interests under sections 544(a) and following. Section 544(a) allows the Trustee in bankruptcy or DIP to set aside a security interest that is not perfected at the time the petition is filed. When a creditor's security interest is set aside, the creditor joins the ranks of unsecured creditors and shares pro rata in the assets of the debtor; the collateral that would have gone only to the secured creditor is now shared by all of the unsecured creditors. In many cases the trustee or DIP can also get back payments made or avoid security interests perfected within 90 days of the petition. In rare cases the trustee or DIP can reach back even farther on the ground that a particular payment or transfer constituted a fraudulent conveyance that can be avoided by a combination of 544(b) and state fraudulent conveyance law or by the use of 548 that allows certain direct avoidance of fraudulent conveyances under the federal law. We will spend considerable time and effort with sections 544(a), (b) and 547 in chapter 7 of this book.

The final phase of the Chapter 11 is the negotiation and approval of the plan of reorganization. Plans and their negotiations take many forms. In some cases the bankruptcy is "prepackaged", i.e., a tentative plan is negotiated by the debtor and its creditors even before the petition is filed. In those cases various creditors, secured and unsecured, give their tentative approval to the plan and it is contemplated that the debtor will be in bankruptcy for less than six months.

Usually the proposal and the negotiation of a plan comes long after the petition is filed. The plan might take the form (as is apparently true of Enron at this writing) of a sale by the estate of the principal operating assets of the former company. More often the plan takes the form of a recapitalization of the debtor and of the debtor's coming out of bankruptcy with most, if not all, of its assets, with many of its debts reduced or changed into equity and with its equity holders cut off or given only a small sliver of the new company. In a negotiated plan each class of creditors (though not necessarily each creditor) votes for the plan, and the plan is so approved under the terms of section 1129(a). Almost all Chapter 11 plans approved by a bankruptcy court are "negotiated plans" not "cram downs". A small minority of plans are "cram downs," those approved by the court notwithstanding the contrary vote of at least one class.

Turn now to section 1129(a) and look at the requirements for a plan. Note that a plan can be approved over the objecting vote of a class only if section 1129(b) is satisfied. Subsection 1129(b) is a substitute for a favorable vote by the dissenting class or classes that would otherwise satisfy 1129(a)(8). For this course we concern ourselves with 1129(b)(2)(A); it describes what has to be done in order to impose a plan on a non-agreeing class of secured creditors. While there are several ways to satisfy subsection (A), the central requirement is stated in (A)(i)(II), the provision of "cash payments totaling at least the allowed amount of [secured claims]". This means that a secured creditor who holds a security interest in an asset with a value of $10M must be given rights in the plan of reorganization that are worth $10M on the date the plan is confirmed. Alternatively, the secured creditor may be made to take "the indubitable equivalent" of its claim under (A)(i)(II).

To reiterate, it is rare for a debtor successfully to "cram down" a plan on a class of creditors who vote against it. On the other hand it is equally rare for the negotiation between the DIP and individual secured creditors to proceed without consideration (and doubtless a threat) about how a plan might be crammed down under section 1129(b)(2)(A). So the negotiation that may be extensive and intense will take place in the shadow of section 1129, and no lawyer for a secured creditor or a debtor in Chapter 11 dares ignore it.

Now return to the bankruptcy cases in this chapter. *Hardage* shows the debtor's seeking to avoid the creditor's security interest and the creditor's trying to keep hold of it in order to increase its leverage in negotiation for a reaffirmation. *Lykes* probably foretells a negotiation about the lessor/secured creditor's right to payment; these would be the large agreed payments if the agreement is a lease but small payments if the obligation is debt secured by measly assets (for in the latter case there could be a cram down under 1129(b)(2)(A) by the payment of a modest sum which by hypothesis would be equal to the "allowed amount of such claim"). In *A–1 Paving* we see a person who claims to be a perfected secured creditor asking the estate to abandon those assets and return them to him and a competing secured creditor asserting that the moving party has no perfected security interest. *In re Vic* is a priority dispute between two secured creditors that happens to be litigated in bankruptcy court.

When you read the foregoing, beware the reaction of the little boy who received the book about penguins for Christmas: "this book tells me more than I wish to know about penguins". Only by knowing something about bankruptcy can one understand the importance of Article 9 or appreciate the practical concerns of a secured creditor.

Chapter Two

SECURITY IN INVENTORY
AND ITS PROCEEDS

---

§ 1. INTRODUCTION

Taking security in inventory and its proceeds is far more complex than taking security in business equipment. In the first place, inventory changes every day a business is open, and money is collected on the sale of inventory every day. That means the proceeds of sales will often be paid to the lender to reduce the loan, and the loan will then be increased when the debtor has to buy new inventory. Thus, the security agreement must take into account the fact that there will be "future advances," i.e., new extensions of credit, and that much of the collateral will be "after-acquired". This claim of the creditor against the debtor's assets is sometimes called a "floating lien," because it floats on top of a river of inventory and proceeds.

But what are "proceeds"? Proceeds are whatever the debtor receives on the sale or other disposition of the collateral. In the case of a car dealer, the proceeds are the personal check, cashier's check, or possibly the note and security agreement the car dealer gets back when he sells a car to a purchaser. In the case of a department store, the proceeds are likely to be not only cash and checks, but also payment obligations on a credit card issued by the store or a bank. Life is further complicated by the fact that some lenders lend against inventory, and others lend against promises of payment. Sometimes promises of payment are embodied in notes and other security agreements that are called "chattel paper". So, there is a potential conflict in many cases between the secured creditor's claim in proceeds and the claim in those same proceeds as the *original collateral* of a second lender. To accommodate all of this, the security agreement typically is quite complicated, for it has to cover not only proceeds, the original collateral and original loan, but also new loans, after-acquired property and proceeds derived months or years after the initial loan.

We also confront a new form of security interest—a purchase money security interest. The purchase money security interest might occur when a second creditor, or seller, offers to finance a new line of merchandise for the merchant debtor. If that secured creditor complies with certain conditions, it can have priority over the earlier perfected secured creditor, despite the fact that it is second in time, and comes much later. There are complexities in defining what is purchase money, understanding the priority rule and understanding the conditions that have to be satisfied.

It will not surprise you to know that buyers of inventory take free of secured creditors' interest even if that interest in the inventory is perfected. This makes sense; think about it. When you last bought something at Sears, JC Penney's or Bloomingdales, did you inspect the filings at the Secretary of State's office to determine whether there was a perfected security interest that would prevail over your claim? No. Section 9–320 allows a buyer in the ordinary course to take free of even a perfected security interest in inventory.

Consider a security agreement that an inventory lender might ask its debtor to sign:

Security Agreement

(All Assets)

For value received, DEBTOR, INC. ("Debtor") grants to LENDER, INC, a Michigan banking corporation ("Bank"), a continuing security interest and lien (any pledge, assignment, security interest or other lien arising hereunder is sometimes referred to herein as a "security interest") in the Collateral (as defined below) to secure payment when due, whether by stated maturity, demand, acceleration or otherwise, of all existing and future indebtedness ("Indebtedness") to the Bank of "Borrower" and/or Debtor. Indebtedness includes without limit any and all obligations or liabilities of the Borrower and/or Debtor to the Bank, whether absolute or contingent, direct or indirect, voluntary or involuntary, liquidated or unliquidated, joint or several, known or unknown; any and all obligations or liabilities for which the Borrower and/or Debtor would otherwise be liable to the Bank were it not for the invalidity or unenforceability of them by reason of any bankruptcy, insolvency or other law, or for any other reason; any and all amendments, modifications, renewals and/or extensions of any of the above; all costs incurred by Bank in establishing, determining, continuing, or defending the validity or priority of its security interest, or in pursuing its rights and remedies under this Agreement or under any other agreement between Bank and Borrower and/or Debtor or in connection with any proceeding involving Bank as a result of any financial accommodation to Borrower and/or Debtor; and all other costs of collecting Indebtedness, including without limit attorney fees. Debtor agrees to pay Bank all such costs incurred by the Bank, immediately upon demand, and until paid all costs shall bear interest at the highest per annum rate applicable to any of the Indebtedness, but not in excess of the maximum rate permitted by law. Any reference in this Agreement to attorney fees shall be deemed a reference to reasonable fees, costs, and expenses of both in-house and outside counsel and paralegals, whether or not a suit or action is instituted, and to court costs if a suit or action is instituted, and whether attorney fees or court costs are incurred at the trial court level, on appeal, in a bankruptcy, administrative or probate proceeding or otherwise. Debtor further covenants, agrees and represents as follows:

1. Collateral shall mean all of the following property Debtor now or later owns or has an interest in, wherever located:

   (a) all Accounts Receivable (for purposes of this Agreement, "Accounts Receivable" consists of all accounts; general intangibles; chattel paper (including without limit electronic chattel paper and tangible chattel paper); contract rights; deposit accounts; documents; instruments; rights to payment evidenced by chattel paper, documents or instruments; health care insurance receivables; commercial tort claims; letters of credit; letter of credit rights; supporting obligations; and rights to payment for money or funds advanced or sold),

   (b) all Inventory,

   (c) all Equipment and Fixtures,

   (d) all Software (for purposes of this Agreement, "Software" consists of all (i) computer programs and supporting information provided in connection with a transaction relating to the program, and (ii) computer programs embedded in goods and any supporting information provided in connection with a transaction relating to the program whether or not the program is associated with the goods in such a manner that it customarily is considered part of the goods, and whether or not, by becoming the owner of the goods, a person acquires a right to use the program in connection with the goods, and whether or not the program is embedded in goods that consist solely of the medium in which the program is embedded),

   (e) specific items listed below and/or on attached Schedule A, if any, is/are also included in Collateral:

   _____

   _____

   (f) all goods, instruments, documents, policies and certificates of insurance, deposits, money, investment property or other property (except real property which is not a fixture) which are now or later in possession or control of Bank, or as to which Bank now or later controls possession by documents or otherwise, and

   (g) all additions, attachments, accessions, parts, replacements, substitutions, renewals, interest, dividends, distributions, rights of any kind (including but not limited to stock splits, stock rights, voting and preferential rights), products, and proceeds of or pertaining to the above including, without limit, cash or other property which were proceeds and are recovered by a bankruptcy trustee or otherwise as a preferential transfer by Debtor.

In the definition of Collateral, a reference to a type of collateral shall not be limited by a separate reference to a more specific or narrower type of that collateral.

2. Warranties, Covenants and Agreements. Debtor warrants, covenants and agrees as follows:

2.1 Debtor shall furnish to Bank, in form and at intervals as Bank may request, any information Bank may reasonably request and allow Bank to examine, inspect, and copy any of Debtor's books and records. Debtor shall, at the request of Bank, mark its records and the Collateral to clearly indicate the security interest of Bank under this Agreement.

2.2 At the time any Collateral becomes, or is represented to be, subject to a security interest in favor of Bank, Debtor shall be deemed to have warranted that (a) Debtor is the lawful owner of the Collateral and has the right and authority to subject it to a security interest granted to Bank; (b) none of the Collateral is subject to any security interest other than that in favor of Bank; (c) there are no financing statements on file, other than in favor of Bank; (d) no person, other than Bank, has possession or control (as defined in the Uniform Commercial Code) of any Collateral of such nature that perfection of a security interest may be accomplished by control; and (e) Debtor acquired its rights in the Collateral in the ordinary course of its business.

2.3 Debtor will keep the Collateral free at all times from all claims, liens, security interests and encumbrances other than those in favor of Bank. Debtor will not, without the prior written consent of Bank, sell, transfer or lease, or permit to be sold, transferred or leased, any or all of the Collateral, except for Inventory in the ordinary course of its business and will not return any Inventory to its supplier. Bank or its representatives may at all reasonable times inspect the Collateral and may enter upon all premises where the Collateral is kept or might be located.

2.4 Debtor will do all acts and will execute or cause to be executed all writings requested by Bank to establish, maintain and continue an exclusive, perfected and first security interest of Bank in the Collateral. Debtor agrees that Bank has no obligation to acquire or perfect any lien on or security interest in any asset(s), whether realty or personalty, to secure payment of the Indebtedness, and Debtor is not relying upon assets in which the Bank may have a lien or security interest for payment of the Indebtedness.

2.5 Debtor will pay within the time that they can be paid without interest or penalty all taxes, assessments and similar charges which at any time are or may become a lien, charge, or encumbrance upon any Collateral, except to the extent contested in good faith and bonded in a manner satisfactory to Bank. If Debtor fails to pay any of these taxes, assessments, or other charges in the time provided above, Bank has the option (but not the obligation) to do so and Debtor agrees to repay all amounts so expended by Bank immediately upon demand, together with interest at the highest lawful default rate which could be charged by Bank on any Indebtedness.

2.6 Debtor will keep the Collateral in good condition and will protect it from loss, damage, or deterioration from any cause. Debtor has and will maintain at all times (a) with respect to the Collateral, insurance under an "all risk" policy against fire and other risks customarily insured against, and (b) public liability insurance and other insurance as may be required by law or reasonably required by Bank, all of which insurance shall be in amount, form and content, and written by companies as may be satisfactory to Bank, containing a lender's loss payable endorsement acceptable to Bank. Debtor will deliver to Bank immediately upon demand evidence satisfactory to Bank that the required insurance has been procured. If Debtor fails to maintain satisfactory insurance, Bank has the option (but not the obligation) to do so and Debtor agrees to repay all amounts so expended by Bank immediately upon demand, together with interest at the highest lawful default rate which could be charged by Bank on any Indebtedness.

2.7 On each occasion on which Debtor evidences to Bank the account balances on and the nature and extent of the Accounts Receivable, Debtor shall be deemed to have warranted that except as otherwise indicated (a) each of those Accounts Receivable is valid and enforceable without performance by Debtor of any act; (b) each of those account balances are in fact owing, (c) there are no setoffs, recoupments, credits, contra accounts, counterclaims or defenses against any of those Accounts Receivable, (d) as to any Accounts Receivable represented by a note, trade acceptance, draft or other instrument or by any chattel paper or document, the same have been endorsed and/or delivered by Debtor to Bank, (e) Debtor has not received with respect to any Account Receivable, any notice of the death of the related account debtor, nor of the dissolution, liquidation, termination of existence, insolvency, business failure, appointment of a receiver for, assignment for the benefit of creditors by, or filing of a petition in bankruptcy by or against, the account debtor, and (f) as to each Account Receivable, except as may be expressly permitted by Bank to the contrary in another document, the account debtor is not an affiliate of Debtor, the United States of America or any department, agency or instrumentality of it, or a citizen or resident of any jurisdiction outside of the United States. Debtor will do all acts and will execute all writings requested by Bank to perform, enforce performance of, and collect all Accounts Receivable. Debtor shall neither make nor permit any modification, compromise or substitution for any Account Receivable without the prior written consent of Bank. Debtor shall, at Bank's request, arrange for verification of Accounts Receivable directly with account debtors or by other methods acceptable to Bank.

2.8 Debtor at all times shall be in strict compliance with all applicable laws, including without limit any laws, ordinances, directives, orders, statutes, or regulations an object of which is to regulate or improve health, safety, or the environment ("Environmental Laws").

2.9 If Bank, acting in its sole discretion, redelivers Collateral to Debtor or Debtor's designee for the purpose of (a) the ultimate sale or exchange thereof; or (b) presentation, collection, renewal, or registration of transfer thereof; or (c) loading, unloading, storing, shipping, trans-shipping, manufacturing, processing or otherwise dealing with it preliminary to sale or exchange; such redelivery shall be in trust for the benefit of Bank and shall not constitute a release of Bank's security interest in it or in the proceeds or products of it unless Bank specifically so agrees in writing. If Debtor requests any such redelivery, Debtor will deliver with such request a duly executed financing statement in form and substance satisfactory to Bank. Any proceeds of Collateral coming into Debtor's possession as a result of any such redelivery shall be held in trust for Bank and immediately delivered to Bank for application on the Indebtedness. Bank may (in its sole discretion) deliver any or all of the Collateral to Debtor, and such delivery by Bank shall discharge Bank from all liability or responsibility for such Collateral. Bank, at its option, may require delivery of any Collateral to Bank at any time with such endorsements or assignments of the Collateral as Bank may request.

2.10 At any time and without notice, Bank may (a) cause any or all of the Collateral to be transferred to its name or to the name of its nominees; (b) receive or collect by legal proceedings or otherwise all dividends, interest, principal payments and other sums and all other distributions at any time payable or receivable on account of the Collateral, and hold the same as Collateral, or apply the same to the Indebtedness, the manner and distribution of the application to be in the sole discretion of Bank; (c) enter into any extension, subordination, reorganization, deposit, merger or consolidation agreement or any other agreement relating to or affecting the Collateral, and deposit or surrender control of the Collateral, and accept other property in exchange for the Collateral and hold or apply the property or money so received pursuant to this Agreement; and (d) take such actions in its own name or in Debtor's name as Bank, in its sole discretion, deems necessary or appropriate to establish exclusive control (as defined in the Uniform Commercial Code) over any Collateral of such nature that perfection of Bank's security interest may be accomplished by control.

2.11 Bank may assign any of the Indebtedness and deliver any or all of the Collateral to its assignee, who then shall have with respect to Collateral so delivered all the rights and powers of Bank under this Agreement, and after that Bank shall be fully discharged from all liability and responsibility with respect to Collateral so delivered.

2.12 Debtor delivers this Agreement based solely on Debtor's independent investigation of (or decision not to investigate) the financial condition of Borrower and is not relying on any information furnished by Bank. Debtor assumes full responsibility for obtaining any further information concerning the Borrower's financial condition, the status of the Indebtedness or any other matter which the undersigned may deem necessary or appropriate now or later. Debtor waives any duty on the part of Bank, and agrees that Debtor is not relying upon nor expecting Bank to disclose to Debtor any fact now or later known by Bank, whether relating to the operations or condition of Borrower, the existence, liabilities or financial condition of any guarantor of the Indebtedness, the occurrence of any default with respect to the Indebtedness, or otherwise, notwithstanding any effect such fact may have upon Debtor's risk or Debtor's rights against Borrower. Debtor knowingly accepts the full range of risk encompassed in this Agreement, which risk includes without limit the possibility that Borrower may incur Indebtedness to Bank after the financial condition of Borrower, or Borrower's ability to pay debts as they mature, has deteriorated.

2.13   Debtor shall defend, indemnify and hold harmless Bank, its employees, agents, shareholders, affiliates, officers, and directors from and against any and all claims, damages, fines, expenses, liabilities or causes of action of whatever kind, including without limit consultant fees, legal expenses, and attorney fees, suffered by any of them as a direct or indirect result of any actual or asserted violation of any law, including, without limit, Environmental Laws, or of any remediation relating to any property required by any law, including without limit Environmental Laws.

3.   Collection of Proceeds.

3.1   Debtor agrees to collect and enforce payment of all Collateral until Bank shall direct Debtor to the contrary. Immediately upon notice to Debtor by Bank and at all times after that, Debtor agrees to fully and promptly cooperate and assist Bank in the collection and enforcement of all Collateral and to hold in trust for Bank all payments received in connection with Collateral and from the sale, lease or other disposition of any Collateral, all rights by way of suretyship or guaranty and all rights in the nature of a lien or security interest which Debtor now or later has regarding Collateral. Immediately upon and after such notice, Debtor agrees to (a) endorse to Bank and immediately deliver to Bank all payments received on Collateral or from the sale, lease or other disposition of any Collateral or arising from any other rights or interests of Debtor in the Collateral, in the form received by Debtor without commingling with any other funds, and (b) immediately deliver to Bank all property in Debtor's possession or later coming into Debtor's possession through enforcement of Debtor's rights or interests in the Collateral. Debtor irrevocably authorizes Bank or any Bank employee or agent to endorse the name of Debtor upon any checks or other items which are received in payment for any Collateral, and to do any and all things necessary in order to reduce these items to money. Bank shall have no duty as to the collection or protection of Collateral or the proceeds of it, nor as to the preservation of any related rights, beyond the use of reasonable care in the custody and preservation of Collateral in the possession of Bank. Debtor agrees to take all steps necessary to preserve rights against prior parties with respect to the Collateral. Nothing in this Section 3.1 shall be deemed a consent by Bank to any sale, lease or other disposition of any Collateral.

3.2   Debtor agrees that immediately upon Bank's request (whether or not any Event of Default exists) the Indebtedness shall be on a "remittance basis" as follows: Debtor shall at its sole expense establish and maintain (and Bank, at Bank's option may establish and maintain at Debtor's expense): (a) an United States Post Office lock box (the "Lock Box"), to which Bank shall have exclusive access and control. Debtor expressly authorizes Bank, from time to time, to remove contents from the Lock Box, for disposition in accordance with this Agreement. Debtor agrees to notify all account debtors and other parties obligated to Debtor that all payments made to Debtor (other than payments by electronic funds transfer) shall be remitted, for the credit of Debtor, to the Lock Box, and Debtor shall include a like statement on all invoices; and (b) a non-interest bearing deposit account with Bank which shall be titled as designated by Bank (the "Cash Collateral Account") to which Bank shall have exclusive access and control. Debtor agrees to notify all account debtors and other parties obligated to Debtor that all payments made to Debtor by electronic funds transfer shall be remitted to the Cash Collateral Account, and Debtor, at Bank's request, shall include a like statement on all invoices. Debtor shall execute all documents and authorizations as required by Bank to establish and maintain the Lock Box and the Cash Collateral Account.

3.3 All items or amounts which are remitted to the Lock Box, to the Cash Collateral Account, or otherwise delivered by or for the benefit of Debtor to Bank on account of partial or full payment of, or with respect to, any Collateral shall, at Bank's option, (a) be applied to the payment of the Indebtedness, whether then due or not, in such order or at such time of application as Bank may determine in its sole discretion, or, (b) be deposited to the Cash Collateral Account. Debtor agrees that Bank shall not be liable for any loss or damage which Debtor may suffer as a result of Bank's processing of items or its exercise of any other rights or remedies under this Agreement, including without limitation indirect, special or consequential damages, loss of revenues or profits, or any claim, demand or action by any third party arising out of or in connection with the processing of items or the exercise of any other rights or remedies under this Agreement. Debtor agrees to indemnify and hold Bank harmless from and against all such third party claims, demands or actions, and all related expenses or liabilities, including, without limitation, attorney fees.

4. Defaults, Enforcement and Application of Proceeds.

4.1 Upon the occurrence of any of the following events (each an "Event of Default"), Debtor shall be in default under this Agreement:

(a) Any failure to pay the Indebtedness or any other indebtedness when due, or such portion of it as may be due, by acceleration or otherwise; or

(b) Any failure or neglect to comply with, or breach of or default under, any term of this Agreement, or any other agreement or commitment between Borrower, Debtor, or any guarantor of any of the Indebtedness ("Guarantor") and Bank; or

(c) Any warranty, representation, financial statement, or other information made, given or furnished to Bank by or on behalf of Borrower, Debtor, or any Guarantor shall be, or shall prove to have been, false or materially misleading when made, given, or furnished; or

(d) Any loss, theft, substantial damage or destruction to or of any Collateral, or the issuance or filing of any attachment, levy, garnishment or the commencement of any proceeding in connection with any Collateral or of any other judicial process of, upon or in respect of Borrower, Debtor, any Guarantor, or any Collateral; or

(e) Sale or other disposition by Borrower, Debtor, or any Guarantor of any substantial portion of its assets or property or voluntary suspension of the transaction of business by Borrower, Debtor, or any Guarantor, or death, dissolution, termination of existence, merger, consolidation, insolvency, business failure, or assignment for the benefit of creditors of or by Borrower, Debtor, or any Guarantor; or commencement of any proceedings under any state or federal bankruptcy or insolvency laws or laws for the relief of debtors by or against Borrower, Debtor, or any Guarantor; or the appointment of a receiver, trustee, court appointee, sequestrator or otherwise, for all or any part of the property of Borrower, Debtor, or any Guarantor; or

(f) Bank deems the margin of Collateral insufficient or itself insecure, in good faith believing that the prospect of payment of the Indebtedness or performance of this Agreement is impaired or shall fear deterioration, removal, or waste of Collateral; or

(g) A default shall occur under any instrument, agreement or other document evidencing, securing or otherwise relating to any of the Indebtedness.

4.2 Upon the occurrence of any Event of Default, Bank may at its discretion and without prior notice to Debtor declare any or all of the Indebtedness to be immediately due and payable, and shall have and may exercise any one or more of the following rights and remedies:

(a) Exercise all the rights and remedies upon default, in foreclosure and otherwise, available to secured parties under the provisions of the Uniform Commercial Code and other applicable law;

(b) Institute legal proceedings to foreclose upon the lien and security interest granted by this Agreement, to recover judgment for all amounts then due and owing as Indebtedness, and to collect the same out of any Collateral or the proceeds of any sale of it;

(c) Institute legal proceedings for the sale, under the judgment or decree of any court of competent jurisdiction, of any or all Collateral; and/or

(d) Personally or by agents, attorneys, or appointment of a receiver, enter upon any premises where Collateral may then be located, and take possession of all or any of it and/or render it unusable; and without being responsible for loss or damage to such Collateral, hold, operate, sell, lease, or dispose of all or any Collateral at one or more public or private sales, leasings or other disposition, at places and times and on terms and conditions as Bank may deem fit, without any previous demand or advertisement; and except as provided in this Agreement, all notice of sale, lease or other disposition, and advertisement, and other notice or demand, any right or equity of redemption, and any obligation of a prospective purchaser or lessee to inquire as to the power and authority of Bank to sell, lease, or otherwise dispose of the Collateral or as to the application by Bank of the proceeds of sale or otherwise, which would otherwise be required by, or available to Debtor under, applicable law are expressly waived by Debtor to the fullest extent permitted.

At any sale pursuant to this Section 4.2, whether under the power of sale, by virtue of judicial proceedings or otherwise, it shall not be necessary for Bank or a public officer under order of a court to have present physical or constructive possession of Collateral to be sold. The recitals contained in any conveyances and receipts made and given by Bank or the public officer to any purchaser at any sale made pursuant to this Agreement shall, to the extent permitted by applicable law, conclusively establish the truth and accuracy of the matters stated (including, without limit, as to the amounts of the principal of and interest on the Indebtedness, the accrual and nonpayment of it and advertisement and conduct of the sale); and all prerequisites to the sale shall be presumed to have been satisfied and performed. Upon any sale of any Collateral, the receipt of the officer making the sale under judicial proceedings or of Bank shall be sufficient discharge to the purchaser for the purchase money, and the purchaser shall not be obligated to see to the application of the money. Any sale of any Collateral under this Agreement shall be a perpetual bar against Debtor with respect to that Collateral. At any sale or other disposition of Collateral pursuant to this Section 4.2, Bank disclaims all warranties which would otherwise be given under the Uniform Commercial Code, including without limit a disclaimer of any warranty relating to title, possession, quiet enjoyment or the like, and Bank may communicate these disclaimers to a purchaser at such disposition. This disclaimer of warranties will not render the sale commercially unreasonable.

4.3   Debtor shall at the request of Bank, notify the account debtors or obligors of Bank's security interest in the Collateral and direct payment of it to Bank. Bank may, itself, upon the occurrence of any Event of Default so notify and direct any account debtor or obligor. At the request of Bank, whether or not an Event of Default shall have occurred, Debtor shall immediately take such actions as Bank shall request to establish exclusive control (as defined in the Uniform Commercial Code) by Bank over any Collateral which is of such a nature that perfection of a security interest may be accomplished by control.

4.4 The proceeds of any sale or other disposition of Collateral authorized by this Agreement shall be applied by Bank first upon all expenses authorized by the Uniform Commercial Code and all reasonable attorney fees and legal expenses incurred by Bank; the balance of the proceeds of the sale or other disposition shall be applied in the payment of the Indebtedness, first to interest, then to principal, then to remaining Indebtedness and the surplus, if any, shall be paid over to Debtor or to such other person(s) as may be entitled to it under applicable law. Debtor shall remain liable for any deficiency, which it shall pay to Bank immediately upon demand. Debtor agrees that Bank shall be under no obligation to accept any noncash proceeds in connection with any sale or disposition of Collateral unless failure to do so would be commercially unreasonable. If Bank agrees in its sole discretion to accept noncash proceeds (unless the failure to do so would be commercially unreasonable), Bank may ascribe any commercially reasonable value to such proceeds. Without limiting the foregoing, Bank may apply any discount factor in determining the present value of proceeds to be received in the future or may elect to apply proceeds to be received in the future only as and when such proceeds are actually received in cash by Bank.

4.5 Nothing in this Agreement is intended, nor shall it be construed, to preclude Bank from pursuing any other remedy provided by law for the collection of the Indebtedness or for the recovery of any other sum to which Bank may be entitled for the breach of this Agreement by Debtor. Nothing in this Agreement shall reduce or release in any way any rights or security interests of Bank contained in any existing agreement between Borrower, Debtor, or any Guarantor and Bank.

4.6 No waiver of default or consent to any act by Debtor shall be effective unless in writing and signed by an authorized officer of Bank. No waiver of any default or forbearance on the part of Bank in enforcing any of its rights under this Agreement shall operate as a waiver of any other default or of the same default on a future occasion or of any rights.

4.7 Debtor (a) irrevocably appoints Bank or any agent of Bank (which appointment is coupled with an interest) the true and lawful attorney of Debtor (with full power of substitution) in the name, place and stead of, and at the expense of, Debtor and (b) authorizes Bank or any agent of Bank, in its own name, at Debtor's expense, to do any of the following, as Bank, in its sole discretion, deems appropriate:

  (i) to demand, receive, sue for, and give receipts or acquittances for any moneys due or to become due on any Collateral (including without limit to draft against Collateral) and to endorse any item representing any payment on or proceeds of the Collateral;

  (ii) to execute and file in the name of and on behalf of Debtor all financing statements or other filings deemed necessary or desirable by Bank to evidence, perfect, or continue the security interests granted in this Agreement; and

(iii) to do and perform any act on behalf of Debtor permitted or required under this Agreement.

4.8 Upon the occurrence of an Event of Default, Debtor also agrees, upon request of Bank, to assemble the Collateral and make it available to Bank at any place designated by Bank which is reasonably convenient to Bank and Debtor.

4.9 The following shall be the basis for any finder of fact's determination of the value of any Collateral which is the subject matter of a disposition giving rise to a calculation of any surplus or deficiency under Section 9.615 (f) of the Uniform Commercial Code (as in effect on or after July 1, 2001): (a) the Collateral which is the subject matter of the disposition shall be valued in an "as is" condition as of the date of the disposition, without any assumption or expectation that such Collateral will be repaired or improved in any manner; (b) the valuation shall be based upon an assumption that the transferee of such Collateral desires a resale of the Collateral for cash promptly (but no later than 30 days) following the disposition; (c) all reasonable closing costs customarily borne by the seller in commercial sales transactions relating to property similar to such Collateral shall be deducted including, without limitation, brokerage commissions, tax prorations, attorneys' fees, whether inside or outside counsel is used, and marketing costs; (d) the value of the Collateral which is the subject matter of the disposition shall be further discounted to account for any estimated holding costs associated with maintaining such Collateral pending sale (to the extent not accounted for in (c) above), and other maintenance, operational and ownership expenses; and (e) any expert opinion testimony given or considered in connection with a determination of the value of such Collateral must be given by persons having at least 5 years experience in appraising property similar to the Collateral and who have conducted and prepared a complete written appraisal of such Collateral taking into consideration the factors set forth above. The "value" of any such Collateral shall be a factor in determining the amount of proceeds which would have been realized in a disposition to a transferee other than a secured party, a person related to a secured party or a secondary obligor under Section 9–615(f).

5. Miscellaneous.

5.1 Until Bank is advised in writing by Debtor to the contrary, all notices, requests and demands required under this Agreement or by law shall be given to, or made upon, Debtor at the first address indicated in Section 5.15 below.

5.2 Debtor will give Bank not less than 90 days prior written notice of all contemplated changes in Debtor's name, location, chief executive office, principal place of business, and/or location of any Collateral, but the giving of this notice shall not cure any Event of Default caused by this change.

5.3 Bank assumes no duty of performance or other responsibility under any contracts contained within the Collateral.

5.4 Bank has the right to sell, assign, transfer, negotiate or grant participations or any interest in, any or all of the Indebtedness and any related obligations, including without limit this Agreement. In connection with the above, but without limiting its ability to make other disclosures to the full extent allowable, Bank may disclose all documents and information which Bank now or later has relating to Debtor, the Indebtedness or this Agreement, however obtained. Debtor further agrees that Bank may provide information relating to this Agreement or relating to Debtor to the Bank's parent, affiliates, subsidiaries, and service providers.

5.5 In addition to Bank's other rights, any indebtedness owing from Bank to Debtor can be set off and applied by Bank on any Indebtedness at any time(s) either before or after maturity or demand without notice to anyone. Any such action shall not constitute an acceptance of collateral in discharge of the Indebtedness.

5.6 Debtor waives any right to require the Bank to: (a) proceed against any person or property; (b) give notice of the terms, time and place of any public or private sale of personal property security held from Borrower or any other person, or otherwise comply with the provisions of Section 9–504 of the Uniform Commercial Code in effect prior to July 1, 2001 or its successor provisions thereafter; or (c) pursue any other remedy in the Bank's power. Debtor waives notice of acceptance of this Agreement and presentment, demand, protest, notice of protest, dishonor, notice of dishonor, notice of default, notice of intent to accelerate or demand payment of any Indebtedness, any and all other notices to which the undersigned might otherwise be entitled, and diligence in collecting any Indebtedness, and agree(s) that the Bank may, once or any number of times, modify the terms of any Indebtedness, compromise, extend, increase, accelerate, renew or forbear to enforce payment of any or all Indebtedness, or permit Borrower to incur additional Indebtedness, all without notice to Debtor and without affecting in any manner the unconditional obligation of Debtor under this Agreement. Debtor unconditionally and irrevocably waives each and every defense and setoff of any nature which, under principles of guaranty or otherwise, would operate to impair or diminish in any way the obligation of Debtor under this Agreement, and acknowledges that such waiver is by this reference incorporated into each security agreement, collateral assignment, pledge and/or other document from Debtor now or later securing the Indebtedness, and acknowledges that as of the date of this Agreement no such defense or setoff exists.

5.7 Debtor waives any and all rights (whether by subrogation, indemnity, reimbursement, or otherwise) to recover from Borrower any amounts paid or the value of any Collateral given by Debtor pursuant to this Agreement.

5.8 In the event that applicable law shall obligate Bank to give prior notice to Debtor of any action to be taken under this Agreement, Debtor agrees that a written notice given to Debtor at least ten days before the date of the act shall be reasonable notice of the act and, specifically, reasonable notification of the time and place of any public sale or of the time after which any private sale, lease, or other disposition is to be made, unless a shorter notice period is reasonable under the circumstances. A notice shall be deemed to be given under this Agreement when delivered to Debtor or when placed in an envelope addressed to Debtor and deposited, with postage prepaid, in a post office or official depository under the exclusive care and custody of the United States Postal Service or delivered to an overnight courier. The mailing shall be by overnight courier, certified, or first class mail.

5.9 Notwithstanding any prior revocation, termination, surrender, or discharge of this Agreement in whole or in part, the effectiveness of this Agreement shall automatically continue or be reinstated in the event that any payment received or credit given by Bank in respect of the Indebtedness is returned, disgorged, or rescinded under any applicable law, including, without limitation, bankruptcy or insolvency laws, in which case this Agreement, shall be enforceable against Debtor as if the returned, disgorged, or rescinded payment or credit had not been received or given by Bank, and whether or not Bank relied upon this payment or credit or changed its position as a consequence of it. In the event of continuation or reinstatement of this Agreement, Debtor agrees upon demand by Bank to execute and deliver to Bank those documents which Bank determines are appropriate to further evidence (in the public records or otherwise) this continuation or reinstatement, although the failure of Debtor to do so shall not affect in any way the reinstatement or continuation.

5.10 This Agreement and all the rights and remedies of Bank under this Agreement shall inure to the benefit of Bank's successors and assigns and to any other holder who derives from Bank title to or an interest in the Indebtedness or any portion of it, and shall bind Debtor and the heirs, legal representatives, successors, and assigns of Debtor. Nothing in this Section 5.10 is deemed a consent by Bank to any assignment by Debtor.

5.11 If there is more than one Debtor, all undertakings, warranties and covenants made by Debtor and all rights, powers and authorities given to or conferred upon Bank are made or given jointly and severally.

5.12 Except as otherwise provided in this Agreement, all terms in this Agreement have the meanings assigned to them in Article 9 (or, absent definition in Article 9, in any other Article) of the Uniform Commercial Code, as those meanings may be amended, revised or replaced from time to time. "Uniform Commercial Code" means Act No. 174 of the Michigan Public Acts of 1962, as amended, revised or replaced from time to time, including without limit as amended by Act No. 348 of the Michigan Public Acts of 2000. Notwithstanding the foregoing, the parties intend that the terms used herein which are defined in the Uniform Commercial Code have, at all times, the broadest and most inclusive meanings possible. Accordingly, if the Uniform Commercial Code shall in the future be amended or held by a court to define any term used herein more broadly or inclusively than the Uniform Commercial Code in effect on the date of this Agreement, then such term, as used herein, shall be given such broadened meaning. If the Uniform Commercial Code shall in the future be amended or held by a court to define any term used herein more narrowly, or less inclusively, than the Uniform Commercial Code in effect on the date of this Agreement, such amendment or holding shall be disregarded in defining terms used in this Agreement.

5.13   No single or partial exercise, or delay in the exercise, of any right or power under this Agreement, shall preclude other or further exercise of the rights and powers under this Agreement. The unenforceability of any provision of this Agreement shall not affect the enforceability of the remainder of this Agreement. This Agreement constitutes the entire agreement of Debtor and Bank with respect to the subject matter of this Agreement. No amendment or modification of this Agreement shall be effective unless the same shall be in writing and signed by Debtor and an authorized officer of Bank. This Agreement shall be governed by and construed in accordance with the internal laws of the State of Michigan, without regard to conflict of laws principles.

5.14   To the extent that any of the Indebtedness is payable upon demand, nothing contained in this Agreement shall modify the terms and conditions of that Indebtedness nor shall anything contained in this Agreement prevent Bank from making demand, without notice and with or without reason, for immediate payment of any or all of that Indebtedness at any time(s), whether or not an Event of Default has occurred.

5.15   Debtor represents and warrants that Debtor's exact name is the name set forth in this Agreement. Debtor further represents and warrants the following and agrees that Debtor is, and at all times shall be, located in the following place [mark applicable provision]:

— Debtor is an individual, and Debtor is located (as determined pursuant to the Uniform Commercial Code) at Debtor's principal residence which is (street address, state and county or parish):

_____.

— Debtor is a registered organization which is organized under the laws of one of the states comprising the United States (e.g. corporation, limited partnership, registered limited liability partnership or limited liability company), and Debtor is located (as determined pursuant to the Uniform Commercial Code) in the state under the laws of which it was organized, which is (street address, state and county or parish): _____.

— Debtor is a domestic organization which is not a registered organization under the laws of the United States or any state thereof (e.g. general partnership, joint venture, trust, estate or association), and Debtor is located (as determined pursuant to the Uniform Commercial Code) at its sole place of business or, if it has more than one place of business, at its chief executive office, which is (street address, state and county or parish): ___.

— Debtor is a registered organization organized under the laws of the United States, and Debtor is located in the state that United States law designates as its location or, if United States law authorizes the Debtor to designate the state for its location, the state designated by Debtor, or if neither of the foregoing are applicable, at the District of Columbia. Debtor is located (as determined pursuant to the Uniform Commercial Code) at (street address, state and county or parish): _____.

— Debtor is a foreign individual or foreign organization or a branch or agency of a bank that is not organized under the laws of the United States or a state thereof. Debtor is located (as determined pursuant to the Uniform Commercial Code) at: _____.

If Collateral is located at other than the address specified above, such Collateral is located and shall be maintained at

---

STREET ADDRESS

CITY, STATE, ZIP CODE, COUNTY

Collateral shall be maintained only at the locations identified in this Section 5.15.

5.16 A carbon, photographic or other reproduction of this Agreement shall be sufficient as a financing statement under the Uniform Commercial Code and may be filed by Bank in any filing office.

5.17 This Agreement shall be terminated only by the filing of a termination statement in accordance with the applicable provisions of the Uniform Commercial Code, but the obligations contained in Section 2.13 of this Agreement shall survive termination.

6. DEBTOR AND BANK ACKNOWLEDGE THAT THE RIGHT TO TRIAL BY JURY IS A CONSTITUTIONAL ONE, BUT THAT IT MAY BE WAIVED. EACH PARTY, AFTER CONSULTING (OR HAVING HAD THE OPPORTUNITY TO CONSULT) WITH COUNSEL OF THEIR CHOICE, KNOWINGLY AND VOLUNTARILY, AND FOR THEIR MUTUAL BENEFIT WAIVES ANY RIGHT TO TRIAL BY JURY IN THE EVENT OF LITIGATION REGARDING THE PERFORMANCE OR ENFORCEMENT OF, OR IN ANY WAY RELATED TO, THIS AGREEMENT OR THE INDEBTEDNESS.

7. Special Provisions Applicable to this Agreement. (*None, if left blank)

Debtor: _____

By: _____
   Signature of:
Its: _____

By: _____
   Signature of:
Its: _____

———

Article 9 Goes Digital

1999 Article 9 includes numerous changes to facilitate electronic commerce. The Code now permits parties to maintain "records" (including both financing statements and security agreements) in either written or electronic form. According to Comment 9(a) to 9–102, a record "need not be permanent or indestructible," * * * but "[t]he information must be stored on paper or in some other medium." The Comment lists the following examples of current technologies that would qualify: "magnetic media, optical discs, digital voice messaging systems, electronic mail, audio tapes, and photographic media, as well as paper."

Former Article 9 required the debtor to sign the security agreement; 1999 Article 9 substitutes "authentication." Under 9–102(a)(7), "authenticate" means "to sign" or "to execute or otherwise adopt a symbol, or encrypt or similarly process a record in whole or in part, with the present intent of the authenticating person to identify the person and adopt or accept a record."

Authentication may be as complex as including a digital rendering of a handwritten signature or as simple as typing one's initials at the end of an email. Clearly "digital signatures" electronically recorded by a dedicated pen on an electronic screen (of the kind now widely used by Sears) qualify as an authentication. These indicate the intention of the party to be bound and have the virtue of a manual signature. Like a manual signature, these signatures can be examined by a document examiner to determine whether they have the unique qualities associated with a particular person's signature. Other authentications, such as typing one's name at the end of an email, do not have these qualities, yet if they are done with the intention of authenticating, they too are an authentication. For example, a typed name at the end of an email would show that it came from a particular person only by showing that it came from his or her computer and only then if one could show that others could not readily access that computer.

How would one show the "present intent" to "adopt or accept a record"? It probably would be enough to combine the words "John Smith" with a statement such as "I agree to be bound by this security agreement." Typing the words "authorized signature" after the name would also suffice, at least if one can show that the "authorized signature" was done contemporaneously with the typing of the person's name.

How does one put a security agreement into an electronic format in a way that insures neither party can alter it after it has been authenticated? One possibility is to involve a third party who deals with the debtor and the creditor and retains an electronic copy in its possession. Several companies, including Surety Technologies and Cohasset Associates, offer services of this kind. For example, using Surety's Digital Notary™ Service, one can provide proof of the existence of any document at a fixed time. Once a party selects the file(s) it wishes to notarize, Surety's software creates a unique digital fingerprint for each file. Two files that differ by only a single character will have different digital fingerprints. The digital fingerprint then takes the place of the file it represents for the remainder of the notary process. This insures that the fingerprint will always remain confidential. Since only the fingerprint is sent to Surety, the contents of the notarized document also remain confidential. Next, Surety creates a Notary Record for each digital fingerprint. Notary Records contain the exact moment of notarization, as well as the information needed to validate the original file at any time in the future. At the same time the Notary Record is being created in binary form, Surety's Universal Registry is updated with an entry for that specific moment. To validate a file, Surety simply generates a new fingerprint based on that file and then compares it with the fingerprint on record. One can request a printed version of the Digital Notary Record at any time. Thus, a party could present nearly indisputable evidence that the document in question is the same as the document that the parties authenticated.

If the debtor and creditor do not wish to use such a service, there are alternatives. A less sophisticated but sufficient method is to use the security tools already provided in most word processing and email software. In Microsoft Word, for example, a party may password protect a file so that a third party may read the file but cannot make any changes. By saving or storing its email containing the document, the recipient can guard against the other party's unauthorized modification. In addition, Microsoft Outlook provides easy-to-use digital signatures and encryption which can secure documents while they are being transported online. While these security methods are far less sophisticated than use of a third party such as Surety, they may be more than adequate for many secured transactions where the amount at stake does not justify an expensive three party procedure.

§ 2. PRIORITY IN AFTER–ACQUIRED COLLATERAL AND PROCEEDS

After-acquired Collateral

Section 9–204 states that a security agreement "may create or provide for a security interest in after-acquired collateral." This rule does not extend to commercial tort claims nor, with limitations, to consumer goods, but in general a debtor and creditor may agree that a security interest automatically attaches to after-acquired collateral. The section adopts the principle of a "continuing general lien" or "floating lien" and it does that even though the debtor "has liberty to use or dispose of collateral without being required to account for proceeds or substitute new collateral." That the priority in after-acquired collateral relates back to the original time of priority (filing or other method of perfection) is clear from the words of subsection (a). The point is made explicitly by Comment 5 and example 4 to section 9–322.

Future Advances

Future advances have earned an entire section (9–323) in the 1999 Article 9. The language of subsection (a) does its best to obscure the general rule of priority as to future advances. It appears to say on first reading, that priority as to a future advance dates from the time of that advance not from the time of an earlier filing or perfection. Of course, that is not what subsection (a) *really* says; the drafters state the rule much more clearly in Comment 3 as follows:

> Under a proper reading of the first-to-file or perfect rule of section 9–322(a)(1) (and former section 9–312(5)), it is abundantly clear that the time when an advance is made plays no role in determining priorities among conflicting security interests except when a financing statement was not filed and the advance is the giving of value as the last step for attachment and perfection. Thus, a secured party takes subject to all advances secured by a competing security interest having priority under section 9–322(a)(1).

To understand the general rule, assume the secured creditor takes a security interest and perfects it by filing a financing statement. Assume further that the debtor makes periodic payments and that the creditor allows the debtor to make periodic draws on the underlying line of credit. These draws will be "future advances". Under section 9–322 the secured creditor's priority as to each advance will relate back to the time of the original filing. Section 9–323(a) will not apply to these advances because they have been perfected by a prior filing. In rare circumstances a lien creditor under subsection 9–323(b), or a buyer of goods under 9–323(d), might achieve priority over the secured creditor as to some of these future advances.

The real role of section 9–323 is to state several intricate—but rather unimportant—*exceptions* to the general rule. In limited cases identified in 9–323(b) and (d), lien creditors and buyers will gain priority over certain later advances.

Problem 2–1

Ajax Sisters, a famous private banking concern, had filed a financing statement covering "inventory existing and after-acquired" of Neiman Marcus. You are counsel for Ajax and they ask you the following questions:

1. If we file on January 15 with respect to inventory as above, but neither lend nor make any agreement to lend at the time, and on January 20 a second creditor files and lends on the same inventory, will that lender have priority over us if we lend money on January 30?

2. If in the foregoing example we make a series of non-obligatory advances to Neiman Marcus, will we continue to have priority over the intervening creditor or after we have knowledge of its loan, or will we be subordinated to the extent of our subsequent non-obligatory advances?

3. What will be our relative ranking with respect to collateral that is acquired one month, six months or one year after our financing statement is filed? Do we continue to have the same relative priority?

4. If Neiman Marcus goes into Chapter 11 (don't laugh, Macy's and Federated Department Stores went into bankruptcy not long ago) and if they continue to do business as we understand they are entitled to do even in Chapter 11 and sell off all old inventory and buy new inventory, will our after-acquired rights continue to accrue? That is, will our security interest continue automatically to attach to new inventory? We have been told that section 552 (look at it) keeps that from happening. How would we protect ourselves before or during bankruptcy from the possibility that our collateral would be sold off and our security interest would not attach to new collateral? Consider not only section 552, but also 361 on adequate protection and 363(c)(1) and (c)(2).

Problem 2–2

Assume that Macy's grants a security interest to Chase in all of the inventory and proceeds of its four New York stores. Chase lends $10 million initially. Assume the collateral that is subject to a security interest is in the $10–$15 million range. Over time the debt is reduced to $100,000.

1. When the debt stands at $100,000, an unsecured creditor gets a judicial lien on all of Macy's inventory. Chase learns of the lien that was created by a levy on November 30 and asks on that same day whether it can safely advance another $5 million to its customer and enjoy priority over the intervening lien creditor. Consider 9–323(b).

2. Macy's sells half of its New York assets to Bloomingdales (and assigns the leases on two stores). Three months after the sale, Chase advances an additional $5 million to Macy's at a time when some people at Chase knew of the sale. Later it claimed that its security interest attaches to the property that was allegedly sold and has priority over the rights of the purchaser. What do you think? See 9–323(d). The combination of sections 9–201 and 9–315 makes clear that a sale does not usually cut off a perfected security interest.

3. Chase has a perfected security interest in all of Macy's inventory in new York but its loan has been paid down to $100,000. Finance Company has a subordinate perfected security interest in all the inventory to secure a $10 million loan. Bank of America has a $5 million unsecured loan and proposes to buy Chase's loan and take an assignment of its security interest. If it does that, will it enjoy priority over Finance Company to the extent of its entire $5 million loan? If you have doubts about the outcome, could you arrange the transaction in a different way to ensure success for Bank of America?

§ 3. PERFECTION

Perfection for inventory is not significantly different from perfection for business equipment that we considered in Chapter 1. In almost all cases, the creditor will file a financing statement. Invariably, the financing statement will specify that it claims after-acquired collateral and the creditor will suffer exactly the same problems here as in the cases in Chapter 1 concerning the appropriate description of collateral, the appropriate debtor's name and the consequences in change in the nature of the collateral and the name of the debtor.

LMS HOLDING COMPANY v. CORE–
MARK MID–CONTINENT, INC.

United States Court of Appeals, Tenth Circuit, 1995.
50 F.3d 1520.

BALDOCK, CIRCUIT JUDGE:

Coremark and Amcon ("Coremark") appeal the district court's grant of summary judgment in favor of Retail Marketing Company ("RMC"). The district court held that Coremark did not have a perfected security interest in RMC's after-acquired inventory. We exercise jurisdiction pursuant to 28 U.S.C. § 1291 and affirm.

In 1988, MAKO, Inc. ("MAKO"), a chain of convenience stores, granted Coremark a security interest in its inventory, after-acquired inventory, and inventory proceeds. Coremark perfected its security interest by filing a financing statement naming MAKO as the debtor. MAKO subsequently filed a Chapter 11 bankruptcy petition.

As part of MAKO's reorganization plan, RMC, an unrelated third party entity, agreed to acquire certain assets in MAKO's convenience stores and take over store operations. The acquired assets included specific inventory subject to Coremark's perfected security interest. The plan provided that Coremark would retain its lien in the "assets * * * acquired by RMC pursuant to [the] Plan" and that this lien would "continue in full force and effect in accordance with [its] terms." The bankruptcy court confirmed the MAKO plan in August 1989–

Following confirmation of the MAKO plan, RMC executed a new promissory note and security agreement in order to assume the indebtedness of MAKO. The security agreement granted Coremark a security interest in RMC's inventory, after-acquired inventory, and inventory proceeds. Coremark, however, did not file a new financing statement naming RMC as the debtor to perfect its security interest in RMC's inventory. Thereafter, RMC sold the MAKO inventory in the regular course of business and commingled the proceeds from the sale with other RMC assets. These proceeds are no longer identifiable. RMC replaced the MAKO inventory with after-acquired inventory. On September 21, 1991, RMC filed a Chapter 11 bankruptcy petition.

On November 20, 1991, Coremark filed a proof of claim in the bankruptcy proceeding. Thereafter, on July 29, 1992, RMC commenced this adversary proceeding seeking inter alia to avoid Coremark's asserted security interest in its after-acquired inventory pursuant to 11 U.S.C. § 544(a)(1). On December 10, 1992, RMC filed a motion for summary judgment arguing that Coremark's security interest in its after-acquired inventory was unperfected because Coremark did not file a financing statement naming RMC as the debtor after RMC acquired the MAKO assets and took over store operations under the MAKO plan.

The bankruptcy court rejected this argument and denied the motion. In so holding, the bankruptcy court relied on Okla.Stat.Ann. tit. 12A, § 9–402(7), which provides in pertinent part that "[a] filed financing statement remains effective with respect to collateral transferred by the debtor even though the secured party knows of or consents to the transfer." Under this provision, the bankruptcy court concluded that the term "collateral" encompassed after-acquired property. Thus, the court held that Coremark's financing statement covering the MAKO collateral remained effective and served to perfect its security interest in RMC's after-acquired inventory "without the necessity of refiling a financing statement in [RMC's] name."

RMC appealed to the district court which reversed the bankruptcy court's holding. Specifically, the district court held that under § 9–402(7), Coremark's financing statement remained effective only as to the collateral actually transferred by MAKO under the bankruptcy plan. Thus, the district court concluded that Coremark's security interest in RMC's after-acquired inventory was unperfected because Coremark failed to file a new financing statement naming RMC as the debtor. Consequently, the district court granted summary judgment in favor of RMC. This appeal followed.

On appeal, Coremark argues the district court erred in granting summary judgment in favor of RMC. Specifically, Coremark contends that under § 9–402(7), the financing statement it filed naming MAKO as the debtor served to perfect its security interest in RMC's after-acquired inventory. We review the district court's grant of summary judgment de novo. Eaton v. Jarvis Products Corp., 965 F.2d 922, 925 (10th Cir.1992). Summary judgment is appropriate when there is no genuine dispute over a material fact and the moving party is entitled to judgment as a matter of law. Id.

Pursuant to 11 U.S.C. § 544(a)(1), a debtor-in-possession (RMC in this case) may assert the rights of a hypothetical lien creditor once it files a bankruptcy petition. The rights of a lien creditor are determined by state law. Woodson v. Utica Square Nat'l Bank of Tulsa (In re McClain), 447 F.2d 241, 243–44 (10th Cir.1971). Under Oklahoma law, a lien creditor has priority over an unperfected, secured creditor. Okla. Stat.Ann. tit. 12A, § 9–301(1)(b), (3). Thus, in a bankruptcy proceeding, if the creditor's security interest is not perfected, the creditor " 'stands as [a] general unsecured creditor who must defer to the trustee.' " Jones v. Small Business Admin. (In re Cohutta Mills, Inc.), 108 B.R. 815, 817

(N.D.Ga.1989) (quoting In re Merts Equipment Co., 438 F.Supp. 295, 298 (M.D.Ga.1977)).

Under Oklahoma law, a secured creditor perfects a security interest in part by preparing and filing a financing statement describing the collateral subject to the security interest and naming the debtor. Okla. Stat.Ann. tit. 12A, 9–302(1). Once a financing statement is filed, the security interest becomes perfected, id. 9–303, protecting the secured party against conflicting interests in the same collateral. Id. 9–312.

Section 9–402 covers the formal requisites of the initial filing and subsequent amendment of a financing statement. Subsection (7) addresses a secured party's duty to refile a financing statement in certain enumerated instances:

> A financing statement sufficiently shows the name of the debtor if it gives the individual, partnership or corporate name of the debtor, whether or not it adds other trade names or the names of partners. Where the debtor so changes his name, or in the case of an organization, its name, identity, or corporate structure that a filed financing statement becomes seriously misleading, the filing is not effective to perfect a security interest in collateral acquired by the debtor more than four (4) months after the change, unless a new appropriate financing statement is filed before the expiration of that time. A filed financing statement remains effective with respect to collateral transferred by the debtor even though the secured party knows of or consents to the transfer. Okla.Stat.Ann. tit. 12A, § 9–402(7) (emphasis added).

Under this section, the second sentence addresses a secured creditor's obligation to refile a financing statement in instances where there has been a "change[ ] in the identity or structure of the debtor in which the 'new' debtor is a successor enterprise of the original debtor." Bluegrass Ford–Mercury, Inc. v. Farmers Nat'l Bank of Cynthiana (In re Bluegrass Ford–Mercury, Inc.), 942 F.2d 381, 388 (6th Cir.1991) (citing Bank of the West v. Commercial Credit Fin. Serv., 852 F.2d 1162, 1169 (9th Cir.1988)). In contrast, the third sentence applies only to those instances where there has been a "bona fide transfer[ ] [of collateral] to third parties unrelated to the transferor." Bank of the West, 852 F.2d at 1169–70 n. 6.

Applying these principles to the instant case, the parties agree that the only provision applicable to the facts before us is the third sentence of 9–402(7). Under this provision, the parties agree that Coremark's security interest remained perfected in the collateral actually transferred to RMC under the MAKO plan. The parties disagree, however, as to whether the financing statement naming MAKO as the debtor operated to perfect Coremark's security interest in collateral acquired by RMC after the MAKO transfer. Thus, the central issue we must resolve in this appeal is whether under the last sentence of § 9–402(7), Coremark's financing statement perfected its security interest in collateral acquired by RMC after the MAKO transfer.

Courts which have addressed the scope of 9–402(7) have reached differing conclusions. For example, in In re Taylorville Eisner Agency, 445 F.Supp. 665 (S.D.Ill.1977), a bank made a loan to individual debtors secured by fixtures, equipment, inventory, and after-acquired property. In order to perfect its security interest, the bank filed a financing statement naming the individuals as debtors. On the same day as the note and security agreement were signed, the individual debtors transferred the collateral to a corporation they had previously formed and the corporation assumed the bank loan. The bank did not file a new financing statement naming the corporation as the new debtor. After selling the inventory which had been transferred and replacing it with after-acquired inventory, the corporation declared bankruptcy. Id. at 666–67.

Relying on the last sentence of § 9–402(7), the trustee argued that because the bank had not filed a new financing statement naming the corporation as the new debtor, the bank did not have a perfected security interest in the corporation's after-acquired inventory. The district court disagreed, stating in pertinent part:

> [T]he final sentence speaks of collateral transferred by the debtor, which must mean the property subject to the security interest as defined in UCC § 9–105(1)(c). In this case the security interest covered existing fixtures and equipment as well as acquired inventory and merchandise.

> * * * The third sentence of subsection 7 is clear that the filed statement remains effective with respect to collateral transferred by the debtor regardless of the knowledge or consent of the secured party. This also means collateral which is after-acquired property. Id. at 669 (emphasis added). Consequently, the district court held that the bank did not have to file a new financing statement naming the corporation as the new debtor in order to retain its perfected security interest in after-acquired property. Id. at 670.

The Sixth Circuit reached a contrary result in Bluegrass, 942 F.2d at 386. In Bluegrass, a bank made a loan to Bluegrass–Ford, a car dealership. The bank perfected its security interest by filing a financing statement which covered "all new cars and demonstrators in the inventory of Bluegrass Ford, Inc." The assets of the dealership were subsequently sold to an individual who then transferred the assets to a new, unrelated corporate entity called Bluegrass Ford–Mercury, Inc. The bank did not file a new financing statement naming Bluegrass Ford–Mercury as the new debtor. The new dealership subsequently filed bankruptcy. Id. at 383.

On appeal, the bank argued that the financing statement filed in the name of Bluegrass Ford perfected its security interest in the after-acquired inventory of Bluegrass Ford–Mercury. The Sixth Circuit rejected this argument. The court noted that the last sentence of 9–402(7) applies only "to collateral transferred by the debtor." Id. at 387. The court then held that this language did not "encompass collateral not yet acquired by the transferee debtor." Id. Consequently, the court concluded that the bank's financing statement originally filed in the name of Bluegrass Ford did not perfect its security interest in Bluegrass Ford–Mercury's after-acquired inventory. Id. at 388.

In accordance with the Sixth Circuit, other court's have concluded that pursuant to § 9–402(7), after-acquired property cannot constitute "collateral transferred by the debtor," see In re Cohutta Mills, 108 B.R. at 820 n. 4, and that a creditor perfects a security interest in after-acquired property of the debtor's transferee by filing a new financing statement in the name of the debtor's third party transferee. See Steinberg v. American Nat'l Bank & Trust Co. of Chicago (In re Meyer–Midway, Inc.), 65 B.R. 437, 444 (Bankr.N.D.Ill.1986) ("The Court agrees with the Trustee that the Bank would be obligated to file a revised financing statement to be perfected in new collateral or collateral intended to secure the Bank under the after-acquired property clause."); Citizens Savings Bank v. Sac City State Bank, 315 N.W.2d 20, 28 (Iowa 1982) (same); see also William M. Burke, The Duty to Refile Under Section 9–402(7) of the 1999 Article 9, 35 Bus.Law. 1083, 1089 (1980) ("In order to perfect any security interest in the new property acquired by the transferee, the secured creditor must either file a financing statement signed by the transferee or take possession of the new property.").

We conclude the Sixth Circuit's reasoning is correct. As the court noted, under § 9–402(7) a filed financing statement remains effective only as "to collateral transferred by the debtor." Bluegrass, 942 F.2d at 387. Inventory purchased by the transferee after the transfer cannot constitute property "transferred by the debtor." See id.; In re Cohutta Mills, 108 B.R. at 820 n. 4. Thus, a financing statement filed prior to a transfer of collateral in the name of the transferor does not serve to perfect a security interest in the transferee's after-acquired property. See Bluegrass, 942 F.2d at 387; In re Meyer–Midway, 65 B.R. at 443–44.

Applying this reasoning to the instant case, we conclude the financing statement Coremark filed in the name of MAKO did not perfect its security interest in RMC's after-acquired inventory. Rather, in order to perfect its security interest in RMC's after-acquired property, Coremark should have filed a new financing statement naming RMC as the debtor. Because Coremark failed to do so, its security interest in RMC's after-acquired inventory remained unperfected.

Coremark contends this result would contravene the express provisions of the MAKO bankruptcy plan which provided that Coremark's lien would "continue in full force and effect in accordance with [its] terms." Aplt.App. at 26. Coremark contends this provision of the bankruptcy plan relieved it from the requirement of filing a financing statement in the name of RMC to perfect its security interest in RMC's after-acquired inventory. We disagree.

The plan provided that Coremark's lien would continue as to assets "to be acquired by RMC pursuant to [the] Plan." As noted above, the assets to be acquired consisted of the inventory transferred by MAKO to RMC. Consequently, under the express terms of the plan, Coremark's lien remained perfected only as to property acquired by RMC under the MAKO plan. Thus, contrary to its assertions otherwise, the MAKO plan did not relieve Coremark of the requirement that it file a financing statement naming RMC as the debtor in order to perfect its security interest in RMC's after-acquired inventory.

AFFIRMED.

How does 1999 Article 9 deal with the problems in the LMS case?

Problem 2–3

Chase files a financing statement with respect to Macy's, a Delaware corporation, in Dover. The financing statement identifies Macy's as the debtor and identifies the collateral as "all inventory located in Macy's Manhattan stores". Assume the security agreement gives Chase a right to "all inventory located in Macy's Manhattan stores" and includes after-acquired property.

1. If the inventory is moved to Macy's New Jersey store, is Chase unperfected as to that inventory?

2. What if it is not only moved but also sold to a Macy's subsidiary that has no security agreement with Chase?

3. The DIP suggests Chase is unperfected in any case because its financing statement failed to mention after-acquired property. What do you think?

§ 4. PURCHASE MONEY SECURITY INTEREST, SECOND IN TIME, FIRST IN RIGHT

Section 9–324 grants priority to purchase money security interests over a prior conflicting security interest even though the purchase money security interest is later perfected; we sometimes call this "super priority". The purchase money secured creditor is often the seller of a product who has retained a security interest to secure its purchase price; however, a bank or other financing agency can also be a purchase money secured creditor. The priority of purchase money secured creditors has long been recognized in real estate transactions and in pre-Code rules for personal property. What is the justification for this special priority?

First, one might argue that a seller of goods (who is going to retain a security interest) should not be obliged to inspect public filings with respect to its purchaser in order for the seller to maintain priority in goods which it owns and proposes to sell; yet the Code does not consistently follow any such principle. A purchase money secured creditor claiming inventory (including a seller) must inspect the files to be sure of priority under section 9–324.

A second possible justification for purchase money priority is that the debtor needs some protection from an earlier secured creditor who may have filed a financing statement with respect to many of debtor's assets (including after-acquired), but who is unwilling to advance additional funds. Absent purchase money priority, an earlier filing with broad after-acquired coverage would give the prior creditor priority over other lenders, leaving the debtor unable to borrow despite the fact that other lenders might be willing to finance new purchases if they could have priority as to the goods purchased. The possibility of priority for purchase money lenders gets the debtor out from under the thumb of an original creditor; it may enable the debtor to borrow notwithstanding the reluctance of the original lender.

Finally, law and economics scholars maintain that purchase money lenders should be permitted to go to the head of the line because they do not threaten preceding creditors in ways that general creditors might. In an article in the Virginia Law Review (80 VA.L.Rev. 2103 (1994)), Professors Kanda and Levmore make a sophisticated argument on behalf of purchase money lenders. First they argue that the justification for a first in time rule for secured creditors is to keep the debtor from "altering the risk" to the debtor's advantage and to the creditor's disadvantage after the deal has been struck. For example a debtor in financial difficulty might choose to engage in risky activity with the knowledge that most of the risk will be borne by his creditors and little of the risk will be borne by him (because he does not have far to fall). First in time rules inhibit that behavior. Kanda and Levmore hypothesize that creditors who come later in time may have better information than earlier creditors and so know which loans should be made (efficient) and which are too risky (inefficient). They suggest that purchase money lenders are often better informed than creditors who have made earlier loans and that they will not undermine the position of earlier secured creditors because their claim will be limited to the collateral purchased with their loan.

IN RE SMITH

United States Bankruptcy Court, Western District of Missouri, 1983.
29 B.R. 690.

PELOFSKY, BANKRUPTCY JUDGE:

* * * In this petition the Bank sought a determination of priorities as between it and FmHA as to certain collateral and for other relief. The Bank also filed Count II to a complaint, precisely which of the three then pending being unknown, again naming debtors and FmHA as defendants, seeking a determination of priorities and asking that the proceeds of the sale of cattle repossessed by FmHA be used to satisfy the Bank's debt.

* * *

The evidence shows that debtor Lloyd Smith was borrowing money from the Bank's predecessor in 1970. In August of 1976 the Bank took a security interest in "All livestock now owned and after acquired". No significant amount of money was advanced to debtors at this time. There is no evidence that debtors had any livestock in August of 1976. In March of 1979 debtors borrowed money from FmHA and executed a security agreement in favor of FmHA identifying cattle and hogs as collateral. Just prior to the advance a financing statement was filed and designated as security, inter alia, " * * * proceeds and products thereof: (a) * * * livestock * * * ". Debtors deposited the funds in their account at the Bank and purchased the cattle and hogs called for in the security agreement.

During the period June 1981 through January 1982 debtors borrowed $20,222.59 from the Bank. During the period from April 17, 1981 through January 1982 debtors gave the Bank four financial statements. Debtors gave a statement in September of 1980 but this, the court finds, is too remote in time to be of probative value except that it also, as do the others, omits any reference to the FmHA debt. On August 24, 1981 the Bank filed a continuation statement of its 1976 UCC filing.

According to an affidavit filed by FmHA, an agent searched the UCC filings in Pulaski County on September 1, 1981 and found no continuation filing by the Bank. In late September 1981, debtors executed a security agreement in favor of FmHA identifying cattle and hogs as collateral. No financing statement was filed in connection with this security agreement. In March of 1982 FmHA foreclosed its security interest in the cattle and sold them, applying the proceeds against the loan. Debtors filed for relief under Chapter 7 of the Code on March 18, 1982, after the foreclosure. This adversary was filed shortly thereafter.

Section 400.9–312, R.S.Mo.1969, deals with "[p]riorities among conflicting security interests in the same collateral". The section provides, in part, that * * * [quoting 9–312(3) and (4)]

Section 400.9–109(3) R.S.Mo.1969 classifies goods as "[f]arm products" if they are " * * * livestock * * * used * * * in farming operations * * *. If goods are farm products they are neither equipment nor inventory." The statutory comment notes that:

> 4.   Goods are 'farm products' only if they are in the possession of a debtor engaged in farming operations. Animals in a herd of livestock are covered whether they are acquired by purchase or result from natural increase.

The evidence shows that FmHA filed its financing statement prior to the funds being paid to debtor. Debtor used a substantial part of the money to purchase pigs and cattle. The purchases were made within two months of the advance. The purchase money security interest therefore was perfected when debtors received the collateral.

Debtors were engaged in farming at all times herein set out and § 400.9–109(3) excludes, therefore, these animals from the definition of inventory. The question of priority of creditors consequently is determined by reference to § 400.9–312(4). That section does not require notice to a creditor holding a prior filing in the same product with an after acquired clause and allows the creditor making a purchase money advance to have priority over the creditor holding "after acquired" rights. Thus, in May of 1979, FmHA had a priority in the purchased cattle over the claim of the Bank.

In its brief the Bank concedes that FmHA had a purchase money security interest in the collateral until September 27, 1981. The Bank argues that the security agreement dated September 28, 1981, destroyed that status and gave FmHA a security interest for an antecedent debt, thus restoring the Bank to its first filed priority status. There is no evidence that FmHA released its first security agreement or UCC filing or advanced new funds in return for execution of this September, 1981 security agreement. No financing statement was filed in connection with the 1981 security agreement.

There was no testimony explaining the 1981 agreement. It would appear that it was taken after the FmHA agent ran a lien search and discovered, or so it seemed, that the Bank lien had expired. The 1981 agreement may have been taken to identify the then existing security.

There are a number of reasons why execution of the 1981 security agreement is immaterial. The Bank had filed a continuation statement and the court so finds. The Bank is not charged with FmHA's failure to discover such a filing or the apparent failure of the Recorder to index or file. The Bank continued to occupy a secured position in some respects. Nonetheless, as to the purchased cattle, FmHA's purchase money position was a priority without regard to the prior Bank filing and needed no subsequent action to maintain that priority even if the Bank's filing had lapsed.

The court concludes that execution of the 1981 security agreement, without more, is of no significance. The 1979 agreement was perfected and not altered by the subsequent agreement. Section 400.9–108 does not apply. In this instance the secured party made no advance, incurred no obligation, released no specific security interest and gave no value when the 1981 agreement was executed. [Citations omitted.]

The Bank also contends that the FmHA security agreement loses its purchase money character and priority as to cattle produced from those purchased. Calves which are bred are not purchased. They are "after acquired" in a general sense. The FmHA security agreement also covers all increases. The question then is whether cattle bred from security for a purchase money security interest are themselves purchase money security.

Section 400.9–107, R.S.Mo.1969, defines a purchase money security interest as one "taken by a person who by making advances * * * gives value to enable the debtor to acquire rights in or the use of collateral if such value is in fact so used." Here there is no question that debtors used the FmHA advance to purchase cattle which they used for their benefit. The advance ultimately, through a natural process, also enabled debtors to have the use of calves, i.e., the products of the purchase money collateral.

The Uniform Commercial Code enables a security interest to follow collateral even if it is transformed. See § 400.9–314, R.S.Mo.1969, as to rules concerning accessions and § 400.9–315, R.S.Mo.1969, as to rules concerning commingled or processed goods. But these statutes, while preserving a security interest, do not resolve the issue as to whether the interest retains its purchase money character but there are clear suggestions that the character remains unchanged. See, for example, § 400.9–315(1)(b) which provides that a financing statement covering goods "also covers the product into which the goods have been manufactured, processed or assembled." See also Holzman v. L.H.J. Enterprises, Inc., 476 F.2d 949 (9th Cir.1973) where the court held that inventory purchased from the sale of inventory subject to a purchase money security interest retained the character of purchase money security.

The purchase money security interest as an exception to the rules of priority of filing allows the creditor to have a security interest in identified collateral which it enabled the debtor to obtain. While such collateral may be transformed, as through manufacturing, it does not expand through its own effort. Cattle do (ignoring the biological act). The purchase money security interest is maintained by keeping the collateral intact or tracing the proceeds. Cattle as collateral expand by natural process.

In a case styled In re Ingram, 11 UCC Reporting Service 605 [468 F.2d 564] (5th Cir.1972) the court held a security interest in progeny of leased cattle was not a purchase money security interest because the creditor only enabled the debtor to acquire "rights in and use of the breeder stock" and not the progeny. The suggestion in § 400.9–204, R.S.Mo.1969 is that since the debtor had no rights in unconceived progeny at the time the security agreement was executed, no security interest could attach and therefore the creditor acquired no rights in such unconceived animals.

The purchase money security interest priority is an exception to the general rule and should be construed narrowly even though the application to a cattle situation is inexact. Compare Index Store Fixture Co. v. Farmers' Trust Co., 536 S.W.2d 902 (Mo.App.1976). It must be remembered, in support of a narrow reading, that even the natural process of herd growth does not proceed without assistance not provided by the purchase money creditor. The result could be different if the evidence showed that some part of the purchase money collateral was sold and new animals purchased, but that is not the case here. Similarly this could be a variation if the calves only replaced cattle that had died. Again, while the herd has diminished here, there is no evidence that diminution occurred from the aging process.

The evidence shows that debtors purchased 19 cows and 20 pigs with the FmHA loan. FmHA sold 13 cows and 7 calves. Debtors owned no pigs at the time of the foreclosure. There is no evidence as to disposition of the other cows. The sale price was not allocated among the animals, although it appears that all of the cows could have been part of the purchase money herd. The parties are directed to confer and to advise the court whether a further hearing would be necessary to resolve the issue of allocation.

The court also reserves the question of the nondischargeability of the debt to the Bank until the issue of allocation is resolved. Further evidence may be necessary on that question.

The court concludes, therefore, that the purchase money security interest does not apply to the calves. FmHA is entitled to the proceeds of the sale of those cattle which retained purchase money character at the time of foreclosure but the Bank is entitled to the proceeds from the sale of any others.

Note

Section 9–324(d) changes things considerably. Among other things the new purchase money claim will cover not only proceeds but also "products". So the purchase money lender might have fared better under the new Code rather than the old.

Problem 2–4

The Great Outdoors Company operated five large department stores in Indiana. In 1999 Bank One took a security interest in all of the Great Outdoors inventory and proceeds and properly perfected that security interest by filing in Indianapolis. In 2001 Hart Schaffner & Marks lent the Great Outdoors $2,000,000 to finance the purchase of Hart Schaffner & Marks clothing. Hart Schaffner & Marks also filed a financing statement in Indianapolis and received a proper security agreement. This security agreement covered all Hart Schaffner & Marks clothing sold to the Great Outdoors together with accounts receivable arising from the sale of such clothing, all such proceeds and the like. In September 2004 Great Outdoors went bankrupt and at the time of its bankruptcy it held $1,200,000 of Hart Schaffner & Marks clothing, and $500,000 of credit card receivables arising from the sale of Hart Schaffner & Marks clothing. Who has priority between Bank One and Hart Schaffner & Marks in each of the following cases?

1.   If Hart Schaffner & Marks gave no notice of its interest to Bank One.

2.   If Hart Schaffner & Marks gave proper notice of its interest to Bank One.

3.   Would Bank One's rights vis-à-vis Hart Schaffner & Marks be the same as to the first loan it made (before it knew of Hart Schaffner & Marks) and as to another $1,000,000 advance after it had learned of Hart Schaffner & Marks' security interest either by examining the records again or by being told?

4.   Assume Bank One's filing had been made on March 4, 1999. Assume Hart Schaffner & Marks had examined the files and had seen Bank One's filing in 2001. Assume further that Bank One never filed a continuation statement and that the Great Outdoors filed for bankruptcy on April 1, 2004.

Is Bank One subordinate to Hart Schaffner & Marks, the DIP, both, or neither?

5.   Assume Bank One has a fully perfected security interest securing its $5 million loan. Assume Bank Two has a fully perfected but subordinate security interest also securing a $5 million loan. In order to get Bank Three to make a loan, Bank One agrees to subordinate its security interest to Bank Three's claim. Accordingly Bank Three makes a $4 million unsecured loan. If upon liquidation the inventory and proceeds are sold for $7 million, how is the $7 million divided among Banks One, Two and Three and a trustee in bankruptcy?

Problem 2–5

Bank has a security interest in car dealer's inventory of automobiles. Bank has properly perfected its security interest and claims all after-acquired inventory as well as proceeds. Several years ago dealer purchased assets of a failed Toyota dealer and your client, Toyota Finance, lent it $2 million to purchase Lexus and Toyota automobiles. Your client went through the proper procedure to notify Bank and to achieve priority over them. The dealer has now gone into bankruptcy and Bank claims your client is not a purchase money lender as to approximately $1 million of Toyota Camrys. It seems that the Lexus cars, although later acquired, were first sold because they were a hot item, whereas the Camrys remained on the lot for a long period of time. Bank claims that when the Lexus cars were sold, the money received from them under Toyota Finance's accounting procedure went to pay off the earlier acquired Camrys and thus there is at best a non-purchase money security interest in those cars which would be subordinate to Bank's interest. What do you think?

MBANK ALAMO NATIONAL ASSOCIATION
v.
RAYTHEON COMPANY D/B/A RAYTHEON MEDICAL SYSTEMS
v.
E.I. DUPONT DE NEMOURS COMPANY

United States Court of Appeals, Fifth Circuit, 1989.
886 F.2d 1449.

REAVLEY, CIRCUIT JUDGE:

MBank Alamo National Association ("MBank") and E.I. DuPont de Nemours Company, Inc. ("DuPont") pressed this conversion action against Raytheon Company ("Raytheon"), claiming that Raytheon collected certain accounts receivable, in which MBank and DuPont had security interests superior to those of Raytheon. Raytheon's defense was that it had a purchase money security interest in the accounts receivable. Concluding that Raytheon had no purchase money security interest in the accounts, the district court held that Raytheon's security interests were subordinate to those of MBank and DuPont, and granted MBank's and DuPont's motions for summary judgment. We affirm.

I. Background

MBank and DuPont entered various security agreements with Howe X-ray ("Howe"). By January 10, 1983, in accordance with these agreements, both DuPont and MBank held perfected liens in Howe's present and future accounts receivable. MBank also held a perfected security interest in Howe's present and after acquired inventory.

Beginning in January 1983, Raytheon, an x-ray equipment manufacturer, entered a series of transactions with Howe who was one of its distributors. Raytheon agreed to ship x-ray equipment to Howe after Howe contracted with one of its customers for the sale, delivery, and installation of certain Raytheon equipment. In exchange, Howe agreed to assign the specific accounts receivable to Raytheon. Subsequent to the assignments, Raytheon filed financing statements in specific accounts receivable of Howe. Between July 1983 and December 1984, Raytheon collected over $850,000.00.

By November 1984, Howe had defaulted on its obligations to MBank and DuPont. MBank and DuPont, pursuant to their security interests, demanded payment from Raytheon from the accounts receivable that it had collected. Raytheon refused, claiming that it had a purchase money security interest ("PMSI") in the accounts receivable and that its interests were therefore superior to those of MBank and DuPont.

In addition to its contention that it had a PMSI in the accounts receivable, Raytheon claimed that even if it did not have a PMSI in those accounts, MBank waived its security interest in the accounts. The district court granted MBank's and DuPont's motions for summary judgment, deciding that Raytheon had no PMSI in the accounts receivable and that Raytheon had not raised an issue of MBank's alleged waiver.

Raytheon appeals the district court's determination that it did not have a PMSI in the accounts receivable. In the alternative, Raytheon contends that if our construction of the PMSI statutory provisions excludes the Raytheon–Howe transaction, the ruling should not apply to this case under the doctrine of nonretroactivity. Raytheon also appeals the district court's finding that Raytheon failed to produce sufficient evidence of waiver to overcome MBank's motion for summary judgment.

II. Analysis

A. Purchase Money Security Interests

The rules governing the rights of creditors are set out in Chapter 9 of the Texas Business and Commerce Code ("Code"), which essentially adopted the provisions of the Uniform Commercial Code—Secured Transactions. See Tex.Bus. & Com.Code Ann. § 9–101 et seq. (Vernon 1989). These provisions were enacted "to provide a simple and unified structure within which the immense variety of present-day secured financing transactions can go forward with less cost and with greater certainty." § 9–101, 1972 Official UCC Comment. In keeping with these goals, rules were enacted prioritizing conflicting security interests in the same property.

The general rule provides that the first perfected security interest to be filed has priority and other perfected interests stand in line in the order in which they were filed. See § 9–312(e). PMSIs are excepted from the first-to-file rule and take priority over other perfected security interests regardless of the filing sequence. § 9–312(c), (d). The district court found that Raytheon did not fall within the PMSI exception, that MBank had priority as the first to file, under § 9–312(e)(1), and that DuPont takes second priority since it filed next.

Raytheon claims the district court erred by not recognizing its priority in the accounts receivable as a PMSI under § 9–312(d). Section 9–312(d) provides that "[a] purchase money security interest in collateral other than inventory has priority over a conflicting security interest in the same collateral or its proceeds if the purchase money security interest is perfected at the time the debtor receives possession of the collateral or within 20 days thereafter."

As a threshold matter, Raytheon must establish that it meets the statutory definition of a PMSI. Raytheon contends that it fits the statutory requirements of a PMSI under § 9–107(2), which provides:

A security interest is a "purchase money security interest" to the extent that it is * * *.

(2) taken by a person who by making advances or incurring an obligation gives value to enable the debtor to acquire rights in or the use of collateral if such value is in fact so used.

To meet these requirements Raytheon must show: (1) that it gave value; (2) that the value given enabled Howe to acquire rights in the accounts receivable; and (3) that the accounts receivable qualify as collateral within the meaning of the statute.

The value requirement is satisfied by any consideration sufficient to support a simple contract. See Thet Mah and Assoc. v. First Bank of North Dakota, 336 N.W.2d 134, 138 (N.D.1983); § 1.201(44)(D) (Vernon 1968). Assuming arguendo that Raytheon gave value by extending credit to Howe in exchange for Howe's promise to assign the accounts receivable to Raytheon, see Thet Mah, 336 N.W.2d at 138, Raytheon has failed to satisfy the other two requirements.

To create a PMSI, the value must be given in a manner that enables the debtor to acquire interest in the collateral. This is accomplished when a debtor uses an extension of credit or loan money to purchase a specific item. See Ingram v. Ozark Prod. Credit Assoc., 468 F.2d 564, 565 (5th Cir.1972); In re Dillon, 18 B.R. 252, 254 (Bkrtcy.E.D.Cal.1982) (PMSI lien attaches to item actually purchased); Jackson & Kronman, Secured Financing and Priorities Among Creditors, 88 Yale L.J. 1143, 1165 (1979) (PMSI priority limited "to loans that can be traced to identifiable, discrete items of property.").

The collateral at issue here is the accounts receivable. In an attempt to force its interest into the PMSI mold, Raytheon has characterized the transaction as follows: "Raytheon, by agreeing to extend credit on its equipment, enabled Howe X–Ray to enter into subsequent contracts of sale with its customers, thereby acquiring rights in the contract accounts which, upon the specific advance and delivery of equipment, blossomed into a right to the collateral accounts receivable." Raytheon, however, cannot force this transaction to fit. To accept this characterization, we would have to close our eyes to the true nature of the transaction.

Raytheon, in essence, is claiming that it advanced x-ray machines to Howe on credit, which then enabled Howe to purchase accounts receivable from its customers. This, however, does not comport with our view of commercial reality. While, as Raytheon suggests, it may be theoretically possible to create a PMSI in accounts receivable by advancing funds for their purchase, see Northwestern Nat'l Bank Southwest v. Lectro Systems, 262 N.W.2d 678, 680 (Minn.1977); Gilmore, The Purchase Money Priority, 76 Harv.L.Rev. 1333, 1372 (1963), the same cannot be done by advancing x-ray machines. We view this as a two-step transaction in which Raytheon first advanced machines to Howe for retail sale and, once these machines were sold, Howe then assigned the accounts receivable to Raytheon. Through the credit advance, Howe acquired an interest in the machines, not the accounts receivable. Raytheon's credit advance, therefore, did not enable Howe to acquire an interest in the accounts receivable, as collateral within the meaning of the statute.

Additionally, in its characterization of the transaction, Raytheon is attempting to benefit from the PMSI's preferred status in a manner that was not contemplated by the UCC drafters. PMSIs provide an avenue for heavily burdened debtors to obtain credit for specific goods when creditors who have previously loaned money to the debtor may be unwilling to advance additional funds. Jackson & Kronman, Secured Financing and Priorities Among Creditors, 88 Yale L.J. 1143, 1145 & n. 9 (1979). By giving a PMSI holder a priority interest in the specific goods purchased, there is some incentive for a lender to advance funds or credit for the specific transaction. The scope of a PMSI holder's preferred interest, however, is specifically limited by the Code.

Under § 9–312(c), a PMSI in inventory is limited to that inventory or to "identifiable cash proceeds received on or before the delivery of the inventory to a buyer * * *." The drafters noted that general financing of an inventory business is based primarily on accounts resulting from inventory, chattel paper and other proceeds. § 9–312, Official UCC Reasons for 1972 Change comment (4). Reasoning that "[a]ccounts financing is more important in the economy than the financing of the kinds of inventory that produce accounts, and [that] the desirable rule is one which makes accounts financing certain as to its legal position," id., they specifically excluded accounts resulting from the sale of inventory from the protections of a PMSI. Thus, financing statements that are filed on a debtor's accounts take precedence over any subsequent claim to accounts as proceeds of a PMSI in inventory. Additionally, to protect lenders who make periodic advances against incoming inventory, the PMSI holder is required to notify other secured parties before it can take priority. § 9–312(c)(2); see id., 1972 Official UCC Comment comment 3.

The priority scheme, however, differs in the context of collateral other than inventory. Under § 9–312(d), a PMSI in collateral other than inventory entitles the holder to a superior interest in both the collateral and its proceeds regardless of any intervening accounts. The differing entitlement to proceeds is due to differences in the expectations of the parties with respect to the collateral involved.

Collateral other than inventory generally refers to equipment used in the course of business. See id., Official UCC Reasons for 1972 Change comment (4); Gilmore, The Purchase Money Priority, 76 Harv.L.Rev. 1333, 1385 (1963). Since, unlike inventory, "it is not ordinarily expected that the collateral will be sold and that proceeds will result, [the drafters found it] appropriate to give the party having a purchase money security interest in the original collateral an equivalent priority in its proceeds." § 9–312, Official UCC Reasons for 1972 Change comment (3).

Howe's business primarily involved the sale of inventory, which included the Raytheon x-ray machines. See § 9–109(4). The accounts receivable are proceeds resulting from the sale of the machines. MBank and DuPont took security interests in the accounts receivable, in accordance with their expectation that sale of the inventory would generate the accounts. If we were to accept Raytheon's argument that it holds a PMSI in Howe's accounts receivable, we would be giving Raytheon a priority interest in the proceeds of inventory, in direct contravention to the express intent of the drafters. Additionally, Raytheon would have successfully avoided the notice requirements of § 9–312(c)(2).

Raytheon argues, however, that the policies underlying PMSIs actually favor recognizing Raytheon's priority interest in Howe's accounts. It points out that Howe could find no other source of financing besides Raytheon and that "MBank and DuPont benefited by the financing arrangements because the extension of [credit] by Raytheon helped Howe X-ray stay in business thereby servicing its debts." Raytheon also contends that if the Code is interpreted to limit the security interests of creditors, such as Raytheon, to a mere promise of repayment and the grant of a PMSI in inventory, a "valuable source of credit" to similarly encumbered debtors would "dry up." This is because the risk of default is too great in the face of prior liens on the debtor's accounts.

The Code itself, however, answers this argument. The drafters were apparently well aware that the failure to extend a PMSI holder's priority status to the resulting accounts would provide less incentive for inventory financiers to provide credit. See § 9–312, 1972 Official UCC Comment comment 8. Yet, they did not extend the protections of a PMSI and merely noted that "[m]any parties financing inventory are quite content to protect their first security interest in the inventory itself, realizing that when inventory is sold, someone else will be financing the accounts and the priority for inventory will not run forward to the accounts." Id.

The drafter's recognition of the problem and the statutory favoring of accounts financing demonstrate that the drafters were not overly concerned that this source of financing would "dry up."

Additionally, Raytheon had alternative means of securing its right to receive payment. Besides obtaining a PMSI in the inventory by complying with the § 9–312(c)(2) notice requirements, it could have entered subordination agreements with MBank and DuPont on the specific accounts resulting from the sale of Raytheon's x-ray machines. It also could have sold the machines to Howe's customers who would have paid Raytheon directly, with Howe receiving a commission on the sale. If Raytheon had followed either of these courses, it would not have subverted the notice and filing requirements of the Code. As this transaction goes beyond that contemplated by the PMSI provisions, we decline "to expand the scope of special protection afforded a purchase money security interest, lest in so doing we defeat the underlying purposes of the Code: to bring predictability to commercial transactions." Mark Prod. U.S., Inc. v. Interfirst Bank Houston, N.A., 737 S.W.2d 389, 393 (Tex. App.—Houston [14th Dist.] 1987).

Since Raytheon did not have a PMSI in Howe's accounts receivable, the first-to-file priority rules govern. See Ford Motor Credit Co. v. First State Bank of Smithville, 679 S.W.2d 486, 487 (Tex.1984). As the last to file, Raytheon's interest is subordinate to those of MBank and DuPont.

B.   The Doctrine of Nonretroactivity

Having concluded that Raytheon did not have a PMSI, Raytheon now contends that because this case presented a novel question of law, the doctrine of nonretroactivity should apply. Under the doctrine of nonretroactivity a court deciding a question of first impression, in a manner that was not clearly foreshadowed, makes the ruling inapplicable to the parties before it. See Chevron Oil Co. v. Huson, 404 U.S. 97, 106, 92 S.Ct. 349, 355, 30 L.Ed.2d 296 (1971). This is no case for nonretroactivity. The holding that Raytheon did not have a PMSI in the accounts receivable is required by the statute and commentary, given the PMSI restrictions and the Code's clear mandate that first-to-file rules establish the priorities in accounts resulting from the sale of inventory. The goal of providing predictability in commercial transactions is furthered by the present application of our holding. Moreover, we find no inequity in applying the rule to Raytheon. Raytheon's credit managers were well aware of the first-to-file rule yet, at no time, attempted to notify MBank or DuPont about its purported interest in the accounts. It did not pursue alternative means of securing payment, but merely claimed a priority right in the absence of any authority to do so.

C.   Waiver

Lastly, Raytheon contends that the district court erred in holding that Raytheon failed to produce sufficient evidence that MBank waived its security interest in the accounts to overcome MBank's motion for summary judgment. To support its claim, Raytheon presented evidence that MBank was informed that Howe and Raytheon were engaged in ongoing credit negotiations and that Howe was assigning the accounts receivable to Raytheon. Additionally, while MBank was aware that it was not receiving full payment of Howe's accounts receivable, MBank never requested that the accounts proceeds be segregated or held in trust for the bank.

Waiver is a valid defense to an action to enforce a security interest. Weisbart & Co. v. First Nat'l Bank of Dalhart, Texas, 568 F.2d 391, 396 (5th Cir.1978); Montgomery v. Fuquay–Mouser, Inc., 567 S.W.2d 268, 270 (Tex.Civ.App.1978). Under Texas law, "[w]aiver is the intentional relinquishment of a known right or intentional conduct inconsistent with claiming it, with full knowledge of the material facts." Montgomery, 567 S.W.2d at 270.

Although Raytheon's evidence suggests that MBank knew about the assignment of the accounts receivable, the assignment alone did not interfere with MBank's rights, because any assignment would be subordinate to MBank's security interest. MBank's rights were not infringed until Raytheon collected the accounts receivable. To raise the issue of whether MBank intended to relinquish its security interest in the accounts receivable, Raytheon would at least have to present evidence that MBank knew Raytheon was collecting the accounts. Raytheon did not do so. The district court properly granted the motions for summary judgment. See Anderson v. Liberty Lobby, Inc., 477 U.S. 242, 248–49, 106 S.Ct. 2505, 2510–11, 91 L.Ed.2d 202 (1986); Washington v. Armstrong World Indus., 839 F.2d 1121, 1122–23 (5th Cir.1988) (per curiam). The judgments for MBank and DuPont are AFFIRMED.

GOLDBERG, CIRCUIT JUDGE, dissenting:

What we confront today is another nettle in the thicket of the Texas Uniform Commercial Code. A thorny question of statutory interpretation that could cause scratch and abrasion if not reconnoitered under the illumination provided by the Texas Supreme Court. After examining the relevant statutes and commentaries, however, I believe that the majority has not construed the code as would the Texas Supreme Court in the face of the same problem. So because the scratch of a thorn may cause infection if not properly treated, I must respectfully DISSENT.

The nettle of this case is whether an account receivable should be considered "collateral" in the words of the purchase money security interest statute so that the purchase money interest has priority over a security interest previously perfected in an identical account. My belief is that accounts receivable are an appropriate form of collateral because they can be used to invigorate marginal businesses. I would thus hold that Raytheon established a purchase money security interest in the specified accounts of Howe x-ray.

I. THE FACTS

Both MBank and DuPont had loaned money to Howe, a dealer in medical equipment including expensive x-ray machines. To guard against the possibility that Howe would default on these loans, MBank, whose loan was made before DuPonts, perfected a security interest in Howe's accounts receivable then existing and subsequently arising and also perfected a similar security interest in Howe's inventory. DuPont's security interest was also perfected in Howe's accounts receivable then existing and subsequently arising but was filed after MBank's interest.

While the MBank/DuPont loans were outstanding, Raytheon entered into a series of transactions with Howe. Each transaction was executed according to a preexisting distribution agreement which allowed Howe to contract with customers for the sale of Raytheon x-ray machines. Under this agreement, Raytheon promised to supply an x-ray machine to Howe in exchange for Howe's promise to assign the account receivable that arose from the sale of the machine to Raytheon. Raytheon gave notice of its security interest in each account by filing a financing statement within the applicable 20 day period after the creation of the account. The structure of this agreement between Howe and Raytheon arose because Howe had begun to experience difficulty in obtaining additional financing and was spiraling down toward bankruptcy, its final fate.

II. DISCUSSION

Before I get involved in the details of Raytheon's purchase money security interest, however, a momentary step back is in order to scan the general landscape of security interests. As a general observation, the usual method for growth in the area of commercial law has been the daring creativity of a company pushing out beyond the boundaries of "normal practice" in response to business exigencies. The history of trust receipts, the factor's liens, and the eventual adoption of Article 9 of the Uniform Commercial Code illustrates this general observation in the area of security interests. See G. Gilmore, Security Interests in Personal Property, Ch. 1–8 (1965).

> "The idea which the draftsmen [of Article 9] started with was that the system of independent security devices [developed in different area of commerce] had served its time; that the formal differences which separated one device from another should be scrapped and replaced with the simple concept of a security interest in personal property; that all types of personal property, whether held for use or for sale, should be recognized as available for security." Id. at 290 (emphasis added).

Article 9 was thus intended to be a flexible statute that could respond to divergent commercial needs.

The facts of this case present exactly the type of problematic situation which demands a creative solution. Raytheon, as a manufacturer of expensive x-ray equipment, often does not seek out customers itself but instead uses local distributors such as Howe to make sales. But Howe had to borrow money for it to function as a merchant of medical equipment. MBank and DuPont provided this money protecting themselves by with security interests in the collateral Howe had available,

Howe's present and future accounts receivable and inventory. This type of security interest in a borrower's intangibles such as accounts receivable is extremely common. The key to who has priority is to determine who filed the security interest in the collateral first. First in time, first in line goes the rhyme.

The problem with this situation is that a manufacturer will not loan or give a heavily indebted merchant any goods to sell on credit because once the merchant sells the goods, the banker, not the manufacturer, will have priority in the resulting accounts under the first in time first in line principle. Raytheon would thus not advance any x-ray machines to Howe because MBank and DuPont would have priority in any accounts that arose from the sale of the machines. Yet it is these very sales which would enable Howe to make profits to pay off its loans to MBank and DuPont. So how does an indebted merchant, who is unable to pay a manufacturer for goods that the merchant must sell to service the banker's loan, stay in business? Often what occurs is a scenario where the banker's loan is not paid, the merchant goes out of business, and the manufacturer loses an opportunity to distribute its goods on the market.

Article 9 provides a solution: the purchase money security interest. This device, with its root in the Railroad Car Trusts of the Nineteenth Century, has priority over security interests filed earlier because of its specific transaction oriented function. Id. at 743–53 (citing U.S. v. New Orleans R.R., 79 U.S. (12 Wall.) 362, 364–65, 20 L.Ed. 434 (1871) (pre Erie commercial case giving priority to the later in time party)). The purchase money security interest operates outside the notice principle which favors early interest holders over later ones. Notice is not the driving force behind the purchase money security interest.

It was this purchase money device that allowed Howe an opportunity to continue doing business to the benefit of MBank, DuPont and Raytheon. Howe did not have enough money to purchase a $140,000 x-ray machine for inventory but Raytheon would not advance a machine on credit to Howe. A creative alternative was necessary. Raytheon agreed to advance a machine to Howe in exchange for Howe's enforceable purchase order or account receivable. Raytheon thus used the account as a vehicle to ensure Howe's payment for the machine. It was a creative solution to the meeting of two creditors, a manufacturer of expensive equipment, and a heavily indebted retailer, that allowed commerce to continue to flow.

But for the law to recognize this creativity, it must be determined whether Raytheon has complied with the elements of the Texas purchase money security interest statute. Admittedly this arrangement does not present a paradigmatic purchase money security interest, but I believe that creativity, when in harmony with the statutory requirements, should be encouraged.

A. The Value Requirement

Purchase money security interests are defined in section 9–107 of the Texas Uniform Commercial Code. Section 9–107, states, in pertinent part:

A security interest is a "purchase money security interest" to the extent that it is * * *

(2) taken by a person who by making advances or incurring an obligation gives value to enable the debtor to acquire rights in or the use of collateral if such value is in fact so used.

Under the statute, Raytheon must satisfy three requirements. Raytheon must demonstrate that: (1) it gave value to Howe by making advances or incurring an obligation; (2) its extension of value enabled Howe to acquire rights in the collateral-the account receivable in each particular transaction; and, (3) the Texas UCC recognizes an account receivable as collateral for the purposes of a purchase money security interest.

There is no question that Raytheon extended value. Raytheon gave value when it shipped, according to the purchase order, an x-ray machine that a particular customer had ordered. This interpretation of the value requirement is consistent with the definition of value as set out in section 1.201(44) of the Texas Uniform Commercial Code. Section 1.201(44) is applicable through the direction of the definitional cross reference of section 9–107. It states in pertinent part, that: "[a] person gives 'value' for rights if he acquires them * * * (D) generally, in return for any consideration sufficient to support a simple contract." Raytheon satisfied section 1.201(44) because the advance of the x-ray machine in exchange for a promise from Howe to assign an accounts receivable arising from the sale of that x-ray machine is consideration sufficient to support a contract. Moreover, under section 9–107(2) itself, " 'A secured party may give value by committing * * * to supply goods or [by] actually supply[ing] the goods.' " Thet Mah and Associates Inc. v. First Bank of North Dakota, 336 N.W.2d 134, 138 (N.D.1983) (citing 1 Bender UCC Service, Secured Transactions, section 4.05(4) p. 304 (1983)).

This advance also satisfied the limitation on the type of value that may be given as defined in comment 2 of section 9–107. Comment 2 states, in pertinent part:

[t]his section * * * provides that the purchase money party must be one who gives value " 'by making advances or incurring an obligation' ": the quoted language excludes from the purchase money category any security interest taken as security for or in satisfaction of a preexisting claim or antecedent debt.

This antecedent debt limitation is satisfied here because Howe's debt to Raytheon was not preexisting but was instead created by the advance of the machine. Only then was Howe indebted to Raytheon for the machine's value. In turn, the debt was secured by the accounts receivable that Howe assigned to Raytheon pursuant to their agreement.

B.   The Enabling Requirement

The second element of a purchase money security interest is the requirement that Raytheon give value "to enable" Howe to acquire rights in the particular account receivable. This requirement means that the advance made by Raytheon must have made it possible for Howe X-ray to obtain the collateral. In the present case, the enabling requirement is satisfied because Raytheon's agreement with Howe, which preceded all of the particular transactions, was that Raytheon would advance an x-ray machine to Howe in exchange for an accounts receivable generated by Howe's sale of the machine to a customer. This preexisting agreement, together with the advance of the machine by Raytheon, enabled Howe to make the sale. At the same moment in time, in the twinkling of an eye, the sale created the particular account receivable payable to Howe which Howe then assigned to Raytheon pursuant to their preexisting agreement. "If the loan transaction appears closely allied to the purchase transaction, that should suffice. The evident intent of paragraph (b) [UCC 9–107(b)] is to free the purchase-money concept from artificial limitations; rigid adherence to particular formalities and sequences should not be required." G. Gilmore, I Security Interests in Personal Property, 782 (1965).

C.   The Collateral Requirement

The thorny question in this case centers on whether accounts receivable should be considered collateral for the purpose of a purchase money security interest under Section 9–107(b). To my mind, Raytheon has jumped this hurdle.

Under section 9–105(a)(3), which is listed in the definitional cross references of section 9–107, collateral is defined as "the property subject to a security interest and includes accounts and chattel paper which have been sold * * *." Moreover, under section 9–106, which is also listed in the definitional cross references of section 9–107, "[a]ccount means any right to payment for goods sold or leased or for services rendered which is not evidenced by an instrument or chattel paper, whether or not it has been earned by performance." The comment to 9–106 states that the section is referring to "ordinary commercial accounts receivable." By reading these two definitional sections in tandem, it is clear that an account receivable can be collateral for the purposes of a purchase money security interest under section 9–107.

There is, however, no other authority to our knowledge that expressly states that accounts receivable should be considered collateral for the purpose of a purchase money security interest. The Supreme Court of Minnesota has suggested that a purchase money security interest in accounts could validly arise. See Northwestern National Bank Southwest v. Lectro Systems, 262 N.W.2d 678, 680 (Minn.1977) ("This is not a case in which funds were advanced and used for purchase of a receivable."). And, Professor Grant Gilmore, one of the original drafters of article 9, has stated in his treatise on security interests, that the purchase money concept might apply to intangible property in occasional cases. G. Gilmore, I Security Interests in Personal Property, 781 (1965) ("There seems to be no reason, however, why the term 'collateral' should have other than its normal meaning: the purchase-money concept may thus, in an occasional case, apply to intangible property * * *.").

MBank and DuPont have asserted that accounts receivable should not be considered collateral for the purpose of defining a purchase money security interest under Section 9–107(2). Their argument, adopted by the majority, is that because accounts receivable financing has been accorded a special importance by the Texas Uniform Commercial Code, its legal position should not be made less certain by the operation of Sections 9–107(2) and 9–312(d). Once a security interest has been created under section 9–107(2), section 9–312(d) grants it special status. Section 9–312(d) states that "a purchase money security interest in collateral other than inventory has priority over a conflicting security interest in the same collateral or its proceeds if the purchase money security interest is perfected at the time the debtor receives possession of the collateral or within 20 days thereafter."

The significance of this special priority granted to purchase money security interests in subsection (2) becomes apparent when compared to the general priority rule in section 9–312(e). Under section 9–312(e)(1), conflicting security interests in the same collateral rank according to the time of filing. The first party to file notice of its interest in an account has priority over any subsequently filed interests in the identical account.

Because of the operation of section 9–312(d), however, the first party to file notice of a security interest in an account would not necessarily have priority under section 9–312(e)(1). Section 9–312(d) would grant priority over any interest filed previously in the same account if purchase money status in the account was first established under section 9–107. The legal position of accounts receivable financing might thus be made less certain if a purchase money security interest could be claimed in accounts receivable under section 9–107(2). Diminished certainty could result in the sense that the first party to file notice of its interest in an account under section 9–312(e) would be uncertain as to whether it had priority in the account or whether another party has priority because the latter established purchase money status in the same account under 9–107(2).

MBank and DuPont argue that this uncertainty in the legal position of accounts receivable financing should be prohibited because of the special importance accorded to accounts receivable financing under the code. They find this importance in the history of section 9–312(c) which prohibits the establishment of purchase money security interests in accounts receivable, derivatively, as proceeds of inventory. The argument points out that this prohibition was created due to the importance of accounts receivable financing in the economy. Based on these premises, the argument concludes that the possibility of a purchase money security interest in accounts receivable under section 9–107(2) should also be prohibited. The fallacy of this logic, however, is that it equates the value of accounts receivable as applied to a problem that arose in the area of inventory financing with the values behind the section 9–107 purchase money security interest.

The argument thus rests upon MBank and DuPont's interpretation of section 9–312(c). Section 9–312(c) provides that "a perfected purchase money security interest in inventory has priority over a conflicting security interest in the same inventory and also has priority in any identifiable cash proceeds received on or before the delivery of inventory to a buyer." This section of the code was changed in 1972 to address the problem of priority conflicts between a claim to accounts receivable derivatively as proceeds of inventory and a claim to the accounts established by the filing of a direct security interest. The conflict arose between inventory financiers who claimed priority in the accounts as proceeds of the inventory that they helped the debtor to acquire and lenders who had taken a direct security interest in the accounts as collateral for money loaned to the debtor.

Section 9–312(c) offered a solution to this conflict. It states that a prior right to the inventory of a debtor does not confer a prior right to any proceeds that arise from the sale of the inventory except for identifiable cash proceeds. There is no prior right to accounts receivable as proceeds from the sale of the inventory. Under this section, it would not be possible to establish a purchase money security interest in inventory and then claim a purchase money security interest in any of the accounts that arose from the sale of that inventory. This exclusion of accounts receivable as proceeds of inventory under section 9–312(c) rests upon the assumption that accounts receivable financing is more important in the economy than the financing of the types of inventory that produce accounts when sold.

MBank and DuPont thus argue that a purchase money security interest in accounts receivable should not be permitted under section 9–107(2) because a purchase money security interest in accounts receivable may not be claimed derivatively as proceeds of the sale of inventory under section 9–312(c). However, when this argument is examined in light of the policy interests underpinning section 9–107(2), the argument's core assumption, the importance of accounts receivable financing in the economy, dictates precisely the opposite result.

The most important policy justification for a purchase money security interest under section 9–107(2) is the protection that it gives to a debtor who is unable to raise additional funds to remain in business. Creditors who have previously loaned money to the debtor and taken a security interest in the debtor's goods may be unwilling to advance additional value or funds. These additional funds, however, could enable a debtor to purchase goods, make sales, and in turn, generate profits. Profits which could not only be used to create more business, but also, to allow the debtor to pay off the creditor's loans. The purchase money security provisions thus enable a leveraged debtor who is able to find a new lender to give that new lender a first claim on the new collateral purchased notwithstanding a prior filing by another creditor.

The arrangement between Raytheon and Howe exemplifies the use of accounts receivable to advance the policy rationale behind the purchase money security interest. It was the use of the accounts receivable by Raytheon as collateral for the x-ray machines that allowed Howe to continue to do business. The additional business that Howe was able to generate with the advance of the x-ray machines, at minimum, gave Howe an additional opportunity to stay in business. This opportunity was a benefit to creditors such as MBank and DuPont whose loans would not be repaid unless Howe had the ability to generate profits. It also demonstrated the importance of accounts receivable financing in another forum, the creation of purchase money security interests.

The use of accounts receivable as collateral in this case benefited MBank and DuPont as creditors because the consequences of an unpaid account were relatively greater to Raytheon. Raytheon, MBank and DuPont would each have been harmed if Howe's customers failed to pay their accounts. If an account receivable were to remain unpaid, Raytheon would lose the entire value of the x-ray machine advanced to Howe. In contrast, it is unlikely that the failure of one account would drive Howe into bankruptcy so that Howe would be unable to repay MBank and DuPont. Yet it is this additional risk taken by Raytheon which allowed Howe a profit that could be used to fund its business to the advantage of MBank and DuPont.

Finally, any obligation imposed on MBank and DuPont to determine whether Howe was using its accounts receivable to collateralize purchase money security transactions is diminished in two respects. First, as stated, it is these very purchase money transactions that allowed Howe an additional opportunity to service its debts to these creditors. Second, MBank and DuPont as creditors had already established relationships with Howe. In future transactions, it would not have been difficult for them to ascertain whether Howe was using any accounts to collateralize purchase money transactions with other creditors and draft the loan contracts accordingly.

D.   The Limit of Raytheon's Purchase Money Security Interest

I would, however, posit a serious limit on the extent of Raytheon's purchase money security interest. Under section 9–107, a security interest has purchase money character only to the extent of the value given to acquire the collateral. In the present case, the value given by Raytheon was the price of the x-ray machine as measured by the difference in the price Howe charged customers and the price Raytheon charged Howe. This price measures the extent of Raytheon's purchase money security interest in the specific accounts receivable of Howe. I do not mean to imply that the value given to a distributor such as Howe will always be measured by the wholesale price. In some situations, it could be the retail price depending upon what the debtor was meant to gain by the transaction. I would leave these transactional details for the district court.

The difference between the price Raytheon charged Howe and the price Howe charged its customers would thus not be a part of Raytheon's purchase money security interest. There is evidence to the effect that

Howe used a portion of this difference, Howe's profit margin, to pay a preexisting debt owing from Howe to Raytheon. This money could not be a part of Raytheon's purchase money security interest because a purchase money security interest may not be used to secure a preexisting debt.

There is also evidence which suggests that Raytheon may have loaned money to Howe to cover Howe's costs of installing the x-ray machine. Any such money would not be a part of Raytheon's purchase money security interest. There should not be any additional opportunities created under the code to give simple loans purchase money character.

To my mind, Raytheon has established a valid purchase money security interest under section 9–107(2) of the Texas Uniform Commercial Code. The x-ray machine advanced by Raytheon constituted the value that enabled Howe to acquire accounts receivable, the collateral, for the purposes of section 9–107(2). As such, this case should be reversed and remanded, where the issue of waiver could be examined with a headlight's incandescence and the retroactivity issue appropriately explored.

I therefore respectfully DISSENT.

Problem 2–6

Analyze the MBank case under 1999 Article 9. Your partner has suggested that changes in the Code from the prior Code would change the outcome of the case. He refers you to 9–330, 9–331 and 9–332.

Problem 2–7

Could the seller have protected its interest by taking a purchase money security interest? (Note that a purchase money secured creditor's priority in inventory does not carry over to the accounts that arise on the inventory's sale. This would have been a problem for the seller.)

§ 5. PROCEEDS, ETC.

Proceeds, Attachment and Definition

Like the former Code, 1999 Article 9 provides automatic attachment of a security interest to the "rights to proceeds provided by section 9–315", 9–203(f). This rule, codified for the first time in 1972, presumes that the parties intend the security interest to attach to proceeds of the collateral even where their agreement is silent. To understand the effect of section 9–203, one must understand the meaning of "proceeds" and the reach of section 9–315. Proceeds are defined as follows in section 9–102(a)(64):

> whatever is acquired upon the sale, lease, license, exchange, or other disposition of collateral;

With experience under the 1962 and 1972 versions of Article 9, the definition of proceeds has gradually changed and expanded. For example, subsection (E) clearly covers insurance proceeds that are payable on injury to, or destruction of, collateral. Likewise subsection (B) covers distributions such as cash and stock dividends. Both of these provisions reverse court decisions under the former Code. Under the 1972 version, the debtor apparently had to "receive" personal property for that property to be "proceeds". There was no reason for the requirement and the drafters of the 1999 Code have omitted the word "receive".

What if the debtor *sells* collateral but denominates the transaction a "lease"? In that case the "lease" is a security agreement taken by the debtor and is chattel paper. According to PEB Commentary No. 9, the chattel paper itself constitutes proceeds. The same commentary states that payments to the debtor under true leases are proceeds. Even a true lease itself could be considered proceeds. One can argue that a lessor of goods for a limited time does not "dispose" of the collateral but there is a disposition not so? Even though only a portion of the debtor's rights are disposed of (for example, a two-year right to use out of a ten-year useful life of a commodity), one can argue that the lease itself is a disposition and that both the lease and the payments under the lease are proceeds.

There are other transactions that look like sales or dispositions, but are not. What if a cow gives milk or bears a calf? There is, of course, no sale or other disposition of the cow, but the production of the milk or a calf looks like a stock dividend—something that now constitutes proceeds under the new third sentence. Until the drafters expand the definition, and, notwithstanding the third sentence, such natural production and reproduction are not proceeds. Presumably that is the reason why many security interests dealing with animals include the term "product", i.e., milk, eggs and young.

Further, to test the boundaries of "disposition" under 9–102(a)(64), assume a debtor has given a security interest in a valuable piece of industrial machinery. Because the debtor wishes to sell the machinery or move it to another location, the debtor proposes that the creditor's security interest be transferred from that machine to another. The other machine becomes subject to the security interest not because it is proceeds of the first, but because of the agreement of the parties. The second machine is not proceeds of the first. The "exchange, disposition" and the like probably contemplate a transfer by the debtor to a *third party*, not the transfer of a security interest from one asset of the debtor to another.

Under section 9–315(a)(2) the security interest attaches only to "identifiable" proceeds. In most cases proceeds will be easily identifiable as having come from particular collateral. For example, if a secured creditor had a security interest in an automobile that was sold and if the purchaser gave the seller a security interest and a note, the security interest would make a specific reference to the automobile and would be directly traceable to that particular piece of collateral.

By far the most common trouble comes when collateral is sold for cash, for a check or for some other form of payment, and the proceeds of that payment or the payment itself are deposited into a bank account. If there are other funds in that account, one will need some accounting fiction to determine which part of the account should be regarded as proceeds and which part as something else. Prior to 1999 the courts allowed creditors to use various tracing methods to identify their collateral in deposit accounts. A common method was the "lowest intermediate balance". Assume a secured creditor could prove the debtor had deposited $10,000 of proceeds into its bank account, assume that thereafter the lowest balance in the account was $8,000. In that case, the lowest intermediate balance fiction would treat the remaining $8,000 as identifiable proceeds of the secured creditor. Revised 9–315(b)(2) blesses such fictional tracing doctrine:

> [I]f the proceeds are not goods, to the extent that the secured party identifies the proceeds by a method of tracing, including application of equitable principles, that is permitted under law other than this article with respect to commingled property of the type involved.

Subsection 9–315(b)(1) allows a secured creditor to claim commingled goods to the extent provided by section 9–336, a provision that deals explicitly with commingled collateral such as grain and the like.

Proceeds, Perfection

Subsections (c) and (d) of 9–315 state the rules for perfection of proceeds:

> (c) [Perfection of security interest in proceeds.] A security interest in proceeds is a perfected security interest if the security interest in the original collateral was perfected.

> (d) [Continuation of perfection.] A perfected security interest in proceeds becomes unperfected on the 21st day after the security interest attaches to the proceeds unless:

>> (1) the following conditions are satisfied:

>>> (A) a filed financing statement covers the original collateral;

>>> (B) the proceeds are collateral in which a security interest may be perfected by filing in the office in which the financing statement has been filed; and

>>> (C) the proceeds are not acquired with cash proceeds;

>> (2) the proceeds are identifiable cash proceeds; or

>> (3) the security interest in the proceeds is perfected other than under subsection (c) when the security interest attaches to the proceeds or within 20 days thereafter.

The reassuring starting point is that the interest in the proceeds is automatically perfected if the security interest "in the original collateral was perfected". Under subsection (d) that perfection continues for 20 days; if the creditor wishes to continue its perfection beyond 20 days, it must either fit within one of the other subsections or take whatever action would be necessary to perfect a security interest in the particular assets involved.

Consider two cases where perfection continues without any act on the part of the secured creditor. First are the cases in 9–315(d)(1): the creditor has filed as to the original collateral at the same office where one would file with respect to these proceeds if one were perfecting an original security interest in them. There is an additional condition that these proceeds cannot have been purchased with earlier cash proceeds. To see how this provision might work and how pervasive its reach, consider an example. Assume the debtor is a Kentucky corporation and the secured creditor has filed a financing statement covering the debtor's inventory at the state capital in Frankfort. Assume further that the financing statement covers only "debtor's inventory of used automobiles" and the proceeds are chattel paper received on the sale of some of those automobiles. Since one originally perfecting as to the debtor's chattel paper would file a financing statement in the "same office" and since the proceeds have not been acquired with "cash proceeds", the secured creditor is perfected as to the chattel paper without taking any action and despite the fact its financing statement does not list chattel paper. Since almost all filings under the 1999 Code will be at the place of a corporate debtor's incorporation, the general rule will be that perfection continues as to proceeds without any action by the secured creditor. Presumably the drafters assumed that anyone who searches in the name of the debtor will find the filing as to inventory and will understand that the prior secured creditor likely claimed proceeds as well.

The second indefinite extension of perfection covers "identifiable cash proceeds", 9–315(d)(2). Section 9–102(a)(9) defines cash proceeds as "money, checks, deposit accounts, or the like". The good news is that the secured creditor is indefinitely perfected with respect to these identifiable cash proceeds; the bad news is that money, checks, and the like are seldom long in the hands of a troubled debtor. Of course, this section does mean that our secured creditor has a continuously perfected security interest in the debtor's bank account, at least if the secured creditor can "identify" the proceeds portion of that account.

Note

It is no surprise to learn that operating businesses that grant security interests in their inventory and intangibles fill their bank (deposit) accounts with proceeds of those security interests. Under the provisions of section 9–315, creditors who hold perfected security interests in the collateral that produced the money deposited in these accounts will have a perfected security interest in the deposit accounts.

Under 9–315(a)(1) the security interest in the retailer's refrigerator, washing machine or accounts receivable attaches to the "identifiable proceeds of the collateral". The consumer's check or promise to pay will be identifiable. Section 9–315(b) appears to indorse the case law methods of tracing proceeds into deposit accounts and thus of making those proceeds still "identifiable" after deposit. The section specifically refers to identification "by a method of tracing, including application of equitable principles that is permitted under law other than this article...". Comment 3 to 9–315 refers to the "lowest intermediate balance rule" as a permissible method of tracing. Assume an account with a balance of $1M; assume an additional $1M from the sale of collateral is deposited; assume that the balance then goes down to $900,000 and back up to $5M. The lowest intermediate balance rule tells us that $900,000 of the $5M in the account is "identifiable" as coming from the $1M of proceeds that were earlier deposited. Nevermind that the rule might be more generous to the secured creditor than you think it should be, that is the rule.

These security interests in deposit proceeds continue to be perfected without any new filing under the terms of 9–315(d) as identifiable "cash" proceeds. Section 9–102(a)(9) explicitly includes "deposit accounts" as "cash" proceeds. Note finally that this method of perfection continues indefinitely but, of course, it will be completely defeated if the account balance goes to zero each night or at any time between the deposit and the time of the creditor's claim to the proceeds. So it is common for a secured creditor to have a perfected security interest in its debtor's deposit account.

Under pre–1999 Article 9 one could not take a direct security interest in a deposit account. The only security interest recognized was an interest in proceeds that might have been deposited there. For that reason the depositary bank (assuming it was not the person financing the debtor's inventory or intangibles) had to rely upon its rights of set-off to challenge a third party who claimed a perfected proceeds interest in a deposit account with the bank. The conventional learning on the priority of set-off is that a set-off is not effective until some act is taken by the bank to do the set-off (i.e., putting a hold on the account, reducing the balance in the account or the like). For those reasons a depositary bank who lent money to its depositors in reliance on a deposit account was likely to lose to a third party secured creditor who was lending on other assets whose proceeds were funding the account.

Two parts of 1999 Article 9 have almost completely reversed the former rules. It is now permissible to take a direct security interest in the deposit account. The priority rules with respect to that security interest, stated in section 9–327, elevate the rights of the depositary bank over any creditor who does not have control (the bank invariably has control) or for that matter over almost every other secured creditor even in the unusual case in which the depositary bank gets perfection by a proceeds claim. If that were not enough, sections 9–340 and 9–341 appear to give the bank's set-off rights priority over competing security interests even when the set-off is exercised after the perfection of the competing secured creditor. Note that sections 9–340 and 9–341 do not explicitly say there is priority, but that must be the meaning of the language stating that a competing security interest does not "affect the right of recoupment or set-off" and that the depositary bank's rights are not "terminated, suspended or modified" by another's perfected security interest in a deposit account.

Presumably most depositary banks will be able to claim the benefit of 9–327 (as one holding a security interest perfected by control) for control will come automatically by having the deposit and the attachment will come because the typical deposit account agreement of the future will have a clause that grants the bank a security interest in the deposit account when and if the depositor borrows money from the bank.

Problem 2–8

Your client, Buckeye Finance, has a security interest in the inventory of a regional department store. The department store runs tens of thousands of dollars through bank accounts at Bank One each week. Your client is fearful that Bank One might lend money to the store and then prime it under section 9–327 as to amounts in the deposit accounts or defeat its interest by set-off (under sections 9–340 and 9–341). You may assume that Buckeye has put all the normal provisions in its security agreement that prohibit its debtor from borrowing from Bank One or from any other bank where it deposits money, but it recognizes that a mere promise does not insure priority vis-à-vis a third party.

In view of sections 9–327, 9–340 and 9–341, how can you assure Buckeye of priority to its proceeds in the deposit account when bankruptcy or other trouble comes?

Problem 2–9

General Merchandise, a regional department store that does business in New England and is incorporated in Connecticut sells furniture, hardware and a variety of other home furnishings. It has granted a security interest in all of its inventory to Bank One. Bank's security agreement covers not only inventory but proceeds and after-acquired inventory. Its financing statement, filed in Hartford, identifies only inventory as collateral. Consider two alternatives:

1. Bank Two lends $2 million to General Merchandise and takes a security interest in and files a financing statement as to "accounts, chattel paper and other intangibles".

2. Alternatively, assume that Bank Two takes a purchase money security interest in a new line of inventory, i.e., Herman Miller furniture. Bank Two complies with the requirements of 9–324(b) and lends $2 million.

Problem 2–10

Upon the bankruptcy of General Merchandise, analyze the rights of Bank and Bank One and Bank Two in both of the above scenarios if each claims the $700,000 of retail installment sales contracts written for the purchase of individual pieces of furniture (a retail installment sales contract typically is a security agreement granted by the consumer purchaser to the seller, together with a promise to pay). Assume that $250,000 of these contracts came from the sale of Herman Miller furniture and another $450,000 came from the sale of other goods.

————

To understand how devilishly complex proceeds claims can be, consider the following problem. Do not overlook the special priority that is granted to security interests in deposit accounts.

Problem 2–11

Assume Bank One takes a security interest in Debtor's "inventory" and perfects its security interest by proper filing. Assume Bank Two does the same but files after Bank One, and that Finance Company takes and perfects a security interest by filing after both Bank One and Two have filed. Bank One, Bank Two and Finance Company each lend $10 million.

1.   On Debtor's failure, the inventory has a value of only $3 million but there is a $1 million bank account located at Bank Two. Who gets that account? (Assume the $1 million in the account is proceeds of the collateral subject to the security interest of Bank One, Bank Two and Finance Company and that the secured creditors have done everything a smart lawyer would advise.)

2.   If Debtor does not fail until it has used the $1 million from the bank account to purchase a large piece of equipment for use in its business, who gets that equipment?

§ 6.   CONSIGNMENT, AN ALTERNATIVE TO CONVENTIONAL INVENTORY SECURITY

Consignments as Security Interests

In a typical consignment an owner puts goods in the possession of a consignee with instructions to sell those goods to third parties. Normally, the consignor agrees to take the goods back if they are not sold. If the goods are sold, the consignee takes a percentage (say 20%) of the sales price and remits the proceeds. Consignments are common with respect to certain goods, such as diamonds and books. A typical consignment has some of the economic characteristics of a loan against inventory, for the consignor's capital enables the consignee to display inventory on its sales floor and to make sales the consignee could not otherwise make.

Prior to the 1999 revision, most of the Code law on the rights of consignees and their creditors was found in section 2–326 of Article 2. In general that section subordinated the consignor's interest to rights of the creditors of the consignee in any case in which the consignee did business under a different name than the consignor, unless the consignor could prove that the consignee was "generally known to be dealing in goods of another", or the consignor complied with a relevant sign law showing its interest or filed a financing statement under Article 9–

In addition, former Article 9 contemplated transactions where the parties used consignment language, but the deals were truly "secured transactions", not conventional consignments. If, for example, a debtor borrowed money from a creditor, granted a security interest in inventory and promised to repay the sum *whether or not the goods were sold*, that transaction would be treated in all respects like a secured transaction even if the parties labeled it a "consignment". The foregoing type of transaction differs from the usual consignment in which the consignee has no obligation to pay if it returns the goods. If a court concluded the transaction was in fact intended as security, then knowledge by the consignee's creditors would not save it from the claim of a trustee or a judicial lien creditor, for it would be treated in all respects like a security interest. This division left some "consignments" entirely within Article 9 but some only partly there, and left the courts in doubt about what parts of Article 9 applied to which transactions.

The 1999 amendments to Article 9 and conforming amendments of 2–326 are substantial improvements. First, section 9–102(a)(20) defines consignment as follows:

(a)(20) "Consignment" means a transaction, regardless of its form, in which a person delivers goods to a merchant for the purpose of sale and:

(A) the merchant:

(i) deals in goods of that kind under a name other than the name of the person making delivery;

(ii) is not an auctioneer; and

(iii) is not generally known by its creditors to be substantially engaged in selling the goods of others;

(B) with respect to each delivery, the aggregate value of the goods is $1,000 or more at the time of delivery;

(C) the goods are not consumer goods immediately before delivery; and

(D) the transaction does not create a security interest that secures an obligation.

The definition incorporates most of the conditions of former 2–326. In a second important definitional change, section 1–201(37) states that any consignment (as that term is defined in 9–102(a)), is a "security interest". This means all consignors who are not explicitly excluded by the definition in 9–102(a)(20) hold security interests that are subject to subordination by lien creditors and others under 9–317 if their interests are unperfected. To protect their interests, consignors will have to perfect them like any other security interest. The combination of 9–102(a)(20) and 1–201(37) has moved almost all commercial consignments into Article 9 at least for most purposes.

Certain transactions a layperson would describe as consignments are not consignments as that term is used by Article 9. Thus, a consignment of used clothing or used furniture to a consignment store is not a "consignment". So, there will still be a subset of transactions regarded as "consignments" to laypersons, but not consignments under 9–102(a)(20) (e.g., consignment of consumer goods).

What of the other cases excluded from 9–102(a)(20) by 9–102(a)(20)(D) not because they are not sufficiently secured transactions but because they secure "an obligation"? The drafters here have preserved a distinction between a conventional commercial consignment, defined in 9–102(a)(20), which in almost all cases, is a "security interest", and the unusual commercial consignment which creates a security interest "that secures an obligation". But if all consignments under 9–102(a)(20) must be perfected and enjoy more or less the same priority as any other security interest, who cares whether a transaction is merely a consignment subject to Article 9 or whether it is a security interest "that secures an obligation"? If it secures an obligation, Article 9 will apply anyway.

Part 6 of Article 9 on foreclosure treats these transactions differently. A consignor whose interest also "secures an obligation" under 9–102(a)(20)(D) must follow the restrictive rules on repossession, resale and the like. If, on the other hand, the transaction is a consignment that creates a security interest in the consignor but does not "secure an obligation" (i.e., if it is a mine run consignment of diamonds or books with a duty of sale or return but no duty to pay for unsold goods) then the consignor must protect its interest by filing a financing statement and is, for the purposes of perfection and priority, treated like a secured creditor but is not so treated for the purpose of foreclosure. The consignor may get its goods back by whatever method is permitted under the state law outside of Article 9. One way to think of the two transactions is to say that a classic consignment creates an interest that behaves like a security interest for the first five parts of Article 9 but not for the sixth, whereas a consignment "that secures an obligation" is a security interest for all parts of Article 9.

That leaves a third type of consignment. These transactions-consignments of consumer goods to a consignment store, consignments of items of less than $1,000, and consignments to a person generally known by its creditors to be substantially engaged in selling the goods or to a consignee who acts in the name of consignor—are not within Article 9. They are governed by Revised 2–326(1) which, in its amended form, reads as follows:

> (1) Unless otherwise agreed, if delivered goods may be returned by the buyer even though they conform to the contract, the transaction is:
>
> > (a) a "sale on approval" if the goods are delivered primarily for use, and
>
> > (b) a "sale or return" if the goods are delivered primarily for resale.

The most obvious way to read section 2–326 is to find that 2–326(2) subordinates the consignor's claims because of the last clause: "goods held on sale or return are subject to such claims while in the buyer's possession". So the poor starving artist puts paintings in the hands of fly-by-night consignees and loses them to fly-by-night creditors, true? That seems unfair; presumably the drafters cut the small time consignor out of the rules in Article 9 to protect him, not to injure him.

A way to avoid the conclusion suggested above is to find that the paintings were not delivered to a "buyer" under the terms of section 2–326(1) and therefore that section 2–326 does not govern this transaction at all. If, for example, the agreement between the consignor and the consignee was that the consignee was acting merely as the agent of the consignor, the consignee would never get title so the consignee would not be a "buyer", and the section would not apply. If that is so, one is out in the common law; presumably the common law will protect the right of the starving artist, consignor, or bailor. This argument hardly stands on firm ground, for "consignment" as defined in 9–102(20) includes cases where title might pass through the consignee's hands at the time of the transfer to a third person as well as cases in which the consignee is merely a distributor acting as the consignor's agent.

To summarize the post–1999 law, if goods are consigned to a merchant in a conventional commercial transaction (where the merchant operates in its own name and not that of the consignor, is not an auctioneer, and is not "generally known by such creditors to be substantially engaged in the selling the goods of others"), the transaction is a consignment and the consignor's interest is a security interest. The consignor must perfect a security interest under Article 9 to protect itself from the consignee's trustee in bankruptcy and from other and later perfected secured creditors. If the transaction falls out of the definition in 9–102(a)(20) because the transaction creates a security interest "that secures an obligation", the rules are practically the same. The consignor is still the holder of a security interest who must perfect it under Article 9. The only difference, and probably an insignificant one, is that on default this latter consignor must comply with Part 6 of Article 9. We suspect there will be little need under the new law to distinguish between garden variety commercial consignments under Article 9 and those which are in every respect security agreements because they secure "an obligation". The law is at least as complicated as before but, at least for the diligent, more certain.

Problem 2–12

General Motors is having a problem with one of its suppliers. It purchased a large quantity of copper to assist a struggling supplier. The supplier took that copper and put it on its manufacturing floor, commingling it with its own copper. It then manufactured radiator cores out of its copper and General Motors' copper and sold the completed radiators back to General Motors (less a credit for the supplied copper). During manufacturing, it was impossible to tell which copper belonged to the supplier and which to General Motors.

General Motors never filed a financing statement and the supplier has now gone bankrupt. The supplier's trustee in bankruptcy claims that General Motors' rights to the $1.5 million worth of copper were lost by its failure to file a financing statement. According to the trustee, General Motors has an unsecured claim for $1.5 million against the bankrupt estate. Is there any way out for General Motors?

§ 7. BUYERS OF GOODS

In one way or another, many sections of the Code pose the question whether a buyer takes free of a prior security interest. Many buyers will take free of a security interest because the secured party has "authorized the disposition free of the security interest", see 9–315(a)(1). Thus the starting point for any analysis about the rights of a buyer vis-à-vis a prior secured creditor is the security agreement itself. The general statutory rule stated in section 9–201 is that the security agreement "is effective * * * against purchasers of the collateral". The rule of that section is confirmed by 9–315(a)(1) which states that the security interest "continues in collateral notwithstanding sale * * * or other disposition". There are also major exceptions to the general rule. Thus, subsection 9–317(b) states that a buyer who gives value and receives delivery of collateral without knowledge of a prior security interest and "before it is perfected" takes free of the security interest. Section 9–320 goes even further-it allows certain buyers to take free even of certain perfected security interests.

CHRYSLER v. ADAMATIC, INC.

Supreme Court of Wisconsin, 1973.
59 Wis.2d 219, 208 N.W.2d 97.

This action was commenced on October 21, 1970, by Appellant Chrysler Corporation, seeking to replevin certain goods which it had contracted to purchase from Defendant Adamatic, Inc. Respondent Lakeshore Commercial Finance Corporation was subsequently permitted to intervene on the basis that it claimed a perfected security interest in the goods in question. During the pendency of this action, Adamatic went into receivership and, consequently, Adamatic's receiver, Russell A. Eisenberg, was also permitted to intervene. On February 9, 1972, judgment was entered giving Chrysler possession of the goods but requiring it to pay certain sums to Lakeshore. Chrysler, Lakeshore, and the receiver have all appealed.

The facts of this lawsuit are largely undisputed.

Chrysler owns and operates a plant in Indianapolis, Indiana, where it manufactures alternators and other electrical components for the motor vehicles it assembles elsewhere. Construction of the alternators requires a "stator winder," a highly specialized machine which can wind copper wire around a component part known as the "stator." For several years Chrysler had been purchasing this equipment from an Ohio manufacturer but had been seeking to find a more efficient winding machine. Chrysler engineers discovered that Adamatic was producing an advanced machine at its Milwaukee plant which, while designed for a different purpose, potentially could be converted for use as a stator winder in the Chrysler plant. Chrysler's interest in utilizing the Adamatic machine led to the transactions forming the basis of this lawsuit.

In 1967, Adamatic had entered into various security agreements with Lakeshore, whereby the latter agreed to finance Adamatic's operations and in return took a security interest in Adamatic's inventory and various other assets. The security agreements were duly filed, and it is undisputed that Lakeshore had a valid security interest in Adamatic's inventory at all relevant times.

Chrysler's first transaction with Adamatic, in March 1969, involved a contract calling for Adamatic to produce a prototype six-coil stator winder. Although the proposed machine was based on designs already formulated by Adamatic, it was to be custom built to Chrysler's specifications. The contract also required Adamatic to manufacture a "cell inserter," a separate machine, which was to be used in conjunction with the winder. The original purchase order quoted a price of $77,150 for the two units, but the price was later increased by $4,000 to cover an additional accessory for the cell inserter.

The agreement required Chrysler to make progress payments as the work neared completion. By the time the machines had been completed for shipment, Chrysler had paid 90 percent of the original purchase price. The remaining 10 percent was to be withheld until the goods were delivered and made to perform satisfactorily. Adamatic has never requested payment of this retainage, and it has not been paid.

On February 9, 1970, the completed winder and cell inserter were delivered to the Chrysler plant in Indianapolis. Although the cell inserter evidently performed to contract specifications, the six-coil winder failed to function well enough for production-line use. Over the next few months, Adamatic employees were in almost constant attendance at Chrysler's plant assisting Chrysler engineers in trying to get the winder working. Their attempts were unsuccessful, and on June 9, 1970, Chrysler sent a telegram to Adamatic threatening to cancel the second contract, executed in April 1970, between the parties if the winder could not be made to perform.

Finally, upon Adamatic's suggestion, it was decided to ship the units back to Milwaukee for additional work by Adamatic. By this time, Chrysler had decided that the six-coil winder should be converted for twelve-coil operation. On August 12, 1970, the cell inserter and six-coil winder were shipped back to Adamatic under a non-negotiable bill of lading. On August 20, 1970, Adamatic sent a quotation giving an additional price of $22,410 for the conversion. The quotation was accepted by Chrysler on a change order dated September 11, 1970. Subsequently, the parties executed a "Consigned Material Receipt Agreement," drafted by Chrysler, in which Chrysler purported to retain title to the goods.

Previously, in February, Chrysler had decided to enter into a second transaction with Adamatic involving additional machines of the same type. During that month, personnel from Lakeshore and Adamatic met with Chrysler in Detroit to discuss the financing of the second transaction. At that time, Chrysler was informed of Adamatic's shaky financial condition and the fact that Lakeshore held a security interest in Adamatic's inventory. Lakeshore told Chrysler that it was prepared to lend up to $300,000 to Adamatic if Chrysler would make progress payments on the proposed, second contract.

Chrysler's second contract with Adamatic was entered into in April 1970. A Chrysler purchase order requested Adamatic to produce three twelve-coil stator winders at a price of $83,646.43 per unit. The order, which was accepted by Adamatic, specified that the first machine was to be delivered on September 7, 1970, with the second and third twelve-coil winders to follow at thirty-day intervals. Chrysler agreed to make progress payments after the work was 25 percent complete, in an amount up to 80 percent of the value of the labor and materials put into the machines at that time.

In August 1970, Adamatic requested the first progress payment on the second contract. Chrysler sent an engineer to Milwaukee, who checked the work done and approved a progress payment of $105,761.55, representing 80 percent of the value which had been put into the machines. A payment in that amount was subsequently given to Adamatic, which immediately turned the money over to Lakeshore.

The six-coil winder had been returned in August, and by mid-September, 1970, the three twelve-coil winders were in various stages of construction. Adamatic's financial condition had long been shaky; by September, it had reached a perilous point. Its current balance sheet indicated a net deficit of $135,624.95. In addition, Adamatic had been delinquent for several months in making federal withholding tax payments to the Internal Revenue Service, and the I.R.S. was threatening Adamatic with a tax lien. Moreover, Adamatic was no longer able to pay its suppliers for parts going into the Chrysler machines, and construction was being slowed by suppliers who were withholding delivery. It appears that Adamatic was still operating only because Lakeshore was continuing to make cash advances sufficient to meet Adamatic's payroll.

On September 15, 1970, Lakeshore and Adamatic personnel met to discuss Adamatic's progress on the Chrysler contracts and the company's general financial prospects. At this time, Lakeshore advised Adamatic that it was in default and that unless it found some other source of financing, Lakeshore would be forced to liquidate its loan. Nevertheless, Lakeshore advanced an additional $30,000 to $50,000 to Adamatic, and by October 15, 1970, the loan balance was approximately $340,000. By the time of trial, however, Lakeshore had foreclosed on other secured assets still in Adamatic's possession, and Adamatic presently owes Lakeshore more than $200,000. It was stipulated that Adamatic was in default under its security agreements when this action commenced.

On October 12, 1970, Chrysler sent one of its engineers to Milwaukee in an attempt to expedite delivery of the twelve-coil winders, since the delivery dates for the first two machines had passed. He was told to return at the end of the week, when he could expect to receive the first machine. He returned on Friday, October 16th, and the following day the first twelve-coil winder was given a test run at the Adamatic plant. The machine was intended to handle two stators at once, but the tooling for one phase of the operation did not function. Moreover, the machine lacked a paint job and safety guards. Nevertheless, the engineer indicated that he would accept delivery and directed Adamatic to prepare the machine for shipment. Chrysler had arranged for a common carrier truck to be present that day, and the cell inserter was loaded on. Adamatic employees continued to work on the first twelve-coil winder during Saturday, October 17th, and on Sunday, the 18th, it operated properly. On Monday, October 19th, the truck returned, and the winder was skidded to the Adamatic dock for loading.

At this point, Lakeshore learned that Chrysler was trying to take delivery of the first twelve-coil winder. By telephone, Lakeshore's president directed Adamatic not to ship the machines. Accordingly, Adamatic personnel removed the cell inserter from the truck and moved the winder back into the plant.

Chrysler sought legal advice, and a meeting was held between the attorneys and representatives of Lakeshore and Chrysler on October 20, 1970. The participants in this meeting differ as to what transpired. According to Chrysler's witnesses, Lakeshore demanded that Chrysler renegotiate the price if it wanted delivery of the machines. Lakeshore's president testified, however, that he told Chrysler that Lakeshore had a perfected, security interest in the machines and was asserting its rights to possession.

Chrysler then commenced this replevin action to obtain possession of the machines. On October 21st, the sheriff seized the three twelve-coil winders and the cell inserter. At the time of the seizure, the first of the twelve-coil winders was substantially completed. The second was only about half finished, and the third was little more than a naked frame. The sheriff also seized the original six-coil winder, which had been completely stripped of usable parts after its return to Adamatic. In its original complaint, Chrysler declared the value of the goods to be $190,000 and put up a surety bond in twice that amount. Lakeshore immediately sought, and was granted, leave to intervene. Nevertheless, Lakeshore failed to file a sufficient redelivery bond, and the goods were turned over to Chrysler and removed to Indianapolis on or about October 27, 1950.

Adamatic, which had been insolvent for some time before the replevin, shortly thereafter went into receivership.

The trial of this action was held before a jury from November 16 to 23, 1971, and questions were submitted on a special verdict. The jury found that, as to the second contract for the twelve-coil winders, Chrysler had been a buyer in ordinary course of business. The jury further found that Lakeshore wrongfully caused Adamatic to detain the property involved in both transactions and that Chrysler's damages as a result of the detention were $40,000. It also found that Adamatic had been insolvent on the date this action commenced. The parties stipulated that issues regarding the first transaction (six-coil winder and cell inserter) were to be decided by trial judge, who determined that Chrysler had the right to possession of these machines.

The jury further found that the total value of the three twelve-coil winders was $220,000. It valued the cell inserter at $20,350, and the six-coil winder at $27,900. The trial judge changed the jury's answer with respect to the six-coil winder to $8,300 and reduced the finding of damages to Chrysler from $40,000 to $4,800.

Judgment was entered accordingly. The judgment essentially provided that Chrysler is entitled to all the goods involved in the action but denied Chrysler damages for the retention. For reasons not readily apparent, however, the trial judge ordered that Chrysler pay to Lakeshore (by way of the receiver) the value of the machines less the amounts which Chrysler had already paid Adamatic. In effect, he found that Chrysler held the goods subject to Lakeshore's security interest, despite the fact that he found Chrysler to be a buyer in ordinary course of business.

* * *

HEFFERNAN, JUSTICE:

It should be emphasized that the cause of action is for replevin. The action was brought by Chrysler to gain possession of the machines and for damages against Lakeshore for their wrongful detention. Although there is evidence in the record indicating a breach of contract by the manufacturer, Adamatic, no relief is sought for that. Lakeshore, on the other hand, asserts ownership of the machines because of its prior perfected security agreement with Adamatic. The receiver, representing the general creditors, bases its claim upon Lakeshore's rights as a secured creditor, but in addition asks for an accounting by Lakeshore for any excess which Lakeshore may receive from Chrysler. As an alternative only, the receiver argues that Chrysler's taking of the goods was an avoidable preference as against the unsecured creditors. No claim is asserted by either creditor against Chrysler for amounts unpaid on the contract price.

The legal issues fall into the natural division between the first contract involving the six-coil winder and the subsequent contract concerned with the three machines that are designated as twelve-coil winders.

The First Contract—Six–Coil Winder

As recited in the statement of facts, the six-coil winder and the cell inserter were returned to Adamatic for alterations on August 12, 1970. Chrysler asserts, in respect to the six-coil winder, that it had title and possessory rights to the machine from the time it was first delivered to the Chrysler plant in February 1970. It asserts that the machine was returned to Adamatic on a bailment, by which Adamatic was to hold the winder for repair and alteration. Both creditors, Lakeshore and the receiver, assert that the return of the machine revested the title in Adamatic and made it subject to their claims.

Under sec. 402.401(1), Stats., subject to the provisions of ch. 409 and other limitations not applicable here, "title to goods passes from the seller to the buyer in any manner and on any conditions explicitly agreed on by the parties." The contract between Chrysler and Adamatic explicitly agreed that title to the six-coil winder and the cell inserter would vest in Chrysler upon the completion of manufacture and shipment to the Chrysler plant. Chrysler, therefore, obtained title to this machine when it was shipped from the Adamatic plant in early February 1970. At that time, under the terms of sec. 402.106(1), Stats., there was a completed sale. It is undisputed that this sale was in good faith and in the ordinary course of business. There is no claim that the original sale was in violation of Lakeshore's security interest or constituted a preference against the unsecured creditors.

In accordance with the provisions of sec. 409–307(1), Stats., Chrysler took the machines free of Lakeshore's security interest. The creditors, however, assert that Chrysler never "accepted" the goods or, if there were an initial acceptance, such acceptance was subsequently revoked. They rely upon sec. 402.401(4) for the proposition:

> "A rejection or other refusal by the buyer to receive or retain the goods, whether or not justified, or a justified revocation of acceptance revests title to the goods in the seller. Such revesting occurs by operation of law and is not a 'sale.'"

This question was fully litigated, and the trial judge made the finding that Chrysler had title to the six-coil winder and the cell inserter at all times after their initial delivery to Chrysler. A review of the record reveals that this finding is fully supported by the applicable law and the evidence adduced at trial.

The fact that title passed when the goods were first delivered, however, does not ipso facto evince Chrysler's acceptance of them. A sale of goods does not necessarily imply the buyer's acceptance. White & Summers, Uniform Commercial Code, p. 249, sec. 8–2. While the delivery of the goods completed the sale, whether Chrysler accepted the machine depends on Chrysler's conduct after the delivery. Sec. 402.606, Stats., delineates conduct that constitutes the acceptance of goods. A buyer accepts goods if he notifies the seller that he accepts them, if he fails to make an effective rejection, or does an act inconsistent with the seller's ownership. There is no evidence that Chrysler expressly notified Adamatic that it was accepting the goods. On the other hand, Chrysler retained the six-coil winder for over six months without rejecting it. Under sec. 402.602, the rejection of goods must be made within a reasonable time after delivery and rejection will be ineffective unless the buyer seasonably notifies the seller.

No notification was ever given of the rejection of the six-coil winder. While there was evidence that Chrysler was displeased with the performance of the initial winder, there was no intimation that the winder was being rejected, although a letter from Chrysler to Adamatic carried the suggestion that, if the six-coil winder did not operate satisfactorily, the second contract-the contract for the three twelve-coil winders-would be cancelled. Chrysler in fact retained the six-coil winder for at least two months following the threat to cancel the other contract.

There was also evidence that Chrysler, during the period of possession, treated the six-coil winder as its own. It tagged the machine with a brass plate, giving it a Chrysler inventory serial number. Such conduct alone has been found to be evidence of acceptance. Julian C. Cohen Salvage Corp. v. Eastern Electric Sales Co. (1965), 205 Pa.Super. 26, 206 Atl.2d 331, 2 UCC 432. The cell inserter was completely acceptable to Chrysler, but it, too, was returned to Adamatic. There is no contention that the mere return of the cell inserter constituted a rejection; rather, it was needed by Adamatic to run tests on other winders that were being manufactured. The documents that passed between Chrysler and Adamatic at about the time of the return of the six-coil winder and cell inserter show that Chrysler wished to retain title and possession of the machine and was returning it merely for adjustment and modification.

The questions of acceptance or rejection of goods are questions to be resolved by the finder of fact and depend upon the ascertainment of the intent of the parties. * * *

There is sufficient evidence to show that Chrysler acquired full title in the six-coil winder and cell inserter at the time of their initial delivery, and that Lakeshore's security interest could not re-attach to the goods in absence of a rejection by Chrysler. The rights acquired by Adamatic were those of a bailee, who had possessory interest for a limited purpose, but did not amount to "rights in the collateral." Sec. 409–204(1), Stats.; Cain v. Country Club Delicatessen of Saybrook, Inc. (1964), 25 Conn.Sup. 327, 203 Atl.2d 441, 2 UCC 247. See, also, 1 Gilmore, Security Interests in Personal Property (1965), p. 353, sec. 11–5; 4 Anderson, Uniform Commercial Code (2d ed.), p. 179, sec. 9–204:7.

* * *

We hold that Chrysler, under the applicable law, was entitled to replevin of the six-coil winder and cell inserter. * * *

The Second Contract—Twelve–Coil Winders

The situation in respect to the three twelve-coil winders is markedly different from that of the six-coil winder and the cell inserter. In respect to the twelve-coil winders, although there had been a contract entered into at an earlier time, the delivery of the goods was occasioned only by the replevin seizure itself. In the absence of Chrysler's claim, Lakeshore's right to the possession of the twelve-coil winders would be unquestioned.

It was conceded that Lakeshore had loaned substantial sums to Adamatic and, under ch. 409, Stats., had perfected a valid security interest in Adamatic's inventory. It was stipulated by the parties that, prior to the replevin, the twelve-coil winders were a part of that inventory. Had Chrysler not seized the machines under its claim of right, upon Adamatic's default Lakeshore could have taken possession of the machines under sec. 409–503 and sold them under the provisions of sec. 409–504 to satisfy, in part at least, Adamatic's obligations.

The mere physical transfer of the machines from Adamatic to Chrysler does not defeat Lakeshore's right to foreclose on the collateral. A perfected security interest gives the secured creditor rights in the goods themselves, and under the rule of sec. 409–201, Stats., those rights follow the collateral into the hands of subsequent owners.

Applying the principles of the Uniform Commercial Code, it is apparent that Chrysler took physical possession of the machines at a time when Lakeshore would ordinarily be entitled to their possession. Chrysler's possession of the goods is, therefore, subject to Lakeshore's security interest unless some other provision of the Code is sufficient to supersede the rights of Lakeshore.

Chrysler relies upon sec. 409–307(1), Stats., as an exception to the general rule that a purchaser is subject to an outstanding security interest. * * *

Chrysler claims to be "a buyer in ordinary course of business." That term is defined by sec. 401.201(9), Stats. * * *

Chrysler claims that it became a buyer in ordinary course of business at the time it originally contracted to purchase the twelve-coil winders. It further argues that Lakeshore's security interest was cut off at the time of entering into the contract and, at the time it took possession of the machines by replevin, its possession was free and clear of any claims of the secured creditor. Lakeshore and the receiver for the general creditors are united in disputing this claim. They argue that nothing less than a bona fide transfer of the goods could cut off the security interest, and that a replevin cannot constitute a transaction in ordinary course.

The initial question posed is whether one can become a buyer in ordinary course before a sale has occurred. While it is apparent that the contract was a contract to sell, only the position of the creditors can be reconciled with the language of the Uniform Commercial Code.

Under sec. 401.201(9), Stats., "buying" includes receiving goods under a pre-existing contract for sale. The statute is silent on the question of whether "buying" encompasses a situation where there has been a nonreceipt of the goods; but the enumeration in the statute, when reasonably construed, limits buying in ordinary course of business to those situations where a "sale," defined by sec. 402.106(1) as "the passing of title from the seller to the buyer for a price," has occurred. There is no contention that title passed to Chrysler prior to the physical transfer occasioned by the replevin, but, under sec. 401.201(9), the buyer in ordinary course must buy without knowledge that the sale is in violation of the rights of a third party. In the instant case Chrysler, at the time of the replevin, had full knowledge of the perfected security interest of Lakeshore.

The commentators who have written on sec. 401.201(9), Stats., shed but confused elucidation on whether one can become a buyer in ordinary course merely by entering into a contract to buy. Professor Gilmore notes that the Uniform Commercial Code, unlike prior uniform acts, does not require that a buyer actually take delivery to attain the status of buyer in ordinary course of business. 2 Gilmore, Security Interests in Personal Property, p. 696, sec. 26.6. * * *

It seems clear that, if there is a sale and the buyer has obtained title to the goods, his status as a buyer in ordinary course will not be defeated merely because he has not taken possession. Such is not our situation here, where Chrysler buttresses its claim as a buyer in ordinary course by asserting the replevin action was a part of the process by which title passed. Moreover, in the contract between the parties, delivery was envisaged as an integral part of the title-passing process.

Although both parties have treated all three twelve-coil winders as being "identified to the contract," the state of the record reveals grave doubt that this is really the fact. Only one machine was in a deliverable state. The other two, at the most, were but incompletely assembled component parts. While the Commercial Code, as pointed out above, does not require that in all cases the buyer actually take delivery in order to have a buyer in ordinary course of business status, sound policy considerations in the instant situation would seem to dictate that the rights of a secured creditor ought not be impaired in the absence of a physical transfer or assignment of the goods. We agree generally with the position submitted by the National Commercial Finance Conference as amicus curiae. It points out that the Code generally gives preference to property interests which are evidenced either by recording or possession and that, to adopt the view of Chrysler, the financier of an inventory would no longer be able to rely on recorded interests and the status of his debtor's inventory. We recognize that this policy argument has been criticized by writers who contend that the commercial reality is that lenders rely not upon inventories or recorded instruments but rather upon the credit ratings of prospective debtors. * * *

This court, in Columbia International Corp. v. Kempler, *supra*, p. 559 of 46 Wis.2d, p. 469 of 175 N.W.2d, took a different position, stressing the policy of this jurisdiction—to place major reliance upon "apparent or ostensible ownership: People should be able to deal with a debtor upon the assumption that all property in his possession is unencumbered, unless the contrary is indicated by their own knowledge or by public records."

Thus, if Chrysler is to be afforded a status as a buyer in ordinary course of business, we conclude that such status must be determined as of the time he actually took possession of the goods.

The remedy of replevin is an unusual and drastic mode of recourse to secure the rights of a purchaser; and, from the viewpoint of common knowledge, it is almost absurd to argue that the acquisition of possession by replevin is in the ordinary course of business. It is certainly so in the instant case when we consider sec. 402.402, Stats. (the buyer's right of replevin) and sec. 402.716. Sec. 402.402(3)(a) provides:

"Nothing in this chapter shall be deemed to impair the rights of creditors of the seller:

"(a) Under the provisions of ch. 409 * * *."

The Commercial Code itself specifically negates Chrysler's contention that the replevin alone can in any way affect the rights of a prior secured creditor. Even if it is argued that these three machines were identified to the contract, sec. 401.201(37), Stats., states:

" * * * the special property interest of a buyer of goods on identification of such goods to a contract for sale under sec. 402.401 is not a 'security interest' * * *."

Chrysler thus makes the anomalous and unacceptable claim that its buyer's interest gives it a right superior to the holder of an antecedent perfected security interest.

Chrysler is not a buyer in ordinary course of business and holds the machines subject to the security interest of Lakeshore. From the viewpoint of equity, this is an unsatisfactory result, for the record shows that, prior to the replevin, Chrysler had substantially paid the contract price for all the goods involved. Our conclusion, however, is supported by the writings of distinguished commentators, who have pointed out that the Code itself affords but little protection for the prepaying buyer. The Code, however, gives broad latitude whereby a prepaying buyer, acting timely, can enter into suitable arrangements for his own protection.

In the instant case Chrysler was fully aware of the fact that it was not only a buyer but was financing the manufacturing process. It was for that reason it made progress payments on the basis of the work and materials as the manufacturing progressed. By proper negotiations with the other creditors, it might well have protected itself by obtaining a security interest in the goods it had contracted to buy. Lakeshore as a substantial creditor interested in the well being of Adamatic, might well have been amenable to a Chrysler proposal that Lakeshore in part subordinate its security interest. In view of the size of this contract in proportion to the limited assets of the manufacturer, it was almost foolhardy for Chrysler to proceed in the face of the perfected security interest of Lakeshore.

Numerous law review articles discuss the problems posed for the prepaying buyer by the Code and various methods that may be used to obviate the very situation which resulted here. * * * The taking of the machines by Chrysler under the circumstances was unlawful. Lakeshore, not Chrysler, was entitled to possession of the twelve-coil winders.

Note

The main issue in *Adamatic* can be summarized by the question: when does one become a "buyer?" Only a buyer can be a buyer in the ordinary course and only a buyer in the ordinary course takes free of prior perfected security interests under section 9–320. In *Adamatic* the court concluded that one was not a buyer "in the absence of a physical transfer or assignment of the goods". Accordingly it decided that Chrysler, who had paid for but never received possession of the twelve-coil winders, was not a buyer and thus not a buyer in the ordinary course of those machines. On the other hand it concluded that Chrysler was a buyer and a buyer in the ordinary course of the six-coil winder and cell inserter that had made the roundtrip from Wisconsin to Indiana and there rested in Chrysler's possession.

In a later case, Daniel v. Bank of Hayward, 144 Wis.2d 931, 425 N.W.2d 416 (1988), the Wisconsin Supreme Court could not stomach its *Adamatic* rule as applied to a consumer non-possessor. In *Bank of Hayward*, the Bank had a security interest in the automobile inventory of a car dealer. The Daniels prepaid $8675.55 for a van that was delivered to the car dealership shortly before the Bank repossessed all of the dealer's inventory including the van. Under the ruling of *Adamatic*, the dealer's secured creditor, Bank of Hayward, claimed priority over the Daniels. Since the Daniels never had possession of the van, they were not a buyer and thus not a buyer in the ordinary course entitled to take free of Bank of Hayward's perfected security interest. The court reversed *Adamatic* and gave the Daniels' their van.

The two Wisconsin cases lay bare both the difficulties of defining "buyer" and the policies (or sympathies) that might be invoked in particular cases.

Before asking how 1999 Article 9 might apply in these cases, consider the more general question about when one might become a buyer. A typical sales transaction proceeds in an irregular movement from the making of a sales contract through payment of a portion of the price through possession or disposition by the buyer. Almost always the contract comes first but possession might come before or after payment and payment might be in installments. The court must determine, as it did in *Bank of Hayward* and *Adamatic*, how far one must proceed down this spectrum before the potential buyer becomes truly a buyer as that term is used in the Code. One analogy, that of a holder in due course, might say one does not get these super priority rights that attach to a buyer in the ordinary course or to the holder in due course status until one has not only given value but also taken possession. On the other hand there are buyers, even more sympathetic than the Daniels, who never expect to take possession and where it would be inappropriate to make that a condition of the status. Assume for example that the goods to be sold are bulk oil or gravel that are expensive to move and that might be resold by the buyer in place without their ever being moved. In those circumstances it is inappropriate to say that the prospective buyer himself must take possession in order to become a "buyer" under the UCC.

Apparently aware of the conflict between cases like *Bank of Hayward* and *Adamatic*, the drafters of 1999 Article 9 added a sentence to 1–201(9) that reads in full as follows: "Only a buyer that takes possession of the goods or has a right to recover the goods from the seller under Article 2 may be a buyer in the ordinary course of business". The significant language in that sentence identifies the person who "has a right to recover the goods from the seller under Article 2". To see who might have a "right to recover" from a seller, see 2–502(1). Section 2–716(3) might also have something to say about these cases.

Problem 2–13

How do *Adamatic* and *Bank of Hayward* come out under 1999 Article 9? Consider not only 9–320, but also 2–502, 2–716, and the new language in 1–201(9).

Problem 2–14

Daisy Bank and Trust has a security interest in refrigerators, stoves, appliances and all other hard goods of Marie Louise, Inc., a department store. Assume that the security agreement purports to continue the security interest in the goods even after they have been sold. Now consider the following transactions in goods covered by the perfected security interest.

1. Wilbur buys a washing machine for cash. Wilbur takes free of Daisy's security interest. True or false?

2. Wilbur buys a washing machine on credit and signs a security agreement giving Marie Louise a security interest in the machine. Wilbur takes free of Daisy's security interest, true or false?

3. Wilbur buys a refrigerator on credit from Marie Louise and signs a security agreement. A month later Wilbur sells the refrigerator to his next-door neighbor, Charlotte. Identify the correct statement or statements:

    a. Charlotte takes free of the security interests of both Daisy and Marie Louise;

    b. Charlotte takes free of Daisy's security interest because she qualifies under subsection 9–320(a);

    c. Charlotte takes free of Marie Louise's security interest because she qualifies under 9–320(a);

    d. Charlotte does not qualify for the protection of 9–320(a), nevertheless she takes free of both security interests.

Note: Federal Limitation on the Farmer Exception to UCC 9–320

By 1985 legislation, Congress has provided a mechanism which can override the "farm products" exception of former 9–307(1). Enacted within the Food Security Act of 1985, 7 U.S.C. 1631 (Supp.1985), the statute grants federal protection to purchasers of farm products. In relevant part the statute provides:

> (d) Except as provided in subsection (e) and notwithstanding any other provision of Federal, State, or local law, a buyer who in the ordinary course of business buys a farm product from a seller engaged in farming operations shall take free of a security interest created by the seller, even though the security interest is perfected; and the buyer knows of the existence of such interest.

This general prohibition against lien enforcement is relatively straightforward. However, lengthy and complex exceptions may swallow the rule. The most important exceptions to the protection of purchasers of farm products are found in section 1631(e).

The first exception concerns buyers in the ordinary course with "actual knowledge" of the security interest. The general rule protects buyers with mere knowledge of the existence of a prior security interest. On the other hand, 1631(e)(1) provides that a buyer will take the purchased farm products subject to the existing security interest if the buyer receives written notice from the seller or secured party of the security interest within one year of sale and the buyer defaults on his obligation to pay for his purchase. At first blush the traditional notice system seems to have been turned on its head. No longer can a secured party depend on a centralized filing system for protection; if the secured party desires priority, he must send notice of his security interest to all potential purchasers of farm products from his debtor.

Of greater interest are the provisions creating a *second* filing system which permits the secured party to gain priority over purchasers of farm products. The second and third exceptions to 1631(d) concern the operations of a new creature called a "central filing system." Defined in 1631(c)(2), a central filing system is a centralized information system which registers secured creditors, debtors and purchasers of farm products. The central filing system is to be administered by the Secretary of State of each state, and each system is to be certified by the United States Department of Agriculture. Under the central filing system the Secretary of State periodically distributes all registered financing information to all registered buyers. If a state adopts a central filing system into its zoo of regulatory animals, an ordinary course purchaser of farm products will lose the general protections of 1631(d) if he is either not registered in the system or if he has received notice of a prior security interest from the Secretary of State. Thus, a state's enactment of a central filing system can return to the farm products exception contained in section 9–320(a).

Finally, a secured party in a non-central filing system jurisdiction may reduce the number of potential purchasers which he must notify if he requires his debtor to identify specifically all potential purchasers of the debtor's farm products. See 7 U.S.C. § 1631(h) (Supp.1985). If the debtor sells to a party not listed on the "accredited" purchaser list and neither gives prior notice to the secured creditor of the potential sale nor forwards the proceeds of the sale to the secured party, section 1631(b)(3) subjects the debtor to a fine of the greater of $5,000 or 15% of the proceeds of the sale. Note, however, that the *purchaser* will still receive the protection of 1631(d).

The basic effect of section 1631 is to shift the burden of informing. The purchaser's burden to seek out information regarding prior security interests is shifted either to the secured party (to notify all potential purchasers in non-central filing system states) or to the Secretary of State (to notify all registered purchasers in central filing system states).

§ 8. BUYERS OF CHATTEL PAPER AND THE LIKE

Section 9–330 governs the rights of most buyers. The classic case involves a secured creditor with a floating lien on inventory with a proceeds claim in chattel paper. That interest conflicts with that of a "purchaser" of this very chattel paper. In some cases the inventory lender may have expected the debtor to sell the chattel paper and to remit the proceeds as payment on its secured debt. When the debtor sells the chattel paper but fails to use the proceeds to reduce the inventory loan, the inventory lender and the purchaser of the chattel paper may assert conflicting claims to that paper. In other cases, the original secured creditor may have lent money against specific items of chattel paper and may therefore assert an even more credible claim against that paper in competition with the purchaser of the paper.

Section 9–330 states rules that allow a buyer of chattel paper to take free of such an earlier claim if the buyer meets a certain set of conditions.

(a) [Purchaser's priority: security interest claimed merely as proceeds.] A purchaser of chattel paper has priority over a security interest in the chattel paper which is claimed merely as proceeds of inventory subject to a security interest if:

(1) in good faith and in the ordinary course of the purchaser's business, the purchaser gives new value and takes possession of the chattel paper or obtains control of the chattel paper under section 9–105; and

(2) the chattel paper does not indicate that it has been assigned to an identified assignee other than the purchaser.

(b) [Purchaser's priority: other security interests.] A purchaser of chattel paper has priority over a security interest in the chattel paper which is claimed other than merely as proceeds of inventory subject to a security interest if the purchaser gives new value and takes possession of the chattel paper or obtains control of the chattel paper under Section 9–105 in good faith, in the ordinary course of the purchaser's business, and without knowledge that the purchase violates the rights of the secured party.

Subsection (a) deals with the case where the original secured creditor claims chattel paper "merely as proceeds"; subsection (b) covers the case where the original secured creditor claims something more than "proceeds". In the latter case, the original secured creditor has loaned money to the debtor somehow in reliance upon the chattel paper. The 1999 revision does not elaborate on "merely as proceeds", rather it directs one to PEB Commentary No. 8:

A lender who agrees to lend up to a specified percentage of the cost of inventory and receivables, has more than a mere proceeds interest in the chattel paper which is a part of the receivables covered by the security agreement.

In other words, if the value of the chattel paper was included in the formula to determine the amount of the loan, the Commentary suggests that a person making the loan is asserting a claim greater than a "proceeds" claim in the chattel paper and, therefore, is entitled to the greater protection of subsection (b).

Assume an original secured creditor lent principally against inventory. That is, assume its claim to the chattel paper was *merely* a proceeds claim. Under former section 9–308, a buyer took free of the original secured creditor's interest if it gave new value and took possession in the ordinary course of business and even if the buyer knew "the specific paper" was "subject to a security interest". If, on the other hand, the claim of the original secured creditor was considered to be something *more than a mere* proceeds claim, the buyer had to act "without knowledge that the specific paper" was "subject to a security interest".

The rules in section 9–330 are similar but different. Under 9–330(a) the secured creditor beats the buyer of chattel paper if the chattel paper itself "indicates that it has been assigned". Thus a stamp on chattel paper showing ownership in an assignee-secured creditor will protect a secured creditor even though that creditor has only a proceeds claim. Unlike former 9–308, new subsection (a) makes no mention of the knowledge of the buyer. Thus, by subordinating the buyer where there is a legend on the face of the paper, the new law cuts back on the buyer's rights. On the other hand, it expands the buyers rights by allowing the buyer to take free even if the buyer knows that its purchase may violate the rights of the prior secured creditor. (The only restriction on buyer's knowledge is the requirement that it act in good faith.)

Subsection 9–330(b) allows a buyer of chattel paper to take free of a prior perfected security interest claimed "other than merely as proceeds" if that buyer meets the usual conditions (new value, possession, ordinary course) and is "without knowledge that the purchase violates the rights of the secured party". The change from the former law (which subordinated the buyer when the buyer had "knowledge that the *specific paper*" was "subject to a security interest") is to conform to what the drafters believe to be the current practice. In Comment 6 the drafters note that it is insufficient to subordinate a purchaser of chattel paper simply because that purchaser has "seen a financing statement covering the chattel paper" (and so knows it is probably subject to a security interest). The Comment goes on to state that a purchaser who has seen a statement in a financing statement with an indication that a purchase "would violate the rights of the filed party" has the kind of knowledge that would and should subordinate the purchaser.

Subsection (f) states that if "chattel paper * * * indicates that it has been assigned to an identified secured party", this will be conclusive proof of the purchaser's knowledge that its purchase "violates the rights of the secured party". So a legend on the face of the paper protects a secured creditor whether that creditor claims "merely as proceeds" or otherwise.

The changes in 9–330 point in opposite directions. They give safe harbor to the inventory lender who wishes to insure that no buyer of chattel paper will gain priority. If the inventory lender stamps the chattel paper to show that the paper has been assigned to it, the purchaser's claim is subordinated, see 9–330(a) and (f). The changes also expand the rights of a purchaser. First, subsection (b) allows the purchaser to take free of a prior perfected security interest even though the purchaser knows of the existence of a security interest in the particular paper as long as the purchaser does not know that its purchase will "violate" the rights of the prior secured party. Second, subsection (a) omits any reference to the knowledge of the purchaser.

Problem 2–15

Great Bank had a perfected security interest in the inventory and proceeds of a large Arizona mobile home dealership, Raising Arizona ("Raising"). In 2002 Raising sold ten mobile homes on retail installment contracts (security interests with notes) to ten different consumers who took possession of the homes and moved into them in various mobile home parks around Phoenix. Raising then sold all ten of those contracts to GMAC but it did not, as GMAC apparently expected, pay the proceeds to Great Bank. Rather, it used the funds to pay other creditors. When Raising went bankrupt, both GMAC and Great Bank claimed first rights in the stream of payments that came from the ten purchasers. GMAC claims priority over the bank under section 9–330. Bank responds with the following arguments:

1. Section 9–330 does not apply in this case because GMAC, as it admits, knew of Bank's prior perfected security interest.

2. The rights here are not chattel paper because the dealer never gave the Certificate of Origin to GMAC (a document the dealer gets from the manufacturer).

3. In one case no security agreement was signed and the only document transferred to GMAC was a non-negotiable note. As to this transaction, Bank is particularly insistent that 9–330 does not apply.

4. There is a second dispute between the parties. When the dealer went bankrupt, there were two mobile homes on its lot that had been returned upon default of the original purchasers. Great Bank claims a perfected security interest in these assets as after-acquired property of the dealer, but GMAC also asserts a right in them. Great Bank points out that GMAC never had a security agreement with Raising that granted a security interest in mobile homes, therefore, GMAC has no claim.

Chapter Three

SECURITY INTERESTS IN RIGHTS TO PAYMENT AND OTHER INTANGIBLES

---

§ 1. INTRODUCTION

Rights to payment come in at least 9 different forms under Article 9. The most common of these would be accounts, instruments and chattel paper. But other rights to payment might be described as general intangibles, payment intangibles, health care receivables, letter of credit rights, deposit accounts or even investment property. Each of these forms of collateral is defined in 9–102; it is not too soon to turn there and try to figure out how an account might be different from chattel paper and how the two of them might be different from instruments, for example.

There are at least two reasons to understand the technical definitions of a particular intangible one is considering. First, the modes of perfection are different for many of the intangibles. Most can be perfected by filing a financing statement but that is not true, for example, of deposit accounts or letter of credit rights. Security interests arising from "sales" of instruments and payment intangibles are automatically perfected upon attachment of the security interest, see 9–309.

A second reason is to be sure the terms used in legal documents such as the security agreement or the financing statement correctly indicate what the parties intend. A secured creditor who takes a security interest in "instruments" that turn out to be "accounts" is likely to find itself unperfected because its documents do not describe the collateral properly.

In many ways a security interest in rights to payment is the best of all security. By hypothesis, these rights turn into cash and, if collected directly from the account debtor are self liquidating. In most cases, they bring with them the promises of payment from third parties known as "account debtors" with whom the creditor has not dealt directly. This multitude of payors means that neither the failure of the debtor itself

150

nor of some small fraction of the account debtors will degrade the value of the collateral.

To understand the basic modes of perfection, take a quick walk through the relevant sections. Section 9–309 gives automatic perfection with respect to a "sale of payment intangibles" and a "sale of a promissory note". Automatic perfection is also permitted for certain assignments of health care insurance receivables at least to the "provider of health care goods and services".

The general rule stated in 9–310(a) is that filing is the appropriate method of perfection for intangibles, and, except in a few circumstances, is normally adequate. Section 9–312(a) states that one can perfect a security interest in "chattel paper ... instruments or investment property" by filing. (To permit one to perfect a security interest in instruments by filing is a change from the prior law.) Despite their absence from the list in 9–312, filing is also a permissible method of perfection for accounts, general intangibles and payment intangibles but not for deposit accounts or letter of credit rights. The latter two may be perfected (except as proceeds) only by control. A security interest in investment property may be perfected either by control or by filing (we consider investment property in Chapter 6). Finally, possession under 9–313 is a permissible method of perfection for "instruments, money or tangible chattel paper".

There are reasons, in most cases good reasons, for the foregoing rules that permit certain acts, require others and prohibit yet others. As we go through the chapter, be sure to consider why a certain mode of perfection is required with respect to certain assets and prohibited with others and vice versa.

Section 9–102 of the 1972 Code covered not only transactions intended to create conventional security interests but also "any sale of accounts or chattel paper." This provision recognized historical forms of financing that had long been practiced in many industries called "factoring." The factor was a person who "bought" accounts; the factor would pay the owner of the account 85, 90 or even 95 cents on the dollar in return for an assignment of 100% of the account. The factor would then make its money by collecting 100 cents on the dollar. The spread (100–90) was the payment for the loan, the equivalent of an interest charge. The classic factor's bargain was "non-recourse": the buyer of the account agreed to take the full credit risk that the account debtor would or could not pay and so would have no recourse against the original owner of the account. Thus the factor got both the full upside (100 cents) and the full downside (0). In practice, there are many variations between full recourse (the debtor promises to pay the full amount if the account debtor defaults) and sale completely without recourse (no claim against the seller/debtor even if all account debtors default).

Modern practice has grandly expanded the factoring business; the new practice is called "securitization." In a securitization transaction the creditor sells its accounts to a trustee who in turn sells "shares" or "participations" in the trust to investors. We discuss this in section 3.

In section 7 we discuss security interests in general intangibles. "General intangibles" is the catchall of intangible rights. They are copyrights, patents, trademarks, and the rights associated with those forms of property. Everything that is intangible but is not an account, instrument, chattel paper, etc., is a "general intangible". General intangibles also include exotic rights such as the right to breed a mare to a particular stud.

As collateral, general intangibles present two significant problems to the secured creditor. First many general intangibles carry anti-assignment provisions, for example, it is common for software licenses to prohibit their assignment to a third person or use by anyone other than the licensee. As we will see, section 9–408 deals with that issue, but in a way that is not likely to be satisfactory to the typical secured creditor. The second major problem with taking security interests in general intangibles is that the most valuable general intangibles, copyrights, patents and trademarks, are subject to federal law. The federal law that governs those rights have their own filing provisions and it is often argued (and sometimes held) that a UCC filing is inadequate to perfect a security interest in such collateral. Congress may eventually delegate security filing to the states but until that happens, a UCC filing may not be adequate to perfect.

§ 2. PERFECTION OF SECURITY INTERESTS IN RIGHTS TO PAYMENT

To test your ability to distinguish among different forms of intangible rights and to understand the legal consequences that flow from those differences, consider the following problem:

Problem 3–1

Debtor is a large metropolitan hospital located in Manhattan. On any given day, it will have thousands of patients; some of them are paying out of their own pockets, some of them are members of HMOs who are paying, and some of them are Medicare or Medicaid patients whose fees are paid by state or federal governments. Bank intends to give hospital a $5 million revolving line of credit and to take a security interest in all of its intangibles. Bank currently has a financing statement on file in Albany claiming all "accounts and proceeds". There is some possibility that the hospital could go bankrupt and you think that at least two other creditors have filed as to certain receivables. The receivables consist of the following:

    1.   Claims against current and former patients who have no insurance.

    2.   Claims against current and former patient's credit cards who have paid by drawing on their credit cards.

    3.   Rights to payment from HMOs and private insurers

    4.   Rights to payment from Medicare and Medicaid

5.   Rights to rentals arising from transactions in which the hospital pharmacy leases wheelchairs, crutches and other devices.

6.   Rights to payment from sales by the hospital store that sells knee braces, wheelchairs, and various home-health devices. Many of these are sold on 24–month contracts under which the hospital retains a security interest and the former patient promises to pay in installments.

7.   Right to payment to the hospital from one of its subsidiaries of a million dollar loan the hospital made to the subsidiary two months ago.

8.   A seven figure deposit account maintained at Citibank in Manhattan.

9.   Right to the rent from a five year real estate lease of a building adjacent to the hospital that is now leased to a large group of doctors.

If the hospital fails tomorrow and files a petition in bankruptcy, in which assets will the Bank have a perfected security interest?

––––––––––

Creditors often seek security not only in the intangibles, but also in a related asset. Subsections 9–203(f) and (g) and 9–308(e) facilitate these claims in the related assets when those assets are "liens" or "supporting obligations". The following case shows that 9–203(f) and (g) will not cover all cases where the secured creditor wants the related asset.

IN RE LEASING CONSULTANTS, INC.

United States Court of Appeals, Second Circuit, 1973.
486 F.2d 367.

Jameson, District Judge:

Respondent–Appellant, First National City Bank (Bank), appeals from an order of the district court affirming, on a petition for review, the order of a referee in bankruptcy directing the Bank to turn over to the Petitioner–Appellee, George Feldman, Trustee in Bankruptcy (Trustee) of Leasing Consultants, Incorporated, (Leasing) the proceeds from the sale of equipment which had been leased by Leasing, located in New York, to Plastimetrix Corporation, located in New Jersey. The leases covering the equipment had been assigned to the Bank as security for a loan to Leasing.

The district court held, 351 F.Supp. 1390, on the basis of stipulated facts, that the perfection by the Bank by filing and possession in New York of its security interest in the lease/chattel paper was not a perfection of the Bank's security interest in Leasing's reversionary interest in the leased property, located in New Jersey. Consequently, the Trustee's lien was held superior to the Bank's unperfected security interest in the leased equipment.

Summary of Facts

In March and June of 1969 Leasing entered into eight leases with Plastimetrix covering heavy equipment. The leased equipment was at all relevant times located in New Jersey. Leasing filed financing statements with the Secretary of State of the State of New Jersey covering each transaction, each statement bearing the legend: "THIS FILING IS FOR INFORMATIONAL PURPOSES ONLY AS THIS IS A LEASE TRANS-ACTION."

On December 15, 1969 Leasing entered into a "Loan and Security Agreement" with the Bank for the financing of its business of purchasing and leasing equipment. The agreement provided in part for the assignment of "a continuing security interest in the lease(s) and the property leased" as collateral security for advances and loans not to exceed 80% of aggregate unpaid rentals.

Pursuant to the security agreement Leasing borrowed money from the Bank in December, 1969 and February, 1970 and assigned as collateral security the eight Plastimetrix leases, each assignment covering all moneys due or to become due under the lease and the "relative equipment" described in the lease. The lease documents were delivered to the Bank.

On December 30 and 31, 1969 the Bank filed financing statements against Leasing with the Secretary of State of the State of New York and the Registrar of the City of New York, Queens County, where Leasing had its principal place of business.[1] No financing statements were filed by the Bank in New Jersey; nor did the Bank take possession of the leased equipment.

On October 14, 1970 Leasing was adjudicated bankrupt by the United States District Court for the Eastern District of New York. On October 30, 1970 Plastimetrix filed a petition under Chapter XI of the Bankruptcy Act in the United States District Court for the District of New Jersey.

The leases were in default and an offer was made to purchase the Bank's interest in the property for $60,000. On May 21, 1971 the Trustee, the Bank, and the purchaser entered into a stipulation providing for acceptance of the offer and execution of bills of sale by the Trustee and Bank covering all "right, title and interest" in the property, and that the sum of $60,000 "be substituted for the Property" and the "respective rights of the Trustee and of the Bank * * * be impressed upon and relegated to said fund of $60,000 with the same priority and to the same extent as they now have against the Property."

The Trustee petitioned the Referee in Bankruptcy for an order directing the Bank to turn over to the Trustee the sum of $60,000. Under stipulated facts the Trustee and Bank agreed that the question presented was solely one of law—involving the construction of Article 9 of the Uniform Commercial Code—and that the precise issue was:

---

1. The financing statement covered "continuing security interest in leases and any and all rents due and to become due thereunder, including all related equipment described therein, chattel paper represented thereby, accounts receivable therewith and proceeds arising therefrom."

Was the Bank required to file a financing statement against the Bankrupt with the Secretary of State of New Jersey in order to perfect a security interest in the leases assigned to it and the equipment leased thereunder by the Bankrupt to Plastimetrix?

The Referee answered in the affirmative and ordered the Bank to turn over the $60,000, with interest, to the Trustee. On review the district court affirmed.

DECISION OF DISTRICT COURT

As the district court recognized, the aim of Article 9 of the Uniform Commercial Code, relating to "Secured Transactions", is "to provide a simple and unified structure within which the immense variety of present-day secured financing transactions can go forward with less cost and with greater certainty". Uniform Commercial Code, § 9–101, Official Comment. The drafters of this article eliminated many distinctions among security devices based on form alone. On the other hand, distinctions based on the type of property constituting the collateral were retained. Id.

Based on the stipulation of counsel, the court assumed that the agreements between Leasing and Plastimetrix were "true leases" and not "conditional sales agreements" or devices intended to create only a security interest.[2] Accordingly the court found that the Bank acquired "a security interest in both the right to receive rental payments under the lease and in the reversionary interest in the underlying equipment."

The court held, and the parties agree, that the leases themselves were "chattel papers" (9–105(1)(b)) and the Bank's security interest in the chattel paper was perfected by filing financing statements in New York and taking possession of the leases. UCC 9–304(1), 9–305, and 9–102(1).

The court held further: "By contrast, the machines themselves constituted 'equipment' located in New Jersey and hence, for perfection purposes, came within the scope of the New Jersey requirements." The Bank having failed to perfect its interest in the reversion in New Jersey, the court concluded that the Trustee—"a lien creditor within the meaning of Uniform Commercial Code 9–301(3)—has priority over an unperfected security interest under 9–301(1)(b)."

Emphasizing the distinction between rights under the chattel paper and the reversionary interest in the equipment, the court quoted from Professor Levie as follows:

In one situation the purchaser of a security agreement may have an advantage over the purchaser of a lease. Where [he] purchases equipment leases, he takes only an assignor's interest in the equipment lease itself. If [he] wishes to be secured by an interest in the

---

2. Where a lease is intended as a security device the lessee usually becomes the owner or has the option to become owner of the property at the end of the lease term. UCC § 1–201(37). The lessor holds merely a security interest and has no reversionary right in the leased property.

goods as well, he must obtain a security interest * * * [in the goods] and perfect it. Levie, Security Interests in Chattel Paper, 78 Yale L.J. 935 (1969).[3]

The district court concluded:

The distinction between the rights represented by the lease and those represented by the reversionary interest in the equipment is a real one, supported by logic and precedent. To ignore the distinction contributes neither to clarity nor uniformity under the Uniform Commercial Code. Moreover, it may mislead third party creditors. The simple solution for a bank in the situation of petitioner is to file notices as to its interest in the reversion in accordance with the law of the state where the equipment is located.

CONTENTIONS OF APPELLANT

Appellant Bank contends that (1) whether the leases be considered "true leases" or security devices, the filing of the security interest in New York (where lessor and the chattel paper were located) covered all of the lessor's rights in the rentals and related equipment wherever located, without a separate filing against the equipment; or (2) alternatively, if a distinction is recognized between a "true lease" and a security device, appellant is entitled to an evidentiary hearing to determine whether the instruments were "true leases" or security interests in the equipment through the device of a lease; and (3) in any event, Leasing in fact had no "reversionary" interest in the property leased to Plastimetrix.

FAILURE TO FILE FINANCING STATEMENT IN NEW JERSEY

In contending that the filing and physical possession of the lease instruments in New York were sufficient to cover the leased equipment located in New Jersey, appellant argues that the "reversionary interest" of Leasing is "an intangible interest, sited at Leasing's domicile in New York, and not in New Jersey." If the reversionary interest in the equipment were characterized as a "general intangible", the Bank's security interest in the equipment would have been perfected when it filed with the New York Department of State and in the county in which Leasing had a place of business. N.Y.UCC §§ 9–103(2), 9–401(1)(c) (McKinney 1964).

---

3. The court continued:

"Practical considerations support this conclusion. The property leased was heavy manufacturing equipment. A potential creditor observing these complicated and non-portable machines should be entitled to believe that he could discover all non-possessory interests by consulting the files in the state where the equipment is located. The equipment was obviously of great value; the New Jersey files revealed only that the lessee held it under a lease. Since the lease agreement required each piece of equipment to have a plate affixed indicating that it was the 'property' of the lessor, judgment creditors of the lessor might assume that its reversionary interest in the equipment was of substantial value. Not being alerted to the diminution of value which would be effected by the creditor's security interest, they might then, for example, attach the lessor's interest, relying on an apparently unencumbered and valuable reversionary interest."

The policies of the Code, however, militate against such an interpretation. We agree with the district court that the reversionary interest is an interest in "goods" rather than an interest in intangibles, and that to perfect the security interest in the reversionary interest in the equipment it was necessary to file a financing statement in New Jersey where the equipment was located. N.J.Stat.Anno. 12A:9–102(1) (1962), 9–302, 9–401(1)(c) (Supp.1972).

Obviously the leased property itself is "goods". We conclude, as did the district court, that the future reversionary interest is likewise an interest in goods, whether it represents "equipment" or "inventory" collateral. The drafters of the Code classified collateral mainly according to the nature or use of the underlying entity, rather than the character of its ownership at any given time. Significantly, the examples of "general intangibles" given in the Official Comment to § 9–106 are all types of property that are inherently intangible. And several Code sections and comments suggest that a collateral interest in "goods" remains such even when the goods are leased. See §§ 9–103(2); 9–109(4) and Official Comment 3; 9–304(3); N.Y.UCC 9–109, Practice Commentary 2 (McKinney 1964) (Kripke).

We conclude accordingly that if the instruments were "true leases", the security interest in the leased equipment was not perfected because of the failure of the Bank to file financing statements in New Jersey.[4]

[The court concluded that the case should be remanded to determine whether the lease instrument was a "true lease" or intended as security. If the district court determined that the agreements were "true" leases, then it will also be necessary to consider the effect of stipulations by the parties and whether the $60,000 fund "represents the sale of the leasehold as well as the sale of the reversionary interest in the equipment." The case was then remanded for determination of these and other matters. Hays, Circuit Judge, dissented. Some footnotes omitted.]

Problem 3–2

1. The 1999 revision would have saved First National City Bank. Why?

2. Your client wants not only the stream of payments but also an interest in the underlying equipment of a lessor who leases goods nationwide. Taking possession of the leases and filing at the debtor's (lessor's) place of incorporation will give you a perfected security interest as to the leases and the leased goods. Is that correct? Client would prefer to leave the leases in the debtor's hands. Does it risk its perfection or its priority by doing so?

---

4. Appellant alternatively contends that since "Leasing had assigned all of its interest in the machinery and equipment to the Bank" it had preferential rights to the equipment under "the law of bailment leases" regardless of the Code provisions. The assignment of the equipment from Leasing to the Bank, however, was expressly made "as security for any and all obligations of [Leasing] to the Bank under and pursuant to the Loan and Security Agreement * * *." This assignment clearly created a security interest in the Bank and made the requirements of Article 9 applicable to the Bank's interest in the equipment. UCC § 9–102(1)(a).

Problem 3–3

1.   Greater Chicago Mortgage Co. makes mortgage loans to individual home owners in the Chicago area and also purchases documents that are variously called "land sale contracts" or "contracts for deed". These are contracts made between a buyer and seller of real estate; they do not include a note, but they can be recorded and when they are, will have the same effect as a mortgage under state law. If the debtor executes a mortgage, it will be recorded and the debtor will also sign a note. Greater Chicago wishes to sell some of these interests to your client, Bank, in these various assets. In order to have a first claim not only on the stream of payments but also on the underlying real estate, Bank understands that it need do nothing more than sign a security agreement with Greater Chicago. It understands that it is automatically perfected under 9–309 as to both the underlying real estate assets and the stream of payments. Is that correct?

2.   Would your conclusion in 1 change if your client told you that it proposed to "buy" the receivables on a nonrecourse basis and then to have Greater Chicago execute a separate document called "Guaranty" under which Greater Chicago would be obliged to buy back any loan on which the account debtor defaulted?

3.   Assume that Greater Chicago has failed and its trustee in bankruptcy has challenged your client on the ground that Bank did not have a valid and perfected security interest in the underlying mortgages and property. The trustee suggests your client was obliged to record an assignment of mortgage or a land sale contract in the real estate records in order to enjoy priority. Secondly, it notes that to some of the mortgage transactions, Greater Chicago failed to record the mortgage. How will that affect the outcome of the case described above?

§ 3.   SECURITIZATION

Before 1999, Article 9 rights to payment that arose from a *loan* by a creditor to a debtor were "general intangibles" not "accounts"; "accounts" arose only on the sale of goods or services. Thus, for example, a securitization of $100 million of commercial loans or $200 million of credit card receivables would not have been covered by Article 9 since they would have amounted to the "sale of general intangibles" not the "sale of accounts or chattel paper." The change in the definition of accounts (to include credit card receivables, 9–102(a)(2)(vii)) and the expansion of Article 9's coverage (to include sales of payment intangibles and promissory notes, 9–109(a)(3)), brings almost all securitization within Article 9. The new definition of payment intangibles and their inclusion in 9–109(a)(3) brings the sale of loan participations into Article 9 as well.

To understand how Article 9 might apply to the sale of various intangibles, consider four cases. First, assume that General Motors Acceptance Corp. (GMAC) makes 1,000 car loans (complete with perfected security interests) to 1,000 consumer car buyers, then sells those loans (constituting in this case "chattel paper", a security agreement and a note) to a trust or other Special Purpose Vehicle (SPV) that issues shares to investors. Second, assume the original lender is not GMAC but a mortgage company that takes notes secured by real estate mortgages from 1,000 account debtor homeowners and transfers its notes and mortgages to a trustee. Third is a credit card company that sells its receivables. Fourth, is Chase Manhattan Bank who lends $100 million to a debtor and then sells off $90 million of "participations" in its $100 million loan to 9 other banks so each of the ten banks now owns only $10 million of the loan.

All of these cases are covered by Article 9. The collateral transferred in GMAC's case was "chattel paper"; that transferred by the real estate lender was "instruments" or "payment intangibles"; the credit card company sold "accounts"; and Chase Manhattan transferred "payment intangibles." Although each of these four transactions is covered under Article 9, they do not get identical treatment. Under 9–309, the banks who bought loan participations and the purchaser of the notes from the mortgage company are automatically perfected without filing or possession. The buyer from GMAC, however, will either have to file in GMAC's name or take possession of the chattel paper. The buyer of accounts from the credit card company will have to file in the name of the credit card company to perfect its interest.

One might ask why the sale of anything is ever treated as though it were a secured loan. Part of the reason is that the sale of intangibles that produce payments behave economically like loans against those same assets. If, for example, GMAC had $100M of receivables from consumers who had purchased cars, it could either "sell" the receivables to a bank or it could borrow from the bank and grant the bank a security interest in the receivables. The two transactions have almost the same economic consequences for GMAC. The sale of loans or other receivables is almost exactly like a "nonrecourse" loan against those assets. A nonrecourse loan is a loan in which the creditor agrees to lend money and to limit its claims for satisfaction of the loan to particular assets of the debtor. For example, by law most purchase money mortgages on residential homes in California are nonrecourse loans. By law the mortgagee can foreclose on the residence and sell it to satisfy its debt but is prohibited from going after the wages or any other assets of the homeowner. At certain times and in certain industries, nonrecourse loans have been commonplace. For a time for example, it was common for banks to make nonrecourse loans against commercial buildings and thus to limit themselves to the right to foreclosure and sale of the building.

An historical reason why it is easy for commercial lenders to regard securitizations as loans is that securitizations are no more than an exaggerated version of an ancient transaction called "factoring". As early as 1900 it was common for a factor to purchase the accounts receivable of sellers in certain industries. The factors would pay $.80 or $.95 for $1.00 of account receivable and would enjoy the entire upside (i.e., collect one hundred cents on the dollar from the account debtors) and suffer the entire downside (i.e., bear the loss with respect to any account debtor who failed to pay). Factoring, securitization and every form of nonrecourse lending comes in increments; it is not bi-modal. For example, a bank that was willing to purchase an automobile dealer's paper might require the dealer to take back (i.e., guarantee) any loan on which there was a default within six months of the transfer. Such limited recourse against the automobile dealer would diminish his incentive to make loans to noncreditworthy debtors and then sell those loans completely free of recourse to the bank.

Whether something is a "sale" as opposed to a "loan" accompanying security interest is often a function of the amount of recourse. If there is full recourse, the transaction is a loan with a security interest. If there is none, it is not a loan and a security interest but only a sale. Whether one ounce, a quart or a gallon of recourse is enough to cause the transaction to go across the line from sale to loan and security cannot be predicted, but it is something that should concern everyone who wishes to be treated as a purchaser, not as a lender.

Whether one is a seller or borrower is usually not important for the purpose of Article 9, for whatever the transaction is called, the "creditor" or "buyer" will normally take whatever action is necessary to perfect a security interest under Article 9. However the distinction between a sale and a loan may be critical for the purpose of bankruptcy law. If there is a sale, the asset is not "property of the estate" under section 541 of the Bankruptcy Code and thus is not subject to interference by the DIP or by the seller's trustee in bankruptcy.

The key to securitization (and perhaps the only significant thing about securitization) is to remove the assets that are securitized beyond the reach of any DIP. One step in this transaction is to transfer the assets to a trust or other SPV. This SPV will have no creditor other than the investors themselves who purchase shares or interests in the pool of assets. If the SPV has no other creditors, it cannot fail to pay other obligations and thus cannot itself be put into bankruptcy.

The greater concern is the DIP or trustee of the seller (debtor). As suggested above in the discussion of bankruptcy in chapter 1, section 8, the trustee or DIP has a variety of ways, under sections 362 and 363, to jack around a secured creditor, even a fully perfected one. The DIP can use the creditor's collateral and can sometimes substitute other collateral as adequate protection, can stop paying interest when the value of the collateral is less than the debt, etc. The way to free the assets (the accounts receivable that GMAC is selling) from the reach of GMAC's DIP is to insure that there is a "sale" as that term is defined in section 541 and that the assets are not in the estate of GMAC should it go bankrupt.

If the securitization is properly done so that the credit rating agencies and the investors believe that the assets are beyond the reach of all DIPs and trustees, the rating agency will give a higher rating to the SPV than they would give to the seller of the receivables who, by hypothesis, has many other creditors. If the rating agencies give a better rating to the SPV than to the original seller, it means that the SPV can borrow at a lower interest rate or, alternatively, that its investors will pay more for debt it issues than they would pay for the parent's debt. In addition to this benefit there may be other small ones that are unrelated to the effect on bankruptcy. In the material that follows consider the eight claimed benefits of securitization. I suspect that most of those are merely reiterations of number one in different words, namely that the cost of funds is lower if the assets are far from the hand of the bankruptcy trustee.

The following article provides a good introduction to the practice of securitization. It refers to the pre–1999 Code, but the issues are generally the same under the 1999 Code.

Gregory M. Shan and John T. Gaffney, "Certain Legal Considerations in Connection with the Securitization of Retail Motor Vehicle Installment Contracts", 314 PLI/Real 501 (1988)

I. INTRODUCTION

A. General

This outline discusses certain legal issues associated with the securitization of motor vehicle retail installment sale contracts ('Loan Receivables') and motor vehicle leases ('Lease Receivables' and, together with Loan Receivables, 'Receivables'). Securitization consists of isolating a pool of Receivables and packaging them into securities which can be traded in the capital markets as either 'pass-through' securities, where payments of principal and interest received on the underlying receivables are paid through to security holders in the same amounts and form as received, or 'pay through' securities, where interest and principal are paid to security holders based on the cash flow of the underlying receivables, but not necessarily in the same amounts or form as received. Many of the legal issues discussed in this outline will also apply to the securitization of other financial assets.

B. Rationale for Securitization

The benefits of securitization to the seller of the financial assets (the "Seller") may include:

(1) lower cost of funds, particularly if the asset-backed securities enjoy a higher credit rating than the Seller itself (i.e., securitization represents the opportunity to create a 'AAA' or 'AA' credit instead of borrowing on the basis of the Seller's own credit rating);

(2) improved asset/liability management (securitization permits the Seller to match its assets and liabilities perfectly);

(3) off balance sheet treatment (securitization may permit the Seller to avoid the consequences of direct borrowing, such as compliance with certain restrictive borrowing covenants and preserving the Seller's direct borrowing capacity);

(4) improved liquidity (securitization represents an additional method of raising funds by the Seller from the capital markets);

(5) new sources of funds (securitization may permit the Seller access to new lenders not otherwise available to the Seller and to whom the credit rating of the investment is particularly important, such as pension funds, insurance companies and foreign investors);

(6) spreading of credit risks (securitization permits the Seller to transfer all or part of the credit risk associated with certain financial assets to a third-party);

(7) increased fee income (if the Seller is a depository institution, securitization may lower its dependence on interest income by increasing fee income); and

(8) assistance in meeting increased capital adequacy standards (securitization assists a financial institution in meeting its capital adequacy standard by shrinking the size of its balance sheet or permitting it to reinvest the proceeds of the securitization transaction in new assets without increasing the size of its balance sheet).

C. Securitization Structures

The securities backed by Loan Receivables or Lease Receivables (hereinafter referred to as the "Securities") are generally in the form of (i) participation interests in a passive "grantor" trust or (ii) debt securities of a limited purpose finance corporation or of a limited purpose business or "owner" trust.

(1) "Grantor" Trust. The trust is generally created pursuant to a pooling and servicing agreement between the Seller and a fiduciary. The Seller transfers the Receivables to the trust, which issues participation certificates representing undivided fractional interests in the trust. The trust transfers the proceeds of the sale of the participation certificates to the Seller in exchange for the Receivables. Ordinarily, the trustee does not hold the documentation for the Receivables or service the Receivables; instead, the documentation is held by the Seller or an affiliated entity, as custodian, and serviced by the Seller or affiliated entity.

(2) Limited Purpose Finance Corporation or "Owner Trust". The Seller or an unaffiliated third-party (typically an investment bank) may create a separately incorporated limited purpose finance corporation or business trust for the purpose of issuing debt securities collateralized by Receivables. Generally, the Seller transfers the Receivables to the finance entity, although in some circumstances a finance corporation may originate the Receivables itself. The finance entity will transfer the proceeds received from the sale of the debt securities to the Seller either as the purchase price for the Receivables or as a dividend or return of capital. The principal and interest payments on the debt securities issued by the finance entity are paid out of the cash flow resulting from payments on the Receivables and reinvestment income thereon. Any funds remaining after payment of the debt and expenses of the finance entity are available to the equity holders of the finance entity. The

equity of the finance entity may either be retained by the Seller or the parent corporation or sold to investors in a private placement.

(3) Credit Support. Supplemental credit support against payment defaults is usually provided in order to obtain the desired credit rating for the Securities. The credit enhancement may support payments by the obligors of the underlying Receivables or payments on the Securities themselves. The extent of the credit support required by the rating agencies will vary from transaction to transaction based upon, among other things, the characteristics of the Receivables to be securitized, the performance of the portfolio of Receivables from which the Receivables to be securitized will be drawn and the structure and terms of the transaction. There are many forms of credit support available for securitization transactions involving Receivables including:

(a) letters of credit from banking institutions which generally support payments on the underlying Receivables;

(b) surety bonds issued by financial insurers which insure payment on the Securities;

(c) limited guarantees of payments on the underlying Receivables by the Seller (if its rating is sufficient);

(d) reserve accounts or spread accounts; and

(e) overcollateralization of the Securities.

II. BANKRUPTCY LAW CONSIDERATIONS

A. General

The principal bankruptcy law issues involved in the securitization of Loan Receivables and Lease Receivables relate to the isolation of the Receivables, including the underlying security interest in the motor vehicle, from credit risk of the Seller. If the objective of the transaction is to obtain a higher credit rating for the Securities than the credit rating of the Seller and the Seller is subject to the Bankruptcy Code (i.e., is not a banking institution or other exempt entity), it will be necessary to structure the transaction so that the Receivables will not be included in the bankruptcy estate of the Seller if it becomes insolvent. In all transactions, it is necessary that the security interest or ownership interest in the Receivables of the grantor trust or finance entity issuing the Securities (the 'Issuer') be perfected.

B. Theories for Including Receivables in the Seller's Bankruptcy Estate

The Seller isolates Receivables by either selling them to the Issuer or by contributing them as capital to the Issuer. This transfer may be subject to attack by creditors or a trustee in bankruptcy of the Seller under any of the following theories:

(1) True Sale Versus Secured Loan. The transfer of the Receivables is described in the operative documents of the securitization transaction as a sale or capital contribution of the Receivables; however, such characterization is subject to recharacterization as a secured loan by the

bankruptcy court in the event of the bankruptcy of the Seller. If the Seller subsequent to the transfer of the Receivables to the Issuer is subject to bankruptcy proceedings and the purported sale is recharacterized as a secured financing, the transferred Receivables will remain the property of the Seller's estate, subject to various provisions of the Bankruptcy Code, including the automatic stay and provisions permitting substitution of collateral. Bankruptcy Code §§ 362 and 541. This result is usually unacceptable because of the expectation of security holders that an uninterrupted cash flow from the Receivables will provide for timely payment on the Securities. By contrast, if the transfer is a 'true sale', the subsequent bankruptcy of the Seller should have no effect on future cash flow from the Receivables. Bankruptcy Code § 541(d). A variety of factors may affect the characterization of the transfer of the Receivables from the Seller to the Issuer as a 'true sale' rather than a secured financing.

(a) The principal factor is the Issuer's direct or indirect recourse against the Seller in the event of nonpayment by the obligor of the underlying Receivables. If the security holders purchased the Securities on the basis of the Seller's credit through the recourse obligation of the Seller to the Issuer, the Issuer is more likely to be treated in bankruptcy as a creditor, together with the Seller's other creditors.

(b) A second factor in characterizing a transfer is the Seller's right, as servicer, to manage the Receivables underlying the Securities and control the payments received from the obligors of the underlying Receivables. Commingling of payments on the Receivables with those of the Seller without careful control is an element of a financing rather than a sale.

(c) A third factor is the extent to which the Seller has retained the economic benefits of the Receivables through a right to repurchase the underlying obligations or through contingent servicing compensation in excess of market rates. Thus, one indication of a financing is if the Issuer is only entitled to receive proceeds of the Receivables to the extent of its 'purchase price' plus interest accrued on the remaining outstanding balance of the purchase price.

(d) A fourth factor is the accounting and tax treatment of the transaction. If the transfer is treated as a financing rather than a sale under generally accepted accounting principles, it is likely to be treated as a secured loan for bankruptcy purposes. Treatment of the transfer as a financing for tax purposes is also an indication that the transfer should be recharacterized as a secured loan. The tax treatment is less compelling, however, because creditors of the Seller do not rely on (and are generally not aware of) the tax characterization of the transfer and because the public policies underlying the tax characterization of the transaction can be different from those underlying its characterization in bankruptcy.

(e) Other less important factors include: whether the security holders made an independent evaluation of the creditworthiness of the obligors on the underlying Receivables; whether the obligors on the underlying Receivables receive notice of the sale; whether the security holders are purchasing an interest in a pool of specifically identifiable Receivables or merely an interest in unspecified Receivables; and whether the Seller retains the documents covering the Receivables and if so, the nature of the Issuer's right to inspect and/or require delivery of such documents.

(2) Parent Bankruptcy. The issuance of Securities through a limited purpose finance entity owned by the Seller does not necessarily insulate security holders from the subsequent bankruptcy or insolvency of the Seller, even if the transfer is a valid sale or capital contribution, rather than a loan. Under certain circumstances a bankruptcy court may order the 'substantive consolidation' of the assets and liabilities of this type of entity with those of the Seller. Substantive consolidation may occur without regard to the solvency of the subsidiary. In general, substantive consolidation may result if the limited purpose finance entity fails to comply with corporate formalities or if the entity's business or operations are so intermingled with those of the Seller as to make separation impractical or inequitable. The following factors support recognition of the 'separateness' of the entity from the Seller:

(a) the presence of independent officers and directors;

(b) a separate business office, even if space is subleased from the Seller;

(c) separate books and records and no commingling of assets; and

(d) the "holding out" of the subsidiary as a separate entity and not as a division or branch of the Seller.

(3) Fraudulent Conveyance. A trustee in bankruptcy may recover, as a fraudulent conveyance, any amount transferred for less than a "reasonably equivalent value" if the debtor was insolvent or rendered insolvent at the time of the transfer. Bankruptcy Code § 548. The various state fraudulent conveyance statutes differ in detail, but generally are to the same effect as the Bankruptcy Code provision.

C. Perfection of Security Interests in the Receivables and the Underlying Collateral

(1) General. The Receivables are 'chattel paper' for purposes of the New York Uniform Commercial Code (the 'UCC'). UCC Section 9–105(b). Under Section 9–102(1)(b) a sale of chattel paper, as well as a loan secured by chattel paper, is subject to Article 9 of the UCC. Accordingly, the Issuer must perfect its interest in the Receivables in accordance with Article 9 of the UCC in order to avoid attack by the trustee in bankruptcy or creditors of the Seller. Because security interests in motor vehicles are typically governed by state certificate of title statutes rather than the provisions of the Uniform Commercial Code,

there may exist some uncertainty as to the method required for perfecting the Issuer's interest in the motor vehicle securing Loan Receivables and as to the ability of the Issuer to obtain a perfected interest in a motor vehicle which is the subject of a Lease Receivable.

(2) Perfection of Loan Receivables. Under the UCC, an interest in chattel paper may be perfected either by filing a financing statement (Section 9–302) or by taking possession of the chattel paper (Section 9–305). Generally, it is not feasible for the Issuer to take possession of the motor vehicle retail installment sale contracts; instead, the seller-servicer of the Receivables generally takes possession of such contracts, as custodian for the Issuer, and files a UCC–1 financing statement with respect to the Loan Receivables. Under certain circumstances, a secured party which obtains possession of the chattel paper may have priority over a secured party which has filed a financing statement with respect to such chattel paper. * * *

(3) Perfection of Security Interests in the Motor Vehicles Underlying Loan Receivables. Each motor vehicle retail installment sale contract is secured by the grant by the obligor to the Seller of a security interest in the vehicle financed. Virtually all states have enacted motor vehicle certificate of title statutes under which security interests in motor vehicles must be noted on the certificates of title or otherwise reflected on state motor vehicle records. The Seller will assign its security interest in the motor vehicles to the Issuer. However, because of the administrative burden and expense, it will not be feasible to deliver the certificates of title to the Issuer, to endorse the certificates of title to reflect the interest of the Issuer therein or to notify the owner of the motor vehicle or the relevant state office of the assignment of the security interest. Accordingly, the Seller will continue to be named as the secured party on the certificates of title relating to the motor vehicles. There is some confusion as to the legal effect of transferring the security interest in a motor vehicle without noting the transfer on the certificate of title. The certificate of title statutes of some states provide that the assignment of a security interest in a motor vehicle must be noted on the certificate of title. On the other hand, as described above, Article 9 of the Uniform Commercial Code governs the assignment or sale of the 'chattel paper' of which the security interest is a part. Absent specific authority in any particular state regarding the interpretation of these overlapping requirements, perfection of the transfer of the chattel paper under Article 9 should be sufficient to protect the Issuer from claims of the bankruptcy trustee and creditors of the Seller even though the transfer of the security interest in the vehicle may not comply with the literal requirements of the applicable certificate of title statute. In addition, the notation of the lien of the Seller on the certificate of title should be sufficient to protect the Issuer against the rights of a subsequent purchaser of the motor vehicle or subsequent creditors of the vehicle owner who take a security interest in the motor vehicle. There is a risk that because the Issuer is not identified as the secured party on the

certificate of title the Seller through administrative error, inadvertence or fraud could release or impair the security interest of the Issuer.

(4) Perfection of Security Interests in Motor Vehicles Underlying Lease Receivables. In the typical lease transaction, the Seller is the owner of the motor vehicle being leased and is named as such on the certificate of title. Under the terms of the most common form of lease, the Seller typically receives regular monthly payments amortizing a portion of the cost of the motor vehicle over a fixed term. At the end of the lease term the lessee of the motor vehicle has a right to purchase the motor vehicle for a fixed price representing the unamortized portion of the cost of the motor vehicle, the 'residual value'. If the lessee does not exercise its option to purchase, the motor vehicle is returned to the Seller and is generally sold for its wholesale value. There are significant difficulties in securitizing leases of this type because the Seller's objectives normally include financing the entire cost of the motor vehicle, including the residual value, through the securitization transaction. Securitizing the residual value creates two problems. First, there is no assurance that the market value of the motor vehicle at the end of the lease term will be equal to the residual value and, second, the Issuer of the Securities must be able to isolate the right to receive the proceeds from the sale of the motor vehicle at the end of the lease term from credit risks of the Seller. The first problem can sometimes be solved through the use of residual value insurance or other credit enhancements. The second problem may be difficult to overcome in cases where the Seller is the titled owner of the vehicle and is not a highly rated entity. As was the case for Loan Receivables, the Issuer will be again claiming an interest in the vehicle without having the interest reflected on the certificate of title. This case differs from Loan Receivables, however, because the transfer of Loan Receivables involves the transfer of a security interest in the motor vehicle, which was noted on the certificate of title, from one holder to another, while the transfer of the residual value associated with the Lease Receivables involves a transfer of the ownership of the motor vehicle, without any notation. An argument can be made that the Seller of Lease Receivables has retained title to the motor vehicle solely for the purpose of servicing the leases and that it has transferred all equitable ownership rights in the motor vehicle to the Issuer. This argument might be sufficient under Section 541(d) of the Bankruptcy Code to protect the Issuer from claims of the Seller's trustee in bankruptcy. * * *

Problem 3–4

You have been hired by Mutual Fund who proposes to buy several sets of receivables and wants your opinion about its rights in each of the circumstances. In one case, Merchandise Company, a midwestern department store, has a subsidiary known as M–Credit that issues credit cards to Merchandise Co.'s customers. Credit card receivables will be assigned to a trust and your client proposes to buy several millions of dollars of receivables from the trust. In the second case, All American Credit Card and Loan Company, makes loans in various ways: it has credit card receivables; it makes automobile loans and takes security interests in the automobiles; it makes automobile leases; and it makes unsecured consumer loans. It proposes to assign all of these to a trustee and your client proposes to buy "participations" from the trust. How would the following play out?

1.   Representatives of Merchandise Co. and All American claim that the trust's interest is either outside of Article 9 or is automatically perfected under the terms of 9–309. Moreover, they maintain there is no problem because the trust is "bankruptcy remote", i.e., the trust will have no obligations to any creditor except for the obligation it might have to your investor and to others and so could not be forced into bankruptcy. To be particularly safe, they have filed a financing statement in the name of Merchandise Co. and one in the name of All American covering all of debtor's "receivables and their proceeds". Do you think they are adequately perfected? Should your client file in the trust's name?

2.   What bankruptcy risk do you see, if any, if either of the trusts, Merchandise Co., its subsidiary or All American goes into bankruptcy?

3.   What action is necessary to insure perfection as to the automobiles that were leased or sold by All American. As to the cars sold, All American normally would have put its name on the Certificate of Title as "Secured Party" and would have signed a security agreement with the purchasers. In the case of the leased cars, All American's name appears as the owner on the Certificate of Title. Does the purchaser have to take any further action to protect itself as to the underlying collateral? How can one tell whether All American has a perfected security interest in the automobiles?

4.   Can different tranches of receivables be set up for different investors with different tastes for risk (e.g., some receivables with lower return and risk and others with greater returns but greater risk)? What problems does it pose?

Problem 3–5

It is now 18 months after you were asked for your advice. It turns out that Merchandise Co. was not as solvent as it could have been. It and its subsidiary have gone into Chapter 11 and their bankruptcy has been consolidated. The debtor in possession (DIP) has recently proposed to keep several months of payments that are passing through its hands. (After the securitization, the subsidiary continued to service the loans by collecting the payments from the customers.) The DIP claims the right to keep the payments for a limited period of time "in order to make the bankruptcy estate more liquid". He notes that the bankruptcy estate will give "adequate protection" under section 361 (in the form of a mortgage on some property that is unencumbered) He asserts that section 541 brings these assets into the bankruptcy estate. Moreover, he notes that section 362 keeps your client and the trust from suing Merchandise Co. and its subsidiary. His claim under section 541 depends in part upon section 9–318(b). He argues that that section necessarily means that a seller of a receivable under Article 9 has retained title sufficient to bring it into the bankruptcy estate. He also notes that under the arrangement between the trust and the subsidiary, the trust could return any receivable to the debtor on which there was a default within 6 months of the assignment to the subsidiary. He says this makes the transaction into a "secured loan" (with title to the receivables remaining in the subsidiary) not a "sale".

What do you think of the DIP's argument? Consider the excerpts from LTV, Octagon Gas and PEB 14 that are set out below.

Twice in the last decade courts have wandered into securitizors' Garden of Eden. The earlier case, *Octagon Gas Systems*, produced an angry Permanent Editorial Board commentary (PEB 14) almost overnight. The second arose out of LTV Steel's second bankruptcy and caused horror in what is now known as the "securitization industry". Read the two cases and decide for yourself whether they are correct interpretations of the law. If they are correct, the bankruptcy law doubtless should be changed to immunize securitization transactions from bankruptcy—at least if the benefits are as clear as the persons in the trade suggest. Securitization has now grown to a huge industry representing over 2 trillion dollars. I suspect that it is merely a by-product of current bankruptcy law and might quickly disappear or shrink to a shadow if the Congress and the courts could devise a way truly to free a secured creditors' rights from the grasp of the DIP.

IN RE LTV STEEL COMPANY, INC.

United States Bankruptcy Court, Northern District of Ohio, 2001.
274 B.R. 278.

Bodoh, Bankruptcy Judge.

This cause is before the Court on the emergency motion of Abbey National Treasury Services PLC ("Abbey National") for modification of an interim order entered by the Court on December 29, 2000. That order permitted LTV Steel Company, Inc., Debtor and Debtor-in-Possession in these jointly administered proceedings ("Debtor"), to use cash assets that are claimed to be cash collateral in which Abbey National has an interest. * * *

DISCUSSION

A. Facts

Debtor is one of the largest manufacturers of wholly-integrated steel products in the United States. Debtor mainly produces flat rolled steel products, hot and cold rolled sheet metal, mechanical and structural tubular products, and bimetallic wire. Debtor currently employs approximately 17,500 people in various capacities, and Debtor is also responsible for providing medical coverage and other benefits to approximately 100,000 retirees and their dependents. Debtor and 48 of its subsidiaries filed voluntary petitions for relief under Chapter 11 of Title 11, United States Code, on December 29, 2000. These cases are jointly administered.

This is not the first occasion on which Debtor has filed for relief under the Bankruptcy Code. Debtor previously filed a voluntary Chapter 11 petition in the Bankruptcy Court for the Southern District of New

York on July 17, 1986. Debtor successfully emerged from Chapter 11 on June 28, 1993. Indeed, the current controversy stems from a series of financial transactions that Debtor executed after its previous reorganization. The transactions in question are known as asset-backed securitization or structured financing ("ABS"), and are generally designed to permit a debtor to borrow funds at a reduced cost in exchange for a lender securing the loan with assets that are transferred from the borrower to another entity. By structuring the transactions in this manner, the lender hopes to ensure that its collateral will be excluded from the borrower's bankruptcy estate in the event that the borrower files a bankruptcy petition.

Abbey National is a large financial institution located in the United Kingdom. Debtor and Abbey National entered into an ABS transaction in October 1994. To effectuate this agreement, Debtor created a wholly-owned subsidiary known as LTV Sales Finance Co. ("Sales Finance"). Debtor then entered into an agreement with Sales Finance which purports to sell all of Debtor's right and interest in its accounts receivables ("receivables") to Sales Finance on a continuing basis. Abbey National then agreed to loan Two Hundred Seventy Million Dollars ($270,000,-000.00) to Sales Finance in exchange for Sales Finance granting Abbey National a security interest in the receivables. On the date Debtor's petition was filed, Chase Manhattan Bank ("Chase Manhattan") was Abbey National's agent for this credit facility.

In 1998, Debtor entered into another ABS financing arrangement. To that end, Debtor created LTV Steel Products, LLC ("Steel Products"), another wholly-owned subsidiary. Debtor entered into an agreement with Steel Products which purports to sell all of Debtor's right, title and interest in its inventory to Steel Products on a continuing basis. Chase Manhattan and several other banking institutions then agreed to loan Thirty Million Dollars ($30,000,000.00) to Steel Products in exchange for a security interest in Steel Products' inventory. Abbey National is not involved in this ABS facility, and it had no interest in prepetition inventory allegedly owned by Steel Products.

Neither Sales Finance nor Steel Products is a debtor in this proceeding. Nevertheless, Debtor filed a motion with the Court on December 29, 2000 seeking an interim order permitting it to use cash collateral. This cash collateral consisted of the receivables and inventory that are ostensibly owned by Sales Finance and Steel Products. Debtors stated to the Court that it would be forced to shut it doors and cease operations if it did not receive authorization to use this cash collateral. A hearing was held on Debtor's cash collateral motion on December 29, 2000 as part of the first day hearings.

Abbey National was not present at the cash collateral hearing. However, the Court notes that Abbey National had actual notice of the hearing, first, in the form of an e-mail sent by a Chase Manhattan employee to Abbey National on December 28, 2000, and second, in the form of a telephone call made from a Chase Manhattan employee to

Abbey National on December 29, 2000. Furthermore, it is clear that Debtor had given advance notice of its intention to file for bankruptcy protection to Chase Manhattan, Abbey National's agent, in the week prior to December 29, 2000. Chase Manhattan was present at the December 29, 2000 hearing.

On December 29, 2000, Debtor and Chase Manhattan reached an agreement regarding an interim order permitting Debtor to use the cash collateral. Chase Manhattan did not formally consent to the entry of this order, as it could not secure Abbey National's consent to the form of the order, but Chase Manhattan did negotiate some of the terms of the order and did not raise an objection to its entry by the Court. The Court determined that entry of the interim order was necessary to permit Debtor to continue business operations, that the interests of Abbey National and all other creditors who had an interest in the cash collateral were adequately protected by the order, and that entry of the order was in the best interests of the estate and creditors of the estate. Accordingly, the Court entered the order tendered by Debtor, the relevant provisions of which are summarized below:

1. Recognition that there is a dispute between Debtor and the secured lenders of Sales Finance and Steel Products as to whether the transactions between Debtor and those entities were true sales or disguised financing vehicles;

2. An order requiring the secured lenders to turn over to Debtor the cash proceeds of the inventory and receivables which are to be used to provide working capital for Debtor;

3. Recognition that in the event the Court determines these transactions to be true sales, the secured lenders whose cash collateral was used will be entitled to administrative expense claims against the estate;

4. Adequate protection was provided to the secured lenders in the form of senior liens on the inventory and receivables and weekly interest payments to the lenders at pre-petition non-default rates.

It is this order that Abbey National seeks to modify. Specifically, Abbey National asks the Court to modify the interim cash collateral order *nunc pro tunc* to include the following provisions:

a. The Debtors shall transfer to Sales Finance all receivables created on or after December 29, 2000 and not previously sold to Sales Finance and that would have been sold to Sales Finance were it not for the occurrence of a Liquidation Event;

b. Steel Products would continue to purchase Inventory from the Inventory Sellers and Sales Finance would continue to purchase Receivables from the Receivables Sellers, each on the same basis and on the same terms as existed prior to the Petition Date;

c. The respective Collection Accounts would be administered by the Collateral Agent in the same manner as was administered prior to the Petition Date. Therefore, notwithstanding the occurrence of any Termination Date, collection on account of the Receivables would not be required to be applied to principal payments or amortization payments (other than any payments required in connection with the maintenance by the borrowers of their respective borrowing bases);

d. Steel Products and the Collateral Agent under the Inventory Facility would continue to automatically release all liens against the Receivables purchased by Sales Finance from Steel Products;

e. All minimum borrowing base and collateral value requirements set forth in the Receivables Facility and the Inventory Facility will continue in full force and effect;

f. In all other respects, the Receivables Facility and the Inventory Facility will continue to operate as required after the occurrence of a Liquidation Event including without limitation, the reimbursement of all expenses of each Receivables Lender and Inventory Lender. (Abbey National's Emergency Motion to Modify Interim Order at 14–16).

Abbey National argues that the interim cash collateral order should be modified because: 1) it did not receive effective notice of the December 29, 2000 hearing and was thus denied due process of law; 2) there is no basis for the Court to determine that the receivables which are Abbey National's collateral are property of Debtor's estate and 3) that even if the receivables are property of Debtor's estate, that Abbey National's interests are not adequately protected because the pre-petition receivables are diminishing at a rapid rate and will soon be depleted. Debtor argues that Abbey National did receive notice of the December 29 hearing, that Abbey National has failed to state grounds to modify the interim order pursuant to Fed. R. Bankr. P. 9024, and that Abbey National's interests in the receivables are adequately protected.

B. Issue

There are four issues before the Court. These are: 1) the procedural basis for Abbey National's motion; 2) whether the circumstances surrounding the December 29, 2000 hearing deprived Abbey National of its right to due process; 3) whether the interim order should be modified because the cash collateral was not property of Debtor's estate; and 4) whether the interim order failed to adequately protect Abbey National's interest in the collateral.

C. Analysis

1. Procedural Basis for Abbey National's Motion

As a preliminary matter, the Court must address the procedural basis for Abbey National's motion. Abbey National has not cited a single rule of civil or bankruptcy procedure in support of its motion. Debtor contends that because Abbey National's motion seeks to modify a previous order of the Court, it must be construed as a motion for relief from judgment pursuant to Fed. R. Civ. P. 60(b), made applicable to this proceeding pursuant to Fed. R. Bankr. P. 9024. Abbey National has not responded to this contention. Because it is clear that Abbey National is seeking relief from the Court's interim order, we shall treat Abbey National's motion as a motion brought under Rule 60(b).

The decision to grant a motion for relief under Rule 60(b) lies within the Court's discretion. Miller v. Owsianowski (In re Salem Mortgage Co.), 791 F.2d 456, 459 (6th Cir.1986). A Rule 60(b) motion may be granted for the following reasons:

> (1) mistake, inadvertence, surprise, or excusable neglect; (2) newly discovered evidence ... (3) fraud (whether heretofore denominated intrinsic or extrinsic), misrepresentation, or other misconduct of an adverse party; (4) the judgment is void; (5) the judgment has been satisfied, released, or discharged ... or (6) any other reason justifying relief from the operation of the judgment. Fed. R. Civ. P. 60(b).

Because Abbey National has not presented its arguments in conformity with Rule 60(b), we shall address Abbey National's arguments in relation to the subsections of Rule 60(b) that appear to coincide with those arguments. We can safely say at the outset that Abbey National has not raised any argument relating to newly discovered evidence or the satisfaction of a judgment and thus we will not consider those elements of Rule 60(b).

2. Due Process

* * *

Based upon this analysis, the Court concludes that the circumstances surrounding the hearing of December 29, 2000 provided Abbey National with sufficient due process.

* * *

3. Whether the Receivables are Property of Debtor's Estate

Abbey National's next argument is that the receivables which constitute its collateral are not property of Debtor's estate, and thus this Court lacked jurisdiction to enter the interim order. We shall construe this as an argument that the interim order is void pursuant to Rule 60(b)(4).

Section 541(a) of the Bankruptcy Code provides that upon the filing of a bankruptcy petition an estate is created consisting of "all legal or equitable interests of the debtor in property as of the commencement of the case." 11 U.S.C. § 541(a)(1). The estate created by the filing of a Chapter 11 petition is very broad, and property may be included in Debtor's estate even if Debtor does not have a possessory interest in that property. United States v. Whiting Pools, Inc., 462 U.S. 198, 204, 205–06, 103 S.Ct. 2309, 2313–14, 76 L.Ed.2d 515 (1983).

Abbey National contends that the interim order is flawed because, on its face, the transaction between Debtor and Sales Finance is characterized as a true sale. Therefore, Abbey National argues, since Debtor sold its interests in the receivables to Sales Finance, Debtor no longer has an interest in the receivables and they are not property of the estate. However, Abbey National has admitted to the Court, both in its pleadings and in oral argument, that the ultimate issue of whether Debtor actually sold the receivables to Sales Finance is a fact-intensive issue that cannot be resolved without extensive discovery and an evidentiary hearing.

We find Abbey National's argument for "emergency" relief to be not well taken for several reasons. First, Abbey National's position in this regard is circular: we cannot permit Debtor to use cash collateral because it is not property of the estate, but we cannot determine if it is property of the estate until we hold an evidentiary hearing. We fail to see how we can conclude that the receivables are not property of Debtor's estate until an evidentiary hearing on that issue has been held. Because the determination of this issue must await further discovery, we decline to grant Abbey National relief from the interim order.

Furthermore, there seems to be an element of sophistry to suggest that Debtor does not retain at least an equitable interest in the property that is subject to the interim order. Debtor's business requires it to purchase, melt, mold and cast various metal products. To suggest that Debtor lacks some ownership interest in products that it creates with its own labor, as well as the proceeds to be derived from that labor, is difficult to accept. Accordingly, the Court concludes that Debtor has at least some equitable interest in the inventory and receivables, and that this interest is property of the Debtor's estate. This equitable interest is sufficient to support the entry of the interim cash collateral order.

Finally, it is readily apparent that granting Abbey National relief from the interim cash collateral order would be highly inequitable. The Court is satisfied that the entry of the interim order was necessary to enable Debtor to keep its doors open and continue to meet its obligations to its employees, retirees, customers and creditors. Allowing Abbey National to modify the order would allow Abbey National to enforce its state law rights as a secured lender to look to the collateral in satisfaction of this debt. This circumstance would put an immediate end to Debtor's business, would put thousands of people out of work, would deprive 100,000 retirees of needed medical benefits, and would have more far reaching economic effects on the geographic areas where Debtor does business. However, maintaining the current status quo permits Debtor to remain in business while it searches for substitute financing, and adequately protects and preserves Abbey National's rights. The equities of this situation highly favor Debtor. As a result, the Court declines to exercise its discretion to modify the interim order pursuant to Rule 60(b)(4).

4. Adequate Protection

The final argument Abbey National has raised in support of its motion is that its interests in the collateral are not adequately protected.

Specifically, Abbey National contends that the pre-petition receivables in which Abbey National has an interest are being depleted at a rate of Ten Million Dollars ($10,000,000.00) per day, and that the receivables will be entirely consumed in short order. Additionally, Abbey National asserts that the interim order diminished the value of Abbey National's liens. We shall treat this line of argument as one arising under Rule 60(b)(6).

Abbey National's contentions that its interest is not adequately protected can be boiled down to a simple issue. Prior to the filing of Debtor's petition, the outstanding balance on Abbey National's loan to Sales Finance was approximately Two Hundred Twenty–Four Million Eight Hundred Thousand Dollars ($224,800,000.00). This loan to Sales Finance was secured by the receivables transferred to Sales Finance, and this financing arrangement was rated AAA by Standard & Poors. However, the terms of the interim order have altered the nature of Abbey National's liens. Under the terms of the interim order, Abbey National and the other secured lenders have been granted liens on Debtor's post-petition inventory and receivables. Abbey National's loan is thus now secured by inventory and assets which do not have a AAA rating, and Abbey National must now share its liens with Debtor's other secured lenders.

We find Abbey National's arguments to be not well taken. First, we find Abbey National's contention that its collateral is being consumed at a rate of Ten Million Dollars ($10,000,000.00) per day to be disingenuous. It is true that the pre-petition receivables are being used by Debtor to purchase and manufacture more steel. However, Debtor's use of the pre-petition receivables will inevitably lead to an increase in the value of post-petition receivables and inventory, in which Abbey National has a security interest.

This conclusion is amply supported by the affidavit of John T. Delmore, Debtor's Assistant Controller. Mr. Delmore's affidavit indicates that as of January 15, 2001, there was a sufficient equity cushion in both post-petition inventory and receivables to provide adequate protection to all of Debtor's secured lenders. The amount of the respective equity cushions equaled 39% for the receivables lenders and 179% for the inventory lenders. Furthermore, it appears that Debtor's business will continue to generate additional post-petition receivables and inventory sufficient to protect Abbey National's interest in the near future. Because we find that Abbey National's interest in cash collateral is adequately protected by an equity cushion and by the other terms of the interim order, the Court declines to exercise its discretion to modify the interim order pursuant to Rule 60(b)(6).

CONCLUSION

For the reasons stated above, the Court concludes that Abbey National's motion seeking to modify the Court's interim order permitting the use of cash collateral on December 29, 2000 is properly characterized as a motion seeking relief from judgment pursuant to Fed. R. Civ.

P. 60(b). Furthermore, the Court finds that Abbey National has failed to establish that modification of the interim order is warranted. Accordingly, Abbey National's emergency motion is overruled.

An appropriate order shall enter.

EXCERPT FROM OCTAGON GAS SYSTEMS, INC. v. RIMMER

United States Court of Appeals, Tenth Circuit, 1993.
995 F.2d 948.

* * * Finally, acceptance of Rimmer's transfer of ownership or title argument would allow an account buyer to benefit unfairly, at the expense of the bankrupt debtor's other creditors, from the debtor's filing for bankruptcy. For example, it is beyond dispute that, outside the realm of bankruptcy, a lien creditor would have rights in the accounts superior to the rights of the unperfected buyer of the accounts. See Okla.Stat. Ann. tit. 12A, § 9–301 & § 9–312 (West Supp.1993). However, under Rimmer's theory, once the debtor declares bankruptcy, the fact of bankruptcy alone places the accounts sold to the unperfected account buyer beyond the reach of the bankruptcy trustee and all of the bankrupt's creditors. This result is contrary to the similar aims of Article 9 and the Bankruptcy Code. The current Bankruptcy Code was designed, in part, to make bankruptcy law more congruent with the UCC In Re Antweil, 931 F.2d 689, 693 (10th Cir.1991), aff'd sub nom. Barnhill v. Johnson, 503 U.S. 393, 112 S.Ct. 1386, 118 L.Ed.2d 39 (1992). The policy behind Article 9 is to ensure certainty for creditors and provide notice of security interests to third parties. See Okla.Stat.Ann. tit. 12A, § 9–101 (West 1963) (Official Comment). Likewise, certain provisions of the Bankruptcy Code "are designed to protect creditors by eliminating secret liens." In Re Reliance, 966 F.2d at 1344 (citing 11 U.S.C. §§ 544, 546). In keeping with these policies, we hold that because, under Article 9, a sale of accounts is treated as if it creates a security interest in the accounts, accounts sold by a debtor prior to filing for bankruptcy remain property of the debtor's bankruptcy estate.

Accordingly, we hold that the bankruptcy court erred in concluding that Article 9 was inapplicable to Rimmer's interest. The bankruptcy court must therefore readdress, in light of Article 9, the central issue of whether the reorganization plan effectuated a transfer of Rimmer's interest to Octagon, or whether Rimmer's interest survives the Plan. The court must make findings regarding whether Rimmer's account was a perfected security interest—i.e., whether UCC filings were required or made. The court must also determine the effect, if any, of the trustee's actions concerning Rimmer's account, and the effect, if any, of Rimmer's actions. For these reasons, we REVERSE the entry of summary judgment in favor of Rimmer and REMAND to the district court with instructions to vacate its judgment and remand the case to the bankruptcy court for further proceedings consistent with this opinion.

[Dissenting opinion of Judge Seth omitted.]

PEB COMMENTARY NO. 14

SECTION 9–102(1)(b).

ISSUE

Does the application of Article 9 to the sale of accounts and chattel paper prevent the transfer of ownership of accounts or chattel paper?

DISCUSSION

Section 9–102(1)(b) provides, subject to certain exceptions, that Article 9 applies "to any sale of accounts or chattel paper." Comment 2 to § 9–102 explains that "a sale of [accounts or chattel paper is] covered by subsection (1)(b) whether intended for security or not * * *. The buyer then is treated as a secured party, and his interest as a security interest." This Commentary examines whether that application means that ownership of receivables may not be transferred or that a buyer's interest in receivables is limited to one of security.

It is a fundamental principle of law that an owner of property may transfer ownership to another person. Were a statute intended to take away that right, it would do so explicitly and such a significant curtailment of rights would be supported by substantial reason. No such reason is expressed or implied in the Code or the Official Comments. Indeed, the sale of receivables long antedates adoption of the Code, and it cannot be supposed that either the drafters of the Code or the legislatures that enacted it intended to work so drastic a change in existing law without clearly saying so. Moreover, a close reading of the text of Article 9 and its Comments, particularly in the context of the pre-Code history, compels the conclusion that Article 9 does not prevent the transfer of ownership

Article 9 contemplates that sales of receivables may exist, and that the consequences of a sale differ from those of a transfer for security. For example, § 9–502(2) recognizes a distinction in the consequences under Article 9 between sales of receivables and transactions secured by receivables. It provides that, "[i]f the security agreement secures an indebtedness, the secured party must account to the debtor for any surplus * * *. But, if the underlying transaction was a sale of accounts or chattel paper, the debtor [as seller of the receivables] is entitled to any surplus [from collections of the sold receivables] * * * only if the security agreement so provides." (Emphasis added.) Section 9–504(2) has virtually identical language. Furthermore, Comment 4 to § 9–502, after acknowledging that "there may be a true sale of accounts or chattel paper," clarifies that "[t]he determination whether a particular assignment constitutes a sale or a transfer for security is left to the courts."

Why, then, was Article 9 made "applicable" to the sale of receivables? The introductory Comment and Comment 2 to § 9–102 explain that Article 9 applies to both sales and security transfers of receivables to avoid the need to distinguish between such transfers for Article 9 purposes: [C]ertain sales of accounts and chattel paper are brought within this Article [9] to avoid difficult problems of distinguishing

between transactions intended for security and those not so intended.
* * *

2.   * * *

Commercial financing on the basis of accounts and chattel paper is often so conducted that the distinction between a security transfer and a sale is blurred, and a sale of such property is therefore covered by subsection (1)(b) whether intended for security or not. . . .

The reason for subjecting both sales and secured transactions to Article 9 was to inform third parties of existing interests in a debtor's receivables and to provide protection for all types of assignments of receivables:

> There was an obvious reason for the inclusion of sales: it was necessary to protect [transferees] not only [in] straight accounts receivable financing but also [in] arrangements of the factoring type. [Emphasis added.] Article 9 merely follows the pre-Code accounts receivable statutes [covering sales of accounts and chattel paper as well as security transfers].

This is not to say, however, that Article 9 has no impact upon a buyer's ownership rights regarding the purchased receivables. For example, a failure to perfect as required by Article 9 may leave the transferee's ownership of the receivables subject to the claims of third parties, such as the seller's lien creditors or trustee in bankruptcy. This perfection requirement, however, does not by its terms or by implication affect the transfer of ownership as between the seller and buyer.

At least two Circuit Court opinions interpret the Code consistently with this Commentary. In Major's Furniture Mart v. Castle Credit Corp., the Third Circuit considered whether a transfer of a company's receivables should be construed as a sale or a secured loan. By considering that question, the court started from the premise that a transaction that Article 9 calls a security interest could nonetheless be a sale. If the transaction was a sale, the transferee would be entitled to surplus collections of the receivables. If the transaction was only for security, then the transferor would be entitled to the surplus collections. The court followed Comment 4 to 9–502 and looked to non-UCC law to determine whether the transaction was a sale.

In the case of In re Contractors Equipment Supply Co., the Ninth Circuit affirmed a lower court decision by looking to non-UCC law to determine that the transfer of receivables in question was a loan. The court stated that had there been a sale, the transferor would not be entitled to any surplus because "[a] sale entails the passage of title."

In Octagon Gas Systems, Inc. v. Rimmer, however, the Tenth Circuit, after stating that a purchased royalty interest in a natural gas system was an account, erroneously stated that "[t]he impact of applying Article 9 to [the buyer's] account is that Article 9's treatment of accounts sold as collateral would place [the buyer's] account within the property of [the seller's] bankruptcy estate." The court reached this determination despite the transfer of the royalty interest purporting to be an outright sale of all the seller's interest. To the extent the court relied on Article 9 in reaching its determination, this Commentary adopts a contrary position.

CONCLUSION

Article 9's application to sales of receivables does not prevent the transfer of ownership. Official Comment 2 to 9–102 therefore is amended by adding the following paragraph:

> Neither Section 9–102 nor any other provision of Article 9 is intended to prevent the transfer of ownership of accounts or chattel paper. The determination of whether a particular transfer of accounts or chattel paper constitutes a sale or a transfer for security purposes (such as in connection with a loan) is not governed by Article 9. Article 9 applies both to sales of accounts or chattel paper and loans secured by accounts or chattel paper primarily to incorporate Article 9's perfection rules. The use of terminology such as "security interest" to include the interest of a buyer of accounts or chattel paper, "secured party" to include a buyer of accounts or chattel paper, "debtor" to include a seller of accounts or chattel paper, and "collateral" to include accounts or chattel paper that have been sold is intended solely as a drafting technique to achieve this end and is not relevant to the sale or secured transaction determination. * * *

§ 4. ACCOUNTS, MONEY EARNED AND TO BE EARNED BY THE SALE OF GOODS AND THE PERFORMANCE OF SERVICES

There is another universe of "accounts" that is almost completely separate from the one described above. This is the universe composed of construction contracts, defense production contracts, and the like. Here the buyer (often a state or local government, or a federal governmental agency, such as the Department of Defense) has an obligation to pay the debtor, a construction company building a road or an airport, or a manufacturing company making aircraft, ammunition or missiles. Under the 1962 Code these rights were not "accounts" but "contract rights" because the payments had not yet been earned by performance. Later versions of Article 9 made contract rights a subclass of "accounts".

Notwithstanding that definitional change it is a mistake to think of the two kinds of accounts as the same. In many ways the rights to payment under the construction and manufacturing contracts are far more precarious than rights to payment under conventional consumer or business accounts. Moreover, the competitors of the secured creditor are likely to be different persons and the threats to the security come from different directions in the two settings.

Note the first significant difference between the two universes. In regard to conventional business accounts, the seller has completed its performance by delivering the goods to the buyer. But where the loan is made to a debtor construction company, the debtor may not have poured even the first yard of concrete. Months or even years of work may yet need to be done. Those months and years of work before payment carry with them daily opportunities for the construction company to default and for the state or governmental agency's assertion of a defense because of that default. Section 9–404(a)(1) tells that such defenses can normally be asserted (when they arise out of the same contract) by the account debtor not only against the debtor (construction company) but also against the bank that has taken a security interest in the right to payment. For that reason alone, the bank's right in these contract claims is more precarious than a similar right in a set of payments arising from completed sales.

A second characteristic of the latter universe is that the secured creditor has all or most of its eggs in one basket. If a contractor who has agreed to pave two runways defaults, all payments will stop. In classic accounts this ending will not occur. Even if the debtor has delivered shoddy goods in a number of transactions, the large numbers may protect the secured creditor and even a significant number of returns by buyers will not wipe out the security.

A final difficulty relates to bonding companies. With rare exceptions those who manufacture goods for the federal government and those who enter into construction contracts for state, local, or federal governments, must provide bonds to assure their performance and assure payment to those who deal with them (subcontractors). Bonding companies are contingent creditors and when they become actual creditors (upon default of the contractor and payment or performance by the bonding company) they are certain to compete with the bank for any payments owed to the debtor under the broken contract. As the following case will disclose, these companies typically assert rights outside of Article 9 and their rights are often recognized as superior to a banks' Article 9 rights.

There are two types of bonds protecting different interests. The "payment" bond protects the owner from mechanic's liens and the like by assuring that laborers, subcontractors, and materialmen who contribute work and materials to the job will be paid. The "performance" bond assures that the bonding company will hire replacements to complete performance if the original contractor defaults.

The principal claim of the bonding companies will be subrogation. They will claim this equitable right to money to be paid for performance after default and for money already earned at the time of default that has been held back under the terms of the contract. This latter money is sometimes called a "retainage"; it commonly equals ten to fifteen percent of each payment. That is to say, the owner will pay only 85 to 90 percent of the amount due as progress payments at the time of performance and will hold back ten to fifteen percent against the possibility that performance has not been done properly and against the possibility that remaining performance will not be done properly. Although the bonding companies sometimes take assignments from their debtors, usually these companies do not assert claims as assignees or as secured creditors. Frequently a bank or other lender will already have filed a financing statement in the contractor's name before any bond is issued and a later bonding company would be subordinated to that claim in an Article 9 contest. On the other hand, bonding companies frequently win on the equitable battlefield.

To whom are the bonding companies subrogated? (To be "subrogated" to someone is to stand in another's shoes and assert that person's rights.) It depends. To the extent they pay materialmen, subcontractors, and such under their "payment" bond, they are subrogated to the rights of those persons. To the extent those persons held mechanics' liens or other priority claims, they might well have priority over everyone on the job. Obviously the bonding company will also have a right to assert the claims of the defaulted contractor, but—at least against a secured creditor—those claims would seem to do little or no good because, by hypothesis, the contractor has agreed to make payment to the secured creditor and has granted it security. The bonding company may also be subrogated to the rights of the owner (the state, local, or federal government). If that party would have the right to set off vis-à-vis the bank under section 9–404, then the bonding company would too.

The bonding companies have frequently described themselves as purchase money lenders. They, so they argue, advance money so the project can be completed. Without their money the project would not be completed and—so the argument goes—there would be no asset or security for anyone. Thus, they claim the status of purchase money lenders who routinely enjoy priority over prior persons. The purchase money analogy goes only so far. The bank can also claim to be a purchase money lender, for if it had not advanced money, the first mile of concrete would not have been laid and to the extent the retainage has been earned by the laying of that mile of concrete, the bank will argue that it is entitled to the retainage over the rights of the bonding company. The following case traces the history of this continuing dispute. Its outcome is representative.

TRANSAMERICA INSURANCE CO. v. BARNETT BANK OF MARION COUNTY

Supreme Court of Florida, 1989.
540 So.2d 113.

SHAW, JUSTICE:

* * * Petitioner surety and Turner Construction, Inc., entered into an agreement whereby petitioner would provide surety bonds for construction projects which Turner contracted to perform for various government bodies. As required by section 255.05, Florida Statutes (1983),[1] Turner obtained payment and performance bonds for the benefit of each

---

1. All statutory references are to Florida Statutes (1983).

government body and for subcontractors and other persons supplying labor, material, and services in the construction projects. An indemnity agreement assigned accounts receivable to petitioner should Turner default. By its terms, the indemnity agreement constituted a security agreement without abrogating, restricting, or limiting the rights of petitioner under the agreement, under law, or in equity. Turner obtained a series of loans from respondent bank to finance its operations, in return for which Turner gave the bank a security interest in accounts receivable from the construction contracts. The bank's security interest was filed under the Uniform Commercial Code prior to the filing of petitioner's security interest.

Construction contracts customarily provide for progress payments to be made to contractors by the owner as construction proceeds. Two safeguards have been devised to protect owners against default by the contractor, both of which are involved here. The first is a contractual provision under which the owner retains a percentage of the progress payments for the purpose of curing or mitigating subsequent contractor default. The retainage is paid to the contractor upon satisfactory performance and/or payment, but neither the contractor nor its assignees or creditors have any claim on the funds until the contractor performs. The second safeguard is a requirement that the contractor obtain payment and performance surety bonds. Because of their importance, payment and performance bonds are mandatory under section 255.05 for government projects and are commonly employed by prudent private owners.

This case comes to us from a partial summary judgment which was affirmed in the district court. The trial court ruled that the bank's prior perfection of its security interests in Turner's accounts receivable from the construction contracts gave it priority over the claims of the surety based on equitable subrogation. The trial court order noted that it did "not operate as a determination that Turner was in fact owed any monies as a result of accounts receivable or funds earned but unpaid." Consistent with this disclaimer, it also appears that the trial court treated petitioner's equitable subrogation rights as if these rights arose solely from standing in the shoes of the contractor Turner[2] and not from standing in the shoes of the owner/obligee and laborers and materialmen involved in the construction projects. The district court adopted a similar analytical approach in its affirmance by rejecting what it called the "federal view" that sureties had priority by virtue of equitable subrogation arising from owner/obligees, laborers, and materialmen. Accordingly, the district court held: (1) the surety's assignment was a security interest subject to the filing and perfection requirements of the UCC; (2) there is no good faith exception to UCC filing requirements and it

---

2. The trial court order recites "the equitable principle involved is that when one [the surety], pursuant to obligation, not a volunteer, fulfills the duties of another [the contractor], he is entitled to assert the rights of that other against third persons." The order also recites: "Based upon its pri- or compliance with the Florida Uniform Commercial Code, BARNETT has a superior claim to all accounts receivable and contract rights of *TURNER* which were earned or vested, but unpaid, as of the moment of the default by TURNER under any job or contract." (Emphasis added.)

matters not whether the secured party who first perfects its interest knows of any other prior interests; and (3) the remedy of equitable subrogation is not available to a surety because of the filing requirements of the UCC.

The initial question is whether a surety's equitable subrogation rights are limited to rights it obtains by standing in the shoes of the defaulting contractor. On this point we agree with the court in *National Shawmut Bank v. New Amsterdam Casualty Co.,* 411 F.2d 843, 844–45 (1st Cir.1969).

> [T]here is confusion because the tendency is to think of the surety on Miller Act payment and performance bonds as standing in the shoes only of the entity it "insures", the contractor. So long as this one-dimensional concept prevails, logic compels the surety to be assessed as merely one of the contractor's creditors, and to be subject to the system of priorities rationalized by the Uniform Commercial Code. But the surety in cases like this undertakes duties which entitle it to step into three sets of shoes. When, on default of the contractor, it pays all the bills of the job to date and completes the job, it stands in the shoes of the contractor insofar as there are receivables due it; in the shoes of laborers and material men who have been paid by the surety—who may have had liens; and, not least, in the shoes of the government, for whom the job was completed.

The narrow view that a surety acts only for the contractor (principal) is inconsistent with the purpose of a surety bond: to protect the obligees. A surety who performs or pays on behalf of an obligee steps into the shoes of the obligee to the extent of performance or payment.

> Traditionally sureties compelled to pay debts for their principal have been deemed entitled to reimbursement, even without a contractual promise such as the surety here had. And probably there are few doctrines better established than that a surety who pays the debt of another is entitled to all the rights of the person he paid to enforce his right to be reimbursed.

Pearlman v. Reliance Ins. Co., 371 U.S. 132, 136–37, 83 S.Ct. 232, 235, 9 L.Ed.2d 190 (1962) (footnote omitted). These rights of the surety as subrogee are not inferior even to the rights of the obligee and may be asserted against the obligee. *Trinity Universal Ins. Co. v. United States,* 382 F.2d 317 (5th Cir.1967).

The district court held that the surety's assignment was a security interest under the UCC. We disagree for two reasons. First, the UCC itself suggests that a surety's assignment from a contractor, should be excluded from the UCC. Section 679.104(6) excludes a transfer of a right to payment under a contract to an assignee who is also to do the performance under the contract. A surety's assignment is contingent on performance by the surety in the event the contractor defaults. This contingent assignment based on contractual performance contrasts sharply with the non-contingent assignment to a financier which does not call for performance and which is uncontrovertably a security interest. In this connection, we note that a draft provision of the UCC which would have specifically subordinated a surety's assignment to a later perfected security interest was specifically rejected by the Editorial Board which drafted the UCC. *See In re J.V. Gleason Co.,* 452 F.2d 1219, 1221 nn. 5–6 (8th Cir.1971), and *National Shawmut Bank,* 411 F.2d at 846 n. 4. Contrary to the district court below, we see this rejection as evidence that the drafters of UCC did not intend to upset the well-established rules governing the priority of a surety assignment. Respondent is attempting to obtain through court-made law what it and others similarly situated were unable to obtain in the drafting and adoption of the UCC. Second, even if we were to assume that a surety's assignment was a security interest, it does not follow that this would abrogate petitioner surety's rights under the doctrine of equitable subrogation. A security interest and equitable subrogation are not incompatible, indeed the surety contract here contained a provision that the assignments therein of a security agreement did not abrogate the surety's right to protect itself under other theories. This contractual provision is consistent with section 671.103 which provides that general principles of law and equity are applicable unless displaced by particular provisions of the UCC. Equitable subrogation arises from law, not from the provisions of a contract.

The district court acknowledged that statutes requiring filing or recording to give notice usually contain a "good faith" limitation. Nevertheless,

> [a]lthough, admittedly, it is not conclusively clear, it appears to us from the drafting history of UCC section 9–312(5) (Section 679.312(5), Fla.Stat.), that a "good faith" limitation was intentionally omitted from the UCC provision and, therefore, none should be implied by the courts.

Transamerica, 524 So.2d at 445. Although the point is not critical here, we note that section 671.203 imposes an obligation of good faith on performance or enforcement of every contract or duty within the UCC.

On the overall question of subrogation, the district court concluded that equitable subrogation was not available to a surety in Florida because sureties have ample opportunities to make contractual subrogation agreements with contractors, other contractor assignees, and with surety obligees and to file these assignments (security interests) under the UCC. As is obvious from our disposition of the other points above, we do not agree. Nonsurety assignees of a contractor in default have no enforceable claim on funds withheld by the owner/obligee because of contractor default. The interests of all concerned parties, whether they be contractors in default, nonsurety assignees, owners, or other obligees, are best served by prompt performance by the surety. Under these circumstances, it is appropriate to give priority to the claims of the surety, up to the limits of its performance. Section 671.102 provides that the code will be liberally construed and applied to promote its underlying purposes and policies, one of which is to make uniform the law among various jurisdictions. As Chief Judge Sharp pointed out in her dissent below,

> the overwhelming and essentially unanimous post-UCC decisions in this country, federal as well as state courts, have held that (1) the surety's equitable right of subrogation is not a consensual security interest, (2) no UCC filing is necessary to perfect the surety's interest, and (3) the surety's interest continues to be, as it was under pre-Code law, superior to the claim of a contract assignee, such as a bank.

White & Summers, Uniform Commercial Code section 22–5 (2d ed. 1980). Adopting the position of the district court would frustrate uniformity and create conflict in the application of UCC. This conflict of law would also exist in bankruptcy cases where equitable subrogation is recognized. *Pearlman; In re J.V. Gleason Co.; McAtee v. United States Fidelity & Guar. Co.*, 401 F.Supp. 11 (N.D.Fla.1975).

Petitioner also argues that its equitable subrogation rights to priority over the bank in individual contracts combine with common law setoff to give it priority over any excess construction funds from other contracts. We disagree for the reasons stated in Judge Sharp's dissent below. Priority based on equitable subrogation in one contract does not provide priority in excess funds from another contract. This does not mean, however, that an owner cannot prioritize its own common law right of setoff.

We quash the decision below and remand for further proceedings consistent with this decision.

It is so ordered.

EHRLICH, C.J., and OVERTON, McDONALD, BARKETT and KOGAN, JJ., concur. GRIMES, J., did not participate in this case.

§ 5. COLLECTION RIGHTS

The beauty of receivables is that they turn into money even if the secured creditor takes no action. In the case of "notification" lending, where the secured party has notified the account debtors and the account debtors are making payment directly to the secured party, it is possible that default by the debtor will make not a ripple, for, by hypothesis, the account debtors will continue to make payments as they have and those payments will go to reduce the recourse or non-recourse loan that the creditor has made to the debtor. In modern practice notification is unusual; in many cases the debtor, as agent of the buyer, will continue to collect payments from the account debtor after it has sold the rights. Even if it is merely the agent for the secured creditor, in practice it will have the power to control the payments, perhaps even to assert the rights suggested in problem 3–5 above where the debtor in possession asserted the rights to hold the payments for a period of time and to use that money in the bankruptcy estate.

Section 9–607 gives the secured creditor the right to notify the account debtors and to collect those payments on default and to go against the account debtors if necessary. It reads in full as follows:

(a) [Collection and enforcement generally.] If so agreed, and in any event after default, a secured party:

(1) may notify an account debtor or other person obligated on collateral to make payment or otherwise render performance to or for the benefit of the secured party;

(2) may take any proceeds to which the secured party is entitled under 9–315;

(3) may enforce the obligations of an account debtor or other person obligated on collateral and exercise the rights of the debtor with respect to the obligation of the account debtor or other person obligated on collateral to make payment or otherwise render performance to the debtor, and with respect to any property that secures the obligations of the account debtor or other person obligated on the collateral;

(4) if it holds a security interest in a deposit account perfected by control under Section 9–104(a)(1), may apply the balance of the deposit account to the obligation secured by the deposit account; and

(5) if it holds a security interest in a deposit account perfected by control under Section 9–104(a)(2) or (3), may instruct the bank to pay the balance of the deposit account to or for the benefit of the secured party.

(b) [Nonjudicial enforcement of mortgage.] If necessary to enable a secured party to exercise under subsection (a)(3) the right of a debtor to enforce a mortgage nonjudicially, the secured party may record in the office in which a record of the mortgage is recorded:

(1) a copy of the security agreement that creates or provides for a security interest in the obligation secured by the mortgage; and

(2) the secured party's sworn affidavit in recordable form stating that:

(A) a default has occurred; and

(B) the secured party is entitled to enforce the mortgage nonjudicially.

(c) [Commercially reasonable collection and enforcement.] A secured party shall proceed in a commercially reasonable manner if the secured party:

(1) undertakes to collect from or enforce an obligation of an account debtor or other person obligated on collateral; and

(2) is entitled to charge back uncollected collateral or otherwise to full or limited recourse against the debtor or a secondary obligor.

(d) [Expenses of collection and enforcement.] A secured party may deduct from the collections made pursuant to subsection (c) reasonable expenses of collection and enforcement, including reasonable attorney's fees and legal expenses incurred by the secured party.

(e) [Duties to secured party not affected.] This section does not determine whether an account debtor, bank, or other person obligated on collateral owes a duty to a secured party.

Problem 3–6

1. Assume the state of Florida enters into a $20 million contract with Contractor to construct a highway. Contractor grants a security interest in its right to payment to Bank. Ultimately Contractor breaches the contract and the state of Florida refuses to pay under 9–404. Clearly Bank loses. Would the outcome be different if the state of Florida refused to pay not because of the breach of the highway construction contract but because it had recently discovered defective performance in an earlier contract and suffered $2 million of damages on that contract which it now proposes to set off against its obligation to pay on the second contract that has been assigned to the Bank. To answer that question, what do you need to know under 9–404(a)(2)?

2. Assume General Motors Corporation owes $100,000 to Missouri Car Dealer for bonuses and other payments on cars that Dealer has sold and that GMAC, a General Motors subsidiary, owns Dealer's premises and has leased those premises to Dealer. Dealer is now in bankruptcy and is behind approximately $20,000 on its rent to GMAC. The contract between General Motors and Dealer provides that General Motors may set off against the amount Dealer owes to it (General Motors) or to any of its subsidiaries. Bank has taken a security interest from Dealer in the payments owed by General Motors to Dealer. When Dealer defaults and goes into bankruptcy, Bank claims a first right on the $100,000 due from General Motors. General Motors claims the right to set off. What are the best arguments for each?

Problem 3–7

Trust buys $100 million of Debtor's credit card accounts but allows debtor to continue to collect the receivables. Trust properly perfects by filing. When Debtor (seller) files in Chapter 11, it holds back three months of payments and threatens to hold back even more.

The investors' committee (composed of the largest buyers of these receivables) now threatens to sue the Trustee, the Trust's legal counsel and the Trust's advisor, Merrill Lynch.

The committee claims:

1. The defendants should have procured promises from Debtor that it would not take bankruptcy.

2. The defendants should not have allowed the debtor to continue collecting the receivables.

3. Upon the filing in Chapter 11, the defendants should have given the 9–607 notice at once and started direct collections.

How should the defendants respond?

Problem 3-8

If an assignee or buyer of receivables commences direct collection from account debtors, what duty does it owe debtor? If for example the assignee or buyer took $200,000 in settlement of $1 million face amount of accounts, does it have liability to debtor for making such a generous compromise? (Assume alternatively the assignment was with or without recourse.)

§ 6. SECURITY INTERESTS IN GENERAL INTANGIBLES—INTANGIBLE RIGHTS OTHER THAN RIGHTS TO PAYMENT

The most common general intangibles in which a creditor will take a security interest are copyrights, patents, and trademarks. The perfection of security interests in these forms of intellectual property is complicated by the presence of federal statutes governing each. These statutes seem to stand above and to displace, to varying degrees, the Article 9 system for the perfection of security interests in general intangibles. As a result, the current state of the law regarding security interests in copyrights, patents, and trademarks is unsettled. In particular, there is uncertainty as to where and how to file, what constitutes notice of a security interest, who has priority, and what collateral is covered by a security interest.

The primary issue surrounding security interests in copyrights, patents, and trademarks is whether such interests must be perfected by a filing in the appropriate state office, in the appropriate federal office, or both. In general, Article 9 governs perfection of all security interests regardless of the form of the transaction or the intent of the parties. Further, under Article 9, a security interest in "general intangibles," including copyrights, patents, and trademarks, must be perfected by filing a financing statement in the appropriate state office. But according to 9–109(c), Article 9 does not apply "to the extent that a statute, regulation, or treaty of the United States" preempts the Code. A prior version of the UCC Official Comments listed the Copyright Act as a prime example of a regulation that preempts the Code's filing requirements.

Copyrights

The Copyright Act has the most comprehensive scheme for recording of assignments of all the federal intellectual property statutes. Under section 101 of the Copyright Act a "transfer of copyright ownership" includes "assignment, mortgage, exclusive license, or any other conveyance, alienation, or hypothecation of a copyright."

IN RE PEREGRINE ENTERTAINMENT, LTD.

United States District Court, C.D. California, 1990.
116 B.R. 194.

KOZINSKI, CIRCUIT JUDGE:*

This appeal from a decision of the bankruptcy court raises an issue never before confronted by a federal court in a published opinion: Is a security interest in a copyright perfected by an appropriate filing with the United States Copyright Office or by a UCC–1 financing statement filed with the relevant secretary of state?

I

National Peregrine, Inc. (NPI) is a Chapter 11 debtor in possession whose principal assets are a library of copyrights, distribution rights and licenses to approximately 145 films, and accounts receivable arising from the licensing of these films to various programmers. NPI claims to have an outright assignment of some of the copyrights; as for the others, NPI claims it has an exclusive license to distribute in a certain territory, or for a certain period of time.

In June 1985, Capitol Federal Savings and Loan Association of Denver (Cap Fed) extended to American National Enterprises, Inc., NPI's predecessor by merger, a six million dollar line of credit secured by what is now NPI's film library. Both the security agreement and the UCC–1 financing statements filed by Cap Fed describe the collateral as "[a]ll inventory consisting of films and all accounts, contract rights, chattel paper, general intangibles, instruments, equipment, and documents related to such inventory, now owned or hereafter acquired by the Debtor." Although Cap Fed filed its UCC–1 financing statements in California, Colorado and Utah, it did not record its security interest in the United States Copyright Office.

NPI filed a voluntary petition for bankruptcy on January 30, 1989. On April 6, 1989, NPI filed an amended complaint against Cap Fed, contending that the bank's security interest in the copyrights to the films in NPI's library and in the accounts receivable generated by their distribution were unperfected because Cap Fed failed to record its security interest with the Copyright Office. NPI claimed that, as a debtor in possession, it had a judicial lien on all assets in the bankruptcy estate, including the copyrights and receivables. Armed with this lien, it sought to avoid, recover and preserve Cap Fed's supposedly unperfected security interest for the benefit of the estate.

The parties filed cross-motions for partial summary judgment on the question of whether Cap Fed had a valid security interest in the NPI film library. The bankruptcy court held for Cap Fed. See Memorandum of Decision re Motion for Partial Summary Adjudication (Nov. 14, 1989)

---

* Sitting by designation pursuant to 28 U.S.C. § 291(b) (1982).

[hereinafter "Memorandum of Decision"] and Order re Summary Adjudication of Issues (Dec. 18, 1989). NPI appeals.

II

A. WHERE TO FILE

The Copyright Act provides that "[a]ny transfer of copyright ownership or other document pertaining to a copyright" may be recorded in the United States Copyright Office. 17 U.S.C. § 205(a); see Copyright Office Circular 12: Recordation of Transfers and Other Documents (reprinted in 1 Copyright L.Rep. (CCH) ¶ 15,015) [hereinafter "Circular 12"]. A "transfer" under the Act includes any "mortgage" or "hypothecation of a copyright," whether "in whole or in part" and "by any means of conveyance or by operation of law." 17 U.S.C. §§ 101, 201(d)(1); see 3 Nimmer on Copyright § 10.05[A], at 10–43—10–45 (1989). The terms "mortgage" and "hypothecation" include a pledge of property as security or collateral for a debt. See Black's Law Dictionary 669 (5th ed. 1979). In addition, the Copyright Office has defined a "document pertaining to a copyright" as one that has a direct or indirect relationship to the existence, scope, duration, or identification of a copyright, or to the ownership, division, allocation, licensing, transfer, or exercise of rights under a copyright. That relationship may be past, present, future, or potential. 37 C.F.R. § 201.4(a)(2); see also Compendium of Copyright Office Practices II ¶¶ 1602–1603 (identifying which documents the Copyright Office will accept for filing).

It is clear from the preceding that an agreement granting a creditor a security interest in a copyright may be recorded in the Copyright Office. See G. Gilmore, Security Interests in Personal Property § 17.3, at 545 (1965). Likewise, because a copyright entitles the holder to receive all income derived from the display of the creative work, see 17 U.S.C. § 106, an agreement creating a security interest in the receivables generated by a copyright may also be recorded in the Copyright Office. Thus, Cap Fed's security interest could have been recorded in the Copyright Office; the parties seem to agree on this much. The question is, does the UCC provide a parallel method of perfecting a security interest in a copyright? One can answer this question by reference to either federal or state law; both inquiries lead to the same conclusion.

1. Even in the absence of express language, federal regulation will preempt state law if it is so pervasive as to indicate that "Congress left no room for supplementary state regulation," or if "the federal interest is so dominant that the federal system will be assumed to preclude enforcement of state laws on the same subject." Hillsborough County v. Automated Medical Laboratories, Inc., 471 U.S. 707, 713, 105 S.Ct. 2371, 2375, 85 L.Ed.2d 714 (1985) (internal quotations omitted). Here, the comprehensive scope of the federal Copyright Act's recording provisions, along with the unique federal interests they implicate, support the view that federal law preempts state methods of perfecting security interests in copyrights and related accounts receivable.

The federal copyright laws ensure "predictability and certainty of copyright ownership," "promote national uniformity" and "avoid the practical difficulties of determining and enforcing an author's rights under the differing laws and in the separate courts of the various States." Community for Creative Non–Violence v. Reid, 490 U.S. 730, 109 S.Ct. 2166, 2177, 104 L.Ed.2d 811 (1989); H.R.Rep. No. 1476, 94th Cong., 2d Sess. 129 (1976), U.S.Code Cong. & Admin.News 1976, p. 5659. As discussed above, section 205(a) of the Copyright Act establishes a uniform method for recording security interests in copyrights. A secured creditor need only file in the Copyright Office in order to give "all persons constructive notice of the facts stated in the recorded document." 17 U.S.C. § 205(c). Likewise, an interested third party need only search the indices maintained by the Copyright Office to determine whether a particular copyright is encumbered. See Northern Songs, Ltd. v. Distinguished Productions, Inc., 581 F.Supp. 638, 640–41 (S.D.N.Y. 1984); Circular 12, at 8035–4.

A recording system works by virtue of the fact that interested parties have a specific place to look in order to discover with certainty whether a particular interest has been transferred or encumbered. To the extent there are competing recordation schemes, this lessens the utility of each; when records are scattered in several filing units, potential creditors must conduct several searches before they can be sure that the property is not encumbered. See Danning v. Pacific Propeller, Inc. (In re Holiday Airlines Corp.), 620 F.2d 731 (9th Cir.), cert. denied, 449 U.S. 900, 101 S.Ct. 269, 66 L.Ed.2d 130 (1980); Red Carpet Homes of Johnstown, Inc. v. Gerling (In re Knapp), 575 F.2d 341, 343 (2d Cir. 1978); UCC § 9401, Official Comment ¶ 1. It is for that reason that parallel recordation schemes for the same types of property are scarce as hens' teeth; the court is aware of no others, and the parties have cited none. No useful purposes would be served—indeed, much confusion would result—if creditors were permitted to perfect security interests by filing with either the Copyright Office or state offices. See G. Gilmore, Security Interests in Personal Property § 17.3, at 545 (1965); see also 3 Nimmer on Copyright § 10.05[A] at 10–44 (1989) ("a persuasive argument * * * can be made to the effect that by reasons of Sections 201(d)(1), 204(a), 205(c) and 205(d) of the current Act * * * Congress has preempted the field with respect to the form and recordation requirements applicable to copyright mortgages").

If state methods of perfection were valid, a third party (such as a potential purchaser of the copyright) who wanted to learn of any encumbrances thereon would have to check not merely the indices of the U.S. Copyright Office, but also the indices of any relevant secretary of state. Because copyrights are incorporeal—they have no fixed situs—a number of state authorities could be relevant. See, e.g., note 4 supra. Thus, interested third parties could never be entirely sure that all relevant jurisdictions have been searched. This possibility, together with the expense and delay of conducting searches in a variety of jurisdictions, could hinder the purchase and sale of copyrights, frustrating Congress's policy that copyrights be readily transferable in commerce.

This is the reasoning adopted by the Ninth Circuit in Danning v. Pacific Propeller. Danning held that 49 U.S.C.App. § 1403(a), the Federal Aviation Act's provision for recording conveyances and the creation of liens and security interests in civil aircraft, preempts state filing provisions. 620 F.2d at 735–36. According to Danning,

> [t]he predominant purpose of the statute was to provide one central place for the filing of [liens on aircraft] and thus eliminate the need, given the highly mobile nature of aircraft and their appurtenances, for the examination of State and County records.

620 F.2d at 735–36. Copyrights, even more than aircraft, lack a clear situs; tangible, movable goods such as airplanes must always exist at some physical location; they may have a home base from which they operate or where they receive regular maintenance. The same cannot be said of intangibles. As noted above, this lack of an identifiable situs militates against individual state filings and in favor of a single, national registration scheme.

Moreover, as discussed at greater length below, see pp. 205–207 infra, the Copyright Act establishes its own scheme for determining priority between conflicting transferees, one that differs in certain respects from that of Article 9. Under Article 9, priority between holders of conflicting security interests in intangibles is generally determined by who perfected his interest first. UCC § 9312(5). By contrast, section 205(d) of the Copyright Act provides:

> As between two conflicting transfers, the one executed first prevails if it is recorded, in the manner required to give constructive notice under subsection (c), within one month after its execution in the United States or within two months after its execution outside the United States, or at any time before recordation in such manner of the later transfer * * *. 17 U.S.C. 205(d) (emphasis added). Thus, unlike Article 9, the Copyright Act permits the effect of recording with the Copyright Office to relate back as far as two months.

Because the Copyright Act and Article 9 create different priority schemes, there will be occasions when different results will be reached depending on which scheme was employed. The availability of filing under the UCC would thus undermine the priority scheme established by Congress with respect to copyrights. This type of direct interference with the operation of federal law weighs heavily in favor of preemption. See generally Bonito Boats, Inc. v. Thunder Craft Boats, Inc., 489 U.S. 141, 109 S.Ct. 971, 103 L.Ed.2d 118 (1989).

The bankruptcy court below nevertheless concluded that security interests in copyrights could be perfected by filing either with the copyright office or with the secretary of state under the UCC, making a tongue-in-cheek analogy to the use of a belt and suspenders to hold up a pair of pants. According to the bankruptcy court, because either device is equally useful, one should be free to choose which one to wear. With all due respect, this court finds the analogy inapt. There is no legitimate reason why pants should be held up in only one particular manner: Individuals and public modesty are equally served by either device, or even by a safety pin or a piece of rope; all that really matters is that the job gets done. Registration schemes are different in that the way notice is given is precisely what matters. To the extent interested parties are confused as to which system is being employed, this increases the level of uncertainty and multiplies the risk of error, exposing creditors to the possibility that they might get caught with their pants down.

A recordation scheme best serves its purpose where interested parties can obtain notice of all encumbrances by referring to a single, precisely defined recordation system. The availability of parallel state recordation systems that could put parties on constructive notice as to encumbrances on copyrights would surely interfere with the effectiveness of the federal recordation scheme. Given the virtual absence of dual recordation schemes in our legal system, Congress cannot be presumed to have contemplated such a result. The court therefore concludes that any state recordation system pertaining to interests in copyrights would be preempted by the Copyright Act.

2. State law leads to the same conclusion. Article 9 of the Uniform Commercial Code establishes a comprehensive scheme for the regulation of security interests in personal property and fixtures. By superseding a multitude of pre-Code security devices, it provides "a simple and unified structure within which the immense variety of present-day secured financing transactions can go forward with less cost and greater certainty." UCC 9–101, Official Comment. However, Article 9 is not all encompassing; under the "step back" provision of UCC 9–104, Article 9 does not apply "[t]o a security interest subject to any statute of the United States to the extent that such statute governs the rights of parties to and third parties affected by transactions in particular types of property."

For most items of personal property, Article 9 provides that security interests must be perfected by filing with the office of the secretary of state in which the debtor is located. See UCC §§ 9302(1), 9401(1)(c). Such filing, however, is not "necessary or effective to perfect a security interest in property subject to * * * [a] statute or treaty of the United States which provides for a national or international registration * * * or which specifies a place of filing different from that specified in [Article 9] for filing of the security interest." UCC § 9302(3)(a). When a national system for recording security interests exists, the Code treats compliance with that system as "equivalent to the filing of a financing statement under [Article 9,] and a security interest in property subject to the statute or treaty can be perfected only by compliance therewith * * *." UCC § 9302(4).

As discussed above, section 205(a) of the Copyright Act clearly does establish a national system for recording transfers of copyright interests, and it specifies a place of filing different from that provided in Article 9.

Recording in the Copyright Office gives nationwide, constructive notice to third parties of the recorded encumbrance. Except for the fact that the Copyright Office's indices are organized on the basis of the title and registration number, rather than by reference to the identity of the debtor, this system is nearly identical to that which Article 9 generally provides on a statewide basis. And, lest there be any doubt, the drafters of the UCC specifically identified the Copyright Act as establishing the type of national registration system that would trigger the section 9302(3) and (4) step back provisions:

> Examples of the type of federal statute referred to in [UCC § 9302(3)(a)] are the provisions of [Title 17] (copyrights) * * *. UCC § 9302, Official Comment ¶ 8; see G. Gilmore, Security Interests in Personal Property § 17.3, at 545 (1965) ("[t]here can be no doubt that [the Copyright Act was] meant to be within the description of § 9–302(3)(a)").

The court therefore concludes that the Copyright Act provides for national registration and "specifies a place of filing different from that specified in [Article 9] for filing of the security interest." UCC § 9302(3)(a). Recording in the U.S. Copyright Office, rather than filing a financing statement under Article 9, is the proper method for perfecting a security interest in a copyright.

In reaching this conclusion, the court rejects City Bank & Trust Co. v. Otto Fabric, Inc., 83 B.R. 780 (D.Kan.1988), and In re Transportation Design & Technology Inc., 48 B.R. 635 (Bankr.S.D.Cal.1985), insofar as they are germane to the issues presented here. Both cases held that, under the UCC, security interests in patents need not be recorded in the U.S. Patent and Trademark Office to be perfected as against lien creditors because the federal statute governing patent assignments does not specifically provide for liens:

> Applications for patent, patents, or any interest therein, shall be assignable in law by an instrument in writing. The applicant, patentee, or his assigns or legal representatives may in like manner grant and convey an exclusive right under his application for patent, or patents, to the whole or any specified part of the United States.
>
> * * *
>
> An assignment, grant or conveyance shall be void as against any subsequent purchaser or mortgagee for a valuable consideration, without notice, unless it is recorded in the Patent and Trademark Office within three months from its date or prior to the date of such subsequent purchase or mortgage. 35 U.S.C. § 261 (emphasis added).

According to In re Transportation, because section 261's priority scheme only provides for a "subsequent purchaser or mortgagee for valuable consideration," it does not require recording in the Patent and Trademark Office to perfect against lien creditors. See 48 B.R. at 639. Likewise, City Bank held that "the failure of the statute to mention protection against lien creditors suggests that it is unnecessary to record an assignment or other conveyance with the Patent Office to protect the appellant's security interest against the trustee." 83 B.R. at 782.

These cases misconstrue the plain language of UCC section 9104, which provides for the voluntary step back of Article 9's provisions "to the extent [federal law] governs the rights of [the] parties." UCC § 9104(a) (emphasis added). Thus, when a federal statute provides for a national system of recordation or specifies a place of filing different from that in Article 9, the methods of perfection specified in Article 9 are supplanted by that national system; compliance with a national system of recordation is equivalent to the filing of a financing statement under Article 9. UCC § 9302(4). Whether the federal statute also provides a priority scheme different from that in Article 9 is a separate issue, addressed below. See pp. 205–207 infra. Compliance with a national registration scheme is necessary for perfection regardless of whether federal law governs priorities. Cap Fed's security interest in the copyrights of the films in NPI's library and the receivables they have generated therefore is unperfected.

B. EFFECT OF FAILING TO RECORD WITH THE COPYRIGHT OFFICE

Having concluded that Cap Fed should have, but did not, record its security interest with the Copyright Office, the court must next determine whether NPI as a debtor in possession can subordinate Cap Fed's interest and recover it for the benefit of the bankruptcy estate. As a debtor in possession, NPI has nearly all of the powers of a bankruptcy trustee, see 11 U.S.C. § 1107(a), including the authority to set aside preferential or fraudulent transfers, as well as transfers otherwise voidable under applicable state or federal law. See 11 U.S.C. §§ 544, 547, 548.

Particularly relevant is the "strong arm clause" of 11 U.S.C. § 544(a)(1), which, in respect to personal property in the bankruptcy estate, gives the debtor in possession every right and power state law confers upon one who has acquired a lien by legal or equitable proceedings. If, under the applicable law, a judicial lien creditor would prevail over an adverse claimant, the debtor in possession prevails; if not, not. Wind Power Systems, Inc. v. Cannon Financial Group, Inc. (In re Wind Power Systems, Inc.), 841 F.2d 288, 293 (9th Cir.1988); Angeles Real Estate Co. v. Kerxton (In re Construction General Inc.), 737 F.2d 416, 418 (4th Cir.1984). A lien creditor generally takes priority over unperfected security interests in estate property because, under Article 9, "an unperfected security interest is subordinate to the rights of * * * [a] person who becomes a lien creditor before the security interest is perfected." UCC § 9301(1)(b). But, as discussed previously, the UCC does not apply to the extent a federal statute "governs the rights of parties to and third parties affected by transactions in particular types of property." UCC § 9104. Section 205(d) of the Copyright Act is such a statute, establishing a priority scheme between conflicting transfers of interests in a copyright:

As between two conflicting transfers, the one executed first prevails if it is recorded, in the manner required to give constructive notice under subsection (c), within one month after its execution in the United States or within two months after its execution outside the United States, or at any time before recordation in such manner of the later transfer. Otherwise, the later transfer prevails if recorded first in such manner, and if taken in good faith, for valuable consideration or on the basis of a binding promise to pay royalties, and without notice of the earlier transfer. 17 U.S.C. § 205(d) (emphasis added). For the reasons discussed above, see p. 201 supra, the federal priority scheme preempts the state priority scheme.

Section 205(d) does not expressly address the rights of lien creditors, speaking only in terms of competing transfers of copyright interests. To determine whether NPI, as a hypothetical lien creditor, may avoid Cap Fed's unperfected security interest, the court must therefore consider whether a judicial lien is a transfer as that term is used in the Copyright Act.

As noted above, the Copyright Act recognizes transfers of copyright ownership "in whole or in part by any means of conveyance or by operation of law." 17 U.S.C. § 201(d)(1). Transfer is defined broadly to include any "assignment, mortgage, exclusive license, or any other conveyance, alienation, or hypothecation of a copyright * * * whether or not it is limited in time or place of effect." 17 U.S.C. § 101. A judicial lien creditor is a creditor who has obtained a lien "by judgment, levy, sequestration, or other legal or equitable process or proceeding." 11 U.S.C. § 101(32). Such a creditor typically has the power to seize and sell property held by the debtor at the time of the creation of the lien in order to satisfy the judgment or, in the case of general intangibles such as copyrights, to collect the revenues generated by the intangible as they come due. See, e.g., Cal.Civ.P.Code §§ 701.510, 701.520, 701.640. Thus, while the creation of a lien on a copyright may not give a creditor an immediate right to control the copyright, it amounts to a sufficient transfer of rights to come within the broad definition of transfer under the Copyright Act. See Phoenix Bond & Indemnity Co. v. Shamblin (In re Shamblin), 890 F.2d 123, 127 n. 7 (9th Cir.1989) (under the Bankruptcy Code, "[t]his court has consistently treated the creation of liens on the debtor's property as a transfer").

Cap Fed contends that, in order to prevail under 17 U.S.C. § 205(d), NPI must have the status of a bona fide purchaser, rather than that of a judicial lien creditor. See Pistole v. Mellor (In re Mellor), 734 F.2d 1396, 1401 n. 4 (9th Cir.1984) (judicial lien creditor does not have the same rights as a bona fide purchaser); cf. 11 U.S.C. § 544(a)(3) (for real estate in the bankruptcy estate, debtor in possession has the rights of a bona fide purchaser). Cap Fed, in essence, is arguing that the term transfer in section 205(d) refers only to consensual transfers. For the reasons expressed above, the court rejects this argument. The Copyright Act's definition of transfer is very broad and specifically includes transfers by operation of law. 17 U.S.C. § 201(d)(1). The term is broad enough to encompass not merely purchasers, but lien creditors as well. NPI therefore is entitled to priority if it meets the statutory good faith, notice, consideration and recording requirements of section 205(a). As the hypothetical lien creditor, NPI is deemed to have taken in good faith and without notice. See 11 U.S.C. § 544(a). The only remaining issues are whether NPI could have recorded its interest in the Copyright Office and whether it obtained its lien for valuable consideration.

In order to obtain a lien on a particular piece of property, a creditor who has received a money judgment in the form of a writ of execution must prepare a notice of levy that specifically identifies the property to be encumbered and the consequences of that action. See Cal.Civ.P.Code § 699.540. If such a notice identifies a federal copyright or the receivables generated by such a copyright, it and the underlying writ of execution, constitute "document[s] pertaining to a copyright" and, therefore, are capable of recordation in the Copyright Office. See 17 U.S.C. § 205(a); Compendium of Copyright Office Practices II ¶¶ 1602–1603 (identifying which documents the Copyright Office will accept for filing). Because these documents could be recorded in the Copyright Office, NPI as debtor in possession will be deemed to have done so.

Finally, contrary to Cap Fed's assertion, a trustee or debtor in possession is deemed to have given valuable consideration for its judicial lien. Section 544(a)(1) provides:

> The trustee [or debtor in possession] shall have, as of the commencement of the case * * * the rights and powers of, or may avoid any transfer of property of the debtor or any obligation incurred by the debtor that is voidable by * * * a creditor that extends credit to the debtor at the time of the commencement of the case, and that obtains, at such time and with respect to such credit, a judicial lien on all property on which a creditor on a simple contract could have obtained such a judicial lien * * *. 11 U.S.C. § 544(a)(1) (emphasis added). The act of extending credit, of course, constitutes the giving of valuable consideration. See First Maryland Leasecorp v. M/V Golden Egret, 764 F.2d 749, 753 (11th Cir.1985); United States v. Cahall Bros., 674 F.2d 578, 581 (6th Cir.1982). In addition, the trustee's lien—like that of any other judgment creditor—is deemed to be in exchange for the claim that formed the basis of the underlying judgment, a claim that is extinguished by the entry of the judgment.

Because NPI meets all of the requirements for subsequent transferees to prevail under 17 U.S.C. § 205(d)—a transferee who took in good faith, for valuable consideration and without notice of the earlier transfer—Cap Fed's unperfected security interest in NPI's copyrights and the receivables they generated is trumped by NPI's hypothetical judicial lien. NPI may therefore avoid Cap Fed's interest and preserve it for the benefit of the bankruptcy estate.

CONCLUSION

The judgment of the bankruptcy court is reversed. The case is ordered remanded for a determination of which movies in NPI's library are the subject of valid copyrights. The court shall then determine the status of Cap Fed's security interest in the movies and the debtor's other property. To the extent that interest is unperfected, the court shall permit NPI to exercise its avoidance powers under the Bankruptcy Code. IT IS SO ORDERED.

Note

The expansive scope of the Copyright Act led Judge Kozinski to conclude that the Copyright Act completely displaced Article 9 for the purposes of perfecting security interests in copyright collateral. Judge Kozinski's opinion, however, fails to specify whether the copyright in question had been registered with the Copyright Office. For most purposes, a copyright holder enjoys the benefits from the Act without registration. Thus, many copyrights are not registered with the Copyright Office. Judge Tchaikovsky has applied different rules to these unregistered copyrights. Read the following opinion and consider whether Judge Kozinski would agree with her reasoning.

IN RE WORLD AUXILIARY POWER COMPANY

United States Bankruptcy Court, N.D. California, Oakland Division, 1999.
244 B.R. 149.

TCHAIKOVSKY, BANKRUPTCY JUDGE.

MEMORANDUM OF DECISION

In these adversary proceedings, Plaintiff Aerocon Engineering Inc. ("Aerocon") seeks to avoid the security interest of Defendant Silicon Valley Bank (the "Bank") in certain unregistered copyrights (the "Copyright") pursuant to 11 U.S.C. § 544(a)(1).[1] Aerocon and the Bank have filed cross-motions for summary judgment. For the reasons stated below, the Court finds that the Bank's security interest is perfected. Therefore, Aerocon may not avoid it pursuant to 11 U.S.C. § 544(a)(1).

SUMMARY OF FACTS

The above-captioned debtors (the "Debtors") are corporate affiliates. They filed voluntary petitions seeking relief under chapter 11 of the Bankruptcy Code in August 1996. In September 1996, all three cases were converted to chapter 7, and chapter 7 trustees were appointed. Prior to the chapter 11 filings and conversion of the cases to chapter 7,

---

1. Section 544(a)(1) of the Bankruptcy Code provides that: "The trustee shall have, as of the commencement of the case, and without regard to any knowledge of the trustee or of any creditor, the rights and powers of, or may avoid any transfer of property of the debtor ... that is voidable by-(1) a creditor that extends credit to the debtor at the time of the commencement of the case, and that obtains, at such time and with respect to such credit, a judicial lien on all property on which a creditor on a simple contract could have obtained a judicial lien, whether or not such a creditor exists; .... " 11 U.S.C. § 544(a)(1).

the Debtors designed, manufactured, and sold aircraft related products. In the process, the Debtors acquired the Copyright. The Copyright was embodied in drawings, blueprints, and computer software which were used to acquire Supplemental Type Certificates from the Federal Aviation Administration. The Supplemental Type Certificates permitted the Debtors to make modifications to a particular airplane type. The Debtors did not register the Copyright with the United States Copyright Office (the "Copyright Office").

Prior to the commencement of these bankruptcy cases, the Bank loaned money to two of the Debtors. The third Debtor guaranteed the loans. The Debtors executed security agreements (the "Security Agreement"), giving the Bank a security interest in the Copyright, among other things, to secure their obligations under the loan and guaranty agreements. The Debtors also executed UCC–1 financing statements (the "UCC–1") which the Bank filed with the California Secretary of State (the "UCC Office"). The Bank did not record the Security Agreement or UCC–1 in the Copyright Office.

On April 14, 1997, the Court approved the sale by the bankruptcy trustees of most of the assets of the three bankruptcy estates, including the Copyright and the trustees' avoiding powers with respect to the Bank's security interest in the Copyright under 11 U.S.C. § 544(a)(1). Aerocon alleges that it is the successor-in-interest to the parties who purchased the Copyright and the related avoiding powers.

APPLICABLE LAW

A. Summary Judgment Law

The legal principles to be applied in determining a motion for summary judgment are well established and are not in dispute. A motion for summary judgment should be granted when it appears that there is no genuine issue of material fact and that the moving party is entitled to judgment as a matter of law. See Fed.R.Civ.P. 56(c); Celotex Corp. v. Catrett, 477 U.S. 317, 322, 106 S.Ct. 2548, 91 L.Ed.2d 265 (1986). In this instance, the parties agree that summary judgment is appropriate. None of the material facts is in dispute.

B. Copyright Law

The owner of a copyright is permitted to register the copyright with the Copyright Office but is not required to do so. See 17 U.S.C. § 208(a).[2] The transfer of ownership of a copyright may be recorded with the Copyright Office whether or not the copyright is registered. See 17 U.S.C. § 205(c). The Copyright Act defines "the transfer of ownership of a copyright" to include the transfer of a security interest. See 17 U.S.C. § 101.

2. However, the owner of a copyright must register the copyright if it wishes to sue a third party for copyright infringement. See 17 U.S.C. § 211.

If the copyright is registered and the transfer of ownership of a copyright is recorded, the recordation gives third parties constructive notice of the transfer. See 17 U.S.C. § 205(c). In the event of conflicting transfers, priority is given to the first transfer executed provided: (1) the transfer is recorded within 30 days of the date of execution in a manner sufficient to give third parties constructive notice[3] and (2) the transferee: (a) received the transfer in good faith, (b) for valuable consideration, and (c) without notice of the prior transfer. See 17 U.S.C. § 205(d).

DISCUSSION

The question presented by these cross-motions is whether the Bank perfected its security interest in the Copyright by filing the UCC–1 in the UCC Office. If it did, Aerocon cannot avoid the Bank's security interest pursuant to 11 U.S.C. § 544(a)(1). See Cal. Com.Code § 9312(5)(a). If the Bank's security interest is unperfected, Aerocon may avoid it under 11 U.S.C. § 544(a)(1). See Cal. Com.Code § 9302(1)(b), (3).[4] In either instance, as discussed below, because the copyright was unregistered, the priority of the conflicting transfers must be determined under state law. See section A below. For similar reasons, as discussed below, the Court concludes that a secured creditor may perfect a security interest in an unregistered copyright in accordance with state law, by filing a UCC–1 financing statement with the UCC Office. See section B below.

A. Priority Of Conflicting Transfers Of Ownership In Unregistered Copyright

The issues presented here were first addressed in In re Peregrine Entertainment, Ltd., 116 B.R. 194 (C.D.Cal.1990). The Peregrine court held that a security interest in a copyright could not be perfected by filing a UCC–1 financing statement in the UCC Office and could only be perfected by recording the transfer of the security interest in the Copyright Office. Id. at 198–204. The Peregrine court also held that a hypothetical judicial lien holder under 11 U.S.C. § 544(a)(1) could obtain a lien on a copyright superior to an unperfected security interest. Therefore, a trustee could avoid the unperfected security interest under 11 U.S.C. § 544(a)(1). See id. at 204–08.

The Peregrine court failed to specify whether the copyright in that case was registered with the Copyright Office.[5] However, the Peregrine

---

3. The transfer may be recorded within 60 days of the date of execution if the transfer was executed outside the United States.

4. Section 9301(1)(b) of the California Commercial Code provides that an unperfected security interest is subordinate to the interest of a lien creditor. Section 9301(3) defines "lien creditor" to include a creditor who has acquired a lien on the property by levy. As discussed in Peregrine, a hypothetical judicial lien creditor could obtain a lien

on an unregistered copyright by levying a writ of execution in accordance with the procedures set forth under state law with respect to general intangibles. See Peregrine, 116 B.R. at 205–06 n. 16.

5. The Peregrine court does, however, acknowledge that a security interest in a copyright may only be perfected by recordation in the Copyright Office if the copyright is registered. See id. at 200 n. 7.

court's analysis only works if the copyright was registered. This is most obvious in its analysis of the respective priorities of the hypothetical judicial lien holder under 11 U.S.C. § 544(a)(1) and the holder of an unperfected security interest.

The Peregrine court based its priority analysis on 17 U.S.C. § 205(d). It stated that:

> ... the UCC does not apply to the extent a federal statute 'governs the rights of parties to and third parties affected by transactions in particular types of property.' UCC § 9104. Section 205(d) of the Copyright Act is such a statute, establishing a priority scheme between conflicting transfers of interests in a copyright: ... See id. at 205.

It concluded first that, by definition, a hypothetical judicial lien holder under 11 U.S.C. § 544(a) should be deemed to have received its lien in good faith, for valuable consideration, and without notice of the prior transfer. It then stated that the only remaining issue was "whether ... [the hypothetical judicial lien holder] could have recorded its interest in the Copyright Office...." See id. at 206. The Peregrine court concluded that the judicial lien holder could have recorded its interest in the Copyright Office and therefore that it could avoid the security interest of a secured creditor that failed to record its security agreement there. See id. at 206–08.

However, unless the copyright was registered in the Copyright Office, a hypothetical judicial lien holder's recordation of its lien in the Copyright Office would not give it any priority over an unperfected security interest in the same copyright under 17 U.S.C. § 205(d). As noted above, 17 U.S.C. § 205(d) only gives priority to a transfer of a security interest recorded in a manner sufficient to give constructive notice to third parties. Recordation of a security interest only gives constructive notice to third parties if the copyright is registered. See 17 U.S.C. § 205(c).

Subsequent to Peregrine, two bankruptcy courts addressed the issues presented here with respect to copyrights that were clearly unregistered. See In re AEG Acquisition Corp., 127 B.R. 34 (Bankr.C.D.Cal. 1991), aff'd, 161 B.R. 50, 58 (9th Cir.BAP 1993);[6] In re Avalon, 209 B.R. 517 (Bankr.D.Ariz.1997). Both courts followed Peregrine, concluding that a security interest could only be perfected by recordation with the Copyright Office. Neither court considered whether it was appropriate to apply the Peregrine court's analysis to an unregistered copyright. See AEG Acquisition, 127 B.R. at 40–41; Avalon, 209 B.R. at 521–22.

It is unclear whether these two courts based their determinations of the respective parties' priorities on state or federal law. In AEG Acquisition, the court stated that: "The Uniform Commercial Code ... gives

---

6. The bankruptcy appellate decision, affirming the bankruptcy court, contained only a single paragraph directed to this issue. It noted that the bankruptcy court had relied on Peregrine and that that decision appeared well reasoned and on point. See AEG Acquisition, 161 B.R. at 58.

lien creditors priority over holders of unrecorded security interests." 127 B.R. at 43. However, like the Peregrine court, it then addressed the requirements for priority set forth in 17 U.S.C. § 205(d). Like Peregrine, in doing so, it failed to note the requirement that recordation of the judicial lien be in a manner sufficient to give constructive notice to third parties or to discuss how such recordation could be accomplished when the copyright was unregistered. See id. at 43–44.[7]

The Avalon court failed to discuss the priority issue at all. It merely stated that:

> If a security interest is not properly perfected, it becomes subordinate to the rights of a bankruptcy trustee (or debtor-in-possession) whose principal purpose is to maximize a debtor's estate for the benefit of the unsecured creditors. Ariz.Rev.Stat. § 47–9301(A)(2); § 47–9301(C); 11 U.S.C. § 544; National Peregrine, Inc. v. Capitol Federal Savings and Loan Association of Denver (In re Peregrine, Entertainment, Ltd.), 116 B.R. 194 (C.D.Cal.1990). Avalon, 209 B.R. at 521.

Because the Peregrine court based its priority determination on 17 U.S.C. § 205(d), by citing to both state law and Peregrine, the Avalon court also failed to make clear whether it was basing its priority analysis on state or federal law.

However, as discussed above, 17 U.S.C. § 205(d) does not establish a priority scheme between conflicting transfers of interests in an unregistered copyright. Therefore, the relative priorities of the Bank's security interest and the interest of Aerocon as a hypothetical judicial lien creditor under 11 U.S.C. § 544(a)(1) must be governed by Article 9 of the California Commercial Code. As stated above, whether Aerocon can avoid the Bank's security interest under the California Commercial Code depends on whether the Bank's security interest was properly perfected by filing a UCC–1 with the UCC Office.

B.   Perfection Of Security Interest In Unregistered Copyright

The Peregrine court concluded that a security interest in a copyright could only be perfected in accordance with the Copyright Act. However, as noted above, it did not specify whether the copyright in question was registered with the Copyright Office. Its conclusion appears sound only as applied to a registered copyright.

The Peregrine court based its analysis on two grounds. First, it concluded that 17 U.S.C. § 205(c) preempted the perfection provisions of the Copyright Act. See section (1) below. Second, it concluded that section 9302(3)(a) of the Commercial Code precluded perfection of a security interest in a copyright by filing a UCC–1 financing statement

---

7. In fact, the AEG Acquisition court misstated the priority scheme established by 17 U.S.C. § 205(d) as giving priority to a transferee who records first. As discussed above, priority is given to the first transfer executed as long as that transfer is recorded in a manner sufficient to give constructive notice within 30 (or 60) days of the date of execution of the transfer. See 17 U.S.C. § 205(d).

with the UCC Office. See section (2) below. As discussed below, neither ground justifies this conclusion when the copyright is unregistered. The Court concludes that a security interest in an unregistered copyright may be perfected by filing a UCC–1 financing statement with the UCC Office. Thus, the Bank's security interest is perfected and may not be avoided by Aerocon under 11 U.S.C. § 544(a)(1).

(1) Preemption.

As noted above, the Peregrine court based its conclusion that a security interest in a copyright could only be perfected by recordation in the Copyright Office primarily on the doctrine of federal preemption. In this context, the Peregrine court stated as follows:

> Even in the absence of express language, federal regulation will preempt state law if it is so pervasive as to indicate that "Congress left no room for supplementary state regulation," or if "the federal interest is so dominant that the federal system will be assumed to preclude enforcement of state laws on the same subject." [Citation and footnote omitted] Here, the comprehensive scope of the federal Copyright Act's recording provisions, along with the unique federal interests they implicate, support the view that federal law preempts state methods of perfecting security interests in copyrights and related accounts receivable. 116 B.R. at 199.

However, the Copyright Act's recording provisions are not comprehensive as applied to an unregistered copyright. They contain no means by which a security interest in an unregistered copyright may be perfected.

As the Peregrine court recognized, federal law preempts state law only to the extent that it contains provisions that govern the rights of the parties. See id. at 203. Section 9104 of the California Commercial Code provides a "voluntary step back" of state law governing security interests only "to the extent [federal law] governs the rights of [the] parties." See id. As stated in Official Comment § 1 to Uniform Commercial Code § 9104, "... [the Federal Copyright Act] would not seem to contain sufficient provisions regulating the rights of the parties and third parties to exclude security interests in copyrights from the provisions of ... [Article 9]." See id. at 203 n. 11. Since federal law provides no means by which a security interest in an unregistered copyright may be perfected, that means must be supplied by state law.

The Peregrine court also based its conclusion that the Copyright Act preempted state law methods of perfection of security interest in copyrights on policy grounds. It rejected the secured creditor's contention that Article 9 of the Uniform Commercial Code and the Copyright Act provided "parallel" perfection schemes. The court stated that:

> A recording system works by virtue of the fact that interested parties have a specific place to look in order to discover with certainty whether a particular interest has been transferred or encumbered. To the extent there are competing recordation

schemes, this lessens the utility of each; when records are scattered in several filing units, potential creditors must conduct several searches before they can be sure that the property is not encumbered. [Citations omitted.] It is for that reason that parallel recordation schemes for the same types of property are scarce as hens' teeth; . . . . Id. at 200.

However, permitting a security interest in an unregistered copyright to be perfected by filing a UCC–1 financing statement with the UCC Office does not create a parallel or competing recordation scheme. Rather, the UCC recordation scheme serves as a supplement or backup to the Copyright Act recordation scheme. If a copyright is registered, recordation in the Copyright Office is the only effective method by which to perfect the security interest. Only if a copyright is unregistered does filing a UCC–1 financing statement with the UCC Office perfect the security interest.[8]

Parties conducting searches for encumbrances on copyrights would not be unduly burdened by this supplementary or backup recordation scheme. A party wishing to determine whether a copyright was encumbered would first search the Copyright Office. If the copyright was registered, the party need search no further. Only if the copyright was unregistered, would the party need to search the UCC Office. This burden seems slight compared to depriving a secured creditor of any means of perfecting its security interest.

"Federal law preempts state law when state law 'conflicts with federal law, would frustrate a federal scheme, or where Congress clearly intended to occupy the field. Saridakis v. United Airlines, 166 F.3d 1272, 1276 (9th Cir.1999).' "In re Cybernetic Servs., Inc., 239 B.R. 917, 920 (9th Cir.BAP 1999). Congress has clearly not indicated an intention to occupy the field of a secured creditor's rights with respect to a copyright. See Peregrine, 116 B.R. at 203 n. 11. The Copyright Act contains no express provision prohibiting a secured creditor from perfecting its security interest in an unregistered copyright in accordance with state law. Therefore, the filing provisions of Article 9 of the Commercial Code do not conflict with federal law.

Finally, as discussed above, the Court does not believe that permitting a secured creditor to perfect its security interest in an unregistered copyright by filing a UCC–1 financing statement with the UCC Office frustrates any federal policy reflected in the Copyright Act. Therefore, the Court concludes that the doctrine of federal preemption does not prevent a secured creditor from perfecting its security interest by filing a UCC–1 with the UCC Office.

8. Granted, perfection in this manner would be vulnerable to invalidation if a copyright were later registered and a competing security interest in the copyright had been recorded in the Copyright Office. For that reason, a prudent secured creditor would record its security agreement in the Copyright Office at the same time it filed its UCC–1 financing statement in the UCC Office.

(2) Section 9302(3)(a) of the California Commercial Code.

The Peregrine court also based its conclusion that a security interest in a copyright could only be perfected by recording the security agreement in the Copyright Office on section 9302(3)(a) of the California Commercial Code. Section 9302(3)(a) provides as follows:

The filing of a financing statement otherwise required by this division is not necessary or effective to perfect a security interest in property subject to . . . :

> (a) A statute or treaty of the United States which provides for a national or international registration or a national or international certificate of title or which specifies a place of filing different from that specified in this division for filing of the security interest. Cal. Com.Code § 9302(3)(a).

The Peregrine court read this provision to apply to the perfection of a security interest in a copyright because "the Copyright Act provides for national registration and 'specifies a place of filing different from that specified in [Article 9] for filing a security interest.' "See 116 B.R. at 203.[9]

The Court finds section 9302(3) ambiguous. Read literally, its effect would be absurd. It would provide that, whenever a particular type of collateral may be registered nationally, regardless of whether the federal statute specifies a place for filing a security interest different than that provided by the UCC, filing a UCC–1 financing statement would be neither necessary nor effective to perfect a security interest in the collateral.[10] An example of such a federal statute is the Patent Act. See 35 U.S.C. § 1–376. In Cybernetic Servs., the Ninth Circuit Bankruptcy Appellate Panel declined to apply section 9302(3)(a) in this literal manner. See 239 B.R. at 917. The panel noted that:

> Official Comment 8 to UCC 9–302 refers to three specific federal statutes that provide a filing system adequate to supersede the Article 9 filing system for perfection of security interests: 17 U.S.C. §§ 28, 30 (copyrights), 49 U.S.C. § 1403 (now § 44107) (aircraft), and 49 U.S.C. § 20(c) (now § 11301) (railroads). [Footnotes omitted.] Each of those statutes clearly includes the filing of security interests within their scope, each requires that a security interest be filed within the applicable registry to obtain priority and perfection of a security interest, and each provides that a filing provides constructive notice of the security interest.

---

9. The Court notes that, in purporting to apply the plain language of section 9302(3)(a), the Peregrine court replaced the word "or" in the statute with the word "and." In other words, section 9302(3)(a), read literally, states that filing a UCC–1 financing statement will not perfect a security interest when a federal statute either provides for national registration of the property or specifies a different place for filing a security interest. The Peregrine court reads section 9302(3)(a) to preclude perfection by filing a UCC–1 financing statement only when the federal statute contains both provisions.

10. It is also unclear whether the word "provide" means "permit" or "require." If "provide" means "require," the statute would not refer to copyrights at all since a copyright is not required to be registered except as a prerequisite to bringing a copyright infringement suit. See 17 U.S.C. §§ 408, 411.

In contrast, the Patent Act is not sufficiently comprehensive to exclude state methods of perfecting security interests in patents. The Patent Act does not include security interests within any of the scope or definition provisions. Id. at 923.

The Court agrees with the Cybernetic Servs. court that section 9302(3)(a) is ambiguous and may not sensibly be applied in accordance with its plain language.[11] Consistent with the panel's rationale, since the Copyright Act provides no means of perfecting a security interest in an unregistered copyright, the Court concludes that section 9302(3)(a) does not preclude perfection by filing a UCC–1 financing statement with the UCC Office.

CONCLUSION

For the reasons stated above, the Court concludes that, when a copyright is unregistered, a secured creditor may perfect its security interest by filing a UCC–1 financing statement with the UCC Office. Since the Bank did so, the Bank's security interest is perfected. As a result, Aerocon is not entitled to avoid the Bank's security interest pursuant to 11 U.S.C. § 544(a)(1). Counsel for the Bank is directed to submit a proposed form of order in accordance with this decision.

Patents

Section 261 of the Patent Act states that "[a]n assignment, grant or conveyance of a patent, patent application, or interest therein shall be void as against any subsequent purchaser unless it is recorded in the Patent and Trademark Office [PTO] within three months from its date or prior to the date of such subsequent purchase or mortgage." Apparently, the scope of this provision is limited to transfers that carry full title and ownership rights. A security agreement does not normally transfer title to the creditor. Thus, whenever the debtor retains full ownership rights in the collateral, the security agreement will not qualify as an "assignment, grant or conveyance" for the purposes of Section 261. So the federal law does not require a filing with the PTO in order for the creditor to avoid claims made by a later purchaser. Therefore, the perfection of a security interest in a patent and determinations of priority of claims in a patent remain matters of state law under Article 9.

Thus far, however, courts have only addressed the rights of a perfected secured creditor as against the trustee in bankruptcy. In the case of *In re Cybernetic Services, Inc.*, the court held that patent law did not preempt state law governing perfection of security interests in patents. A secured creditor who filed under Article 9 was properly perfected and defeated the trustee in bankruptcy, but no case has

---

11. When the plain language of a statute produces a result demonstrably at odds with its apparent purpose, it should not be interpreted in that manner. See In re Catapult Entertainment, Inc., 165 F.3d 747, 754 (9th Cir.1999)(holding that plain language did not create absurd result); see also In re Century Cleaning Services, Inc., 195 F.3d 1053 (9th Cir.1999).

considered the rights of a perfected secured creditor as against a later good faith purchaser for value or a subsequent lender who has filed a mortgage with the PTO. In theory, the perfected secured creditor should receive the same priority as against a good faith purchaser or a mortgagee. In practice the result could be different. In the first case to examine the issue of security interests in patents, the court stated in dicta that a UCC financing statement may not be effective against a good faith purchaser for value or a mortgagee. In re Transportation Design & Technology, Inc., 48 B.R. 635.

Trademarks

Section 1060 of the Lanham Trademark Act provides that "[a]n assignment shall be void as against any subsequent purchaser for valuable consideration without notice, unless it is recorded in the [PTO] within three months after the date thereof or prior to such subsequent purchase." 15 U.S.C. § 1060. The reference to an "assignment" in Section 1060 applies only to absolute assignments and not to security interests. Thus, courts have uniformly held that the federal law does not preempt Article 9 for the purposes of perfecting a security interest in trademarks. Consequently, a secured creditor who has filed a financing statement in the applicable state office has properly perfected its interest. A perfected secured creditor will prevail over the trustee in bankruptcy and (probably) a later claimant, even if the later claimant has filed its interest with the PTO. If one accepts that a secured creditor with a perfected interest in a patent will prevail over a subsequent good faith purchaser, then, a fortiori, the perfected secured creditor will prevail here also.

Problem 3–9

Your client, Software Bank, was pleasantly surprised to hear about *In re World Auxiliary Power* and to find that it could perfect a security interest in an unregistered copyright by filing in the Secretary of State's office where the debtor is located. The bank has a couple of questions. It wonders what happens if the debtor, unbeknownst to the bank, registers its software with the copyright office. Does that registration render the state filing ineffective? It is also concerned about the statement in *Peregrine* that a security interest in accounts and other proceeds that might arise from the use of a copyright (such as payments due on the showing of a movie) might also be subject to a federal filing and thus might not be perfected by filing with the Secretary of State's office. What is your opinion on that? How can your client address those problems?

* * *

Consider the following problem in light of the Peregrine case.

Problem 3–10

Travelware designs and licenses elaborate computer programs for travel agencies. It has granted a license to TRAVELTOWN, a nationwide travel agency. TRAVELTOWN in turn has made sublicenses with various one office travel agencies whom it franchises. TRAVELTOWN also uses the software in its own offices that are located in every state of the United States. Bank has taken a security interest in TRAVELTOWN'S license and in its rights to payment from its franchisees. Bank Two has taken a security interest in Travelware's license and copyright.

1. Assume that Bank filed a financing statement in TRAVELTOWN'S name and the financing statement claimed only TRAVELTOWN'S "goods, including equipment". Bank claims that it is perfected because software is included in the definition of "goods" in 9–102. What do you think?

2. Assume alternatively that Bank takes a security interest in TRAVELTOWN'S license and files a financing statement covering "general intangibles" at the state capital. Is it perfected?

3. Assume that Bank takes a security interest in TRAVELTOWN'S accounts owed to it by its franchisees and files a financing statement at the state capital that claims "accounts". Is it perfected?

4. Assume that Travelware claims that the term in its license which prohibits transfers to third parties renders the security interest invalid as to the accounts and license. It relies on section 9–408. What is your response?

5. Assume that bank defeats Travelware's claims in number 4. Bank proposes to "seize" the license and to transfer it to a third party. Travelware again cites section 9–408 and the anti-assignment clause. What now?

Problem 3–11

Bank wishes to take a security interest in Travelware's software. How does it do it? What if Travelware has never properly recorded its copyright in the federal system? Does that mean Bank cannot get an effective and perfected security interest?

Chapter Four

SECURITY IN FIXTURES

---

§ 1. INTRODUCTION

In general, Article 9 does not deal with real estate security. The single important exception to that rule is section 9–334 concerning priority of security interests in fixtures. That section governs the conflict between personal property interests in fixtures and real property interest in fixtures.

Typical of the priority conflicts we consider here are those that arise when a real estate mortgagee claims not only the real estate but also all "appurtenances, fixtures, buildings, equipment" (and so on, in a list as long as the mortgagee's lawyer can devise). After the mortgage is on the property, the debtor purchases a furnace or lathes or some other item of industrial equipment that becomes a fixture on the real property and subject to the real estate mortgage under the state real property law. This single transaction comes in a dozen variants depending on when the interests attach, when they are perfected, on the identity of the claimant and on the mode of perfection. Section 9–334 purports to deal with most of the possible conflicts. If the collateral in question is not a fixture, or if it is "building material" that has become so intimately associated with the real property that it no longer constitutes either personal property or a fixture, other law governs the priority dispute.

The secured creditor with a claim to a fixture has a choice; it can either make a filing in the local real estate records (a fixture filing) or do a regular UCC–1 filing in the personal property records at the state capital. As we will see, the former gives the secured creditor protection against certain real estate claimants while the latter gives protection only against lien creditors and certain other claimants where the fixture involved is not considered to be important to mortgagees and the like. For example, subsection (e)(3) grants the secured lender who has done only a personal property filing at the state capital priority over the trustee in bankruptcy (lien creditor) on the theory that a lien creditor is not someone who would rely upon the real estate records. Subsection (e)(2) gives priority to the secured creditor who has only done a personal property filing on certain assets such as factory or office machines on the theory that mortgagees or other purchasers of the real estate do not place any reliance upon such machines when they make loans or buy; thus it is fair and appropriate to grant the secured creditor priority in this case even though the secured creditor does not do a fixture filing.

Fixtures and Fixture Filings, Section 9–102(a)(40) and (41)

Section 9–102(a)(41) defines fixtures as "goods that have become so related to particular real property that an interest in them arises under real property law". Broadly, goods can be classified for the purposes of 9–334 into three categories: those that remain "pure goods"; those so substantially integrated into real estate as to become real estate themselves, i.e., "pure realty"; and those in the gray area that would pass in a deed to the real estate yet remain personal property. This last classification are fixtures. Comment 3 to 9–334 presents this as follows:

> * * * this section recognizes three categories of goods: (1) those that retain their chattel character entirely and are not part of the real property; (2) ordinary building materials that have become an integral part of the real property and cannot retain their chattel character for purposes of finance; and (3) an intermediate class that has become real property for certain purposes, but as to which chattel financing may be preserved.

Goods cross the line from pure goods to fixtures when they become sufficiently related to the real estate such that they would pass in a deed under the local real estate law. What passes by deed in Minnesota may not pass in Wisconsin, and what is sufficiently related to a real estate interest in New York might not be sufficiently related in Georgia. Thus the general definition in section 9–102(a)(41) is no more than a cross reference to state case law and state real estate statutes. What, then, are the state law principles governing when goods become fixtures? Here, we cannot go much beyond posing the question.

Most courts start from the proposition that status of goods as a fixture depends upon the intention of the parties. Of course, "objective manifestations of intention" are the windows through which we view actual intent. One searching for such manifestations might ask: What did the parties say in their agreement? How did they attach the goods to the realty? What is the relationship between the parties? How is the operation of the goods related to the use of the real property? For many courts, intent is most clearly manifested by the firmness with which the goods are affixed to the real estate and the amount of sweat that removal would entail. The American Law of Property puts the matter as follows (emphasis added):

> In the United States, whether a given chattel becomes a fixture is said to depend on intention, but whether it is the unilateral intention of the annexor at the time of annexation, or the bilateral intention of the parties to some transaction relating to the chattel or to the land, and whether it is the actual intention, or the manifested intention, or the imputed intention, is not always clear.

Part of the confusion comes from the various meanings ascribed to the term "fixture". Under the modern cases no more precise definition is possible than this: a fixture is a former chattel which, while retaining its separate physical identity, *is so connected with the realty that a disinterested observer would consider it a part thereof.*

This is not the place to inject order into this chaotic body of law. One must realize only that there is more than one line of authority and the cases must be examined with care to arrive at a reasonable guess about what is and what is not a fixture.

Subsection 9–102(a)(40) states:

A "fixture filing" is "the filing of a financing statement covering goods that are or are to become fixtures and satisfying section 9–502(a) and (b). The term includes the filing of a financing statement covering goods of a transmitting utility which are or are to become fixtures".

The concept of a "fixture filing" was introduced in the 1972 revision of Article 9. The drafters concluded that one should be required to file a fixture filing in the office in which a record of a mortgage for the real property would be filed if one seeks priority over subsequent real estate interests who would typically check in the real estate files and only in those files.

Comment 4 to revised 9–501 explains the two ways in which a secured party may file a financing statement to perfect a security interest in goods that are or are to become fixtures, depending upon the parties against whom protection is sought. First, a secured party may make a non-fixture filing in Article 9 records, as with goods, in accordance with section 9–501(a)(2). Or, a secured creditor may file a "fixture filing" in the office in which a record of a mortgage on the related real property would be filed; see 9–501(a)(1)(b). Given the uncertainty of whether goods are or may become fixtures under applicable real-property law, Comment 3 to 9–334 recognizes that a secured party may make a fixture filing as a precaution. A court may not infer merely from a fixture filing that the secured party concedes that the goods are or will become fixtures.

In addition to the normal information under 9–502(a), a financing statement filed as a fixture filing under subsection (b) must include: (1) a showing that it covers goods which are, or are to become, "fixtures"; (2) a recital that the financing statement is to be filed in the real estate records; (3) a description of the real estate; and (4) the name of the record owner if the debtor has no interest of record. Section 9–502(c) states that the recording of a complying mortgage is equivalent to a fixture filing.

§ 2.   PERFECTION AND PRIORITY IN FIXTURES

CUMMINGS v. BEARDSLEY

Supreme Court of Arkansas, 1980.
271 Ark. 596, 609 S.W.2d 66.

STROUD, JUSTICE:

This is a suit filed in chancery court to foreclose the lien securing the balance of the purchase price and installation charge for two large illuminated motel and restaurant signs. Appellees filed a Motion for Summary Judgment which was granted by the trial court. We affirm the Chancellor as we agree that he properly granted the motion resulting in a dismissal of appellant's complaint.

In 1973, appellant contracted with Erect–O–Therm Structures, Inc., to fabricate and install two large signs on certain premises owned by Erect–O–Therm in Prescott, Arkansas. The signs were to advertise the location of the Stockholm Restaurant and Check Inn Motel. To secure the unpaid balance of the purchase price, Erect–O–Therm granted appellant a security interest in the signs by the execution of a security agreement describing them. A financing statement was filed with the Secretary of State of Arkansas in 1974. The security agreement between appellant and Erect–O–Therm also provided that the signs were not to be so affixed or related to realty as to become a part of the realty. The larger of the two signs was hung some 80 feet from the ground on steel poles anchored in a concrete foundation four feet deep by 16 feet wide by 20 feet long. The smaller sign is supported by steel poles which rise 12 feet from their concrete foundation.

Subsequently, Erect–O–Therm experienced financial difficulties and apparently lost the motel and restaurant property, including the two signs, to Union Planters Bank of Memphis by virtue of the bank's foreclosure of a mortgage on that realty. Appellees Conrad and Lillemore Beardsley then acquired the property from Union Planters. On January 31, 1979, appellant brought this foreclosure suit against appellees for the unpaid balance of the purchase price in the amount of $20,355.35, plus 10% of that amount as attorney's fees, possession of the signs and a deficiency judgment against appellees for any deficit remaining after the proceeds of a resale of the signs are applied to the indebtedness. Appellees denied the material allegations of appellant's complaint by specifically alleging that they had not purchased the signs from appellant nor entered into any agreement with appellant, that they had no knowledge of any indebtedness for the signs nor had they assumed any such debt, and that the financing statement was filed in the wrong place. Appellees also filed a third party complaint against Union Planters, not involved in this appeal, where they allege that they should have judgment over against the bank for any damages they suffer in this suit inasmuch as the bank represented to them that the property was free of liens and encumbrances. Some nine months thereafter, appellees filed a motion for summary judgment which was submitted on the pleadings, deposition of an officer of the appellant company, deposition of appellee Conrad Beardsley, and briefs. From a granting of the motion appellants bring this appeal, urging that the court erred in granting the motion for summary judgment.

It is well-settled that summary judgment should be granted only when a review of the pleadings, depositions and other filings reveals that there is no genuine issue as to any material fact and the moving party is entitled to judgment as a matter of law. Rule 56, Arkansas Rules of Civil Procedure. In the present case, in its order of January 24, 1980, the trial court found as follows:

    1. The Defendants, Conrad Beardsley and Lillemore Beardsley, did not purchase the signs and related property referred to in the complaint from the Plaintiff, and there is no genuine issue as to this fact.

    2. The Defendants, Conrad Beardsley and Lillemore Beardsley, are not personally liable to the Plaintiff under the security agreement referred to in the complaint since these Defendants were not a party thereto and have not assumed the indebtedness referred to in said security agreement, and there is no genuine issue as to this fact.

    3. As between the Plaintiff and Erect–O–Therm Structures, Inc., those parties agreed that the signs in question were not, and would not become fixtures, and so as between them the signs are not fixtures, but as between the Plaintiff and the Defendants, the signs, which include the supporting pipes, are fixtures. The Defendants were entitled to rely on the filings in the Nevada County Circuit Clerk's office at the time they purchased property on which the signs are located on September 28, 1976. Ark.Stat.Ann. § 85–9–401 (addendum 1961) is the applicable statutory section since the filings involved in this case were made prior to the effective date of the 1973 amendment to Article 9 of the Uniform Commercial Code, and thereunder the proper place to file a security instrument in order to perfect securing interest was in the office where a mortgage on the real estate concerned would be filed or recorded. The Plaintiff filed its financing statement with the Secretary of State and not in the office of the Circuit Clerk of Nevada County, Arkansas, being the County where the real estate is located, and thus did not properly perfect its security interest in the signs as between it and the Defendants.

    4. There are no genuine issues as to any material fact as between the Plaintiff and the Defendants, Conrad Beardsley and Lillemore Beardsley, d/b/a Check Inn and Check Inn; consequently, these Defendants are entitled to a judgment as a matter of law.

As to the trial court's first and second rulings, we agree there clearly is no genuine issue as to those matters. The copy of the security agreement attached to appellant's complaint reflects that the signs were purchased by Erect–O–Therm, not appellees, and that appellees were not a party to the agreement. There is nothing in the record to indicate, not even as an allegation, that appellees knew of or assumed the indebtedness when they purchased the motel and restaurant. The third ruling of the trial court, pertaining to the characterization of the signs as fixtures, is the only holding which appellant disputes. The trial court ruled that as between appellant and Erect–O–Therm the signs were not fixtures because of the provision in the security agreement which stated the signs would not be considered part of the realty. However, the trial court further held that, inasmuch as it was undisputed that appellees were not parties to the security agreement and were without knowledge of the aforementioned provision, the signs were fixtures as between appellant and appellees and there is no genuine issue as to that fact. These large signs anchored deep in concrete were so clearly fixtures, appellees had the right to rely on the records in the office of the Circuit Clerk of Nevada County, where filings covering fixtures are to be made, to determine if a lien was in existence at the time of their purchase. A good faith filing made in the wrong place (in this case the office of the Secretary of State) was not constructive notice to appellees as it is notice only to "any person who has knowledge of the contents of such financing statement." Ark.Stat.Ann. § 85–9–401(2) (addendum 1961).

* * * As noted previously, it was undisputed in the record that appellees were not in any way involved with the purchase of the signs from appellant; that they had not assumed the indebtedness referred to in the security agreement; that they had no knowledge of the agreement between appellant and Erect–O–Therm; and that appellant had not filed the financing statement in the Nevada County Circuit Clerk's office prior to appellees' purchase. As appellant failed to file the financing statement in Nevada County, as the security agreement was not determinative of the rights [and] obligations of appellees, and as the security agreement was the only proof offered by appellant to support his contention that summary judgment should not lie, we cannot say that there was a genuine issue as to any material fact or that the trial court erred in granting appellees' Motion for Summary Judgment.

AFFIRMED. [Dissent omitted.]

IN RE FINK

United States Bankruptcy Court, Western District of New York, 1980.
4 B.R. 741.

Hayes, Bankruptcy Judge:

This is an action by the Trustee to avoid a security interest in a mobile house claimed by defendant, Endicott Trust Company of New York hereinafter referred to as "Endicott" and to preserve that lien pursuant to Bankruptcy Rule 611 as to defendant Wemco Corp. hereinafter referred to as "Wemco."

The facts appear to be as follows. The bankrupt, Pauline Fink, purchased a mobile home from Palmer Mobile Homes, Inc. on or about

August 20, 1977. She entered into a retail installment contract. The security interest was transferred by assignment to Endicott on or about August 20, 1977. Endicott filed a financing statement which described the collateral as 24 H 52 1977 Bendix. Thereafter, the mobile home was delivered to Route 415 in the Town of Campbell which the bankrupt was leasing from Wemco. On August 24, 1977, the bankrupt contracted to purchase the real property on which the mobile home was placed from Wemco for $24,000. The realty consisted of about four acres and the only structure thereon was a store. The realty was transferred on December 1, 1977 by Wemco to the bankrupt and the bankrupt gave back to Wemco a purchase money mortgage for the full purchase price of $24,000.

The mobile home or modular home, which ever it may be, was delivered by Palmer Mobile Homes, Inc. and was placed on a foundation of concrete footers, concrete blocks and steel and wooden beams running the width and length of the building.

The details of construction follow. A foundation was evacuated. A septic tank was installed. Concrete footers were installed around the edge of the crawl space and at least one pillar of concrete blocks was erected in the center of the crawl space. Concrete blocks were installed and cemented to the footers. After this was done, the house was delivered to the lot in two sections (12N H 52N) on steel cradles. The sections with cradles were then placed on the cement blocks. The house sections were bolted together. A roof cap was put on over the place in the roof where the sections were joined together and it was cemented and nailed down. Siding was put on the two ends of the house and nailed over the spot where the joinder of the section occurred to give the appearance of a continuous wall. The septic system was hooked up. Water lines were connected. An electrical line was connected to the store's system and the store's electrical system and capacity were increased. At this point, the top course of cinder blocks were placed in but not cemented to the course immediately below. No tie downs were used in the construction. The house even has an open fireplace, although this hangs on the side of the house. From the pictures in evidence, the house appears to be a normal ranch home without front or back steps.

Additional facts which were developed at the trial follow. Palmer, who installed the mobile home on the foundation, testified that he could remove and transport the home for about $500 by removing the roof cap and the siding and shingles from the end, disconnect water lines, electric septic tank and unbolt the sections of the house and transport it on the cradle of steel beams which support each section.

The officer of Wemco said that the house was constructed in the same fashion as any construction and that the attachment to realty was the same as in any stick built house.

Additionally, when Wemco transferred the property to the bankrupt, Fink, in December, 1977, the attorney for Wemco had the abstract redated. There was nothing on the abstract that gave Wemco any notice of an interest by Endicott in the house. Wemco, when it transferred the property to Mrs. Fink, took back a purchase money mortgage for $24,000.

The facts stated above raise the issue as to whether or not the home in question is a chattel that requires perfection by filing pursuant to New York State UCC 9–302(1)(d) or a fixture attached to real property that requires filing in accordance with New York State UCC 9–313(1)(a). Section 9–302(1)(d) of the Uniform Commercial Code holds that a financing statement must be filed to perfect a security interest in a motor vehicle. This section has been held to govern mobile homes * * *. Section 9–313 requires a special filing where the item is a fixture. The filing must be in the office where a mortgage on real estate is filed and it must conform to the requirements of UCC 9–402(5) which requires that a financing statement filed as a fixture must show that it covers this type of collateral, must recite that it is to be indexed in the real estate records and the financing statement must contain a description of the real estate sufficient for its identification and it must show the name of the record owner.

If the home in question is considered to have ceased to be personalty and become a fixture by annexation to the real property, the filing made by Endicott was improper. The case turns upon whether the home is personalty or a fixture.

Section 9–313 states in part that "(1)(a) 'goods' are fixtures when they become so related to particular real estate that an interest in them arises under real estate law." The official comments which accompany this section say in part, "in cases where mobile homes or prefabricated steel buildings are erected by a person having an ownership interest in the land, the question into which category the buildings fall is one determined by local law." The definition of fixture is not an exact one. A recent law review article on the subject of fixtures under the UCC defines the term as follows:

> A fixture is a former chattel which, because of its annexation to and association with realty, has become part and parcel thereof but which has not lost its separate physical identity. A fixture is neither personalty nor realty within a strict definition of those terms. Rather, it partakes of the characteristics of each, since prior to annexation it is movable and not associated with realty, but after annexation it loses its character as personalty and is deemed realty. Various definitions of fixture have been utilized, all of which emphasize the former chattel aspect and the annexation to realty.[1]

23 N.Y.Jur. Fixtures section 2 (1962) says as follows:

> As a general rule, the true criterion of a fixture is based on the united application of three requisites: (1) actual annexation to the

---

1. Trade Fixture—Secured Transactions   Code, 44 Alb.L.Rev. 165, (1979).
Under New York's Uniform Commercial

real property or something appurtenant thereto; (2) application to the use or purpose to which that part of the realty with which it is connected is appropriated; and (3) the intention of the party making the annexation to make a permanent accession to the freehold * * *.

In re Lido Beach Sewage Collection Dist., 40 Misc.2d 384, (County Ct. 1963), page 385:

> Ordinarily for an article to become a fixture the following requisites must be met: Firstly, there must be annexation to the realty. Secondly, there must be adaptability of the article affixed to the use of the freehold. Thirdly, the intention of the party creating the annexation is to make the article a permanent accession to the freehold.

The two cases which have dealt with mobile homes in the context of section 9–313 are In re Foskett, 7 UCC Rep.Serv. 267 (W.D.Wisc.1969) and George v. Commercial Credit Corp., 440 F.2d 551 (7th Cir.1971). They seem to follow the New York State tests set forth above. A recent 1979 Vermont Supreme Court case, Hartford Nat'l Bank & Trust Co. v. Godin, 398 Atl.2d 286, 26 UCC Rep.Serv. 221 (Vt.Sup.Ct.1979), also held a mobile home a fixture based on the same three tests set forth above.

Applying these principles to the case at bar, we find that the bankrupt contracted to purchase the mobile home at about the same time she entered into a contract to purchase the realty. She had a crawl space dug. She had footings installed and she had cinder block cemented to the footings to hold the home. The bankrupt installed a septic tank system, ran water and electric into the home. The bankrupt lived in the home.

Looking at the house, in the pictures that were taken of the house, it looks at least to the uninitiated eye like any other ranch house you might see erected in the country. There would be nothing to warn anyone that this was in fact a trailer or a motor vehicle. If it was a trailer, it came certainly in two parts and had to be separated into two parts to be moved along the road. Should someone wish to move the house, they would have to dismantle it, separate it into two parts, remove part of the roofing and remove five to six feet of the center strips of shingles at either end of the home. The house in the manner in which it was annexed to real property certainly meets the test set forth in the cases cited above. Therefore, this court finds that Endicott is an unsecured creditor and that their filing should have been under section 9–313 rather than under 9–302(1)(d).

With regard to Wemco's interest, it is paramount to the trustee because Wemco had a filed mortgage agreement which is a lien upon the real property.

This Memorandum and Decision shall constitute Findings of Fact and Conclusions of Law in accordance with Rule 752 of the Rules of Bankruptcy Procedure.

Problem 4–1

A general practitioner calls you in as a secured transactions expert for your opinion concerning the rights of his client, IR, who sold a complex manufacturing line to the manufacturer of automotive interiors. The line covers several thousand square feet and runs for nearly 300 yards through a large manufacturing complex. Most of it is bolted to the floor and is composed of overhead trams, rails and attached facilities for spraying and heating. The person who called you in is concerned that the "line" may constitute a fixture. He tells you that IR received a $1 million down payment and has an agreement to be paid for the remaining $4 million of the purchase price over five years. IR took a security interest in the line and filed a financing statement with the Secretary of State's office in Lansing. The debtor is a Michigan corporation and is now in financial difficulty. The lawyer has several questions:

1. If the debtor goes into bankruptcy will IR defeat the trustee in bankruptcy despite the fact that it has not done a fixture filing?

2. Will IR defeat Bank who, after IR's interest attached, lent $1 million to the common debtor and took a mortgage on the premises?

3. Is there anything you can recommend that IR do now to improve its chances?

4. If the mortgage proves superior to IR's security interest and the debtor defaults, what can IR do? Can it repossess?

5. If Bank held a properly perfected security interest in debtor's furnace that was installed in an office building in International Falls, Minnesota, would Bank be within its right to repossess the furnace in the middle of winter? See section 9–604.

Problem 4–2

In October 2001 debtor bought a mobile home and transported it to a lot south of Phoenix. Bank lent the money to buy the mobile home and had its name put on a Certificate of Title. It appears that Bank has done similar transactions with as many as 100 other residents in the mobile home park. It is now 2007, the mobile homes have all been added on to, their wheels taken off and they appear, from the outside, to be conventional stick built homes. Friendly Financial, ignorant of the Certificates of Title, has issued home equity loans to 20 to 30 of the owners of the mobile homes in the mobile home park. Friendly has perfected its interest by taking mortgages and recording them.

1. If the mobile home owners default on the loans to Bank, will Bank have priority over Friendly?

2. One of Friendly's lawyers suggested that the mobile homes are no longer just fixtures. She claims they are real estate just like a stick built house and so not subject to any mode of perfection provided in Article 9. How do you respond?

Problem 4–3

Debtor owns several hundred large, liquid fertilizer tanks that it installs on farms throughout Iowa. Several years ago, Bank loaned $1.4 million to finance the purchase of the tanks. It took a security interest in all of the tanks and did a fixture filing in the county where each tank is located. When Bank consulted you last month you told Bank to file a UCC–1 in Des Moines and it did so.

Last week, Debtor filed in Chapter 11. The lawyer for the DIP has now commenced an adversary proceeding in the bankruptcy court to subordinate Bank's interest. What do you expect the DIP's arguments to be? (One will surely be under 547 of the Bankruptcy Code, not so?)

Chapter Five

SECURITY IN CONSUMER GOODS

§ 1. INTRODUCTION

Most security interests in consumer goods are to finance the purchase price. So we start there at the purchase money loan.

Automatic Perfection—Purchase Money Security Interests in Consumer Goods

Should merchants or banks with security interests in consumers' chairs, stoves, or washing machines be required to file like most other secured creditors? Pre–Code law granted sellers of consumer goods and those who lent the purchase price of consumer goods perfected status even without filing. So, the Code's "automatic" perfection on creation of such interests was no departure. In this case, automatic perfection reduces what would otherwise be heavy transaction costs with slight benefits. If creditors had to file with respect to every consumer credit transaction, the filing offices would be bulging at the seams. Further, the benefits to be gained from filing these security interests are marginal. Since potential creditors have long been aware of automatic perfection of such "conditional sales," they are on guard when a consumer attempts to borrow against consumer goods. Finally, most consumer goods cost little and depreciate quickly; creditors, other than purchase money lenders, seldom rely on such goods in making loans.

The case law has revealed only two significant lawyer problems. First, what is a purchase money security interest? Second, what are "consumer goods"?

Purchase Money Status

In most circumstances identification of a purchase money security interest is easy. If the seller has retained an interest in goods sold to secure payment of some or all of the price, the seller has a purchase money security interest whether the agreement with the buyer is called a "conditional sales contract," a "bailment lease," or something else. Observe also that a third party (for example, a bank or finance company) that lends money to a prospective buyer can, as under prior law, also qualify as a purchase money lender under section 9–103(a)(2). That person must make advances or incur an obligation "to enable the debtor to acquire rights in or the use of collateral," and, the money lent must be "in fact so used." Elsewhere we will consider the importance of the limitations of (a)(2); for now, it suffices to understand that the third party has a purchase money security interest only if that party can show that the money the third party lent was "in fact" used to acquire an interest in the collateral in question.

To be automatically perfected, a security interest must retain its status as a "purchase money" security interest. Thus it is often in the interest of a trustee in bankruptcy or some other competitor to claim that a security interest which was originally "purchase money" has lost that status or, in some cases, never attained that status. The challenge to the purchase money status comes in two forms. First, the challenger might argue that the mixture of a purchase money and non-purchase money security interest in the same security agreement renders the entire security agreement non-purchase money. Second, the challenger might acknowledge the existence of two security interests, one purchase money and one non-purchase money, but argue that the debtor's payments should be allocated first to the purchase money security interest and so reduce that one to the benefit of the trustee (who, by hypothesis, can defeat the non-purchase money unperfected interest but who cannot defeat the purchase money perfected interest). 1999 Article 9 explicitly provides that a single document can create two security interests in business transactions: one purchase money and one non-purchase money, but section 9–103 declines to take a position on that issue in consumer cases. So, unless a court chooses to apply the business rule by analogy to consumer cases too, we are left with the same confusion after the 1999 revision that existed before.

There are two common circumstances in which purchase money status is uncertain. First, is the case where the debtor makes several consecutive purchases from one seller. For example, assume the debtor buys a refrigerator in month one, a television in month two, and a stereo in month three. Assume further that each of the purchases is financed by the seller who takes a security interest in each of the assets purchased. Since each would be financed by the seller, each would be a purchase money security interest and so be automatically perfected. But life is not so simple. In all likelihood our seller will combine the three items into one security agreement and that security agreement will provide that each asset is collateral, not only for its own purchase price but also for the purchase price of the other two items. Now there's a problem. Because the purchase price for the refrigerator was "purchase money" only as to the refrigerator and not as to the television or stereo, to the extent that the television and stereo stand as collateral for the price of the refrigerator, the security is "non-purchase money".

The second circumstance arises when a loan is re-financed or when a debtor makes payments against a loan that is secured by two security interests, one purchase money and one non-purchase money. Assume, for example, the debtor borrows $2,000 from the bank in a purchase money loan to buy a stereo system. Six months later the bank "refinances" the loan; at that time the debtor borrows an additional $1,000. Has the refinancing caused the security interest to lose its purchase money status? For consumer cases, 9–103 declines to give an answer; however, for business cases, 9–103 rules that the purchase money status is retained. So section 9–103 leaves a court free to follow its own rule if it has one, to apply the business rule by analogy, or to reason from other cases.

Even if the original security interest retains its purchase money status, the new loan ($1,000) will not be a purchase money loan and will not be automatically perfected. Now, assume the debtor pays $1,000 against its consolidated debt. Does this $1,000 reduce the loan that is secured by the purchase money security interest, does it extinguish the $1,000 loan that is secured by non-purchase money security interest, or is it allocated pro rata? This will be important if the secured creditor is depending on the automatic perfection provisions associated with purchase money loans. If the $1,000 payment is allocated on a FIFO (first in, first out) basis to the earliest loan, $1,000 of the loan is now secured by a perfected security interest (purchase money) and $1,000 is secured by an unperfected security interest. If, alternatively, the payments are allocated on a LIFO basis to the last loan, the secured creditor retains a perfected security interest as to its entire remaining loan because the payment would have been treated as a payment against the second loan secured by a non-purchase money security interest.

Where there are multiple purchases and later payments, one faces the same allocation problem. If I have paid the price of the item first purchased, do I at least own that? If a court recognizes a "dual status" security agreement, it needs to find an allocation method to determine how a single payment per month by the debtor should be allocated among the various purchase money interests and the non-purchase money interests. Should it be FIFO, LIFO or some other method? Some courts were offended (see, e.g., *Walker Thomas*) by allocation schemes that held every piece of collateral subject to the security interest until the last penny was paid; others found a solution to that problem in state law providing an allocation scheme. In any case the creditor needs to provide an allocation scheme by its agreement or to find one in the law. Finally, there are cases where the loan was rewritten or "consolidated". In those too, the courts have been in confusion and disagreement, some finding that the rewriting or consolidation deprived the new loan entirely of the purchase money status; others concluding the opposite.

Other pitfalls await creditors relying on automatic perfection. For example, if the goods are to become fixtures, the filing exemption will not protect the retailer, see sections 9–334 and 9–604. Observe that purchase money status is important not merely for perfection; it is also necessary to preserve a security interest in consumer goods from extinction in bankruptcy under 522(f).

Consumer Goods

The second question presented by 9–103 involves classification of the collateral: consumer goods or not? Is a stove designed for home use necessarily a consumer good? Is a $50,000 house trailer a consumer good? According to subsection 9–102(a)(23): "[g]oods are 'consumer goods' if they are used or bought for use primarily for personal, family or household purposes * * *." Section 9–102 does not classify goods according to design or intrinsic nature but according to how their owner uses them. It follows that as use changes, either because the owner finds some new task for the goods, or because an owner sells the goods to another who uses them for a different purpose, the classification of the goods will also change. Of course, borderline cases, such as a physician's car or a farmer's jeep, will arise. When they do, the factfinder must determine whether the debtor used the goods "primarily" for personal, family, or household purposes.

Conclusion

Whether a security interest in consumer goods is a purchase money security interest is important for at least three reasons: First, it is important for the purposes of 9–309. If the security interest is a purchase money security interest in consumer goods, it is automatically perfected without filing or any other act; if the security interest is not a purchase money security interest, the creditor will normally have to file a financing statement in order to perfect and achieve priority over a trustee in bankruptcy and many other claimants. Second, in bankruptcy a consumer debtor may be able to avoid certain non-purchase money security interests in household goods and the like under 522(f)(1)(B)— even if they are perfected. Finally, the taking of non-purchase money security interest in certain household goods may be an unfair trade practice under the FTC regulation, 16 C.F.R. § 444.2(a)(4). So, the purchase money status of a security interest in consumer goods has potential significance beyond automatic perfection.

§ 2. PERFECTIONS OF PURCHASE MONEY SECURITY INTEREST

IN RE MANUEL

United States Court of Appeals, Fifth Circuit, 1975.
507 F.2d 990.

NICHOLS, ASSOCIATE JUDGE:

This case originated in the bankruptcy of James Lucius Manuel. On December 7, 1972, he purchased certain household furniture from appellant Roberts Furniture Co. On February 13, 1973, he purchased a television set, also from appellant. The purchase money security agreement he then signed referred to an unpaid balance of $573.32 from the first purchase, deducted $116.03 for refunds, leaving a prior unpaid balance of $457.29 which was added to the unpaid balance on the TV set,

$174.07, making a total balance owed of $631.36. This agreement was never filed for perfection as Georgia law required, nor was perfection obtained by retaining possession. The agreement also failed to indicate the order in which purchases were paid off, and the amounts still due on each item and secured by the paid-up items. The apparent purpose of Roberts Furniture was to ensure that title to nothing passed until title to all passed. The February 13 purchase money agreement provided:

> It is agreed that the contracts, whether one or more, heretofore entered into between Seller and Buyer, having an unpaid balance of $573.32 referred to as "prior balance" shall remain in full force and effect, that Seller's security interest in the goods sold thereunder shall remain perfected, until full payment for said goods has been made, and that the contract evidenced by this instrument shall have no effect on the above mentioned existing contract except to modify the terms of payment thereof.

> It is further agreed, however, that for the purposes of the payment of the said prior balance and total of payments on the contract evidenced by this instrument, that Buyer shall make one payment in the amount and for the period set forth below until the total of payments as set forth has been paid. Upon a default in the contract evidenced by this instrument the said existing contract shall also be deemed to be in default. Until all installment payments and all other amounts due hereunder, have been paid, Seller shall retain a security interest in the Goods and any and all equipment, parts, accessories, attachments, additions and other goods, and all replacements thereof, now or hereafter installed in, affixed to or used in connection with said Goods and, if Buyer sells or otherwise disposes of the Goods in violation of the terms of this agreement, in the proceeds of such sale or disposition. *Goods may secure all present and future liabilities, debts and obligations of whatever nature of BUYER to SELLER or its assigns.* (Emphasis supplied.)

Manuel filed a voluntary bankruptcy petition on May 3, 1973. Roberts Furniture claimed reclamation in bankruptcy on the basis of priority of their "Purchase Money Security Interest." The bankruptcy judge found that except for the TV set Roberts failed to acquire a Purchase Money Security Interest as defined by Georgia Code § 109A–9–107; that Roberts failed to perfect the security interest in any other manner provided by the Georgia and Uniform Commercial Codes; and that Section 70(c) of the Bankruptcy Act, 11 U.S.C. § 110, and Georgia Code § 109A–9–301(3) gave the bankruptcy trustee preference over Roberts' unperfected security interests.

The District Judge would have denied reclamation for the TV set also, except that the point was not preserved by cross appeal. Appellee now stipulates, contrary to the impression of the court below, that the combined value of all the involved merchandise is not equal to the debt owed Roberts Furniture Co. Nevertheless, we affirm.

I

* * *

The issue here is whether Georgia law would allow the arrangement below to be considered a Purchase Money Security Interest, which requires no filing for perfection. Georgia has enacted the Uniform Commercial Code. Georgia Code § 109A–9–107 defines a Purchase Money Security Interest: [court quotes 9–107] Georgia Code § 109A–9–302 provides the exceptions where filing is not required for perfection. One of the exceptions is:

* * *

(d) a purchase money security interest in consumer goods;

There are other exceptions to the filing requirement, not here relevant. Otherwise, if not perfected by filing, under Georgia Code § 109A–9–301, the unperfected security interest is subordinate to the rights of "(1)(b) * * * a lien creditor * * *;" which term includes "(3) * * * a trustee in bankruptcy * * *;" unless all the creditors had actual knowledge of the security interest, which is not contended here.

Roberts Furniture claims the exception for consumer goods. As the judges below noted, citing Allen v. Lokey, 307 F.2d 353 (5th Cir.1962), and National Silver Co. v. Nicholas, 205 F.2d 52 (5th Cir.1953), the burden of proof to establish a security interest is upon the party seeking reclamation, and Roberts has not met that burden. The problem here begins with the fact that the security agreement filed with the court shows about $150 paid on about a $900 total debt, for 7 pieces of furniture and a TV set, with no clues as to what items are paid for and which are not, nor does any rule of first-bought, first-paid for appear.

A plain reading of the statutory requirements would indicate that they require the purchase money security interest to be in the item purchased, and that, as the judges below noted, the purchase money security interest cannot exceed the price of what is purchased in the transaction wherein the security interest is created, if the vendor is to be protected despite the absence of filing. Except as to the TV set, if at all, the interest here is not a "purchase money security interest" because it is not taken or retained by the seller of the collateral solely to secure all or part of *its* (emphasis supplied) price. Roberts attempted to make collateral secure debt other than its own price. The statutory exception does not reach the case.

The judges below drew their conclusion on the statutory language and on authority other than Georgia cases. Appellee has collected and cited to us a number of Georgia cases, which we have examined. We have no doubt that the Georgia courts will henceforward observe the express command of their legislature, but we find it unnecessary to analyze in detail cases which show no more than that they have hitherto done so, with respect to parts of the enactment here involved, other than those to be construed here. The District Judge refers to In re Simpson, 4 UCC 243 (D.C.W.D.Mich.1966). This referee in bankruptcy's opinion is well thought out, and documented with references to the Official Code Comment #2, and to secondary authority. It was a case stronger for the vendor, than the one here, in that the farm machinery item in dispute was sold under the agreement which failed, in the referee's view, to create a purchase money security interest without filing, only because it included a clause making the item security, not only for its own price, but also for future advances. The entire discussion may be regarded as dictum since the referee ends up by holding that the vendor saved its security interest after all by recovering possession before the bankruptcy, without fraud on the creditors. In view of the wide circulation of the referee's opinion by the UCC Reporting Service, the absence of contrary case authority, and its inherent reasonableness, we think our District Judge properly gave much weight to it.

The error of the belief below, that the value of the intended collateral exceeded the debt, is not fatal to the conclusion reached, though it does impair some of the reasoning, and prevents us from adopting the opinion below as our own.

We express no view as to whether a valid purchase money security interest was created with respect to the TV set. Nothing we say is to be taken as a holding as to that.

AFFIRMED.

———

Section 9–103 of the 1999 Code does not overrule *Manuel*. Why?

Problem 5–1

This dispute arises in a state where there is no decision adopting or rejecting the position in the In re Manuel case. The state has adopted a Retail Installment Sales Act which says that payments made on a bill that represents more than one purchase are prorated according to the original principal balance of each. Debtor made three purchases: a TV for $500 on February 2, 2002; a refrigerator for $400 on September 1, 2002; and a stove for $600 on January 5, 2003. After the stove purchase, the principal balance stood at $1,350. From February through May, when the debtor declared bankruptcy, the debtor made three $50 payments on the combined bill. At the time of bankruptcy, the bill stood at $1,340 (most of the payments had been allocated to interest).

1. In the debtor's bankruptcy, the trustee claims the court should follow In re Manuel and that no part of the $1,340 claim is a purchase money claim because, after the rewrite, no part of the loan constitutes valid value given to acquire "rights in the collateral".

2. As a fall back position, trustee argued that the FIFO rule stated in the contract (as opposed to the pro-rata rule stated in the retail installment sales act) should be applied and that the TV should be regarded as completely free of the bank's security interest because the debtor has paid more than $500.

3.   Creditor argues that trustee has no standing because the assets will be claimed as exempt by the debtor if they are not subject to the security agreement and therefore the dispute, if any, is between the debtor and the secured creditor (assume for this purpose that the debtor will claim federal exemptions under 522(d)). In any case, the creditor claims a purchase money security interest in all of the collateral because of the application of 9–103(b)(2). What do you think?

4.   If the trustee declines to challenge the creditor under 544(a) because she knows that the debtor will claim the assets as exempt (and so take them out of the bankruptcy estate), will debtor be permitted to challenge the security interest under 522(h)?

Problem 5–2

Debtor purchases a $60,000 mobile home for her residence. She borrows $50,000 from Bank and gives a security interest. By mistake, Bank fails to file a financing statement.

1.   On Debtor's bankruptcy, Bank claims an automatically perfected security interest. Trustee argues that the automatic perfection provisions do not and should not apply to a commodity with such a large value.

2.   Would trustee prevail if the mobile home had become a fixture since Bank concedes that it did not do a "fixture filing"?

3.   What if one could procure a Certificate of Title on mobile homes in Arkansas where the transaction takes place but Debtor never did so? See 9–311.

4.   What if two months after the sale Debtor moved the mobile home to a construction site where she used it as a construction office?

§ 3.   THE SPECIAL CASE OF AUTOMOBILES AND OTHER GOODS COVERED BY CERTIFICATES OF TITLE

The certificate of title laws that now exist in all states in some form provide a mode of perfection that was in use in many states at the time the original Code was enacted, and which is entirely separate from the Code system of perfection. Section 9–311(a) states that the filing of a financing statement is not necessary or sufficient to perfect a security interest in property subject to a certificate of title statute, and section 9–311(b) provides that satisfying the requirements of such a state statute is equivalent to filing for the purposes of Article 9. In addition to this "step-back" provision, sections 9–316(d) and (e) provide rules for changes in the applicable law. More importantly, 9–303 dictates the law governing perfection and priority of security interests in goods covered by a certificate of title. Section 9–337 provides rules for priority. Although this topic is included in the chapter on Consumer Security Interest, one cannot assume that all automobile security interests are granted by consumers. In fact there are many business security interests in trucks or other vehicles that are covered by certificates of title. For example, getting one's name on the certificate of title would be the common way of perfecting a security interest in a trucking company's over the road vehicles. In general the problems of perfection and priority are the same whether the debtor is a consumer or a business person.

Problem 5–3

Assume Bank One makes a loan to Trucker/Debtor and takes a security interest in Debtor's $70,000 truck. The truck, at the time of the loan, is located in and operated from Tennessee. The Bank perfects its security interest by getting its name listed as the secured creditor on the Tennessee certificate of title. Consider the rights of the Bank vis-à-vis a trustee in bankruptcy or a competing creditor in each of the following cases.

1. Debtor moves to Ohio, establishes his residence there and operates the truck from Cincinnati. He continues to operate the truck under the Tennessee certificate of title and 2 years after the move, files bankruptcy. The trustee argues that the failure of the Debtor to get a certificate of title in Ohio and the creditor to gets its name on such certificate subordinated the creditor. Is the trustee correct?

2. Assume in the former case that Debtor procured a new certificate of title in Ohio one month after the move to Cincinnati. Either because of the Debtor's fraud or because of a mistake in the Ohio Certificate of Title Office, Bank One was not listed as a secured creditor on the new certificate. Six months after the move and five months after the clean Ohio certificate had been issued, assume alternatively that the Debtor sells its truck to a bona fide purchaser or that Debtor files bankruptcy. In the former case the bona fide purchaser defeats the Tennessee secured creditor, correct? What about the competition between the Bank and the Trustee in the latter case? In challenging the trustee, the Bank points particularly to section 9–316(d).

RICHARD G. GREEN, SR. v. ARCADIA FINANCIAL LTD., ET AL.

Supreme Court, Erie County, 1997.
174 Misc.2d 411, 663 N.Y.S.2d 944.

MINTZ, JUSTICE:

Plaintiff moves for declaratory judgment and interim relief. Defendant Arcadia cross-moves for summary judgment dismissing the complaint, and defendant Four M Sales (Four M) also seeks dismissal of the complaint. The facts underlying this action are not in dispute.

Antwan Anderson purchased a 1993 Jeep Cherokee from Master Motors of Buffalo on January 4, 1997. Anderson paid $,2500.00 down and financed the remainder of the purchase price ($18,119.20) through an installment obligation to defendant Arcadia whereby he was to make 72 monthly payments of $424.60 commencing February 4, 1997. Defendant Arcadia secured the installment obligation with a lien which was properly perfected, and such lien was duly noted on Anderson's certificate of title. Anderson made payments in February and March. On February 11, 1997, Anderson submitted a forged release of lien on a piece of stationery which purported to be Arcadia letterhead to the

Department of Motor Vehicles. Through the submission of the release of lien, Anderson obtained on March 4, 1997, a new certificate of title without any lien noted thereon. On March 14, 1997, Anderson sold the vehicle to defendant Four M. On April 21, 1997, Four M sold the vehicle to the plaintiff, who financed its acquisition through defendant Pentagon. On June 13, 1997, the vehicle was repossessed by Arcadia's agent. Defendant Arcadia claims that its lien continues despite the filing of the false release of lien, and despite the issuance by the Department of Motor Vehicles of a certificate of title with no liens noted. Plaintiff claims that he acquired the vehicle from Four M without Arcadia's lien.

New York enacted the Uniform Vehicle Certificate of Title Act in 1971 (Vehicle and Traffic Law, § 2101 et seq.). The Act preempts U.C.C. Article 9 with respect to security interests in automobiles which are created by persons other than dealers; thus, Article 9 has no application to this case. Under § 2118, a security interest in the automobile is perfected by the filing of an application with the Department of Motor Vehicles. It is undisputed that defendant Arcadia properly perfected its security interest by such a filing. Under § 2121, a security interest is released by the filing of a release of lien which has been executed by the lienholder. Although Anderson filed a release of lien, it is undisputed that such release was not executed by Arcadia. While the certificate of title is prima facie evidence of the information contained thereon (§ 2108(c)), the existence of the certificate of title in question is not dispositive of the issue. Anderson could not and did not convey unencumbered title of the Jeep to Four M. This is not, however, determinative of the issue of whether Four M, as a dealer in used automobiles, could deliver unencumbered title to plaintiff, as a buyer in the ordinary course of business, who is a good faith purchaser for value.

U.C.C. 2–403(1) provides in part:

> A purchaser of goods acquires all title which his transferor had or had power to transfer except that a purchaser of a limited interest acquires rights only to the extent of the interest purchased. A person with voidable title has power to transfer a good title to a good faith purchased for value.

A purchaser who purchases a vehicle from a thief, or from a dealer who has purchased from a thief does not acquire title under § 2–403. See, e.g., Candela v. Port Motors, Inc., 208 A.D.2d 486, 617 N.Y.S.2d 49 (2d Dept.1994). However, a person who acquires title by fraud has "voidable" title, and can convey good title so long as the goods are transferred to a good-faith purchaser for value before such title is voided. See, e.g., Sheridan Suzuki, Inc. v. Caruso Auto Sales Inc., 110 Misc.2d 823, 442 N.Y.S.2d 957 (Sup.Ct.Erie Co.1981). A person who acquires a certificate title by fraudulent documents submitted to the Department of Motor Vehicles does not acquire voidable title within the meaning of § 2–403. Alamo Rent–A–Car, Inc. v. Mendenhall, 113 Nev. 445, 937 P.2d 69 (1997). Such a person has no greater title than he did prior to the acquisition of the documents. For this reason, Arcadia's lien continued in the vehicle after its sale to plaintiff. Had Anderson acquired a properly executed release of lien through fraud or through a dishonored check, his resulting unencumbered title would have been "voidable." However, he did not ever acquire a proper release of lien, and his title, encumbered by the Arcadia lien, remained unchanged by the submission of the forged release of lien. Thus, Anderson conveyed title to Four M subject to Arcadia's lien, and Four M could only convey the same title to plaintiff.

Four M, however, as a dealer in automobiles, warrants unencumbered title under U.C.C. 2–312(3). Since the vehicle sold by Four M to the plaintiff was subject to Arcadia's lien, Four M breached its warranty of title, and plaintiff is entitled to recover his damages due to the existence of this lien from Four M. Candela v. Port Motors, supra. The measure of damages is the lesser of the outstanding loan balance owed to Arcadia or the amount paid by plaintiff to Four M including the payments under his installment obligation and the outstanding loan balance owed to defendant Pentagon. In the event that the amount paid by plaintiff is greater than the outstanding loan balance owed to Arcadia, Four M is to pay off that loan balance by payment to Arcadia, and the plaintiff will retain the vehicle, and he may maintain his action against Arcadia for the claimed damage to the vehicle during the repossession and retention of the vehicle by Arcadia. In the event that the amount paid by plaintiff is less than the outstanding loan balance owed to Arcadia, Four M is to return to plaintiff any down payment and any payments made by plaintiff to Pentagon on the installment obligation, and Four M is also to pay the outstanding loan balance to Pentagon. In that case, plaintiff is entitled to recover from Arcadia the value of improvements he made to the automobile after its purchase. Alamo Rent–A–Car v. Mendenhall, supra.

For these reasons, judgment is granted to plaintiff against defendant Four M, and judgment is granted to defendant Arcadia against plaintiff on the issue of the validity of its lien.

TOYOTA MOTOR CREDIT CORP. v. C.L. HYMAN AUTO WHOLESALE, INC.

Supreme Court of Virginia, 1998.
256 Va. 243, 506 S.E.2d 14

Lacy, Justice.

In this appeal, we determine whether a lienholder whose lien was omitted from a duplicate certificate of title of an automobile because of the fraud of the owner can enforce that lien against a subsequent bona fide purchaser of the automobile.

The facts are not in dispute. In February 1996, Traci Bowden purchased a Toyota vehicle pursuant to a retail installment contract. The contract was assigned to Toyota Motor Credit Corporation (TMCC) for value. TMCC's security interest was noted on the certificate of title issued by the Virginia Department of Motor Vehicles (DMV). TMCC retained possession of the certificate of title.

In July 1996, Bowden applied for a duplicate certificate of title from DMV, representing that TMCC's lien had been satisfied and released. Bowden's application was accompanied by a letter purportedly from TMCC releasing its lien. This letter was a forgery. Based on these fraudulent representations, DMV issued a duplicate certificate of title showing "no liens" against the vehicle. Bowden then sold the vehicle to C.L. Hyman Auto Wholesale, Inc. (Hyman).

When Bowden fell behind in her payments on the Retail Installment Agreement, TMCC began efforts to bring the account current or to recover the vehicle. Eventually, TMCC discovered Bowden's fraud and that she had sold the vehicle to Hyman. TMCC asked Hyman to return the vehicle. When Hyman refused, TMCC filed a motion for judgment in detinue against Hyman. Following a hearing, the trial court found that Hyman was a bona fide purchaser for value without notice of the fraud, was "entitled to rely on the certificate issued by the DMV," and was not subject to TMCC's lien. The trial court dismissed the motion for judgment. We awarded TMCC an appeal.

As the trial court recognized, both parties in this litigation are innocent victims of the fraudulent acts of a third party: "Each has followed the law and done everything which could reasonably be expected in order to protect its interests.... However, the case is here, and, like it or not, the loss must fall on one of these two innocent parties." In determining where the loss falls, the trial court concluded that the motor vehicle titling statutes, as interpreted by this Court, require a decision in favor of Hyman. We agree and will affirm the judgment of the trial court.

The motor vehicle titling statutes, Title 42, Chapter 6, were enacted to protect the public by providing for the issuance of certificates of title as evidence of ownership of motor vehicles and to provide potential buyers and creditors with a single place where information about the status of motor vehicles could be found. Maryland Credit Fin. Corp. v. Franklin Credit Fin. Corp., 164 Va. 579, 583, 180 S.E. 408, 409–10 (1935). These statutes, originally enacted in 1924, eliminated any requirement that a lien against a motor vehicle be recorded in the county or city where the purchaser or debtor resides or in any other manner available for recording a security interest in personal property, but imposed the new condition that a security interest in a motor vehicle would not be perfected "as to third parties" unless shown on the certificate of title. Code § 46.2–638; Bain v. Commonwealth, 215 Va. 89, 91, 205 S.E.2d 641, 643 (1974).

Code § 46.2–638 specifically provides that a certificate of title showing a security interest "shall be adequate notice to the Commonwealth, creditors, and purchasers that a security interest in the motor vehicle exists." We have recognized that the converse is also true. [W]hen a certificate of title is issued which fails to show a lien or encumbrance, it is notice to the world that the property is free from any lien or encumbrance, and if transferred to a bona fide purchaser the latter would obtain a good title.

Maryland Credit, 164 Va. at 582–83, 180 S.E. at 409. To hold otherwise would eliminate the ability of potential buyers and lenders to rely on the information contained in certificates of title.

Inevitably, there will be occasions when the information regarding the status of liens contained in a certificate of title will be in error. If the erroneous information is a notation that no liens exist against the vehicle, the interest of the bona fide purchaser for value prevails over the interest of the creditor with a security interest in the motor vehicle. Id. This rule applies whether the error was the result of an innocent mistake or, as in this case, of fraudulent acts by the owner. A rule which allowed reliance on the absence of lien notations on a certificate of title if such absence resulted from an innocent mistake or clerical error but not if such absence resulted from fraud would negate any ability to rely on the certificate of title. Under such a rule, a potential purchaser or **16 lender would always have to conduct an independent search to determine if, in fact, there are no liens against the vehicle, thus defeating the intent of the General Assembly in creating a single repository for recording liens against motor vehicles. In this case, therefore, Hyman was entitled to rely on the absence of any lien notations on the certificate of title, and TMCC cannot enforce its security interest against Hyman.

TMCC asserts that this conclusion is in conflict with established principles underlying the law relating to title expressed in First Nat'l Bank of Waynesboro v. Johnson, 183 Va. 227, 31 S.E.2d 581 (1944), and Code § 8.2–403(1), as well as specific cases decided by this Court in which a lienholder was allowed to enforce its lien against a good faith purchaser for value without notice, Rudolph v. Farmers' Supply Co., 131 Va. 305, 108 S.E. 638 (1921), and McQuay v. Mount Vernon Bank and Trust Co., 200 Va. 776, 108 S.E.2d 251 (1959). Close examination of these cases shows, however, that the conclusion we reach today is not contrary to the authority cited by TMCC.

Longstanding Virginia law provides that one who does not have title to goods cannot transfer title to a buyer, even a bona fide purchaser for value without notice. Johnson, 183 Va. at 236, 31 S.E.2d at 585. Thus, a thief cannot pass title to stolen goods even to an innocent purchaser who pays for the stolen goods. However, Virginia law has also recognized that a person who purchases goods from one possessing only voidable title can nevertheless receive good title to the goods purchased. Oberdorfer v. Meyer, 88 Va. 384, 386, 13 S.E. 756, 756–57 (1891); Old Dominion Steamship Co. v. Burckhardt, 72 Va. (31 Gratt.) 664, 668 (1879). These principles have been implicitly recognized in Code § 8.2–403(1). That subsection states, in pertinent part:

A purchaser of goods acquires all title which his transferor had or had the power to transfer.... A person with voidable title has power to transfer a good title to a good faith purchaser for value. When goods have been delivered under a transaction of purchase the purchaser has such power even though . . .

(d) the delivery was procured through fraud punishable as larcenous under the criminal law.

Citing the principles embodied in Code § 8.2–403, TMCC argues that Bowden could not pass "greater" title in the automobile than she owned. Since her title was subject to the encumbrance of TMCC's lien, Hyman's title must also be subject to the lien.

TMCC's argument, however, misinterprets the purpose and applicability of Code § 8.2–403. The statute deals with the power of an owner with void or voidable title to pass good title to a bona fide purchaser for value. It does not apply to the "rights . . . of lien creditors." Code § 8.2–403(4). In this case, Bowden had a "good" title to the automobile, and she passed a good title to Hyman. She was not a stranger to title, and her title was not made "void" or "voidable" by TMCC's security interest. Code § 8.2–403 and the principle described in Johnson, therefore, simply do not apply.

Finally, the two Virginia cases cited by TMCC in which an innocent lienholder has prevailed over a bona fide purchaser do not require a different result in this case. Both of these cases involve sales to bona fide purchasers for value by motor vehicle dealers and the application of the doctrine of estoppel based on the likelihood that the secured motor vehicle would be put into the stream of commerce. In neither case did the Court consider the impact of the motor vehicle titling statutes or the extent to which potential purchasers are entitled to rely upon a certificate of title which failed to note an existing lien.

Rudolph v. Farmers' Supply Co., as TMCC notes, was decided prior to the enactment of the motor vehicle titling statutes in 1924. Rudolph, therefore, did not consider the effect of a certificate of title issued by DMV showing no liens on the motor vehicle, because the General Assembly had not yet authorized its issuance. Consequently, the decision in Rudolph is not controlling in this case.

The second Virginia case relied on by TMCC, McQuay v. Mount Vernon Bank and Trust Co., was decided after the enactment of the titling statutes. However, it is not clear whether the bona fide purchaser in that case, McQuay, ever saw or received any title certificate from the seller or DMV and he did not assert a defense based on reliance on a certificate of title issued by DMV showing no liens on the vehicle. The ability to rely on a certificate of title issued with no notations of liens, therefore, was not at issue, and thus the holding in McQuay does not control the case before us.

For the above reasons, we conclude that the trial court properly held that TMCC was not entitled to enforce its lien against Hyman because Hyman, a bona fide purchaser for value without notice of the lien, was entitled to rely on a certificate of title which did not contain a notation of the lien.

AFFIRMED.

Problem 5–4

The two previous cases boil down to who, as between two innocent parties, should be made to bear the loss when debtor forges a title. Greene put the loss on the buyer; Hyman put it on the secured creditor. Which court gets it right?

§ 4. BUYERS

The materials in Chapter 2 illustrate substantial rights of buyers in the ordinary course under 9–320(a). The rights of buyers of consumer goods from consumers are almost as insubstantial and unimportant as the rights in subsection (a) are substantial and important. Professor Gilmore described the analogous rights in former section 9–307(2) as sales "by amateurs to amateurs". Sometimes the subsection is called the "garage sale" provision. Note that the seller must use the goods primarily for personal, family or household purposes and the buyer must also purchase the goods primarily for personal, family or household purposes. That is, even if the seller or buyer used the goods or intends to use them for business purposes, the sale does not qualify for 9–320(b) treatment. Equally important, the buyer does not take free if the perfection was not automatic (purchase money sale to a consumer) but rather was by the filing of a financing statement. In effect, subsection 9–320(b) is the appropriate protection for a buyer who could not discover the creditor's security interest even if he tried because, by hypothesis, the creditor has not filed a financing statement and has given the debtor possession of the goods.

Problem 5–5

Recall problem 2–14 in Chapter 2; answer it in light of your new learning about 9–320(b):

Daisy Bank and Trust has a security interest in refrigerators, stoves, appliances and all other hard goods of Marie Louise, Inc., a department store. Assume that the security agreement purports to continue the security interest in the goods even after they have been sold. Now consider the following transactions in goods covered by the perfected security interest.

Wilbur buys a refrigerator on credit from Marie Louise and signs a security agreement. A month later Wilbur sells the refrigerator to his next-door neighbor, Charlotte. Identify the correct statement or statements:

     a.   Charlotte takes free of the security interests of both Daisy and Marie Louise;

     b.   Charlotte takes free of Daisy's security interest because she qualifies under section 9–320(a);

     c.   Charlotte takes free of Marie Louise's security interest because she qualifies under 9–320(a);

d. Charlotte does not qualify for the protection of 9–320(a), nevertheless she takes free of both security interests.

Problem 5–6

Debtor, a lawyer in New York, buys a $20,000 diamond ring. Bank finances $18,000 of the purchase and files a financing statement in Albany. The purchase occurs in January 2002 and in February, debtor moves back to her former residence in New Orleans. On March 10th, she sells the ring to a friend for $14,000 and then defaults on the $18,000 loan. In October Bank discovers the sale of the ring; it asks:

1. Did the purchaser take free of Bank's interest?

2. Would the outcome be different if debtor sold the ring to a diamond merchant for $14,000?

3. Who would get the ring if debtor did not sell it but rather went bankrupt a year after she returned to Louisiana? (For the purposes of this part of the problem, assume Louisiana prohibits the use of the federal exemptions and has no state exemption that allows any part of a $14,000 diamond ring to be claimed as exempt and that Louisiana has adopted a nonuniform amendment that permits automatic perfection under 9–309(1) only on items with a value less than $10,000.) Consider 9–316 and 9–320.

§ 5. RESTRICTIONS ON CONSUMER SECURED CREDIT

In re Manuel shows that certain interests thought to be "purchase money" may not be. Under 522(f) certain non-possessory, non-purchase money security interests in consumer goods can be upset in bankruptcy despite the fact they are perfected. There are similar restrictions adopted by the Federal Trade Commission. Consider 16 CFR, part 444 in answering the following problem.

Problem 5–7

1. Ms. Proctor borrowed $2,500 from your client Local Loan Co. which took a security interest in all of Ms. Proctor's household goods. Ms. Proctor has defaulted on the loan. When Local Loan sued to foreclose on the debt, Ms. Proctor's lawyer responded that Local Loan's security interest is in violation of 16 CFR § 444.2(a)(4), and, therefore, the security agreement is void and unenforceable. What do you think?

2. Furniture Co. sells furniture and electronic appliances to a low income clientele. In separate transactions over a six month period in 2001, Furniture Co. sold a bedroom suite, two televisions and a radio to Ms. Proctor. Furniture Co. retained a security interest in each, and the security agreement contained a cross-collateralization clause. When she defaulted, Furniture Co. sued to recover possession of the goods. Ms. Proctor's lawyer has now responded that the obligations are not enforceable because they constitute non-possessory, non-purchase money security interests taken in violation of FTC rule 16 CFR part 444.2(a)(4). Furniture Co. has asked whether it has a good case. They are fearful because their modus operandi with Ms. Proctor is their general way of doing business.

3. Ms. Proctor's boyfriend co-signed the note, but has denied that he ever received the notice required under § 444.3. If the court believes him, is he free of liability?

4. A young associate in your firm has argued that the security agreement and guarantee are all enforceable regardless of any FTC violations. She notes that a violation of FTC rules need not void the underlying agreement or give rise to damages to Ms. Proctor or her boyfriend. Your associate asserts that the only remedy for an FTC violation is a fine or penalty imposed by the FTC.

5. Finally, assume that the applicable state usury laws prohibit Local Loan from making an unsecured loan to Ms. Proctor because the resulting interest rate would be too high. Local Loan does not want to take a security interest in Ms. Proctor's household goods for fear of violating 16 CFR 444. An officer at Local Loan has proposed instead to arrange for a consumer's sale to Local Loan of all her household goods and then for a lease of the goods back to the consumer. What do you think?

CODE OF FEDERAL REGULATIONS
TITLE 16—COMMERCIAL PRACTICES
CHAPTER I—FEDERAL TRADE COMMISSION
SUBCHAPTER D—TRADE REGULATION RULES
PART 444—CREDIT PRACTICES

§ 444.1 Definitions.

(a) Lender. A person who engages in the business of lending money to consumers within the jurisdiction of the Federal Trade Commission.

(b) Retail installment seller. A person who sells goods or services to consumers on a deferred payment basis or pursuant to a lease-purchase arrangement within the jurisdiction of the Federal Trade Commission.

(c) Person. An individual, corporation, or other business organization.

(d) Consumer. A natural person who seeks or acquires goods, services, or money for personal, family, or household use.

(e) Obligation. An agreement between a consumer and a lender or retail installment seller.

(f) Creditor. A lender or a retail installment seller.

(g) Debt. Money that is due or alleged to be due from one to another.

(h) Earnings. Compensation paid or payable to an individual or for his or her account for personal services rendered or to be rendered by him or her, whether denominated as wages, salary, commission, bonus, or otherwise, including periodic payments pursuant to a pension, retirement, or disability program.

(i) Household goods. Clothing, furniture, appliances, one radio and one television, linens, china, crockery, kitchenware, and personal effects (including wedding rings) of the consumer and his or her dependents, provided that the following are not included within the scope of the term household goods:

(1) Works of art;

(2) Electronic entertainment equipment (except one television and one radio);

(3) Items acquired as antiques; and

(4) Jewelry (except wedding rings).

(j) Antique. Any item over one hundred years of age, including such items that have been repaired or renovated without changing their original form or character.

(k) Cosigner. A natural person who renders himself or herself liable for the obligation of another person without compensation. The term shall include any person whose signature is requested as a condition to granting credit to another person, or as a condition for forbearance on collection of another person's obligation that is in default. The term shall not include a spouse whose signature is required on a credit obligation to perfect a security interest pursuant to state law. A person who does not receive goods, services, or money in return for a credit obligation does not receive compensation within the meaning of this definition. A person is a cosigner within the meaning of this definition whether or not he or she is designated as such on a credit obligation.

§ 444.2 Unfair Credit Practices.

(a) In connection with the extension of credit to consumers in or affecting commerce, as commerce is defined in the Federal Trade Commission Act, it is an unfair act or practice within the meaning of Section 5 of that Act for a lender or retail installment seller directly or indirectly to take or receive from a consumer an obligation that:

(1) Constitutes or contains a cognovit or confession of judgment (for purposes other than executory process in the State of Louisiana), warrant of attorney, or other waiver of the right to notice and the opportunity to be heard in the event of suit or process thereon.

(2) Constitutes or contains an executory waiver or a limitation of exemption from attachment, execution, or other process on real or personal property held, owned by, or due to the consumer, unless the waiver applies solely to property subject to a security interest executed in connection with the obligation.

(3) Constitutes or contains an assignment of wages or other earnings unless:

(i) The assignment by its terms is revocable at the will of the debtor, or

(ii) The assignment is a payroll deduction plan or preauthorized payment plan, commencing at the time of the transaction, in which the consumer authorizes a series of wage deductions as a method of making each payment, or

(iii) The assignment applies only to wages or other earnings already earned at the time of the assignment.

(4) Constitutes or contains a nonpossessory security interest in household goods other than a purchase money security interest.

§ 444.3   Unfair or deceptive cosigner practices.

(a) In connection with the extension of credit to consumers in or affecting commerce, as commerce is defined in the Federal Trade Commission Act, it is:

(1) A deceptive act or practice within the meaning of Section 5 of that Act for a lender or retail installment seller, directly or indirectly, to misrepresent the nature or extent of cosigner liability to any person.

(2) An unfair act or practice within the meaning of Section 5 of that Act for a lender or retail installment seller, directly or indirectly, to obligate a cosigner unless the cosigner is informed prior to becoming obligated, which in the case of open end credit shall mean prior to the time that the agreement creating the cosigner's liability for future charges is executed, of the nature of his or her liability as cosigner.

(b) Any lender or retail installment seller who complies with the preventive requirements in paragraph (c) of this section does not violate paragraph (a) of this section.

(c) To prevent these unfair or deceptive acts or practices, a disclosure, consisting of a separate document that shall contain the following statement and no other, shall be given to the cosigner prior to becoming obligated, which in the case of open end credit shall mean prior to the time that the agreement creating the cosigner's liability for future charges is executed:

Notice to Cosigner

You are being asked to guarantee this debt. Think carefully before you do. If the borrower doesn't pay the debt, you will have to. Be sure you can afford to pay if you have to, and that you want to accept this responsibility.

You may have to pay up to the full amount of the debt if the borrower does not pay. You may also have to pay late fees or collection costs, which increase this amount.

The creditor can collect this debt from you without first trying to collect from the borrower. The creditor can use the same collection methods against you that can be used against the borrower, such as suing you, garnishing your wages, etc. If this debt is ever in default, that fact may become a part of your credit record.

This notice is not the contract that makes you liable for the debt.

§ 6. FORECLOSURE AGAINST AUTOMOBILES AND OTHER CONSUMER GOODS, CONSUMER PROTECTION IN PART 6 OF ARTICLE 9

In certain ways a creditor's rights against a consumer under Part 6 of Article 9 are more limited than they would be against a business debtor in the same circumstances. For example, section 9–620 has a variety of restrictions on taking collateral in satisfaction of the debt without a sale to a third party. Section 9–625(c)(2) grants a consumer debtor punitive damages equal to 10% of the principal amount plus the full amount of the finance charge in certain circumstances and section 9–626 does not impose the rebuttable presumption rule on consumers but it does impose that rule on commercial debtors. In addition, the restrictions on waiver found in 9–602 and on self-help repossession in 9–609 probably apply more frequently to consumer debtors than to business debtors even though those sections do not state separate rules for consumers.

In fact much of the law under the predecessor of Part 6, in the pre–1999 Code, was made from consumer transactions. A common case would be one in which a debtor granted a security interest in his or her automobile, the debtor defaulted and the creditor repossessed without judicial process. In such circumstances, the interaction between the creditor, or the creditor's agent, and the debtor include a large array of possibilities ranging from an outright fist fight in which the debtor beat up the repossessor or shot him, to cases in which the repossessor pretended to be a policeman and made off with a car or boat. These cases were often followed by disputes about the mode of notice and mode of sale and whether the notice was appropriate and the mode of sale was commercially reasonable. Many of these cases arose out of automobile repossessions. Two examples follow.

GILES v. FIRST VIRGINIA CREDIT SERVICES, INC.

N.C. App., 2002.
560 S.E.2d 557.

McGee, Judge.

Richard Giles and Joann Giles (plaintiffs) appeal the trial court's order granting First Virginia Credit Services, Inc.'s (First Virginia) motion for summary judgment in part.

Plaintiffs filed a complaint against defendants First Virginia and Professional Auto Recovery, Inc. (Professional Auto Recovery) for wrongful repossession of an automobile. Plaintiffs alleged in an amended complaint that: (1) First Virginia and Professional Auto Recovery wrongfully converted and/or repossessed the automobile and plaintiffs' personal property located within the automobile; (2) plaintiffs made a payment on the account which First Virginia accepted immediately prior to First Virginia's repossession of the automobile and which First Virginia subsequently cashed and applied to plaintiffs' account *560 after the repossession; (3) removal of the automobile constituted breach of the peace in violation of N.C. Gen.Stat. § 25–9–503; (4) N.C. Gen.Stat. § 25–9–503 is unconstitutional; and (5) First Virginia was negligent in hiring Professional Auto Recovery and committed unfair or deceptive trade practices entitling plaintiffs to treble damages.

First Virginia filed an answer stating the automobile was repossessed due to the default of Joann Giles in making the payments to First Virginia on a loan secured by the automobile. First Virginia stated that N.C. Gen.Stat. § 25–9–503 permitted a secured lender to peaceably repossess its collateral upon default by a debtor and that such repossession could not, as a matter of law, constitute conversion of the collateral or an unfair or deceptive trade practice. First Virginia moved to dismiss plaintiffs' complaint for failure to state a claim pursuant to N.C. Gen. Stat. § 1A–1, Rule 12(b)(6).

Joann Giles entered into an installment sale contract on or about 18 January 1997 for the purchase of an automobile. The contract was assigned to First Virginia, which obtained a senior perfected purchase money security interest in the automobile. The terms of the contract required Joann Giles to make sixty regular monthly payments to First Virginia. The contract stated that Joann Giles' failure to make any payment due under the contract within ten days after its due date would be a default. The contract contained an additional provision agreed to by Joann Giles that stated:

> If I am in default, you may consider all my remaining payments to be due and payable, without giving me notice. I agree that your rights of possession will be greater than mine. I will deliver the property to you at your request, or you may use lawful means to take it yourself without notice or other legal action....
>
>   * * *
>
> If you excuse one default by me, that will not excuse later defaults.

During the early morning hours of 27 June 1999, Professional Auto Recovery, at the request of First Virginia, repossessed the locked automobile from plaintiffs' front driveway. According to First Virginia, the account of Joann Giles was in arrears for payments due on 2 May 1999 and 2 June 1999, and pursuant to the terms of the contract, repossession was permitted.

In an affidavit filed by plaintiffs in opposition to First Virginia's motion for summary judgment, plaintiffs' neighbor, Glenn A. Mosteller (Mr. Mosteller), stated that he was awakened around 4:00 a.m.

> by the running of a loud diesel truck engine on the road outside my house. Evidentially [sic] the truck was stopped because I lay in bed for a while and did not get up. I then became concerned and went to the window to see what was going on. At this time I saw a large rollback diesel truck with a little pickup truck on the truck bed behind it. The truck only had its parking lights on. The truck ... started going toward the Giles' yard. It still only had its parking lights on. About that time, a man jumped out of the truck and ran up the Giles' driveway. Their car was parked up at their house. Then the car came flying out back down the driveway making a loud noise and started screeching off.... At about the same time, the rollback also pulled off real fast making a real loud diesel noise and

went down [the road].... I got to the phone, called the Giles and told them someone was stealing their car.... My lights were on ... and the Giles' lights were on and that portion of our neighborhood had woken up. Richard Giles came out in his yard and we hollared a few words back and forth and I jumped in my truck ... to try to get the police. About 5 minutes later a police car came up and pulled into the Giles' yard. Then another police car came then a Sheriff's Deputy car came. Then another police car came.... There was a great commotion going on out in the street and in our yard all to the disturbance of the quietness and tranquility of our neighborhood.... It scared me and it scared the Giles.

Joann Giles stated in a deposition that she was awakened by Mr. Mosteller's telephone call in which he told her that someone was stealing her car. She stated she ran to see if the automobile was parked outside and confirmed that it was gone. Joann Giles testified she woke up her husband and gave him the telephone; he ran outside into the yard and heard Mr. Mosteller "hollering" at him from across the street. Plaintiffs testified in their depositions that neither of them saw the car being repossessed but were only awakened by their neighbor after the automobile was gone. During the actual repossession, no contact was made between Professional Auto Recovery and plaintiffs, nor between Professional Auto Recovery and Mr. Mosteller.

First Virginia filed a motion for summary judgment pursuant to N.C. Gen.Stat. § 1A–1, Rule 56. Plaintiffs filed a motion to amend their complaint pursuant to N.C. Gen.Stat. § 1A–1, Rule 15. These motions were heard by the trial court on 17 May 2000. In an order dated 15 June 2000, the trial court: (1) granted plaintiffs' motion to amend their complaint; (2) granted First Virginia's motion for summary judgment in part, stating there was no genuine issue as to any material fact as to the conversion or repossession of the motor vehicle; (3) denied First Virginia's motion for summary judgment in part, concluding that there were genuine issues of material fact as to the reasonableness of the taking into possession or conversion of plaintiffs' personal property located within the automobile and related damages; (4) declined plaintiffs' request to declare N.C. Gen.Stat. § 25–9–503 unconstitutional; and (5) ruled on other motions not at issue in this appeal. The trial court certified in an order filed 6 July 2000 that its decisions in the 15 June 2000 order constituted a final judgment as to some of plaintiffs' claims and found the order was immediately appealable pursuant to N.C. Gen.Stat. § 1A–1, Rule 54(b). Plaintiffs appeal.

I.

We must first determine whether plaintiffs' appeal is properly before this Court in that the trial court's order does not resolve all issues among the parties and is therefore interlocutory. * * * The trial court's judgment granting First Virginia's motion for summary judgment determined plaintiffs' claim for wrongful conversion and/or repossession of plaintiffs' automobile, making it a final judgment as to this claim, and we therefore may review this issue on appeal.

* * *

II.

By their first assignment of error, plaintiffs argue the trial court erred in granting in part First Virginia's motion for summary judgment dismissing plaintiffs' claim for wrongful conversion and/or repossession of their automobile. Plaintiffs specifically argue that (1) the determination of whether a breach of the peace occurred in violation of N.C. Gen.Stat. § 25–9–503 is a question for the jury and not one to be determined by summary judgment, and (2) there is a dispute as to whether plaintiffs were in default.

* * *

A.

Plaintiffs first argue the trial court erred in granting partial summary judgment to First Virginia because the issue of whether a breach of the peace occurred is a question for the jury.

Our Courts have long recognized the right of secured parties to repossess collateral from a defaulting debtor without resort to judicial process, so long as the repossession is effected peaceably. See e.g., Rea v. Credit Corp., 257 N.C. 639, 641, 127 S.E.2d 225, 227 (1962); Freeman v. Acceptance Corp., 205 N.C. 257, 258, 171 S.E. 63, 63 (1933). Our General Assembly codified procedures for self-help repossessions, including this common law restriction, in the North Carolina Uniform Commercial Code (UCC). N.C. Gen.Stat. § 25–9–503 (1999), in effect at the time of the repossession in this case, reads in part,

> Unless otherwise agreed a secured party has on default the right to take possession of the collateral. In taking possession a secured party may proceed without judicial process if this can be done without breach of the peace or may proceed by action.

The General Assembly did not define breach of the peace but instead left this task to our Courts, and although a number of our appellate decisions have considered this self-help right of secured parties, none have clarified what actions constitute a breach of the peace.

N.C. Gen.Stat. § 25–9–503, at issue in this appeal, has been replaced by N.C. Gen.Stat. § 25–9–609 (Interim Supp.2000) (Effective 1 July 2001), which states that a secured party, after default, may take possession of the collateral without judicial process, if the secured party proceeds without breach of the peace. In Number 3. of the Official Comment to the new statutory provision, our General Assembly continued to state that, "[l]ike former Section 9–503, this section does not define or explain the conduct that will constitute a breach of the peace, leaving that matter for continuing development by the courts." N.C.G.S. § 25–9–609. The General Assembly clearly may further define and/or limit the time, place and conditions under *563 which a repossession is permitted, but it has not yet done so.

In a pre-UCC case, Rea v. Credit Corp., 257 N.C. 639, 127 S.E.2d 225 (1962), a defaulting debtor left his locked automobile on his front lawn. An agent of the mortgagee went to the debtor's home to repossess the automobile, saw the automobile parked on the lawn, found no one at home, and asked a neighbor where the debtor was. The agent was told no one was at home and he thereafter opened the automobile door with a coat hanger and removed the automobile on a wrecker. Our Supreme Court found that this evidence could not warrant a finding by a jury that the mortgagee's agent wrongfully took possession of the automobile because no breach of the peace occurred. In Rea, although our Supreme Court did not define breach of the peace, it reiterated the common law rule that the right of self-help repossession "must be exercised without provoking a breach of the peace[.]" Id. at 641–42, 127 S.E.2d at 227. Our Supreme Court thought the law "well stated" by the South Carolina Supreme Court in the case of Willis v. Whittle, that

> "if the mortgagee finds that he cannot get possession without committing a breach of the peace, he must stay his hand, and resort to the law, for the preservation of the public peace is of more importance to society than the right of the owner of a chattel to get possession of it."

Rea, 257 N.C. at 641–42, 127 S.E.2d at 227 (quoting Willis v. Whittle, 82 S.C. 500, 64 S.E. 410 (1909)).

In a case addressing the issue of whether prior notice of repossession is required under N.C. Gen.Stat. § 25–9–503, our Court stated that repossession can be accomplished under the statute without prior notice so long as the repossession is peaceable. Everett v. U.S. Life Credit Corp., 74 N.C.App. 142, 144, 327 S.E.2d 269, 269 (1985). Without specifically defining breach of the peace, our Court explained that "[o]f course, if there is confrontation at the time of the attempted repossession, the secured party must cease the attempted repossession and proceed by court action in order to avoid a 'breach of the peace.' "Id. at 144, 327 S.E.2d at 270. This indicates, as argued by First Virginia, that confrontation is at least an element of a breach of the peace analysis.

In that breach of the peace has not heretofore been clarified by our appellate courts, but instead only vaguely referred to, we must construe this term as the drafters intended. "In construing statutes the court should always give effect to the legislative intent." Electric Service v. City of Rocky Mount, 20 N.C.App. 347, 348, 201 S.E.2d 508, 509 (1974) aff'd, 285 N.C. 135, 203 S.E.2d 838 (1974). "The intent of the Legislature may be ascertained from the phraseology of the statute as well as the nature and purpose of the act and the consequences which would follow from a construction one way or another." Campbell v. Church, 298 N.C. 476, 484, 259 S.E.2d 558, 564 (1979). In determining what conduct constitutes a breach of the peace we consider each of these contributing elements.

The phrase "breach of the peace" is defined in Black's Law Dictionary as the "criminal offense of creating a public disturbance or engaging in disorderly conduct, particularly by an unnecessary or distracting noise." Black's Law Dictionary 183 (7th ed.1999). The phrase is also commonly understood to mean a "violation of the public order as amounts to a disturbance of the public tranquility, by act or conduct either directly having this effect, or by inciting or tending to incite such a disturbance of the public tranquility." 12 Am.Jur.2d Breach of Peace § 5 (1997).

In a criminal case, our Supreme Court defined breach of the peace as "a disturbance of public order and tranquility by act or conduct not merely amounting to unlawfulness but tending also to create public tumult and incite others to break the peace." State v. Mobley, 240 N.C. 476, 482, 83 S.E.2d 100, 104 (1954). See also Perry v. Gibson, 247 N.C. 212, 100 S.E.2d 341 (1957) (wrongful death case stating the same definition for breach of the peace). Such " '[a] breach of the peace may be occasioned by an affray or assault, by the use of profane and abusive language by one person toward another on a public street and in the presence of others, *564 or by a person needlessly shouting and making loud noise.' "Mobley, 240 N.C. at 482, 83 S.E.2d at 104 (quoting 4 Am.Jur. Arrest § 30). A breach of the peace, as used in Chapter 19 of our General Statutes, entitled "Offenses Against Public Morals," is defined as "repeated acts that disturb the public order including, but not limited to, homicide, assault, affray, communicating threats, unlawful possession of dangerous or deadly weapons, and discharging firearms." N.C. Gen.Stat. § 19–1.1(1) (1999).

We must also consider the nature and purpose of Chapter 25 of the North Carolina General Statutes, the UCC, which is to be "liberally construed and applied to promote its underlying purposes and policies." N.C. Gen.Stat. § 25–1–102 (1999). Its stated purposes are:

(a) to simplify, clarify and modernize the law governing commercial transactions;

(b) to permit the continued expansion of commercial practices through custom, usage and agreement of the parties;

(c) to make uniform the law among the various jurisdictions.

Id.

In carrying out the policy of uniformity with other jurisdictions, we consider their treatment of the term of breach of the peace. While cases from other jurisdictions are not binding on our courts, they provide insight into how this term has been analyzed by other courts and therefore are instructive.

The courts in many states have examined whether a breach of the peace in the context of the UCC has occurred. Courts have found a breach of the peace when actions by a creditor incite violence or are likely to incite violence. Birrell v. Indiana Auto Sales & Repair, 698 N.E.2d 6, 8 (Ind.App.1998) (a creditor cannot use threats, enter a residence without debtor's consent and cannot seize property over a debtor's objections); Wade v. Ford Motor Credit Co., 8 Kan.App.2d 737, 668 P.2d 183, 189 (1983) (a breach of the peace may be caused by an act likely to produce violence); Morris v. First National Bank & Trust Co. of Ravenna, 21 Ohio St.2d 25, 254 N.E.2d 683, 686–87 (1970) (a physical confrontation coupled with an oral protest constitutes a breach of the peace).

Other courts have expanded the phrase breach of the peace beyond the criminal law context to include occurrences where a debtor or his family protest the repossession. Fulton v. Anchor Sav. Bank, FSB, 215 Ga.App. 456, 452 S.E.2d 208, 213 (1994) (a breach of the peace can be created by an unequivocal oral protest); Census Federal Credit Union v. Wann, 403 N.E.2d 348, 352 (Ind.App.1980) ("if a repossession is ... contested at the actual time ... of the attempted repossession by the defaulting party or other person in control of the chattel, the secured party must desist and pursue his remedy in court"); Hollibush v. Ford Motor Credit Co., 179 Wis.2d 799, 508 N.W.2d 449, 453–55 (Wis.App. 1993) (in the face of an oral protest the repossessing creditor must desist). Some courts, however, have determined that a mere oral protest is not sufficient to constitute a breach of the peace. Clarin v. Minnesota Repossessors, Inc., 198 F.3d 661, 664 (8th Cir.1999) (oral protest, followed by pleading with repossessors in public parking lot does not rise to level of breach of the peace); Chrysler Credit Corp. v. Koontz, 277 Ill.App.3d 1078, 214 Ill.Dec. 726, 661 N.E.2d 1171, 1173–74 (1996) (yelling "Don't take it" is insufficient).

If a creditor removes collateral by an unauthorized breaking and entering of a debtor's dwelling, courts generally hold this conduct to be a breach of the peace. Davenport v. Chrysler Credit Corp., 818 S.W.2d 23, 29 (Tenn.App.1991) and General Elec. Credit Corp. v. Timbrook, 170 W.Va. 143, 291 S.E.2d 383, 385 (1982) (both cases stating that breaking and entering, despite the absence of violence or physical confrontation, is a breach of the peace). Removal of collateral from a private driveway, without more however, has been found not to constitute a breach of the peace. Hester v. Bandy, 627 So.2d 833, 840 (Miss.1993). Additionally, noise alone has been determined to not rise to the level of a breach of the peace. Ragde v. Peoples Bank, 53 Wash.App. 173, 767 P.2d 949, 951 (1989) (unwilling to hold that making noise is an act likely to breach the peace).

Many courts have used a balancing test to determine if a repossession was undertaken at a reasonable time and in a reasonable manner, and to balance the interests of debtors and creditors. See e.g., Clarin v. Minnesota Repossessors, Inc., 198 F.3d 661, 664 (8th Cir.1999); Davenport v. Chrysler Credit Corp., 818 S.W.2d 23, 29 (Tenn.App.1991). Five relevant factors considered in this balancing test are: "(1) where the repossession took place, (2) the debtor's express or constructive consent, (3) the reactions of third parties, (4) the type of premises entered, and (5) the creditor's use of deception." Davenport, 818 S.W.2d at 29 (citing

2 J. White & R. Summers, Uniform Commercial Code § 27–6, at 575–76 (3d ed.1988)).

Relying on the language of our Supreme Court in Rea, plaintiffs argue that the "guiding star" in determining whether a breach of the peace occurred should be whether or not the public peace was preserved during the repossession. Rea, 257 N.C. at 641–42, 127 S.E.2d at 228. Plaintiffs contend "the elements as to what constitutes a breach of the peace should be liberally construed" and urge our Court to adopt a subjective standard considering the totality of the circumstances as to whether a breach of the peace occurred.

Plaintiffs claim that adopting a subjective standard for N.C. Gen. Stat. § 25–9–503 cases will protect unwitting consumers from the "widespread use of no notice repossessions, clandestine and after midnight repossessions" and will protect "our State's commitment to law and order and opposition to vigilante policies, opposition to violence and acts from which violence could reasonably flow[.]" If a lender is not held to such a high subjective standard, plaintiffs contend that self-help repossessions should be disallowed altogether.

First Virginia, in contrast, argues that a breach of the peace did not occur in this case, as a matter of law, because there was no confrontation between the parties. Therefore, because the facts in this case are undisputed concerning the events during the actual repossession of the automobile, the trial court did not err in its partial grant of summary judgment.

First Virginia disputes plaintiffs' contention that a determination of whether a breach of the peace occurred should be a wholly subjective standard, because if such a standard is adopted, every determination of whether a breach of the peace occurred would hereafter be a jury question and "would run directly contrary to the fundamental purpose of the Uniform Commercial Code, which is to provide some degree of certainty to the parties engaging in various commercial transactions." Further, First Virginia argues that applying a subjective standard to a breach of the peace analysis could be detrimental to borrowers, with lenders likely increasing the price of credit to borrowers to cover the costs of having to resort to the courts in every instance to recover their collateral upon default. The standard advocated by plaintiffs would "eviscerate" the self-help rights granted to lenders by the General Assembly, leaving lenders "with no safe choice except to simply abandon their 'self help' rights altogether, since every repossession case could [result] in the time and expense of a jury trial on the issue of 'breach of the peace[.]' "Finally, First Virginia argues that a subjective standard would be detrimental to the judicial system as a whole because "[w]ith a case-by-case, wholly subjective standard ... the number of lawsuits being filed over property repossessions could increase dramatically[.]"

Based upon our review of our appellate courts' treatment of breach of the peace in pre-UCC and UCC cases, as well as in other areas of the law, the purposes and policies of the UCC, and the treatment other jurisdictions have given the phrase, we find that a breach of the peace, when used in the context of N.C. Gen.Stat. § 25–9–503, is broader than the criminal law definition. A confrontation is not always required, but we do not agree with plaintiffs that every repossession should be analyzed subjectively, thus bringing every repossession into the purview of the jury so as to eviscerate the self-help rights duly given to creditors by the General Assembly. Rather, a breach of the peace analysis should be based upon the reasonableness of the time and manner of the repossession. We therefore adopt a balancing test using the five factors discussed above to determine whether a breach of the peace occurs when there is no confrontation.

In applying these factors to the undisputed evidence in the case before us, we affirm the trial court's determination that there was no breach of the peace, as a matter of law. Professional Auto Recovery went onto plaintiffs' driveway in the early morning hours, when presumably no one would be outside, thus decreasing the possibility of confrontation. Professional Auto Recovery did not enter into plaintiffs' home or any enclosed area. Consent to repossession was expressly given in the contract with First Virginia signed by Joann Giles. Although a third party, Mr. Mosteller, was awakened by the noise of Professional Auto Recovery's truck, Mr. Mosteller did not speak with anyone from Professional Auto Recovery, nor did he go outside until Professional Auto Recovery had departed with the Giles' automobile. Further, neither of the plaintiffs were awakened by the noise of the truck, and there was no confrontation between either of them with any representative of Professional Auto Recovery. By the time Mr. Mosteller and plaintiffs went outside, the automobile was gone. Finally, there is no evidence, nor did plaintiffs allege, that First Virginia or Professional Auto Recovery employed any type of deception when repossessing the automobile.

There is no factual dispute as to what happened during the repossession in this case, and the trial court did not err in granting summary judgment to First Virginia on this issue.

B.

Plaintiffs next argue there was a factual dispute over whether or not a default occurred in the repayment of the note and therefore summary judgment was improper.

N.C. Gen.Stat. § 25–9–503 states that "unless otherwise agreed a secured party has on default the right to take possession of the collateral." The contract signed by Joann Giles stated that she would be in default if she "fail[ed] to make any payment within 10 days after its due date." Additionally, she agreed that if the bank chose to excuse a default, that would not excuse later defaults.

Plaintiffs argue in their brief to this Court that Joann Giles was "one payment behind" when her automobile was repossessed on 27 June 1999. They claim a payment was made to First Virginia before the automobile was repossessed, bringing her account up to date, but that payment was cashed and credited to Joann Giles' account two days after the repossession. Plaintiffs thus imply that because the check was ultimately received and cashed, Joann Giles' account was not in default when the repossession occurred. This position, however, is untenable. If a default is not cured before repossession, the fact that the check was mailed before repossession is immaterial when it is not received until after the collateral is repossessed. 10 Ronald A. Anderson, Anderson on The Uniform Commercial Code, § 9–503:52 (3d ed. 1999 Revision).

Plaintiffs also argue in their brief that Credit Co. v. Jordan, 5 N.C.App. 249, 168 S.E.2d 229 (1969) "espouses the proposition that acceptance of late payments along with evidence of unconscionable or improper action on the part of the financial institution would constitute waiver or estoppel." Plaintiffs contend that First Virginia had accepted late payments in the past from Joann Giles and that First Virginia's repossession of the automobile was unconscionable; therefore, First Virginia was estopped from repossessing her automobile on 27 June 1999.

Plaintiffs' reliance on Credit Co., however, is misplaced because the proposition stated by plaintiffs is taken from dicta in that case and is not binding on this Court in the case before us. Further, plaintiffs do not direct us to any evidence in the record supporting a conclusion that First Virginia intended to forbear plaintiffs' payments or that First Virginia acted unconscionably. In fact, Joann Giles agreed in the contract that acceptance of a late payment by First Virginia would not excuse a later default. Plaintiffs' argument of forbearance by First Virginia is without merit.

The trial court found, and we agree, that there is no genuine issue of material fact as to whether Joann Giles' account was in default when the automobile was repossessed. The trial court did not err in granting summary judgment to First Virginia on this issue. Plaintiffs' first assignment of error is overruled.

III.

Plaintiffs next argue that the provisions of N.C. Gen.Stat. § 25–9–503 granting a secured party the right to take possession of collateral without judicial process, without notice and/or a right to be heard, are unconstitutional as applied to the facts in this case. They further argue that the waiver of notice in the contract Joann Giles signed with First Virginia deprived her of her constitutional rights under the Fourteenth Amendment to the United States Constitution.

Plaintiffs claim that the statutory scheme providing for non-judicial repossession under N.C. Gen.Stat. § 25–9–503 constitutes state action sufficient to evoke the protection of the due process clause of the Fourteenth Amendment of the United States Constitution. As support for their position, plaintiffs rely on Turner v. Blackburn, 389 F.Supp. 1250 (W.D.N.C.1975). Turner, however, is distinguishable from the case before us because in Turner, the court's determination that state action was involved, thereby requiring application of the provisions of the Fourteenth Amendment, was based upon the direct participation of the clerk of court in the statutory procedure for foreclosure and sale under deed of trust. Id. at 1254–58. In the case before us, however, plaintiffs cite no participation on the part of any state official in First Virginia's self-help repossession, nor can we find any in our review of the record.

Plaintiffs argue the state action in this case, requiring our Court to declare N.C. Gen.Stat. § 25–9–503 unconstitutional, is based on our state's statutory scheme permitting the Department of Motor Vehicles to title a motor vehicle, to create and perfect a lien on a motor vehicle, to transfer title of a motor vehicle when the motor vehicle is sold pursuant to a repossession, and to transfer title absent the owner's signature. Further, plaintiffs argue state action is present through our statutory scheme which provides for repossession without judicial process, where payment of any surplus from sale of the repossessed vehicle is paid to the clerk of superior court who is liable on a bond for safekeeping the funds. Except for the reference to N.C. Gen.Stat. § 25–9–503, the statutes as recited by plaintiff, do not apply to this case and will not be addressed.

A majority of the federal circuit courts have considered the question before us and are in agreement that self-help repossession pursuant to UCC provisions does not constitute "state action" within the purview of the due process provision of the Fourteenth Amendment. Shirley v. State National Bank of Connecticut, 493 F.2d 739 (2d Cir.1974); Gibbs v. Titelman, 502 F.2d 1107 (3d Cir.1974), cert. denied, Gibbs, et al. v. Garver, Director, Bureau of Motor Vehicles, et al., 419 U.S. 1039, 95 S.Ct. 526, 42 L.Ed.2d 316 (1974); James v. Pinnix, 495 F.2d 206 (5th Cir.1974); Turner v. Impala Motors, 503 F.2d 607 (6th Cir.1974); Nichols v. Tower Grove Bank, 497 F.2d 404 (8th Cir.1974); Nowlin v. Professional Auto Sales, Inc., 496 F.2d 16 (8th Cir.1974), cert. denied, 419 U.S. 1006, 95 S.Ct. 328, 42 L.Ed.2d 283 (1974); Adams v. Southern California First National Bank, 492 F.2d 324 (9th Cir.1973), cert. denied, 419 U.S. 1006, 95 S.Ct. 325, 42 L.Ed.2d 282 (1974). While this Court is not obliged to follow decisions from other jurisdictions, these decisions are instructive in our determination of whether there was sufficient state action in this case to sustain a challenge under the Fourteenth Amendment.

We agree with First Virginia's contention that N.C. Gen.Stat. § 25–9–503 is "wholly self-executing and takes no involvement by any state employee to fully effect its purpose." In enacting N.C. Gen.Stat. § 25–9–503, our General Assembly codified a right existing at common law; it did not delegate to private parties authority previously held by the state. Therefore, plaintiffs' argument that state action was involved in this case is without merit.

Plaintiffs also claim that the waiver of notice in the contract signed by Joann Giles is void because it deprives her of her property without notice and an opportunity to be heard, as required by the Fourteenth Amendment. Because we find that there is no state action under N.C.

Gen.Stat. § 25–9–503, this argument also fails. Plaintiffs' second assignment of error is overruled.

The trial court's order granting partial summary judgment for First Virginia is affirmed.

Judges WALKER and HUDSON concur.

DeMARY v. RIEKER

New Jersey Super. Appellate Division, 1997.
302 N.J.Super. 208, 695 A.2d 294

SHEBELL, P.J.A.D.

Plaintiffs, Marie DeMary and Louis DeMary, instituted the within action for personal injuries they each suffered as a consequence of Chase Manhattan Services Corporation (Chase) ordering repossession of a leased Mercedes automobile. On September 4, 1991 at approximately 5:30 a.m., plaintiffs were awakened by their son, who told them that someone was taking their car. All three went outside, saw William Rieker (Rieker) attaching the Mercedes to a tow truck, and became very upset. Mrs. DeMary was standing on the passenger side of the truck, asking Rieker to allow her husband to remove his possessions from the car, when Rieker began to back out of the driveway. She had her hands on the truck and when Rieker took off, she held on. The truck accelerated to about twenty-five to thirty miles per hour and was driving "erratically, zigzagging," as she pleaded with him to stop. She said "[h]e came to a sudden jerk and for a second he jerked and then I just fell off." As the tow truck continued to drive away, the Mercedes, in tow, ran over Mrs. DeMary's left ankle, resulting in extensive and permanent injury.

Mr. DeMary testified that when he told Rieker to unhook the car, his voice was raised and the exchange of words was heated. He told Rieker that he mailed the check and offered to let him use the phone to verify it. Rieker refused to determine whether a payment had been made. Mr. DeMary had been trying to get some things out of the car at the time his wife went over to the passenger side of the truck. When he realized his wife was hanging onto the side of the truck as it began moving, Mr. DeMary ran after it. During the course of the chase, he fell on the front lawn and broke his ankle.

Mrs. DeMary was taken by ambulance to St. Joseph's Hospital and was later transferred to Meadowlands Hospital, where she remained for approximately two weeks. There she had an operation where twenty-two screws were implanted in her ankle with some bone grafting. Mrs. DeMary had a second surgery in July 1992 to remove some screws and to add more bone to the ankle. The bone was taken from her hip on each occasion, and resulted in scarring in both areas. A third surgery was performed in March 1994 to remove all of the screws in her ankle. Mrs. DeMary received physical therapy each time after surgery, for approximately four to six months each time. Her orthopedic surgeon testified as to the procedures he used to treat her. He gave his prognosis:

I'm very concerned about the prognosis for the ankle because of the possibility of post-traumatic arthritis. I think in all medical probability, I think this patient's looking at an ankle fusion in the future— * * * That means making the foot and ankle unit one, to eliminate any pain. Certainly the patient's a relatively young woman so you would not want to do this in the near future, but in my experience that's probably what it will come to.

He also indicated that Mrs. DeMary would never again have full range of motion in her ankle and would have no range of motion if the ankle were fused.

Both Mr. and Mrs. DeMary testified that their marital relationship deteriorated because of the accident, resulting in their separation about two years before trial. Mrs. DeMary moved in with her mother at that time.

Mr. DeMary's broken ankle was placed in a cast for six weeks. At the time of trial, he complained of pain during bad weather. He has not been jogging since the accident, which was an activity he had done frequently. His doctor testified that Mr. DeMary had a "non-displaced fibial fracture." A short leg cast required the use of crutches for six weeks, and Mr. DeMary walked with a cane for a week after the cast was removed. The doctor opined that Mr. DeMary would have a partial permanent disability as a result of his injury, but did not quantify the extent of disability.

A company owned by Mr. DeMary leased the 1990 Mercedes from Chase and Mrs. DeMary was the guarantor of the lease. The company was responsible for the payments on the vehicle, but had been late making payments. In August 1991, Mr. DeMary spoke with someone from Chase regarding the late payments and promised that he would send a check before the end of the month. He assumed that since the Chase representative did not object, this was acceptable to them. Mr. DeMary testified that a check made out by his company was sent to Chase, however, he had no personal knowledge when the last check to Chase was written and mailed. He assumed it was mailed because his secretary told him it had been mailed. He also testified it was common practice to write checks from his own personal account rather than the company account.

His secretary testified that she had conversations with Chase "[a]ll the time." She added: "[t]hey had my office number and my personal home number." She always spoke with the same Chase employee and would straighten any payment problems out with him. She testified that Mr. DeMary's company was having financial difficulties, but that Chase was one of their priorities and she kept in touch with Chase to let them know when payments were coming. She recalled that in July 1991 she had a telephone conversation with a Chase representative regarding the late car payments and told Chase she was sending a payment then and two more payments would be sent in one to two weeks. She produced a copy of a letter showing that check number 422 for $1,441.25 was sent to

Chase on August 30, 1991 at P.O. Box 5210, New Hyde Park, New York, 11042. The check was drawn on Mr. DeMary's personal account, rather than a company account, and was cashed on September 9, 1991.

Chase's representative testified that the DeMary's account had been more than thirty days delinquent four times since the inception of the loan and that $105 in late fees had been assessed during that period. Chase's records indicated that Mr. DeMary's secretary called Chase on July 29, 1991 to advise that she had sent a single payment on July 26 and that she would be sending another payment on August 2. Chase received a payment on August 2, however, it did not bring the account current. On August 16, a letter was sent to Mr. DeMary's company regarding two payments that were in arrears. On August 29, Chase's record of DeMary's account history showed that the collection agent was gathering all of the paperwork and that repossession was being considered. On September 3, 1991, a Chase representative tried to contact the DeMary's at home, but the phone was not working, and Interstate was assigned to repossess the Mercedes.

Chase's agreement with Interstate was described by Chase's representative at trial as essentially the same as with any repossession company. Under the agreement, Chase could review the books and records of Interstate; stop the repossession at any time; require Interstate to maintain liability insurance with an insurance carrier that is satisfactory to Chase and to notify Chase of any material modification of any insurance policy; and require Interstate to obtain Chase's prior written consent before hiring any subcontractors. The Chase representative also testified that Chase was not in the business of repossessing vehicles; did not supply Interstate with tow trucks, personnel, or any other equipment necessary to effectuate the repossession; and did not pay the salaries of the tow truck operators or have the authority to hire or fire the operators. The Interstate tow truck did not display any Chase identification, and Rieker did not tell the DeMary's that he was hired by Chase. Chase employees are forbidden from participating in an involuntary repossession.

The trial judges were called upon to deal with several issues. The first was how to explain to the jury Interstate's lack of further participation in the case after jury selection. Judge Mochary indicated to the jury that the towing company Interstate and the two employees of that company are no longer in this case. They have been dismissed out by me. You are not to speculate as to why. All you have to know is that it was done by the Court.

Counsel for Chase requested that she be permitted to inform the jury in her opening that Interstate settled the case, but the judge refused her request.

Next, because the Repossession Agreement between Interstate and Chase contained, as noted, a clause requiring Interstate to obtain insurance that named Chase as an additional insured, a dispute arose as to whether the agreement should be redacted to exclude any evidence of insurance from the jury. The judge found it should be redacted to prevent the jury from knowing the amount of insurance, but refused to redact the entire insurance provision. Chase also requested that the agreement be redacted with regard to an indemnification provision. After hearing all of the testimony, Judge Harris decided that the indemnification provision could be viewed by the jury as evidence of Chase's control over Interstate.

Chase made a motion for judgment at the close of all of the evidence, asserting that no agency relationship between Chase and Interstate was proven; that if an agency relationship was proven, Rieker was acting outside the scope of his employment; that the repossession was not the proximate cause of the injury; and that the release of an agent or a finding of no fault on the part of the agent releases the master from liability.

Judge Harris found that there was sufficient indicia of control to allow the jury to decide whether an agency relationship existed between Chase and Interstate, and that there was a sufficient nexus between the negligence alleged and plaintiffs' injuries to allow the jury to decide the issue. The judge reserved decision on whether the settlement was actually a release of Chase's agent requiring that Chase be released as well, but eventually denied relief to Chase.

The jury found Chase liable to Mrs. DeMary in the sum of $2,500,000 and to Mr. DeMary for $500,000. Neither received a per quod award. The jury found Chase to be eighty percent negligent and Interstate/Riekers to be twenty percent negligent.

Chase's motion for Judgment Notwithstanding the Verdict (JNOV) or, in the alternative, for a new trial, was denied. The indemnification action between Chase and Interstate was stayed by consent of the parties, and an order certifying the judgment as final was entered. Chase appeals from the judgments.

On appeal, Chase's first allegation is that Judge Mochary's instruction to the jury that Interstate and the Rieker's were "dismissed out by the Court" resulted in reversible error. Rule 2:10–2, provides:

> Any error or omission shall be disregarded by the appellate court unless it is of such a nature as to have been clearly capable of producing an unjust result, but the appellate court may, in the interests of justice, notice plain error not brought to the attention of the trial or appellate court.

Here, the situation was brought to the attention of Judge Harris when he took over conduct of the trial. He did advise the jury that Interstate and the Riekers had settled with the plaintiffs. He instructed:

> When this action was started, the plaintiff alleged in the complaint that the joint or concurring negligence of William Rieker, Ann Rieker and Interstate Financial Adjustors, Incorporated was a proximate cause of the accident. Before the trial started Rieker and Interstate settled

with the plaintiff in a sum of money, the amount of which is to be of no concern to you.

Your first duty is to determine whether or not the defendants remaining were individually or concurrently negligent in proximately causing the accident. Judge Mochary, in his preliminary instruction, one of his preliminary instructions to you, indicated that the settling defendants were dismissed out of the case and they are dismissed out in terms of the literal meaning of the word as far as your consideration as to ascribing liability to them. They are not in the case and they should not be part of your determination except as I am now indicating.

If you find that any one of the defendants or all of the defendants were guilty of negligence and that such negligence was a proximate cause of the accident, then it becomes your duty to determine the amount of damages you should award to the plaintiffs to compensate them fairly and reasonably for their injuries. In computing these damages, you must not be concerned with the number of defendants who were originally in the case, nor with the number of defendants remaining.

Judge Harris also indicated that counsel for Chase could refer to the settlement in her summation. Indeed, counsel for Chase emphasized Interstate's settlement with plaintiffs at least three times in her summation.

Considering Judge Harris' instruction and Chase's summation, Judge Mochary's preliminary instruction to the jury was not clearly capable of producing an unjust result. R. 2:10–2. The jury was instructed that Interstate/Riekers had settled with plaintiffs for a sum of money rather than having been dismissed by the court. Any error in the initial instruction by Judge Mochary was harmless and did not influence the result. We reject as without merit Chase's contention that Judge Mochary's explanation to the jury prejudiced its trial strategy, compelling its counsel to not focus on the egregiousness of Rieker's conduct.

Chase's assertion that Judge Harris improperly imposed a deadline for the jury's deliberations was not raised below and is unsupported by the record. We spurn the argument as clearly without merit. R. 2:11–3(e)(1)(E).

Chase also asserts that it was an abuse of discretion to allow the jury to consider evidence of insurance contained in the Repossession Agreement. Chase contends that even if the insurance provision was evidence of agency, it should have been excluded as too prejudicial. Chase also argues that the failure to give a limiting instruction as to the use of this evidence requires reversal.

N.J.R.E. 411 states

> Evidence that a person was or was not insured against liability is not admissible on the issue of that person's negligence or other wrongful conduct. Subject to Rule 403, this rule does not require the exclusion of evidence of insurance against liability when offered for

another purpose, such as proof of agency, ownership, control, bias, or prejudice of a witness.

Admission of such evidence of insurance for purposes other than to prove liability is subject to the discretion of the trial judge as to whether the prejudicial impact of the evidence outweighs its probative value. N.J.R.E. 403. However, "[i]f the evidence of liability insurance is admissible as bearing upon some issue other than negligence or culpable conduct, the jury should be charged in accordance with N.J.R.E. 105 as to the limited weight to be given to the evidence." Biunno, Current N.J. Rules of Evidence, comment on N.J.R.E. 411.

The insurance provision contained in the Repossession Agreement reads as follows:

> 1. At its sole cost and expense, the Repossessor will maintain as long as this Agreement is in effect, the following insurance coverage with an insurance carrier or carriers satisfactory to Chase: (a) Automobile Liability Insurance ..., naming Chase as additional insured; (b) Automobile Physical Damage Insurance ..., naming Chase as loss payee; (c) Automobile Collision Insurance ..., naming Chase as loss payee; (d) No Fault Insurance ...; (e) Comprehensive General Liability Insurance ..., naming Chase as additional insured.

All reference as to the amount of insurance was redacted.

Agency was considered an issue at trial, and the language contained in the Repossession Agreement was thought to be evidence of Chase's "control" over Interstate. However, the ability to contractually require another corporation to obtain insurance, and to be named as an additional insured or a loss payee does not, in our view, bear upon whether Chase and Interstate were in a master/servant relationship. Thus, the perceived probative value of this provision on the agency issue was erroneous.

The admission of this evidence was compounded by the fact that the judge did not limit the manner in which the jury could use this evidence of insurance. In deciding to admit the provision, Judge Mochary stated he would give a limiting instruction to the jury that "it is only to be considered ... as indication of or as a possible element of control...." However, this instruction was inadvertently omitted when Judge Harris took over the trial, and neither counsel informed the judge of the omission.

Nonetheless, the failure to give a limiting instruction was harmless error, as was the admission of the agreement requiring insurance. As between insurance coverage and financial responsibility of a corporation the size of Chase, it is debatable which is the "target" defendant of the two. Clearly, the jury would perceive Chase as having the ability to pay regardless of any evidence of insurance. Standing alone, the insurance provision was not here clearly capable of producing an unjust result, even when combined with the failure to give a jury instruction limiting its use. R. 2:10–2.

We turn next to Chase's argument that the provision contained in the Repossession Agreement requiring Interstate to indemnify Chase should not have been made available to the jury and was prejudicial. The relevant portion of the Agreement reads as follows:

INDEMNITIES

1. By Chase. Chase shall have no liability to Repossessor in connection with the transactions contemplated by this Agreement, except Chase shall assume full responsibility for and save the Repossessor, its employees and agents, harmless from any and all claims arising solely in connection with the propriety of Chase's notice to the Repossessor to repossess any Vehicle.

2. By Repossessor. The Repossessor shall assume full responsibility for and save Chase, its employees and agents harmless from and against any and all claims, losses, damages, costs or suits arising in connection with the Repossessor's acts or omissions concerning the pick-up, repossession, transportation, storage or sale of any Vehicle or its contents or any breach of any representation, warranty or covenant in this Agreement.

Chase claims that this provision had little to do with the issue of its control over Interstate or Rieker, and that its probative value was outweighed by its prejudicial nature. See N.J.R.E. 403.

The judge admitted the evidence of indemnification as "a possible indicia of control." However, it is apparent that the indemnification provision is not an indicator of control. Clearly, admission of this evidence was error. The prejudicial effect of this error will be discussed in the damages portion of this opinion.

Chase also claims that the judge should have instructed the jury that "it had to consider the relative fault of all parties, including the plaintiffs and both settling and non-settling defendants." Judge Harris made reference to the possible negligent conduct of Interstate and plaintiffs a number of times. We find no reason to disturb the jury verdict of no negligence on the part of plaintiffs. However, because the jury was asked to apportion fault between Chase and Interstate after the initial verdict, without further explanatory instruction, and because of the lack of sufficient instruction as to the legal standards governing the allegation of negligence against Chase, we have grave doubt as to the propriety of the jury's 80–20% apportionment of fault.

The jury was charged that plaintiffs contended Chase was negligent in ordering the repossession. However, only a general negligence charge was given to cover all allegations of negligence in this case. The jury was given no standard by which to judge whether plaintiffs had proven Chase was negligent in maintaining and reviewing its records prior to causing repossession. However, we see no reason to enter that thicket at this juncture. We leave it for the indemnification trial between Chase and

Interstate, as we are convinced that Chase had a duty to ensure that repossession of the secured property was carried out in a peaceable manner, a duty which could not be delegated to an independent contractor or anyone else. Since the duty is non-delegable, a breach of the peace results in liability on the part of the secured party ordering repossession. Further, discussion of this duty will follow.

Thus, we need not rule upon Chase's contention that there was no probative evidence to support plaintiffs' claim that Interstate was in a master/servant relationship with Chase, although we tend to agree with its position. Under the doctrine of respondeat superior, a master is liable for the negligence of his/her servant that occurs during the scope of the servant's employment. Abbamont v. Piscataway Tp. Bd. Educ., 138 N.J. 405, 416, 650 A.2d 958 (1994); Printing Mart–Morristown v. Sharp Electronics Corp., 116 N.J. 739, 771, 563 A.2d 31 (1989); Prosser and Keaton on Torts, § 69, 499–501 (West 5th ed.1984). The jury was asked to determine whether Interstate was actually a servant of Chase and whether Interstate was an independent contractor. The jury answered "yes" to both questions, which although legally inconsistent, was most likely a function of the manner in which the jury interrogatories were worded. Also contributing to the inconsistency is the possibility that the jury found a non-delegable duty existed.

Regardless, we assume that the evidence does support Chase's assertion that Interstate was an independent contractor, and we agree that usually a hiring party is not liable for the negligence of an independent contractor. Bahrle v. Exxon Corp., 145 N.J. 144, 156, 678 A.2d 225 (1996). However, one may not abdicate a non-delegable duty simply by entering into a relationship with an independent contractor. Prosser, supra, § 71, 511–12.

N.J.S.A. 12A:9–503 only authorizes repossession without judicial process where it is accomplished "without breach of the peace." As this case demonstrates, there is a distinct probability that an involuntary repossession may become a highly confrontational situation. Whenever a person is confiscating the property of another, particularly where the owner believes he/she is entitled to keep the property, the potential for dispute is likely, and injury to person or property is a foreseeable consequence.

New Jersey has never decided whether the duty to repossess without a breach of the peace is non-delegable. However, those jurisdictions that have considered the question do impose such a duty upon parties ordering independent contractors to repossess property. See Clark v. Associates Commercial Corp., 877 F.Supp. 1439, 1445 (D.Kan.1994); James v. Ford Motor Credit Co., 842 F.Supp. 1202 (D.Minn.1994); King v. Citizens Bank of Warrensburg, CIV.A. 88–2576–0, 1990 WL 154210, at (D.Kan. Sept. 19, 1990); General Fin. Corp. v. Smith, 505 So.2d 1045, 1048 (Ala.1987); Nixon v. Halpin, 620 So.2d 796, 798 (Fla.App.1993); Sammons v. Broward Bank, 599 So.2d 1018, 1021 (Fla.App.1992); Massengill v. Indiana Nat'l Bank, 550 N.E.2d 97, 99 (Ind.App.1990); Nichols

v. Metropolitan Bank, 435 N.W.2d 637, 640 (Minn.App.1989); Robinson v. Citicorp. Nat'l Services, 921 S.W.2d 52, 54–55 (Mo.App.1996); Mauro v. General Motors Acceptance Corp., 164 Misc.2d 871, 626 N.Y.S.2d 374, 376–77 (Sup.Ct.1995); MBank El Paso, N.A. v. Sanchez, 836 S.W.2d 151, 153–54 (Tex.1992). We adopt this rule, that an employer has a non-delegable duty to effectuate a repossession without a breach of the peace, as strongly in the public interest.

This theory was presented to the jury as follows:

> An employer of an independent contractor will not—will be held liable if the work was of the kind which the employer should have recognized would during its progress necessarily create a danger of the mishap which occurred and thus contained or involved an unreasonable or peculiar risk of bodily harm to the plaintiff unless special precautions were taken.

> One who employs an independent contractor to do work which the employer should recognize as likely to create during its progress particular risk of physical harm to other, unless special precautions are taken, is subject to the liability for physical harm caused to them by the failure of the independent contractor to exercise reasonable care to take such precautions even though the employer has provided for such precautions and the contractor otherwise.

> If you make a finding of fact that the repossession of plaintiff's vehicle authorized by Chase was likely to create, during its progress a particular risk of harm to others unless special precautions are taken, that is discontinuing the repossession, it cannot be—if it cannot be completed without a breach of the peace or notifying the police to accompany them to plaintiff's home, then you may consider whether Chase is liable for the physical harm caused to the plaintiffs by failure of Interstate to exercise reasonable care to take such precautions.

> A secured party such as Chase on default has the right to take possession of the collateral. In taking possession a secured party may proceed without judicial process if this can be done without breach of the peace or may proceed by action.

> We are willing to assume Chase had a valid security agreement under which repossession was permissible and that the lease was in default. We also assume that Chase and Interstate intended repossession to be effectuated without a breach of the peace. However, we are satisfied the jury properly found that a breach of the peace occurred. The jury was instructed as to this issue and there was ample evidence presented to support a finding of a breach of the peace. As Chase had a non-delegable duty to ensure the repossession was carried out without any breach of the peace, we uphold the liability verdict against Chase. We, however, set aside the apportionment verdict and remand that issue for determination during the indemnification trial between Chase and Interstate.

We now turn to the final issue of whether a new trial should have been ordered because of the excessiveness of the jury awards in favor of each of the plaintiffs. We first note that because the jury made no award to the plaintiffs for any per quod losses, the awards of 2.5 million dollars and five hundred thousand dollars to Mrs. DeMary and Mr. DeMary, respectively, represent compensation only for the personal injuries each suffered resulting from their separate accidents.

We look first at Mr. DeMary's award of a half a million dollars for a simple non-displaced fibial fracture resulting in six weeks of casting and what can be considered at best, some minor permanent disability. Although Judge Mochary was of the opinion that it was not a result which would shock the judicial conscience, we must disagree with that conclusion. The award bears no reasonable relationship to the injury and the need to compensate Mr. DeMary for his losses. There were no medical expenses or out-of-pocket losses such as lost income or future medical expenses to be considered. After six weeks of casting, during which he ambulated with crutches, he used a cane for approximately one week. The only problem he related was that it hurt "like a toothache" in bad weather and that he is unable to jog today as he used to do before the accident.

Turning to Mrs. DeMary's injury and the award of 2.5 million dollars, we note the gravity of the injury, which includes a significant loss of both flexion and extension in the ankle joint, without apparent impairment in lateral movement. In reviewing the propriety of the verdict, we also assume that the jury found credible the testimony of Mrs. DeMary's orthopedist that a fusion of the ankle because of arthritic changes was likely in the future. Certainly the treatment that had taken place prior to trial, involving three surgeries with bone grafts, insertion and removal of screws, and scarring in both the hip and ankle areas, is significant and impressive. We also recognize her complaints of pain when she wakes up in the morning, swelling when she is on the ankle too long, stiffness, and the need to take Advil for relief of the pain.

Nonetheless, even considering the significance of Mrs. DeMary's injuries, the award of 2.5 million dollars is suspect when viewed in the light of Mr. DeMary's clearly excessive verdict, counsels' inflammatory comments, and certain trial error. Remarks made by both plaintiffs' counsel in their summations included references to a "faceless defendant" and Chase as a "weasel." Also a theme in both summations was the notion that Chase was an insulated corporation who should not be allowed to "get away with" what they did to plaintiffs.

We conclude that the jury awards were as a result of prejudice resulting from counsels' inflammatory remarks directed against the "giant" Chase. While we sustain the liability award against Chase based upon a non-delegable duty, we must reverse the damage award. We also have considered that the jury had before it the Repossession Agreement which purported to hold Interstate and Rieker ultimately responsible for such offensive conduct and disregard for human safety. This may have given the jury the impression that in returning a large verdict against Chase, it was also punishing Interstate and Rieker. In any event, only awards which are fair and reasonable should be sustained regardless of the ability of a defendant to pay the freight. See Caldwell v. Haynes, 136 N.J. 422, 442, 643 A.2d 564 (1994); Baxter v. Fairmont Food Co., 74 N.J. 588, 596–97, 379 A.2d 225 (1977).

We add that we have reviewed both trial judges' comments in their rulings on the motion for a new trial as to damages and we find nothing which demonstrates a "feel of the case" sufficient to sustain the verdicts. The observations regarding the credibility of the plaintiffs, and their understating of their injuries, is fully accepted by us. Nonetheless, it does not detract from our conclusion that the verdicts should not stand because they represent a miscarriage of justice under the law.

We are satisfied that a new trial as to damages only is the best method of evaluating the fair compensation to be awarded to plaintiffs for the injuries they have suffered. The removal of inflammatory rhetoric and dispersions cast toward the corporate defendant will permit the jury to fully and fairly evaluate the damages.

We affirm as to Chase's liability, set aside the apportionment of fault as between the defendants, reverse as to the damage awards, and remand for a retrial as to damages. The issue of apportionment may be resolved in the trial on the indemnification issue, if necessary.

Affirmed in part, reversed in part, and remanded for further proceedings.

Question

What is the effect of the plaintiffs' settlement with Interstate on Chase's liability?

FORD MOTOR CREDIT CO. v. MATHIS

Supreme Court of Mississippi, 1995.
660 So.2d 1273

ROBERTS, JUSTICE:

This is an appeal from a summary judgment entered against Ford Motor Credit Company ("FMCC") and in favor of George Mathis ("Mathis") on April 20, 1992, in the Circuit Court of George County, Mississippi. The trial court held FMCC's sale of a truck repossessed from Mathis at a wholesale auction open only to dealers was not commercially reasonable under Miss.Code Ann. § 75–9–504. We reverse.

Facts And Procedural History

On May 22, 1987, George Mathis purchased a used 1984 Mazda B2000 pickup truck which he financed through Ford Motor Credit Company. Mathis signed a Retail Installment Sales Contract whereby he agreed to pay the sum of $4,039.59 over a period of 42 months. He subsequently defaulted on the agreement and voluntarily surrendered the truck to FMCC.

After recovering the truck, FMCC mailed to Mathis via certified mail a notice of repossession prior to sale. The lower court found the notice complied with Miss.Code Ann. §§ 75–9–504 and 75–9–507 in all respects. The truck was sold at the Mississippi Automobile Auction in Hattiesburg, Mississippi, for the sum of one thousand six hundred fifty dollars ($1,650.00), a sale price which was 137% above the National Automobile Dealers Association "Blue Book" wholesale value. After making all "credits, adjustments and offsets" there was a remaining balance of $2,427.29 owing on the contract.

Subsequently, FMCC filed a complaint in the Circuit Court of George County, Mississippi, for recovery of the vehicle's outstanding balance of $2,427.29 plus $364.09 in attorney's fees for a total of $2,791.38. The defendant, Mathis, filed an answer in which he alleged that he was entitled to damages for FMCC's failure to dispose of the repossessed truck in a commercially reasonable manner, and for its failure to sell the truck for its reasonable fair market value. The issues were eventually narrowed to whether the post-repossession sale of the truck at the Mississippi Auto Auction was a commercially reasonable sale as required under the Uniform Commercial Code, Miss.Code Ann. §§ 75–9–504 and 75–9–507.

FMCC filed a Motion for Summary Judgment on April 24, 1990. A hearing on the motion was held on July 6, 1990, before the Honorable Clinton E. Lockard. Judge Lockard denied the motion without prejudice subject to its being reconsidered upon the submission of additional affidavits. The additional affidavits were subsequently filed with the court and FMCC's Motion for Summary Judgment was again heard by the circuit court, the Honorable Darwin Maples presiding. An order was entered on November 21, 1990, denying FMCC's motion. An amended order was filed by Judge Maples on January 3, 1991, in which he set out his findings of fact and conclusions of law upon which he based his decision to deny FMCC's Motion for Summary Judgment.

FMCC was then granted leave to petition this Court for an interlocutory appeal. On March 1, 1991, this Court denied that Petition for Leave to File Interlocutory Appeal. The case was set for trial on three separate occasions. Finally, on April 20, 1992, Mathis filed a Motion for Summary Judgment. On that same date, the circuit court, the Honorable Kathy King Jackson presiding, entered a ruling that Mathis was entitled to summary judgment as a matter of law. In granting summary judgment, Judge Jackson adopted the findings of fact and conclusions of law made by Judge Maples in an earlier order.

During discovery, FMCC submitted affidavits from Gordon Illing, an employee of FMCC, Gary Sells, assistant general manager of Mississippi Auto Auction in Hattiesburg, Rickie Chatagnier, an employee of General Motors Acceptance Corporation in Biloxi, Mississippi, and Al Payne, an employee of Chrysler Credit Corporation in Mobile, Alabama. The facts given in these affidavits were undisputed by Mathis and were therefore accepted as true by the lower court.

The Mississippi Auto Auction, Inc. is a wholly owned subsidiary of Anglo–American Auto Auction, Inc. Anglo–American Auto Auction, Inc. has subsidiaries doing business throughout the United States. These auctions are only open to licensed automobile dealers who are able to meet certain financial and stability criteria.

The Hattiesburg auto auction attracts dealers from all 50 states. However, the sales area primarily targeted by the auction includes 15 states. Those states primarily targeted include all the states bordering Mississippi plus California, Indiana, Texas, Arizona and Missouri. Regularly scheduled auctions are held once a week. In addition, special sales are also held. Prior to a sale approximately 3,500 mail-outs are sent to dealers in the target area. Employees of the Hattiesburg auction also make approximately 300 telephone calls per week to publicize the sales. The auction also has two traveling representatives, each of whom call upon about 75 dealers per week. There is an average weekly attendance of 220 dealers bidding on cars at the Hattiesburg auction. Mississippi Auto Auction, Inc. sold approximately 24,000 cars in 1989. Anglo–American Auto Auction, Inc., through its collective subsidiaries, sells approximately 500,000 cars per year.

In his affidavit, Sells stated that approximately 100 Ford repossessions are sold each week at the Hattiesburg auto auction. The auction also handles "repossession sales for local banks, finance companies, rental companies and some dealer consignments." "Virtually every type of lending entity regularly engaged in financing automobiles uses an auto auction similar to the Hattiesburg Auto Auction."

NADA "Blue Book" wholesale values are determined by the prices bid by dealers at car auctions which are transmitted by computer to the NADA. Auto auctions are virtually the only method used by FMCC, General Motors Acceptance Corporation and Chrysler Credit Corporation for selling repossessed vehicles.

The lower court held that although the data regarding auto auctions was not in dispute, "as a matter of law, that such a sale, calculated to generate a wholesale price [as opposed to a retail price], is not a commercially reasonable sale as is required under Mississippi's adopted version of Article 9 of the Uniform Commercial Code." FMCC was held to have complied with all other requirements of Article 9 in regard to the repossession of Mathis' truck.

Appeal

FMCC argues that the resale of a repossessed automobile through a dealers-only auto auction intended to generate a wholesale price is a commercially reasonable sale under the UCC and the provisions of Miss.Code Ann. Sections 75–9–504 and 75–9–507. § 75–9–504 reads in pertinent part:

(3) Disposition of the collateral may be by public or private proceedings and may be made by way of one (1) or more contracts. Sale or
other disposition may be as a unit or in parcels and at any time and
place and on any terms, but every aspect of the disposition including
the method, manner, time, place and terms must be commercially
reasonable. . . .

The lower court held the repossession and sale of the truck financed
by Mathis through FMCC was proper in all respects with the exception
of the manner of the sale. The trial judge held that since the truck was
sold at an auction open only to dealers and therefore calculated to
generate a wholesale, not a retail, price, it was commercially unreasonable. The lower court found that the price obtained for Mathis' repossessed truck was 137% above the NADA "Bluebook" wholesale price.
The lower court did not find the price obtained for the truck to be
commercially unreasonable. It found instead that the sale was not
commercially reasonable because the auction was intended only to bring
a wholesale price. Because of the lower court's ruling, only the commercial reasonableness of the manner of sale will be addressed here. Commercial reasonableness is discussed in § 75–9–507 as follows:

(2) The fact that a better price could have been obtained by a sale at
a different time or in a different method from that selected by the
secured party is not of itself sufficient to establish that the sale was
not made in a commercially reasonable manner. If the secured party
either sells the collateral in the usual manner in any recognized
market therefor or if he sells at the price current in such market at
the time of his sale or if he has otherwise sold in conformity with
reasonable commercial practices among dealers in the type of property sold he has sold in a commercially reasonable manner. . . .

The wholesale disposition of repossessed collateral is commercially
reasonable if it is "consistent with ordinary commercial practice among
dealers." White & Summers, Uniform Commercial Code (3rd Ed.1988 &
Supp.1994) § 27–11.

Comment 2 to § 9–507 of the U.C.C. reads:

One recognized method of disposing of repossessed collateral is for
the secured party to sell the collateral to or through a dealer—a
method which in the long run may realize better average returns
since the secured party does not usually maintain his own facilities
for making such sales. Such a method of sale, fairly conducted, is
recognized as commercially reasonable under the second sentence of
subsection (2).

The wholesale versus retail issue has not been previously addressed
in Mississippi. The courts of several other states have dealt with this
issue, however, and have as a general rule been unwilling to hold the
sale of repossessed vehicles at wholesale auction to be commercially
unreasonable.

In a case with facts very similar to the case at bar, the Georgia Court of Appeals, in interpreting a statute identical to § 75–9–507(2), held:

> Bank South has shown, by way of affidavit, that the collateral was disposed of at a private auction by a recognized automobile auction company according to standard practice and procedure for sales of this kind. Bank South has disposed of collateral in this manner on a weekly basis for 11 years. . . . Because McMillian has offered no evidence to the contrary, we agree the trial court correctly concluded that the method and manner of sale were commercially reasonable. McMillian v. Bank South, N.A., 188 Ga.App. 355, 373 S.E.2d 61, 62 (1988). See also Lee v. Trust Company Bank, 204 Ga.App. 28, 418 S.E.2d 407, 408 (1992).

The Alabama Civil Court of Appeals has also held the wholesale auction of repossessed vehicles to be commercially reasonable. In Daniel v. Ford Motor Credit Co., 612 So.2d 483 (Ala.Civ.App.1992), FMCC sold a repossessed automobile at a wholesale dealers' auction for a price less than the average wholesale price listed in the NADA appraisal guidebook. In finding the disposition to be commercially reasonable, the Alabama Court opined:

> The testimony has indicated that the wholesale dealer auction is the usual manner of sale of repossessed automobiles and that it is in conformity with the reasonable commercial practices among dealers in repossessed automobiles, in accordance with § 7–9–507(2). In view of the evidence, of the requirements of the statute, and of the proper notice that was given, we cannot hold that the sale was commercially unreasonable. Id. at 485.

In Gaynor v. Union Trust Co., 216 Conn. 458, 582 A.2d 190 (1990), the Connecticut Court held a bank's wholesale disposition of repossessed used cars to be commercially reasonable.

In Union National Bank of Wichita v. Schmitz, 18 Kan.App.2d 403, 853 P.2d 1180 (1993), the Kansas Court of Appeals refused to hold the disposition of repossessed collateral at a dealers-only wholesale auction to be per se commercially unreasonable. The Court opined:

> It is well established that whether a particular disposition was done in a commercially reasonable manner is a question of fact to be determined by the trier of fact. The burden of proving that the collateral was disposed of in a commercially reasonable manner is placed upon the secured creditor. . . .
>
> * * *
>
> The method utilized to dispose of the collateral in this case was a well-known, regularly scheduled, dealer-only wholesale auction. The trial court's findings that this sale was commercially unreasonable are so broad that they virtually declare any dealer-only wholesale auction to be not commercially reasonable. In deciding this issue, the trial court focused solely on the nature of the auction and the

price received for the vehicle. The trial court's decision, if allowed to stand, would mean that a dealer-only wholesale auction could not be commercially reasonable. This is not the law, and the trial court erred in reaching this conclusion.

* * *

We think it apparent from the decisions and the statutes cited that the mere fact collateral is sold at wholesale and not "exposed to the retail market" is not in and of itself sufficient to render a sale commercially unreasonable. The trial court in the instant matter erred in reaching this conclusion. Id. 853 P.2d at 1184–6.

Like the Kansas Court, we find the lower court erred in its holding that the sale of repossessed vehicles at wholesale without first exposing them to the retail market is per se commercially unreasonable. When the factors of manner, method, time, place and terms of sale are considered, the disposition of repossessed property at a dealer-only wholesale auction may very well be commercially reasonable. This is a question for the finder of fact in a particular case. If the debtor challenges the commercial reasonableness of the disposition of his repossessed vehicle, the burden is on the creditor to show through the aggregate of circumstances that the sale met all the factors of commercial reasonableness. Schmitz, 853 P.2d at 1187. See also Northern Commercial Co. v. Cobb, 778 P.2d 205 (Alaska 1989); Villella Enterprises, Inc. v. Young, 108 N.M. 33, 766 P.2d 293 (1988).

We find that the trial court erred in granting summary judgment to Mathis and reverse and remand for a trial on the merits.

Cross-appeal

Since we find the trial court erred in granting summary judgment to Mathis, both issues on cross-appeal are moot and, therefore, need not be addressed.

Conclusion

The trial court erred in holding that the sale of a repossessed vehicle at a dealers-only auction is per se commercially unreasonable. Both issues on cross-appeal are moot. For the foregoing reasons this case is reversed and remanded on direct appeal and cross-appeal is dismissed as moot.

HAWKINS, C.J., PRATHER, P.J., SULLIVAN, PITTMAN, BANKS and SMITH, JJ., concur.

LEE, P.J., concurs in result only.

MCRAE, JUSTICE, dissenting:

Since a "dealer-only" auction is essentially a private sale, I applaud the majority's recognition that the burden belongs on a creditor to demonstrate that the sale of repossessed property has been handled in a commercially reasonable manner. In this case, however, Ford Motor

Credit Company has not met its burden. I would therefore affirm the summary judgment in Mathis's favor.

Although the majority acknowledges that manner, method, time, place, and terms of sale are factors to consider when determining the commercial reasonableness of the sale of repossessed property, it appears to take for granted the reasonableness of a sale based on wholesale, and not retail, price. Why? Because that is how everybody does it. Nothing, however, in our statutes or case law directs us to assume that repossessed property is properly sold in a dealers-only wholesale auction rather than a retail auction. To the contrary, in the analogous situation of a deficiency judgment in a real property foreclosure sale, determination of fair market value does not even contemplate a sale where the public is not in attendance and placing bids. Wansley v. First National Bank of Vicksburg, 566 So.2d 1218, 1224 (Miss.1990); Haygood v. First National Bank of New Albany, 517 So.2d 553, 556 (Miss.1987). While a lending institution, if it so chooses, may sell a vehicle in a private sale through a dealer, it is the dealer who sells the vehicle at retail to the public when the institution does not have the facilities to do so.

Obtaining a fair price for the repossessed property benefits both debtor and creditor. In this case, however, we are given no indication of what a "fair" price for Mathis's vehicle might have been. The NADA Blue Book provides both the wholesale and retail prices of vehicles, as well as the current loan value. That information was not made a part of the record. Instead, the majority relies only on the affidavit of a Ford Motor Credit Company employee, who stated that the sale of the vehicle for $1,650.00 represented 137% of its wholesale value. Further, Ford Motor Credit incurred $198.00 in transporting the vehicle to Hattiesburg for the sale. Might a "fairer" price have been achieved at a lower cost had the car been sold elsewhere?

I would affirm the trial court's decision since Ford Motor Credit Company failed to meet its burden of showing that Mathis's vehicle was sold in a commercially reasonable manner. To the contrary, the creditor proved only that it utilized a closed (private) sale and sold the vehicle for a wholesale price after incurring the unwarranted expense of transporting it outside of the area where it was financed and housed. I do agree with the majority only to the extent that it correctly places the burden of demonstrating reasonableness on the creditor.

Problem 5–8

Assume a peaceful repossession of a pickup truck used as debtor's personal vehicle. The truck is sold at a wholesale dealer auction for $14,000 at a time when the debt outstanding was $20,000 and the wholesale blue book price was approximately $15,000. Assume the only notice given to the debtor was a phone call given by the bank one week before the sale; the bank officer informed debtor that the truck would be sold at a private sale seven days later. The bank has sued for a deficiency under 9–625. The debtor makes the following claims:

1. Where a creditor fails to comply with Part 6, a deficiency is "absolutely barred". Debtor maintains that 9–626 supports that conclusion.

2. Bank was deficient in giving its notice and conducting its sale. Bank should have sold the truck at retail and, in any case, it should have received at least the wholesale price of $15,000.

Bank responds that its sale price was fair and it need not give notice because a sale at a widely recognized Dealer's Auction is a sale in a recognized market of the kind that obviates the need for notice.

What do you think?

Problem 5–9

After the repossession in problem 5–8 but before the truck could be sold, debtor takes bankruptcy. Debtor's lawyer warned the bank against conducting any sale because of the automatic stay under section 362 of the Bankruptcy Code. She has also stated that the debtor intends to exercise his right to redeem the truck under section 722. Debtor proposes to redeem the truck by curing (making the two delinquent payments) and by reinstituting and continuing the payment schedule in effect before the bankruptcy.

Must Bank permit this?

Note

The Repo Man

As seen in both *Giles* and *DeMary*, when a debtor defaults on his car loan, the job of repossessing the car often falls to an independent collection agent, sometimes known as the "repo man." On average, a simple repossession of a typical car will net a repo man $300. However, a repo man may receive as much as $10,000 for a more difficult repossession of an antique car. In any given year, a typical repo man will earn between $30,000 and $60,000. Like any other job, the level of business depends on the state of the economy. Unlike most work, however, the business of a repo man booms when the rest of the economy busts. Layoffs and recession make the repo man smile.

On any given day, most of a repo man's time is spent tracking down cars and investigating the whereabouts of elusive debtors. Creditors often require a repo man to try to get possession voluntarily from the debtor before they attempt to repossess without his acquiescence. A repo man will attempt to get information from the friends and family of the debtor. Often the best source of information will be an ex-wife or ex-girlfriend. Using these sources, a veteran repo man will usually find his car in a matter of days.

Once the car is found the real action begins. Many debtors are slow to accept the fact that their car is going to be repossessed. Debtors often confuse a repo man with a car thief. As a result, repossessing a car can be a dangerous business. Given the law and the danger surrounding each repossession, a good repo man has both personal and economic incentive to avoid breaching the peace.

The best repo men finds ways of getting the car without sparking a confrontation with the debtor. For example, one repo man in San Jose discovered the power of shame. He noted that many still rich-at-heart dot-com executives (now defaulting on loans in increasing numbers) frequented a particular restaurant. The parking lot was a treasure trove. Even when the car owners noticed their car being repossessed, most were too embarrassed to make a scene.

Occasionally even a veteran repo man gets caught in a confrontation. In the last few years, one repo man was stabbed in the chest with a screwdriver and another was shot and killed execution style. Consider also the following account of a repossession gone awry in downtown Philadelphia:

> At 4:00 a.m. Edward Simmons is standing in a dark alley. Rosita Conroy has defaulted on her car loan, and her creditor has hired Simmons to repossess her car. Simmons slips down the alley and opens the car door using a duplicate key given to him by the creditor. He starts the car and drives to a nearby gas station where his partner waits with their tow-truck. Unbeknownst to Simmons, however, Jacques Galin witnesses him driving off with the car and follows him to the gas station armed with a loaded gun. When Galin finds the men loading the car, he approaches the car and shoots Simmons through the windshield. Simmons' partner takes cover behind a dumpster while Simmons attempts to return fire. His gun jams. Simmons then slumps in the seat, and the car, still in gear, rolls into Galin. Now pinned against the hood, Galin continues to fire into the car until Simmons' partner returns and shoots Galin in the head. Simmons suffers multiple gunshot wounds to his face, shoulder, chest, abdomen and hand. Miraculously, all involved survive. Simmons later sued Galin over the incident, and the United States District Court for the Eastern District of Pennsylvania ordered Galin to pay the repo man $1.2 million for battery. See *Simmons v. Galin*, 2002 WL 109611 (E.D.Pa.).

§ 7. VARIATIONS ON AND ALTERNATIVES TO CONVENTIONAL CONSUMER SECURED CREDIT

Consumers often enter into transactions that have some, but not all, of the characteristics of a conventional Article 9 secured loan. First, are "pawn" transactions in which the debtor leaves an item of value in the hands of a pawn broker with the understanding that debtor has a right within a specified time to return and repurchase the item at a specified price, or that the debtor has a right to the return of the item upon the payment of a specified amount together with interest. These transactions are nonrecourse; the debtor is not obliged to return and reclaim the collateral and there is no "default" if the debtor fails to do so. While permissible interest rates vary, some are quite high (20% per month in Georgia) and others more moderate (3% per month in Minnesota).

Yet one step further removed from Article 9 is the rent-to-own contract. In a rent-to-own contract, a consumer "rents" an item with a right to have title transferred at the end of a rental period that may extend for 52 weeks or, in some cases, 18 months. Sometimes the transfer of title occurs only on the payment of an option price that is often nominal. In other cases, there is no option but simply a right to the conveyance of the property upon completion of a specified number of payments. Like the pawn transaction, the rent-to-own transaction is nonrecourse; the debtor has no obligation to continue paying and may return the goods and cancel the transaction at the end of any payment interval (weekly or monthly). Commonly, the total payments under a rent-to-own contract are two or three times the lessor's cost. Typically this transaction is entered into by working class people who have limited credit and those who have no other credit options.

Is either of these transactions a secured loan?

Problem 5–10

Consider the following provisions from the Minnesota Pawn Broker Statute:

325J.06.   Effect of nonredemption

(a) A pledgor shall have no obligation to redeem pledged goods or make any payment on a pawn transaction. Pledged goods not redeemed within at least 60 days of the date of the pawn transaction, renewal, or extension shall automatically be forfeited to the pawnbroker, and qualified right, title, and interest in and to the goods shall automatically vest in the pawnbroker.

(b) The pawnbroker's right, title, and interest in the pledged goods under paragraph (a) is qualified only by the pledgor's right, while the pledged goods remain in possession of the pawnbroker and not sold to a third party, to redeem the goods by paying the loan plus fees and/or interest accrued up to the date of redemption.

(c) A pawn transaction that involves holding only the title to property is subject to chapter 168A or 336.

325J.095.   Motor vehicle title pawn transactions; special provisions

(a) In addition to the other requirements of this chapter, a pawnbroker who holds a title to a motor vehicle as part of a pawn transaction shall:

>   (1) be licensed as a used motor vehicle Dealer under section 168.27, and post such license on the pawnshop premises;

>   (2) verify that there are no liens or encumbrances against the motor vehicle with the department of public safety; and

>   (3) verify that the pledgor has automobile insurance on the motor vehicle as required by law.

(b) A pawnbroker may not sell a motor vehicle covered by a pawn transaction until 90 days after recovery of the motor vehicle.

———

How do the quoted sections treat pawn transactions differently from conventional secured loans? Would a pawn broker who failed to do a public sale or give notice be liable for violating 9–625(c)(2) or any other section in Part 6?

IN RE FREDDY JACK BOWMAN, GLORIA ANN BOWMAN

United States Bankruptcy Court, D. Arizona, 1995.
194 B.R. 227.

Lessor, which had leased household goods on a weekly basis to Chapter 13 debtors, moved for relief from automatic stay after debtors defaulted on the leases. Lessor also moved for dismissal of case as bad-faith filing. The Bankruptcy Court, James M. Marlar, J., held that: (1) under Arizona law, leases were not disguised sales and thus transactions were not secured transactions but were leases that debtors had to assume or reject; (2) lifting of stay would be delayed for 14 days to give debtors opportunity to assume leases and cure defaults; and (3) case would not be dismissed as bad-faith filing.

Motion to dismiss denied.

MEMORANDUM DECISION

MARLAR, BANKRUPTCY JUDGE:

This Court has under advisement the motion filed by Central Rents, Inc. ("Central" or "movant") seeking relief from the automatic stays. A final hearing was conducted on September 18, 1995, at which time Todd Jones appeared for the movant, and the debtor Freddy Bowman appeared. Mrs. Bowman did not appear. The Court has considered the arguments of counsel, the evidence, and the entire file in this matter and now rules.

I. Facts

The basic facts of this case are not in dispute. Between March 10, 1995, and April 14, 1995, the debtors rented two stereo systems, a kitchen set, and a television set from the movant. Each transaction was evidenced by a separate rental agreement on Central's standard form, copies of which were received in evidence (Ex. A, B, C, D). Almost immediately thereafter, the debtors defaulted on their lease obligations. On May 10, 1995, the debtors filed for relief under Chapter 13 of the Bankruptcy Code. The debtors have filed a plan which proposes to recharacterize the rental agreements as secured transactions and bifurcate the movant's claims into secured and unsecured portions. On July 13, 1995, Central Rents, Inc. filed its motion seeking relief from the automatic stays so that it could repossess the rental property. Movant has also asked that this case be dismissed as being filed in bad faith.

II. Legal Discussion

A. Lease vs. Disguised Sale

Central to both the motion for stay relief and the proposed plan of reorganization is the character of the "rental agreements." The debtors contend that the agreements are in the nature of a disguised security agreement and, therefore, appropriately treated as a secured debt. Such treatment, if accurate, would make the Bowmans the owners of the property. The movant, on the other hand, contends that the agreements are true leases and capable only of being assumed or rejected pursuant to § 365. Such treatment, if legally correct, would make movant the owner. After thorough consideration of the matter, the Court must agree with the movant.

The resolution of this dispute begins with an examination of the Uniform Commercial Code as enacted in Arizona. Prior to 1992, the UCC defined a "security interest" as:

[A]n interest in personal property * * * which secures payment or performance of an obligation. The retention or reservation of title by a seller of goods * * * is limited in effect to a reservation of a "security interest" * * *. Unless a lease * * * is intended as security, reservation of title thereunder is not a "security interest" * * *. Whether a lease is intended as security is to be determined by the facts of each case; however: (a) the inclusion of an option to purchase does not of itself make the lease one intended for security, and (b) an agreement that upon compliance with the terms of the lease the lessee shall become or has the option to become the owner of the property for no additional consideration or for a nominal consideration does make the lease one intended for security.

A.R.S. § 47–1201(37) (1967) (amended 1990, 1992, and 1993). Under this provision, if a lessee is obligated to pay, over the term of the lease, the full purchase price of the property, the transaction is a disguised sale, regardless of its form. In contrast, if the lessee is not required to pay the full purchase price or if, to acquire ownership, the lessee must pay more than a nominal amount in order to exercise an option to purchase, the transaction is a "true" lease, rather than a sale. Although the decision did not involve Arizona law, the Ninth Circuit concluded in 1982 that a nominal purchase price at the end of the term is, as a matter of law, the determining factor. See In re J.A. Thompson & Son, Inc., 665 F.2d 941, 947 (1982).

If judged by this definition, the present agreements would have to be characterized as disguised sales capable of cram-down in a plan or reorganization. Central's standard Rental Purchase Agreement sets a weekly rental payment and provides for payments to be made over a period of weeks. If the debtors were to make all of the scheduled weekly payments they would own the property at the end of total lease term. They also have the option to purchase the property at a discount, by paying cash totaling 60% of the remaining lease payments due under the agreement. In other words, the lessee automatically owns the property at the end of the lease term without any additional cash outlay. Moreover, the risk of loss is completely shifted to the "lessee" during the term of the lease. The agreement provides that the lessee is fully responsible for the safety of the property until it is returned. The lessee bears the risk of loss or damage. These terms give the agreement the distinct flavor of a disguised sale.

However, in 1992 the statutory definition of a "security interest" was dramatically changed to provide, in pertinent part, as follows:

(a) Whether a transaction creates a lease or security interest is determined by the facts of each case. However, a transaction creates a security interest if the consideration the lessee is to pay the lessor for the right to possession and use of the goods is an obligation for the terms of the lease not subject to termination by the lessee, and: (i) the original term of the lease is equal to or greater than the remaining economic life of the goods; (ii) the lessee is bound to renew the lease for the remaining economic life of the goods or is bound to become the owner of the goods; (iii) The lessee has an option to renew the lease for the remaining economic life of the goods for no additional consideration or nominal additional consideration upon compliance with the lease agreement; or (iv) the lessee has an option to become the owner of the goods for no additional consideration or nominal additional consideration upon compliance with the lease agreement. (emphasis added)

A.R.S. § 47–1201(37). Under this definition, a transaction is a disguised sale if: (1) the consideration the lessee is to pay the lessor for the right to possession and use of the goods is an obligation for the term of the lease not subject to termination by the lessee; and (2) one of the four conditions described in A.R.S. § 47–1201(37)(a) (UCC § 1–201) is met. These factors require the conclusion that the agreements in this case are true leases. Their redeeming feature is their term. Although it would appear at first blush that the term of the agreements is a period of several weeks, it is actually one (1) week with the following qualification:

You are not obligated in any way to renew this agreement after the first rental period. However, you may renew this agreement weekly or monthly by making another payment before your paid term expires.

Thus, the lessee's obligation does not extend beyond one week and can be terminated and the property returned by the lessee with no further obligation. In light of this, this Court must conclude that this term removes the present contracts from the realm of disguised sales.

While there is apparently no Arizona case law to support this conclusion, the same conclusion has been reached in numerous other jurisdictions. See generally, Powers v. Royce Rentals (In re Powers), 983 F.2d 88 (7th Cir.1993) (construing Illinois law); In re Allen, 174 B.R. 293 (Bankr.D.Or.1994) (construing Oregon law); Rent–A–Center, Inc. v. Mahoney (In re Mahoney), 153 B.R. 174 (E.D.Mich.S.D.1992) (construing Michigan law); In re Morris, 150 B.R. 446, 449 (Bankr.E.D.Mo.1992) (construing Missouri law); Rent–A–Center, Inc. v. Spears (In re Spears), 146 B.R. 772 (Bankr.S.D.Ill.1992) (construing Illinois law); In re Frady, 141 B.R. 600 (Bankr.W.D.N.C.1991) (construing North Carolina law); In re Taylor, 130 B.R. 849 (Bankr.E.D.Ark.1991) (construing Arkansas law); In re Mitchell, 108 B.R. 166 (Bankr.S.D.Ohio 1989) (construing Ohio law). Given this conclusion, it follows that the present rental agreements are terminable leases subject to Bankruptcy Code § 365, and not subject to cram-down in a chapter 13 plan. In other words, the Bowmans are not the owners of the property.

B. Stay Relief

Pursuant to § 365, the debtors must either assume or reject the rental agreements. Because there has admittedly been a default under the agreements, the contracts may only be assumed if the debtors (1) cured the existing defaults; (2) compensate the movant for any actual pecuniary loss resulting from the defaults; and (3) provide adequate assurance of future performance under the rental agreements. 11 U.S.C. § 365(b)(1). Pursuant to § 365(d), a chapter 13 debtor may assume or reject an executory contract at any time before the confirmation of a plan. However, the court may fix a deadline for the debtor to assume or reject.

The movant alleges that there is cause to lift the stay due to the significant default on the agreements. On this point, this Court must agree. The movant further contends that the debtors are unable to cure the defaults and assume these leases. However, there is no evidence to support this contention, because the debtors have proceeded on the assumption that they are the owners of the property and that the agreements could be dealt with in their plan. Accordingly, rather than lifting the stay immediately, the Court finds that it is more equitable to give the debtors 14 days to determine whether they want to assume or reject these agreements. If they elect to assume the contracts, they must notify counsel for the movant, in writing, and cure all defaults by delivering good funds to counsel on or before the deadline. To satisfy the requirement of adequate assurance, the stay will be lifted, upon the expiration of 14 days after the date of this decision. If the debtors fail to timely cure the defaults and/or to make any of the regular weekly payments coming due after the entry of this decision, the movant will be free to pursue its state law remedies. In contrast, if the debtors fulfill their obligations under the agreements, they will be able to retain the rented property. This is a fair result for all.

C. Motion to Dismiss

Central has also alleged that this case was filed in bad faith and, therefore, should be dismissed. In support of this request Central cites In re Eisen, 14 F.3d 469 (9th Cir.1994) for the proposition that it is appropriate to dismiss a case where the debtor has (1) filed serial bankruptcy cases and (2) the second case was filed in response to creditor action. The Court does not read the Eisen case to stand for such a rule. In Eisen there was clear evidence that the debtor had concealed assets and mislead the court and creditors. There is no such evidence in this case. Admittedly, the good faith of these debtors is appropriately placed in question due to their serial filings and the uncomfortably close nexus between their execution of the rental agreements and the commencement of this case. However, the record is not sufficiently clear to allow such a ruling at this juncture. Thus, the motion to dismiss will be denied without prejudice.

Contemporaneously herewith, an Order consistent with this decision will be entered.

Problem 5–11

In the Bowman case the debtors had agreed to lease or buy two stereos, one kitchen set, and one television. Assume the lessor-seller's cost for all of these items was $1,500. Conforming to the typical rent to own practice, the lessor-seller and the lessee-buyer entered into a contract that provided for total payments of $3,500. Assume also that the value of the used goods in buyer's possession would have been $1,000 and that debtors made a payment of only $10 against the total obligation. With this background, understand what each party was arguing in the Chapter 13 proceeding:

Seller-lessor maintains that the transaction is a lease. If the seller-lessor's argument prevails, the lessee-buyer can get title under 365 only by paying the remaining $3,490.

Buyer-lessee maintained that the transaction was in truth a secured loan. In bankruptcy, a debtor may split an unsecured loan into a secured and an unsecured claim (see section 506). The secured claim would be no more than the value of the collateral; in this case, perhaps as little as $1,000. The unsecured claim would make up the remainder, $2,490.

By reviewing sections 1322(b)(2), 1325(a)(4) and (5), and 1325(b)(1)(B) determine what the debtor was trying to do. If the debtor had only enough non-exempt assets to pay 10 cents on the dollar to unsecured creditors, the debtor could propose a plan that paid the present value of 10 cents on the dollar over the three-year plan, true? What is the protection for secured creditors under section 1325? What is the protection for an unsecured creditor?

Chapter Six

SECURITY IN STOCKS, BONDS AND OTHER INVESTMENT PROPERTY

§ 1. INTRODUCTION

It is commonplace to borrow against stocks and bonds. Customers borrow from their brokers; brokers borrow from their banks. It is important to have an inexpensive and certain mode of creating a valid security interest in stocks and bonds. Notwithstanding the importance of establishing a certain mode, changes in the substantive practices of issuing and holding stocks and other securities have resulted in many changes in the way the UCC addressed this issue in the past 25 years.

While rules regarding creation and perfection of security interests in most forms of property are solely the realm of Article 9, important rules and definitions with respect to stocks and bonds are also contained in Article 8: Investment Securities. Article 8 has been subject to two major recent revisions, in 1977 and 1994. Prior to the 1977 amendments, the classic security interest in stocks and bonds was created under Article 9 by the debtors giving the creditor possession of the certificates. This satisfied both the creation and perfection aspects of the security interest. The 1977 amendments, however, excluded "certificated securities" from the scope of Article 9 and placed attachment, perfection, and enforceability of such security interests within the scope of Article 8. Article 8 then defined the steps to create a valid security interest through a dizzying set of cross-references.

At this point, however, the student should understand why Article 8 was modified in 1977. In a sense, shares of stock have gone through one full cycle from being completely intangible, to having tangible form, and back to complete intangibility. Initially, a shareholder's interest in a corporation was evidenced only by his name on the books of the corporation as the owner of a specific number of shares. Later it became useful to have certificates that evidenced those shares and the certificates were passed back and forth among shareholders, creditors (as pledgees), and others. The certificate was treated as representing the ownership in the share in the same way as a certificate of title represents ownership in a car or a note represents ownership of a debt.

As transactions multiplied and much of the transmission of data was done electronically, people began to realize that the certificates sometimes inhibited effective transfer of rights and imposed significant costs on the system. Thus, for example, it is common for a brokerage house customer to permit the brokerage house to keep all of the certificates representing the shares of stock in the broker's name and for the customer to hold no certificates. This enables the customer to direct the broker over the phone to make trades without having to go to the safety deposit box, get out the certificates, and assign them to the broker in each case. If one is able to protect computer memory better than certificates, theft losses may be minimized by keeping only electronic or written records of stock ownership and doing away with certificates that must be safely kept. Accordingly, shares or stock have become "decertificated" and more intangible.

This development presents the question: How can one perfect a security interest in a share of stock that is not represented by a certificate or is represented by a certificate in the name of a trustee? If it is merely represented by the shareholder's name on the books of a corporation, presumably the right is something like a general intangible, not an instrument as a certificated security would be. If it were a general intangible, perfection would call for a filing, yet those in the securities industry historically are not accustomed to searching UCC files, and thus such a method might seem inappropriate or at least disfavored.

With these concerns in mind, the 1977 Article 8 amendments created a complex system in which perfection was effected through the concept of "transfer." The acts necessary to effect "transfer" were complicated, and the nature of these acts depended upon whether there was a certificate outstanding, whether the certificate was held by a financial intermediary or other person, etc. These changes, however, did not deal effectively with the development of commercial practices. For example, the 1977 amendments assumed that changes in ownership would continue to be reflected through transfer of physical certificates or the registration on the books of the issuers, yet that is not how changes in ownership are actually reflected in the modern securities holding system.

Because of these and other inadequacies, Article 8 was again amended in 1994. The 1994 amendments primarily introduced greater flexibility so to allow proper response and accommodation of changing securities industry practices. The amendments also included significant changes in the rules concerning security interests in securities. The revision returned to the pre–1977 structure in which the rules on security interests are set out in Article 9, rather than Article 8. Moreover, the changes were not merely structural, but also effected substantial simplification of the creation and perfection of security interests in securities and other investment property, whether held directly or indirectly.

These new rules were included in pre–1999 Article 9 in a single section, 9–115, addressed to investment property. With the 1999 revisions, these rules were relocated to the appropriate sections of Article 9; for example attachment is defined within 9–203 and priority within 9–328. These rules are discussed below.

§ 2. RULES UNDER ARTICLE 9

Attachment of a security interest is addressed in 9–203 and follows the same basic provisions of attachment for any other type of collateral, with one minor and expected addition. Attachment of a security interest in a "securities account" is also an attachment of a security interest in the "security entitlements" carried in the securities account.

Article 9 provides alternative means of perfection and continues recognition of the general historic practice of perfection through possession of certificates. Section 9–313 provides perfection by "delivery" of a certificated security. Where the debtor has a certificate registered to him, giving possession to the creditor is "delivery", 8–301.

Article 9 also provides that security interests in stocks and other investment property may be perfected by "control." The idea of control as a means of perfection first came to Article 9 via the 1994 revision to Article 8. With the 1999 revision, the concept of control has been expanded beyond investment property to other forms of intangible interests such as deposit accounts. Control is to intangibles as possession is to tangibles. Although many intangibles cannot be "possessed", some may be put under the "control" of a secured creditor to the exclusion of others, and this will put third parties on notice. What is control? Sections 9–104, 9–105, and 9–106 define it. For investment property, Section 9–106 directs one to Article 8, particularly 8–102, 8–106, 8–301, and 8–501.

Another significant change that accompanied the 1994 revision of Article 8 is that a security interest in stocks and other investment property may now be perfected through filing, 9–312(a). Under the priority rules set forth in 9–328 however, a security interest perfected by filing, is inferior to one perfected through delivery or control.

Some Definitional Clarification

We all recognize a bond or a share of stock, but "investment property" must be more than that, true? Section 9–102(a)(49) gives the following definition of investment property, which is only moderately helpful:

> (49) a security, whether certificated or uncertificated, security entitlement, securities account, commodity contract, or commodity account.

The idea of a "security entitlement" will itself be mysterious. As a rough but helpful explanation, most "securities" are stocks and bonds. Typically, "security entitlements" are rights that the customer has against his or her broker as represented by the statement the stockbroker provides the customer monthly or quarterly. See 8–102(a)(15), 8–102(a)(17) and 8–102(a)(9). Also, "investment property" is explicitly removed from Article 9's definitions of "general intangible" (section 9–102(a)(42)) and "instrument" (9–102(a)(47)).

Problem 6–1

A stock certificate covering 1 million shares of IBM common stock was issued to and is registered in the name of the Depository Trust Company and is located in DTC's vault in New York City. DTC's books show that it is holding 100,000 of these shares for Salomon Smith Barney and the remaining 900,000 shares for other banks and brokers who are DTC participants. Salomon's records show it is holding 20,000 shares for M Manufacturing and 80,000 shares for other customers.

On March 1, 2003 M borrowed $100,000 from Lender to acquire equipment. At that time, M signed a written security agreement describing the collateral as "20,000 shares of IBM stock in my account with Salomon Smith Barney."

1. On March 3, Lender sent a copy of the signed security agreement to Salomon. On June 1, Flattened acquired a judicial lien on the stock. Between Lender and Flattened, who has the superior claim?

2. On March 3, Lender filed a financing statement covering "all securities accounts and securities now owned or hereafter acquired by M Manufacturing". Flattened acquired a judicial lien on June 1. Between Lender and Flattened, who has the superior claim?

3. Assume the facts are the same as in 2 above, except that on June 20 M Manufacturing borrowed $5,000 from Salomon Smith Barney under the "margin loan" provisions of their account agreement, identical to the one reproduced below. What are the priorities of Salomon, Lender, and Flattened in the IBM shares?

4. Assume the facts are the same as in 3 above, except that on July 1, Lender presented to Salomon, and Salomon executed, a control agreement identical to the one reproduced below. As of August 1, what are the priorities among Salomon, Lender, and Flattened in the IBM shares?

Account Control Agreement Retail Customer

ABC Bank, having an address at _____ ("Creditor"); John Borrower, residing at _____ ("Debtor"); and Broker–Dealer, having an address at _____ hereby agree as follows:[1]

Preamble:

1. Broker has established a securities account number _____ in the name of _____ (the "Account").[2]

---

1. The arrangement reflected in this agreement is totally voluntary. A securities intermediary is prohibited from entering into a "control agreement" without the consent of the entitlement holder. Conversely, the securities intermediary is not required to enter into such an agreement even though the entitlement holder so directs. Section 8–106(g).

2. The establishment of the account might not be evidenced by a written agree-

2. Debtor has granted Creditor a security interest in the Account pursuant to agreement.[3]

3. Creditor, Debtor and Broker are entering into this Agreement to provide for the control of the Account and to perfect the security interest of Creditor in the Account.

Terms:

Section 1. The Account. Broker hereby represents and warrants to Creditor and Debtor that (a) the Account has been established in the name of Debtor as recited above[4], and (b) except for the claims and interest of Creditor and Debtor in the Account (subject to any claim in favor of Broker permitted under Section 2), Broker does not know of any claim to or interest in the Account. all parties agree that all property held by Broker in the Account will be treated as financial assets under Article 8 of the Uniform Commercial Code of the State of _____.

Section 2. Priority of Lien. Broker hereby acknowledges the security interest granted to Creditor by Debtor. Broker hereby confirms that the Account is a cash account and that it will not advance any margin or other credit to Debtor therein, either directly by executing purchase orders in excess of any credit balance or money market mutual funds held in the Account, executing sell orders on securities not held in the Account or by allowing him to trade in instruments such as options and commodities contracts that create similar obligations, nor hypothecate any securities carried in the Account.[5] Broker hereby [waives and releases/subordinates] all liens, encumbrances, claims and rights of setoff it may have against the Account or any financial asset carried in the Account or any free credit balance in the Account and agrees that, except for payment of its customary fees and commission pursuant to its agreement with Customer and except for payment for financial assets purchased for the Account, it will not assert any such lien, encumbrance, claim or right against the Account or any financial asset carried in the Account or any credit balance in the Account.[6] Broker will not agree with any third party that Broker will comply with entitlement orders concerning the Account originated by such third party without the prior written consent of Creditor and Debtor.[7]

ment. If it is, the law chosen to govern that agreement will be relevant. See text accompanying footnote 14 below.

3. The security agreement need not be written. See 9–203(1)(a). The broker is not required to be a party to the security agreement.

4. If less than all the assets held or to be held in the account are to be subject to the secured party's security interest, a schedule should be provided for. In addition, the secured party should keep in mind that any financial assets which are registered in the name of Debtor, payable to his order, or specially endorsed to him, which have not been endorsed to Broker or in blank, will not be considered part of the securities account (and seek representations or conduct appropriate diligence to determine whether this is an issue). See 8–501(d).

5. This is not a necessary element for the Creditor's security interest—it goes to the issue whether, as a business matter, the Creditor will allow there to be a lien in favor of the Broker. But see note 6.

6. Without this waiver, Broker will have priority over Creditor. See 9–115(5)(c).

7. This provision is essential in order to ensure the securities intermediary does not comply with a later request by the entitle-

Section 3. Control. Broker will comply with entitlement orders[8] originated by Creditor concerning the Account without further consent by Debtor. Except as otherwise provided in Section 2 above and 4 below, Broker shall also comply with entitlement orders concerning the Account originated by Debtor[9] or his authorized representatives, until such time as Creditor delivers a written notice to Broker that Creditor is thereby exercising exclusive control over the Account.[10] Such notice may be referred to herein as the "Notice of Exclusive Control".[11] After Broker receives the Notice of Exclusive Control and has had reasonable opportunity to comply, it will cease complying with entitlement orders [or other directions] concerning the Account originated by Debtor or its representatives.[12]

Section 4. No Withdrawals. Notwithstanding the provisions of Section 3 above, Broker shall neither accept nor comply with any entitlement order from Debtor [withdrawing/making a free delivery of] any financial assets from the Account nor deliver any such financial assets to Debtor nor pay any free credit balance or other amount owing from Broker to Debtor with respect to the Account without the specific prior written consent of Creditor.[13]

Section 5. Statements, Confirmations and Notices of Adverse Claims. Broker will send copies of all statements and confirmations concerning the Account to each Debtor and Creditor at the address set forth in the heading of the Agreement. Upon receipt of written notice of any lien, encumbrance or adverse claim against the Account or in any financial asset carried therein, Broker will make reasonable efforts to notify Creditor and Debtor thereof.

Section 6. Limited Responsibility of Broker. Except for permitting a withdrawal or payment in violation of Section 4 above or advancing margin or other credit to Debtor in violation of Section 2 above, Broker shall have

ment holder that it enter into a control agreement with another lender. In such an event, the secured parties would have equal priority. Section 9–115(5)(b).

8. "Entitlement order" is defined in Section 8–102(a)(8) to mean "a notification communicated to a securities intermediary directing transfer or redemption of a financial asset to which the entitlement holder has a security entitlement". This can be defined in the agreement, or the requirements for an effective communication can be spelled out.

9. The Creditor might wish to limit the nature of the trading or investment permitted by the Debtor, but this is likely to be perceived by the Broker as unduly burdensome from an operational or monitoring perspective. Accordingly, any such limitations are probably best left to the underlying security agreement.

10. Trading rights do not affect perfection or priority; see 8–106(d)(2) and com-

ments; 9–115(4) and (5); but may affect credit decisions as a practical matter.

11. The Debtor and Creditor should provide in the relevant security agreement for the circumstances under which the Creditor is entitled to send such a notice, which may be before or after default.

12. See, in this regard, Section 8–115, which affords a securities intermediary a reasonable opportunity to act on an injunction, restraining order or other legal process before incurring liability to adverse claimants.

13. The use of the term "withdrawal" appears to be understood in the market to refer to "free deliveries" or other instructions by a customer to deliver securities to a named recipient, as opposed to "trading" in an account, which is accomplished by the broker executing a trade with a third party. Prohibiting "withdrawals" by Debtor is a business issue. It is not necessary in order for the Creditor to achieve control as a legal matter.

no responsibility or liability to Creditor for making trades of financial assets held in the Account at the direction of Debtor, or his authorized representatives, or complying with entitlement orders concerning the Account from Debtor, or his authorized representatives, which are received by Broker before Broker receives a Notice of Exclusive Control and has had reasonable opportunity to act on it. Broker shall have no responsibility or liability to Debtor for complying with a Notice of Exclusive Control or complying with entitlement orders concerning the Account originated by Creditor. Broker shall have no responsibility or liability to Creditor with respect to the value of the Account or any asset held therein. Broker shall have no duty to investigate or make any determination as to whether a default exists under any agreement between Debtor and Creditor and shall comply with a Notice of Exclusive Control even if it believes that no such default exists. This Agreement does not create any obligation or duty of Broker other than those expressly set forth herein.

Section 7. Indemnification of Broker. Debtor and Creditor hereby agree to indemnify[14] and hold harmless Broker, its directors, officers, agents and employees against any and all claims, causes of action, liabilities, lawsuits, demands and damages, including without limitation, any and all court costs and reasonable attorney's fees, in any way related to or arising out of or in connection with this Agreement or any action taken or not taken pursuant hereto, except to the extent caused by Broker's breach of its obligations hereunder.[15]

Section 8. Customer Agreement. In the event of a conflict between this Agreement and any other agreement between Broker and Debtor, the terms of this Agreement will prevail. Regardless of any provision in any such agreement relating to the law governing the Account, the parties hereto agree the establishment and maintenance of the Account, and all interest, duties and obligations with respect thereto, shall be governed by the law of the State of _____.[16]

Section 9. Termination. The rights and powers granted herein to Creditor, have been granted in order to perfect its security interest in the Account, are powers coupled with an interest and will neither be affected by the death or bankruptcy of Debtor nor by the lapse of time. [Unless earlier terminated by Broker pursuant to this section,] the obligations of Broker under Sections 2, 3, 4 and 5 above shall continue in effect until Creditor has notified Broker in writing that this Agreement is to be terminated. Upon receipt of such notice the obligations of Broker under Sections 2, 3, 4 and 5 above with respect to the operation and maintenance of the Account after the receipt of such notice shall terminate, Creditor shall have no further right to originate entitlement orders concerning the Account and any previous Notice of Exclusive Control delivered by Creditor shall be deemed to be of no further force and effect. [Broker reserves the right, unilaterally, to

---

14. A creditor's willingness to indemnify the intermediary may be a subject for negotiation. Such indemnities, although apparently not uncommon, are by no means universal.

15. Consideration should be given to the appropriate standard for Broker's loss of

indemnification—ordinary negligence, gross negligence, etc.

16. This is necessary in order to establish the "securities intermediary's jurisdiction" under Section 8–110(b).

terminate this Agreement, such termination to be effective [X] business days' after written notice thereof is given to Debtor and Creditor.[17]]

Section 10. This Agreement. This Agreement, any schedules or exhibits hereto and the instruction and notices required or permitted to be executed and delivered hereunder set forth the entire agreement of the parties with respect to the subject matter hereof.

Section 11. Amendments. No amendment, modification or (except as otherwise specified in Section 9 above) termination of this Agreement, nor any assignment of any rights hereunder, shall be binding on any party hereto unless it is in writing and is signed by each of the parties hereto, and any attempt to so amend, modify, terminate or assign except pursuant to such a writing shall be null and void.[18] No waiver of any rights hereunder shall be binding on any party hereto unless such waiver is in writing and signed by the party against whom enforcement is sought.

* * *

Section 15. Counterparts. This Agreement may be executed in any number of counterparts, all of which shall constitute one and the same instrument, and any party hereto may execute this Agreement by signing and delivering one or more counterparts.

Section 16. Choice of Law. This Agreement shall be governed by and construed in accordance with the law of the State of _____.

> ABC Bank
> By: _____
>
> Debtor:
> By: _____
>
> Investment Securities Corp.
> By: _____

To see the terms a stockbroker might require for a loan, read the following Margin Agreement.

---

17. Some ability of the Broker to cease acting in connection with the Account must be accommodated. On the other hand, simply permitting the Broker to terminate the control arrangement while the Account is still in operation, would pose too great a practical risk to the Creditor, unless the Creditor is free (under its agreement with the Debtor) to move all the financial assets to its own account or the Broker's unilateral right to terminate the control agreement is conditioned upon the Creditor's completion of arrangements to move the financial assets to another securities intermediary with which it has entered into a satisfactory control arrangement. The terms and conditions of any Broker initiated termination will need to be negotiated.

18. Consideration should be given to the possibility of permitting assignment of the Creditor's rights in connection with an assignment of the secured obligations and how best to accommodate such an arrangement. One way would be to permit the Creditor's rights under this agreement to be assigned to any assignee of the underlying security interest. This would presumably require some sort of documented evidence of the assignment satisfactory to the Broker. The Debtor's consent would need to cover such an arrangement, so as not to run afoul of Article 8's prohibition on intermediaries entering into control agreements without their entitlement holders' consent. Section 8–106(g).

Sample Margin Account Agreement

In consideration of your accepting and carrying one or more accounts for the undersigned, the undersigned hereby consents and agrees that:

Applicable Rules and Regulations

1. All transactions shall be subject to the constitution, rules, regulations, customs and usages of the exchange or market and its clearinghouse, if any, on which such transactions are executed by you (Broker) or your agents, including your subsidiaries and affiliates.

Definition

2. For purposes of this agreement, "securities and other property" shall include, but not be limited to, money, securities, financial instruments and commodities of every kind and nature and all contracts and options relating thereto, whether for present or future delivery.

Collateral Requirements and Credit Charges for the Margin Account Service

3. The undersigned will maintain such securities and other property in the accounts of the undersigned for collateral purposes as you shall require from time to time; and the monthly debit balance of such accounts shall be charged, in accordance with your usual custom, with interest at a rate permitted by the laws of the State of New York. It is understood that the interest charge made to the undersigned's account at the close of a charge period will, unless paid, be added to the opening balance for the next charge period and that interest will be charged upon such opening balance, including all interest so added.

Security Interest

4. All securities and other property now or hereafter held, carried or maintained by you or by any of your affiliates in your possession or control, or in the possession or control of any such affiliate, for any purpose, in or for any account of the undersigned now or hereafter opened, including any account in which the undersigned may have an interest, shall be subject to a lien for the discharge of all indebtedness and other obligations of the undersigned to you, and are to be held by you as security for the payment of any liability or indebtedness of the undersigned to you in any of said accounts. You shall have the right to transfer securities and other property so held by you from or to any other of the accounts of the undersigned whenever in your judgment you consider such a transfer necessary for your protection. In enforcing your lien, you shall have the discretion to determine which securities and property are to be sold and which contracts are to be closed.

Representations as to Beneficial Ownership and Control

5. The undersigned represents that, with respect to securities against which credit is or may be extended to you: (a) the undersigned is not the beneficial owner of more than three percent (3%) of the number of outstanding shares of any class of equity securities, and (b) does not control, is not controlled by, and is not under common control with, the issuer of any such securities. In the event that any of the foregoing representations are inaccu-

rate or become inaccurate, the undersigned will promptly so advise you in writing.

Calls for Additional Collateral—Liquidation Rights

6. (a) You shall have the right to require additional collateral:

> (1) in accordance with your general policies for the margin service maintenance requirements, as such may be modified, amended or supplemented from time to time; or

> (2) if in your discretion you consider it necessary for your protection at an earlier or later point in time than called for by said general policies; or

> (3) in the event that a petition in bankruptcy or for appointment of a receiver is filed by or against the undersigned; or

> (4) if an attachment is levied against the accounts of the undersigned; or

> (5) in the event of the death of the undersigned.

(b) If the undersigned does not provide you with additional collateral as you may require in accordance with (a)(1) or (2), or should an event described in (a)(3), (4) or (5) occur (whether or not you elect to require additional collateral), you shall have the right:

> (1) to sell any and all securities and other property in the accounts of the undersigned with you or with any of your affiliates, whether carried individually or jointly with others;

> (2) to buy any or all securities and other property which may be short in such accounts; and

> (3) to cancel any open orders and to close and or all outstanding contracts.

You may exercise any or all of your rights under (b)(1), (2), or (3) without further demand for additional collateral, or notice of sale or purchase, or other notice or advertisement. Any such sales or purchases may be made at your discretion on any exchange or other market where such business is usually transacted, or at public auction or private sale; and you may be the purchaser for your own account. It is understood that your giving of any prior demand or call or prior notice of the time and place of such sale or purchase shall not be considered a waiver of your right to sell or but without any such demand, call or notice as herein provided.

Payment of Indebtedness Upon Demand

7. The undersigned shall at all times be liable for the payment upon demand of any debit balance or other obligations owing in any of the accounts of the undersigned with you, and the undersigned shall be liable to you for any deficiency remaining in any such accounts in the event of the liquidation thereof, in whole or in part, by you or by the undersigned; and the undersigned shall make payment of such obligations and indebtedness upon demand.

* * *

Pledge of Securities and Other Property

9. All securities and other property now or hereafter held, carried or maintained by you in your possession or control in any of the accounts of the undersigned may be pledged and repledged by you from time to time, without notice to the undersigned, either separately or in common with other such securities and other property, for any amount due in the accounts of the undersigned, or for any greater amount, and you may do so without retaining in your possession or under your control for delivery a like amount of similar securities or other property.

Lending Agreement

10. In return for the extension or maintenance of any credit by you, the undersigned acknowledges and agrees that the securities in the under-signed's account, together with all attendant rights of ownership, may be lent to you or lent out to others to the extent not prohibited by applicable laws, rules and regulations. In connection with such securities loans, and in connection with securities loans made to me to facilitate short sales, you may receive and retain certain benefits to which the undersigned will not be entitled. The undersigned understands that, in certain circumstances, such loans could limit the undersigned's ability to exercise voting rights, in whole or part, with respect to the securities lent.

Presumption of Receipt of Communications

11. Communications may be sent to the undersigned at the address of the undersigned or at such address as the undersigned may hereafter give you in writing. All communications so sent, whether by mail, telegraph, messenger or otherwise, shall be deemed given to the undersigned personally, whether actually received or not.

* * *

Agreement to Arbitrate Controversies

13. Arbitration is final and binding on the parties.

- The parties are waiving their right to seek remedies in court, including the right to a jury trial.

- Prearbitration discovery is generally more limited than and different from court proceedings.

- The arbitrators' award is not required to include factual findings or legal reasoning and any party's right to appeal or seek modification of rulings by the arbitrators is strictly limited.

- The panel of arbitrators will typically include a minority of arbitrators who were or are affiliated with the securities industry.

The undersigned agrees that all controversies which may arise between us, including, but not limited to, those involving any transaction or the construction, performance or breach of this or any other agreement between us, whether entered into prior, on or subsequent to the date hereof, shall be determined by arbitration. Any arbitration under this agreement shall be conducted only before the New York Stock Exchange, Inc., the American Stock Exchange, Inc. or arbitration facility provided by any other exchange of which you are a member, the National Association of Securities Dealers, Inc. or the Municipal Securities Rulemaking Board, and in accordance with its arbitration rules then in force. The undersigned may elect in the first instance whether arbitration shall be conducted before the New York Stock Exchange, Inc., the American Stock Exchange, Inc. or arbitration facility provided by any other exchange of which you are a member, the National Association of Securities Dealers, Inc. or the Municipal Securities Rulemaking Board, but if the undersigned fails to make such election, by registered letter or telegram addressed to you at the office where the undersigned maintains the account, before the expiration of five days receipt of a written request from you to make such an election, then you may make such election. Judgment upon the award of arbitrators may be entered in any court, state or federal, having jurisdiction.

No person shall bring a putative or certified class action to arbitration, nor seek to enforce any predispute arbitration agreement against any person who has initiated in court a putative class action, or who is a member or a putative class who has not opted out of the class with respect to any claims encompassed by the putative class action until: (I) the class certification is denied; (ii) the class is decertified; or (iii) the customer is excluded from the class by the court. Such forbearance to enforce an agreement to arbitrate shall not constitute a waiver of any rights under this agreement except to the extent stated herein.

Joint and Several Liability

14. If the undersigned shall consist of more than one person, their obligations under this agreement shall be joint and several.

* * *

Extraordinary Events

16. You shall not be liable for loss caused directly or indirectly by government restrictions, exchange or market rulings, suspension of trading, war, strikes or other conditions beyond your control.

The Laws of the State of New York Govern

17. This agreement and its enforcement shall be governed by the laws of the State of New York; and shall cover individually and collectively all accounts which the undersigned may open or reopen with you; shall inure to the benefit of your successors, whether by merger, consolidation or otherwise, and assigns, and you may transfer the accounts of the undersigned to your successors and assigns; and this agreement shall be binding upon the heirs, executors, administrators, successors and assigns of the undersigned.

Amendments

18. The undersigned agrees that you shall have the right to amend this Agreement, by modifying or rescinding any of its provisions or by adding any new provision. Any such amendment shall be effective as of a date to be established by you, which shall not be earlier than 30 days after you send notification of any such amendment to the undersigned.

* * *

BY SIGNING THIS AGREEMENT, THE UNDERSIGNED ACKNOWL-
EDGES: (1) THAT, IN ACCORDANCE WITH PARAGRAPH 13, THE
UNDERSIGNED IS AGREEING IN ADVANCE TO ARBITRATE ANY
CONTROVERSIES THAT MAY ARISE WITH YOU; (2) THAT, PURSU-
ANT TO PARAGRAPH 10 ABOVE, CERTAIN OF THE UNDERSIGNED'S
SECURITIES MAY BE LOANED TO YOU OR LOANED OUT TO OTH-
ERS; AND (3) RECEIPT OF A COPY OF THIS AGREEMENT.

Signature _____ Date _____

Title _____

Signature _____ Date _____

(Second party if joint account; Co–Trustee)

Title _____

(or special accounts, example: Co–Trustee)

Account No.: _____

§ 3. WHAT IS INVESTMENT PROPERTY?

Whether a specific intangible interest is "investment property" can
be critical to the priority of various claims (for example, no investment
property, no perfection by control). Although the 1994 and 1999 amendments to Article 8 and Article 9 resolve most of these issues, some
uncertainty remains. The following two cases decided under the previous
law show some of the problems. Consider how these two cases would be
resolved under the present law. In any event, what might one do to
insure that a particular interest is treated as investment property?

IN RE WITHERELL CORPORATION
United States Bankruptcy Court, E.D. Michigan, 1992.
144 B.R. 64.

RHODES, BANKRUPTCY JUDGE:

This matter is before the Court on the plaintiff's motion for summary judgment. A response and a reply brief were filed, and a hearing
was held on July 23, 1992.

I.

Witherell Corporation owns 43 shares of Kean Investment Company,
a limited partnership. William E. Turnbull, Sr. is the general partner of
Kean Investment. On March 29, 1990, Mr. Turnbull made two loans to
Witherell. The first loan was for $50,000, was due April 1, 1991, and was
secured by a pledge of 21.5 shares of Witherell's interest in Kean
Investment. The second loan was also for $50,000, was due April 1, 1992,
and was secured by a pledge of Witherell's remaining 21.5 shares of
Kean Investment.

On October 11, 1991, Witherell filed bankruptcy. At that time, it
had not made any payments to Mr. Turnbull. On January 2, 1992,

Witherell filed an adversary proceeding seeking a declaratory judgment that Mr. Turnbull's security interest in Witherell's limited partnership interest is unperfected, and therefore avoidable under 11 U.S.C. § 544(a). This motion for summary judgment was filed on May 5, 1992. The issue before the Court is whether Mr. Turnbull's security interest was properly perfected.

Witherell asserts that Mr. Turnbull has not perfected his security interest in the limited partnership shares. It argues that the perfection of this security interest is governed by Article 9 of the Uniform Commercial Code, and that under this article, perfection can only be accomplished by the filing of a financing statement. Mr. Turnbull admits that he did not file such a statement. Therefore, Witherell asserts, his interest is unperfected.

Mr. Turnbull asserts that the perfection of his security interest is governed by Article 8 of the Uniform Commercial Code. He states that his interest is perfected under this provision, and that this motion for summary judgment should be denied.

II.

Article 8 of the Uniform Commercial Code, set forth in M.C.L.A. § 440.8101 et seq., applies to investment securities. In order for Mr. Turnbull to prevail on his assertion that the perfection of his interest is governed by this Article, Witherell's limited partnership interest must meet the definitional requirements of an investment security. Section 440.8102(1)(c) defines a security as either a certificated or an uncertificated security. Witherell's interest is not represented by an instrument, so the issue becomes whether its interest constitutes an uncertificated security.

An uncertificated security is defined by M.C.L.A. § 440.8102(1)(b) as:

[A] share, participation, or other interest in property or an enterprise of the issuer or an obligation of the issuer which is:

(i) not represented by an instrument and the transfer of which is registered upon books maintained for that purpose by or on behalf of the issuer;

(ii) of a type commonly dealt in on securities exchanges or markets; and

(iii) either one of a class or series or by its terms divisible into a class or series of shares, participations, interests, or obligations.

The plain language of this statute indicates that the issuer is required to maintain records, and register any transfers of the securities. If these records are not maintained, the statutory requirements are not satisfied, and the property interest is not an uncertificated security.

In that event, the transaction between the parties is not governed by Article 8. Instead, Article 9 (M.C.L.A. § 440.9101 et seq.) would determine whether Mr. Turnbull's security interest is perfected. Pursuant to M.C.L.A. § 440.9106, Witherell's interest in Kean Investment would be a general intangible. In re Hartman, 102 B.R. 90, 94 (Bankr.N.D.Tex. 1989). Section 440.9302 requires the filing of a financing statement to perfect an interest in this type of property. It is undisputed that Mr. Turnbull did not file a financing statement. Therefore, his interest in Witherell's shares of Kean Investment would be unperfected.

The Court concludes that the best interests of justice require the Court to give the parties a further opportunity to submit evidence on the issue of whether Kean Investment maintains the type of records contemplated by M.C.L.A. § 440.8102(1)(b), and whether the claimed security interest was registered in those records. Such evidence shall be submitted within 21 days of this date. If it appears that such records are not maintained or that this security interest was not registered as required, the Court will grant the plaintiff's motion for summary judgment.

IT IS SO ORDERED.

IN RE TURLEY

United States Court of Appeals, Ninth Circuit, 1999.
172 F.3d 671.

RYMER, CIRCUIT JUDGE:

Thomas C. Thompson Sports ("Thompson Sports") appeals from a district court order that affirmed summary judgment in favor of Farmers and Merchants Bank of Long Beach ("Bank"). Both the district court and the bankruptcy court held that the Bank has a prior perfected security interest in certain interpleaded funds. We reverse and remand to the bankruptcy court for the entry of judgment in favor of Thompson Sports.

I

The resolution of this priority dispute turns on the characterization of certain proceeds. Both the Bank and Thompson Sports lay claim to funds interpleaded by Championship Auto Racing Teams ("CART") after the termination of its association with the debtor, Norman Turley. Thompson Sports holds a perfected security interest in the debtor's general intangibles and argues that it has priority to the interpleaded funds because they represent proceeds from a general intangible—a franchise agreement between the debtor and CART. The Bank, on the other hand, asserts that it is entitled to the funds because the proceeds stem not from a franchise agreement, but from the redemption of the debtor's CART share certificate, which the debtor pledged to the bank.

CART organizes "Indy Car" auto racing events. The debtor raced Indy cars as a member of CART. To race in CART events, one must be a "franchise member." These memberships are subject to strict requirements. Applicants for the one-season franchise memberships must commit to participate in all "Indy Car World Series" events and make a detailed disclosure of the racing team's ownership, the history of the applicant's principals, and the racing team's financial and operational structure. CART's Board of Directors reviews applicants for suitability to participate competitively in the Indy Car World Series. Franchise memberships are not transferable, each race team is restricted to two memberships, and the membership may only be renewed if the member exhibits "bona fide participation in all racing events" and is "otherwise eligible."

In addition to the restrictive franchise membership provisions, CART's by-laws also contain stringent limitations on stock ownership. Once accepted as a franchise member, applicants must purchase one share of CART stock. If a franchise membership terminates, the member must return the stock certificate in exchange for the share value as determined by the Board, as well as a Board determined franchise value. Shareholders cannot "sell, transfer, encumber or otherwise dispose of any share" without first delivering a "written offer to sell to the corporation." According to the by-laws, that offer must include "the resignation of such shareholder's Franchise Membership in the corporation." And the prospective purchaser "must be another shareholder of the corporation." Confronted with the proposed sale, CART may either redeem the share or allow the transaction to proceed.

Soon after Turley arranged for financing arrangements from both the Bank and Thompson Sports, Turley filed for Chapter 11 bankruptcy protection. After the petition, CART's Board voted to redeem Turley's share of stock for $220,000. Additionally, Turley was entitled to a $29,394 end-of-the-year payment from CART based on his participation in CART-sanctioned races in 1993. Given the competing claims to the funds, CART filed a complaint in interpleader. On cross-motions for summary judgment, the bankruptcy court entered summary judgment in favor of the Bank.

The district court affirmed. See Thomas C. Thompson Sports, Inc. v. Farmers and Merchants Bank, 213 B.R. 857 (C.D.Cal.1997). The court held that Turley's share certificate in CART is a "certificated security" under Article 8 of the UCC. See id. at 861. By gaining possession of the share certificate, the bank perfected its security interest in the share and its proceeds. See id. at 861–62. According to the district court, the interpleaded funds were proceeds attributable to Turley's share in CART, and the Bank is therefore entitled to the funds. See id. at 860–62.

II

* * *

III

The pivotal issue in this appeal is whether Turley's share certificate is a "certificated security" under Article 8 of the UCC. If it is, the Bank, which has possession of the certificate, holds a perfected security interest in all funds attributable to the share. See Cal. Com.Code § 8321(1)

(1993). If it is not, the Bank cannot assert a perfected security interest pursuant to Article 8; this dispute would be governed by Article 9.

A

Under Michigan law, a "certificated security" is "a share, participation, or other interest in property of or an enterprise of the issuer or an obligation of the issuer" that is:

(i) represented by an instrument issued in bearer or registered form;

(ii) of a type commonly dealt in on securities exchanges or markets or commonly recognized in any area in which it is issued or dealt in as a medium for investment; and

(iii) either one of a class or series or by its terms divisible into a class or series of shares, participations, interests, or obligations.

Mich. Comp. Laws Ann. § 440.8102(a) (1993). As the UCC comments explain, the language of subsection (ii) "is intended to cover such interests as the stock of closely-held corporations which, although not in fact dealt in on exchanges or markets, is 'of a type' that is." Id. § 440.8102 note (1998) (Official Reasons for 1977 Change).

Whether Turley's CART share is a certificated security therefore turns on whether it is "of a type" that is generally traded in markets and exchanges. The Bank argues that a CART share is nothing more than a share in a close corporation and that the CART transfer restrictions, being typical for such corporations, do not remove the share from Article 8 purview. But see Motobecane Am., Ltd. v. Patrick Petroleum Co., 600 F.Supp. 1419 (E.D.Mich.1985) (holding under Michigan law that a certificate representing an interest in a limited partnership was not an Article 8 security because of transfer restrictions), aff'd on other grounds, 791 F.2d 1248 (6th Cir.1986). Thus, according to the Bank, there is nothing special about a CART share and Article 8 applies.

We disagree. As a franchise member, Turley was required to purchase one share of CART stock. Upon termination of his franchise membership, CART's by-laws compelled him to return the share certificate. In order to renew his one-season franchise membership, and thus retain his CART share, the by-laws required Turley to participate in the season's racing events and remain "otherwise eligible." With these requirements, the CART share is definitively not "of a type commonly dealt in on securities exchanges or markets or commonly recognized * * * as a medium for investment." Cf. Morton v. Santa Anna Nat'l Bank (In re Bonnema), 219 B.R. 951, 955 (Bankr.N.D.Tex.1998) (noting that the "of a type" test is meant to ensure "that the Article 8 rules do not apply to interests or obligations in circumstances so unconnected with the securities markets that parties are unlikely to have thought of the possibility that Article 8 might apply").

Our conclusion is bolstered by Giuffre Organization, Ltd. v. Euromotorsport Racing, Inc., 141 F.3d 1216 (7th Cir.1998), where the Seventh

Circuit, examining facts nearly identical to those here, held that a CART share is not a certificated security under the pre–1994 amendments version of the UCC. As the court explained, a CART share is no ordinary stock certificate:

> CART is not your everyday close corporation—nor are its shares simple investment vehicles. Once shares of ordinary corporate stock have been paid for, the investors have no rights other than to vote for directors (and to receive dividends if any should be declared) * * *. CART certificates are different. They entail not only a right but also an obligation to participate in races. Id. at 1218. Security instruments that are "commonly dealt in" do not carry with them such affirmative obligations.

B

Given that Turley's share in CART is not a certificated security, we turn to the question of what was Turley's interest in CART, and does the certificate matter.

Since it is not an Article 8 certificated security, Turley's interest is "caught by the 'general intangible' net in Article 9." 4 James J. White & Robert S. Summers, Uniform Commercial Code § 31–12, at 161 (4th ed.1995); see also Bonnema, 219 B.R. at 955 (holding that the certificated capital retains "must fall into the catch-all category of 'general intangibles'"); Cal. Com.Code § 9106 (1993). As a security interest in a general intangible may only be perfected by filing, Cal. Com.Code § 9302 (1993), possession of the share certificate is without consequence. The Bank can have nothing more than an unperfected security interest in Turley's CART share. See Giuffre, 141 F.3d at 1219 (stating that only an Article 9 financing statement could perfect a security interest in a CART share).

The interpleaded funds were proceeds attributable to Turley's interest in CART. That interest is a general intangible and Thompson Sports' perfected security interest in Turley's general intangibles trumps any interest the Bank may have in the proceeds. Judgment must be entered for Thompson Sports. Thompson Sports shall be entitled to post-judgment interest from the date of the entry of judgment in accordance with this opinion.

REVERSED AND REMANDED.

Problem 6–2

Having learned its lesson in the foregoing case, Bank files a financing statement covering general intangibles including Debtor's "CART rights". Later Bank Two takes a security interest in a variety of the Debtor's intangibles including its CART rights. Bank Two requires Debtor to put its CART rights into a securities account opened for that purpose at Bank Two's brokerage subsidiary. The brokerage subsidiary then executes a "control" agreement with Bank Two. When trouble comes, Bank Two claims priority under section 9–328. Among other things, Bank Two claims that Bank's financing statement is now entirely ineffective because the collateral is no longer "general intangibles"; it has become "investment property". Consider 9–507(b).

Who wins?

What if Bank could prove that Bank Two knew of Bank's security interest before it took its security interest?

§ 4. GOVERNMENT SECURITIES

Since U.S. government securities are considered "securities" under Article 8, they are governed by the UCC in the same manner as any other publicly held debt security, except insofar as the UCC is preempted by applicable federal law.

Treasury securities are no longer issued in certificated form; they can be held only through the book-entry systems established by the Treasury and the Federal Reserve Banks. The treasury offers a book-entry system, known as "Treasury Direct" that enables individual investors to have their positions recorded directly on the books of a Federal Reserve Bank (in a manner somewhat similar to the uncertificated system contemplated by the 1977 version of Article 8). The Treasury Direct system is governed by treasury regulations and is not designed for active trading.

The majority of Treasury securities are held not through the Treasury Direct system but through a multi-level indirect holding system. The Federal Reserve Banks maintain records of the holdings of member banks of the Federal Reserve System, and those banks in turn maintain records showing what they are holding for their customers, including government securities dealers, institutional investors, or smaller banks that may in turn act as custodians for individual investors. Under the Treasury regulations, parties who may be securities intermediaries range from Federal Reserve Banks to brokers that maintain security accounts for others in the ordinary course of business. See 31 C.F.R. 357.2. Within this multi-tiered system, the upper tiers are composed of a Federal Reserve Bank, acting as an agent of the Treasury, and "Participants," which are other persons, typically banks, that have direct account relationships with a Federal Reserve Bank. A typical chain of ownership might be as follows:

Treasury

|

Federal Reserve Bank

|

Participant

|

Broker–Dealer

|

Individual Holder/Investor

Regulations of the Treasury, see 61 Fed. Reg. 43,626 (1996), have substantially adopted Article 8 as the rules on perfection and priority of security interests in treasury securities. In cases where states have not adopted revised Article 8, federal law preempts the preexisting state law and applies revised Article 8. (Because provisions on perfection via filing and automatic perfection of interests granted to a securities intermediary—provisions that would otherwise exist under Revised Articles 8 and 9—do not apply, this preemption is not complete.)

31 C.F.R. 357.12

(a) A Participant's Security Entitlement is created when a Federal Reserve Bank indicates by book entry that a Book-entry Security has been credited to a Participant's Securities Account.

31 C.F.R. 357.11

(a) [T]he law * * * of a Securities Intermediary's jurisdiction governs:
* * *

    (5) Except as otherwise provided in paragraph (c) of this section, the perfection, effect of perfection or non-perfection and priority of a security interest in a Security Entitlement.

* * *

(c) [T]he law of the jurisdiction in which the Person creating a security interest is located governs whether and how the security interest may be perfected automatically or by filing a financing statement.

(d) If the jurisdiction specified [as the Securities Intermediary's jurisdiction] is a State that has not adopted Revised Article 8 * * * , then the law for matters specified in paragraph (a) of this section shall be the law of that State as though Revised Article 8 had been adopted by that State.

Problem 6–3

    Borrower requests a loan of $100,000 to purchase an experimental airplane. He states he has $100,000 in U.S. government treasury securities that he can offer as collateral on the loan and will sign a security agreement to that effect. The treasury securities are held for Borrower by his broker.

    What steps do you as the bank need to do to perfect this security interest?

Problem 6–4

    1. Bank of America acts as the depositary for $1 million worth of treasury securities that belong to its depositor janis & Co. The bank wishes to lend $1 million to janis & Co. What must it do to perfect its security interest?

    2. If the treasury securities are held at Bank of America but janis & Co. wishes to borrow from Wells Fargo, Wells Fargo can perfect by filing in the name of janis & Co., true?

    3. Assume that the transaction in 2 will take the form of a "repo" transaction. If you were counsel for Wells Fargo, how would you suggest that

they structure the repo transaction? (You might consider the fact that if janis & Co. fails to make the repurchase, Wells Fargo would like to be able to dispose of the securities on the open market on the day of janis & Co.'s default.)

§ 5. REPOS: SALES OR SECURED TRANSACTIONS?

As the case that follows shows, courts have had considerable difficulty in classifying certain transactions commonly known as "repurchase agreements". Under these transactions a seller (debtor) commonly sells a security to a buyer (secured creditor) and promises to repurchase the security within a specified period of time. If the seller does not make the repurchase, the buyer typically has the right to sell the security on the market to satisfy the liability. Normally, the repurchase price will be slightly higher than the sales price; that difference may be regarded as the lender's interest charge for the loan that is made. As the case shows, some people argue, and some courts hold, that these are outright sales of a security and that rules on personal property security in Article 9 and elsewhere have nothing to say about them. Other courts have held that these are secured loans under which the seller is transferring a security interest to the buyer for a short term loan which will be liquidated by the seller's "repurchase".

How are these transactions to be treated if they are secured transactions and not outright sales? Unless the proper documents are signed and the proper actions are taken, a trustee in bankruptcy or debtor in possession in the bankruptcy of the seller may assert rights against the buyer and the buyer may be regarded as an unperfected secured creditor. That is a particularly troublesome possibility in the modern market where government securities are not certificated and therefore are not subject to perfection by possession. Also, the "buyer" (creditor) will not want to be constrained by Part 6 of Article 9 if the "seller" (debtor) defaults and buyer needs to unload the securities in a falling market.

GRANITE PARTNERS, L.P. v. BEAR, STEARNS & CO. INC.

United States District Court, S.D. New York, 1998.
17 F.Supp.2d 275.

Sweet, District Judge:

Defendants Donaldson, Lufkin & Jenrette Securities Corporation ("DLJ"), Bear, Stearns & Co. Inc., Bear, Stearns Capital Markets Inc. (collectively, "Bear Stearns"), Howard Rubin ("Rubin"), and Merrill Lynch, Pierce, Fenner & Smith Inc. ("Merrill Lynch") (together with DLJ, Bear Stearns, and Rubin, the "Brokers") have moved for partial dismissal of the First Amended Complaint ("Complaint") pursuant to Rules 12(b)(6) and 9(b) of the Federal Rules of Civil Procedure for failure to state a claim upon which relief can be granted and for failure to plead fraud with particularity. * * *

PARTIES

Plaintiff Granite Partners, L.P. ("Granite Partners"), a Delaware limited partnership, was established in January 1990 as an investment fund to invest primarily in mortgage-related securities on behalf of individuals and entities subject to United States taxation.

Plaintiff Granite Corporation ("Granite Corp."), a Cayman Islands corporation, was organized in January 1990 to invest primarily in mortgage-backed securities on behalf of offshore investors and domestic tax-exempt entities, including foundations and pension funds.

Plaintiff Quartz Hedge Fund ("Quartz") (collectively with Granite Partners and Granite Corp., the "Funds"), a Cayman Islands corporation, was established in January 1994 as a vehicle to invest primarily in mortgage-related securities on behalf of offshore investors and others exempt from United States taxation.

The Funds bring this action by and through the Litigation Advisory Board (the "LAB"), which was given the exclusive authority on behalf of and in the name of the Funds' estates to commence, prosecute, settle, or otherwise resolve all unresolved claims and causes of action of the Funds' estates by order of the United States Bankruptcy Court for the Southern District of New York.

DLJ, Bear Stearns, and Merrill Lynch, all Delaware corporations with their principal places of business in New York City, are broker-Dealers that transacted business with the Funds.

Rubin, a resident of New Jersey, was at all relevant times a senior managing director and the head CMO trader at Bear Stearns.

RELEVANT NONPARTIES

At all relevant times to this action, nonparty Askin Capital Management, L.P. ("ACM"), a Delaware limited partnership, was a registered investment advisor, whose exclusive place of business was New York City. ACM was, at all relevant times, controlled by nonparty David J. Askin ("Askin"), who owned and controlled ACM's sole general partner, Dashtar Corporation. Askin also served as ACM's sole limited partner, president, chief executive officer, and chief financial officer. ACM became the investment advisor to Quartz since its formation.

Prior Proceedings

On April 7, 1994, the Funds filed petitions for relief under chapter 11 of the United States Bankruptcy Code. The chapter 11 trustee for the Funds (the "Trustee") initially filed this action in the United States Bankruptcy Court for the Southern District of New York on September 12, 1996. The case was referred to this Court on October 18, 1996. On consent, this Court withdrew the reference from the Bankruptcy Court on December 3, 1966.

On January 27, 1997, the Trustee submitted a Third Amended Joint Plan of Liquidation for the Funds (the "Plan"). Following the Bankruptcy Court's confirmation of the chapter 11 Plan on March 2, 1997, this action has been pursued by the LAB, appointed pursuant to the Liquidation Plan.

The LAB filed the Complaint in this action on August 4, 1997, naming, in addition to Bear Stearns, Rubin, DLJ, and Merrill Lynch as defendants.

In the Complaint, the LAB asserts the following claims: breach of contract, inducing and participating in breach of fiduciary duty, tortious interference with contracts, rescission of unauthorized trades, breach of duty, conversion, federal and state antitrust violations, prima facie tort, common law fraud, negligent and innocent misrepresentation, breach of express warranty, unjust enrichment, objection to claims and interest, and equitable subordination.

* * *

Facts

... [t]he factual allegations considered here and set forth below are taken primarily from the LAB's Complaint and do not constitute findings of fact by the Court. They are presumed to be true only for the purpose of deciding the present motion.

This case arises out of the collapse in early 1994 of the Funds that were managed by Askin and ACM. The major claims brought in this lawsuit fall into two categories: (1) that the Brokers injured the Funds by selling to them inappropriate securities purchased by Askin and ACM, and (2) that the Brokers injured the Funds by making improper margin calls and liquidating the Funds' reverse repurchase positions when the margin calls were not satisfied.

The Funds invested primarily in collateralized mortgage obligations ("CMOs") created by the Brokers and other broker-Dealers. ACM, through its president, Askin, purchased the securities for the Funds. The Brokers are alleged to be "among the principal sellers of CMOs to the Funds." (Compl. § 4.)

CMOs are bonds created from and collateralized by mortgage-backed securities formed from pools of residential mortgages or securities backed by such mortgages. They are divided into various classes, or "tranches," each of which is entitled to a different portion of the principal and/or interest payments made by the underlying mortgage obligors. The tranches differ from one another with respect to their sensitivity to interest rate changes and the certainty with which their reaction to such changes can be predicted. The Brokers referred to the riskiest tranches—those most prone to large and unpredictable swings in value—as "toxic" or "nuclear waste."

The two larger Funds, Granite Partners and Granite Corp., were designed to invest in "market-neutral" portfolios of high-quality CMOs. They were intended to acquire balanced holdings of "bullish" bonds and "bearish" bonds. A bullish security is likely to increase in value when interest rates fall and decrease in value when interest rates rise. A bearish security is likely to decrease in value when interest rates fall and increase in value when interest rates rise. By purchasing offsetting positions in predictable securities, the Funds would enjoy the high returns associated with rate-sensitive CMOs while hedging against the risk attendant upon interest rate fluctuations. Quartz was intended to be "market-directional"—to maintain a bullish or bearish portfolio depending on the predicted direction of interest rates.

Askin and ACM, the Funds' investment advisor, had fiduciary and contractual duties to the Funds to make investments with due care and in accordance with the Funds' stated investment objectives. ACM was to accomplish these respective goals by rigorously and continuously analyzing each proposed acquisition for each Fund with a sophisticated, proprietary computer model that would allow ACM and Askin to determine the impact of interest rate changes on the price and value of each bond.

Askin and ACM, however, managed the Funds negligently and repeatedly breached their contractual and fiduciary duties. They did not perform a rigorous analysis of the securities they bought, and they were unable to gauge how those securities would respond to interest rate movements. Moreover, they did not use, or even have, sophisticated computerized analytical techniques. In fact, "ACM and Askin often made purchase decisions based on little or no analysis or research. They instead relied on Broker recommendations, representations, valuations, and reports, Askin's 'instincts,' and unsophisticated analysis to select the Funds' securities." As a result, ACM and Askin failed to create market-neutral portfolios for Granite Partners and Granite Corp., instead creating portfolios that were dramatically bullish, and that contained a number of highly volatile, unpredictable, toxic CMOs. Similarly, at the time when Askin believed that interest rates would rise, he constructed an inappropriate bullish portfolio for Quartz.

The Complaint alleges that throughout 1993 and early 1994, the Brokers took advantage of Askin's shortcomings. Although they knew of Askin's obligation to create market-neutral portfolios for Granite Partners and Granite Corp., knew of Askin's inability to analyze the impact of interest rate changes on esoteric CMO tranches, and knew of the Funds' dangerous bullish tilt, the brokers induced Askin to buy inappropriate, toxic, bullish CMOs that eroded in value when short-term interest rates rose in early 1994. For example, from January 1993 to February 1994, the Brokers sold the Funds $34 million in bearish CMOs but $740 million in inappropriate securities. The Complaint maintains that the Brokers misrepresented many of these strongly bullish and toxic securities as bearish or only slightly bullish.

The Brokers sold these toxic and inappropriate securities to the Funds because it was profitable for them to do so. The sale of the toxic tranches of a CMO offering makes the entire offering economically feasible. The Brokers are committed to buying any unsold tranches for their own accounts, and they do not wish to own nuclear waste themselves. Accordingly, they are unwilling to market a new offering unless they are assured they will be able to sell the toxic securities. For this reason, the toxic tranches are referred to as the "deal drivers."

To generate demand for the more volatile tranches of their CMO offerings, the Brokers cultivated relationships with a small number of managers of investment funds, including ACM. They steered investors to ACM to enable ACM to purchase the more volatile, esoteric CMOs from the Brokers and granted AMC extensive credit (at times in violation of their own internal credit guidelines) to increase the amount of such CMOs that ACM could purchase. ACM, acting on the Funds' behalf, became one of the largest volume purchasers of these volatile and esoteric tranches from the Brokers. In early 1994, the Funds owned, in the aggregate, more than $1.5 billion of such CMOs, approximately half of which were purchased from the three Brokers (and another quarter from Kidder, Peabody & Co. Inc. ("Kidder")). In short, the Brokers all were "in bed" with ACM. (Compl. § 40.)

As a result of the Brokers' sales of numerous inappropriate securities to the Funds, by the beginning of 1994 the Funds' portfolios were dangerously "tilted" in a way that exposed the Funds to substantial losses in the event of an increase in interest rates. When interest rates rose in February and March 1994, the Funds experienced an erosion in value. In March 1994, the Brokers issued improper margin calls on the Funds, based on arbitrary security valuations.

The Funds acquired most of their securities pursuant to repos, a financing mechanism that allowed the Funds to pay only a fraction of the cost of each CMO in cash, borrowing the balance from the Brokers. In such a transaction, one party to the agreement agrees to sell a security to a buyer/lender for a given sum (the "repo amount") and to buy the security back from the buyer/lender at a later date (the "buy-back date") for the repo amount plus a market rate of interest (the "repo rate"). In effect, the Complaint alleges that the repos were collateralized loans—the Brokers loaned the Funds most of the purchase price for each CMO and took possession of the bonds as collateral. The use of repos benefited the Brokers, allowing the Funds to increase their purchases from the Brokers.

The contracts between the Funds and the Brokers allowed the Brokers to make margin calls on the Funds if the value of the securities on repo fell below the amount that the Funds had borrowed (plus an agreed-upon "haircut"). In that instance, a "margin deficit" exists. In making margin calculations, the market value of the securities must be the price obtained from a "generally recognized source agreed to by the parties or the most recent closing bid quotation from such a source," plus accrued income not included therein. (Compl. § 55.) In March 1994, however, the Brokers issued a blizzard of margin calls that were not based on fair market prices, but on unreasonably low, manipulated valuations.

When the Funds were unable to meet the Brokers' improper margin calls, the Brokers liquidated the Funds' portfolios. Under the PSA Agreements, if a proper margin call is not met, the broker-Dealer may liquidate the collateral upon one business day's notice, including by selling the securities to itself in a "deemed" sale and crediting the customer in an amount equal to the price of the securities obtained from a general recognized source or the most recent closing bid quotation from such a source. According to the Complaint, the liquidations were not conducted in good faith and in a commercially reasonable manner. Instead of seeking to maximize the prices paid for the Funds' securities in the liquidations by soliciting bids from their retail customers, the Brokers in nearly all cases simply "deemed" the CMOs sold to themselves, at unreasonably low prices.

The Brokers agreed to facilitate each other's liquidations by providing each Broker with sham bids for the Fund securities that each of them held. These were not bona fide offers to purchase the securities at market prices, but artificially low "accommodation" bids solicited and provided in an effort to justify the prices at which the Brokers then deemed the Funds' CMOs sold to themselves.

The Complaint alleges that by selling the inappropriate toxic securities to the Funds, by generating artificial and improper margin calls, and then by liquidating the portfolios in a commercially unreasonable and collusive manner, the Brokers netted profits, whereas the Funds lost more than $400 million.

Discussion

* * *

VI.   Count XI Alleging Breach of Duty to Liquidate in a Commercially Reasonable Manner Is Dismissed Only as to Bear Stearns and DLJ

The Brokers held most of the securities they liquidated pursuant to repos. The LAB represents that these repos were the functional equivalent of secured loans and that the Brokers, as secured parties, were obligated by Article 9 of the UCC to exercise their right to liquidate in good faith and a commercially reasonable manner. See N.Y.U.C.C. § 1–203 (McKinney 1993); id. § 9–594 (McKinney 1990). The Complaint also alleges that the common law applicable to pledgees imposes a duty of commercial reasonableness in liquidation. In Count XI, the LAB alleges that the Brokers violated these statutory and common law duties.

Because Article 9 is only applicable to secured transactions, the maintenance of the instant claim depends upon the characterization of the repos. If they are purchase and sales agreements, the UCC is inapplicable and Count XI must be dismissed. If they are secured loans, the claim stands.

A.   Repurchase Agreements Defined

A repurchase agreement, by its terms, involves two separate but related transactions: (1) a sale by a party (the "repo seller") of securities in exchange for cash and (2) an agreement by the repo seller to repurchase the same or equivalent securities for a specified price at a future date. In a reverse repurchase agreement, the party initially buys the securities in exchange for cash, and incurs a forward obligation to resell them. Every repo is also a reverse repo; that is, a reverse repurchase agreement is simply a repurchase agreement viewed from the perspective of the repo buyer. See In re Bevill, Bresler & Schulman Asset Management Corp., 67 B.R. 557, 566–67 (D.N.J.1986).

Repos are creatures of the capital markets. Their purchase-and-sale form reflects a value-for-value exchange designed as such for use explicitly in those markets. The legal status of repo agreements is not easily subject to characterization—the purchase-and-sale framework incorporates characteristics of other transactional forms, including financings. For example, as in a financing, the repurchase price for the securities reflects the time value of the cash obtained by the repo seller in the initial sale. However, the repo structure is distinct from that of a loan in other respects. Unlike a lender taking collateral for a secured loan, a repo buyer "take[s] title to the securities received and can trade, sell or pledge them." SEC v. Drysdale Sec. Corp., 785 F.2d 38, 41 (2d Cir.1986). Such free transferability of repo securities renders repos attractive to securities Dealers whose inventories of securities turn over rapidly and who may require securities to be available for a variety of settlement obligations. At the same time, the adjustability of the term of repo agreements makes them an ideal financial management tool for institutional investors investing cash balances. Thus, for "such entities as state and local governments, public and private pension funds, money market and other mutual funds, banks, thrift institutions, and large corporations, repos have become a vital tool of cash management." S.Rep. No. 98–65, at 45 (1983) [hereinafter 1983 Senate Repo Amendments Report].

Repos are the principal method used by securities Dealers to fund their acquisition of U.S. Treasury securities. See Department of the Treasury, Sec. and Exch. Comm'n, and Bd. of Governors of the Fed. Reserve Sys., Joint Report on the Government Securities Market at A–11 (Jan.1992) [hereinafter 1992 Joint Report]. The Treasury relies heavily on primary Dealers to absorb new government debt issues, and repos are extensively used by Dealers to obtain the cash necessary to permit their underwriting of such issues. See, e.g., Government Securities Act Amendments of 1993, H.R.Rep. No. 255, at 10–11 (1993), reprinted in 1993 U.S.C.C.A.N. 2996, 2997. By maximizing the ease and flexibility with which Dealers can acquire and hold inventories of Treasury securities, repo transactions contribute significantly to the depth and liquidity of the secondary market for Treasury securities. See, e.g., 1983 Senate Repo Amendments Report at 45–46. Together with other trading techniques and transactions, repos and reverse repos "have benefited the market and the taxpayer by increasing liquidity, thereby lowering the government's financing costs." 1992 Joint Report at 1.[1]

---

1. Repos involving U.S. Treasury securities are also used by the Federal Reserve System as its primary tool for implementation of monetary policy. See In re Bevill,

Repo transactions perform a similar function with respect to other fixed-income securities, including federal agency securities such as those issued or guaranteed by the Federal National Mortgage Association ("Fannie Mae") and the Federal Home Loan Mortgage Corporation ("Freddie Mac").[2] They are a vital and cost-efficient mechanism for broker-Dealers to fund their inventory and dealing activities in these securities. The existence of a repo market in a particular type of securities also adds to the liquidity of the underlying cash market for the securities. CMOs, like those involved in the instant case, are securities where cash flows from a securitized mortgage pool are repackaged into classes of interests with different projected maturities and principal repayment schedules which appeal to a broad range of investors with specific investment needs and objectives. CMOs allow their investors to retain the yield and credit quality advantages of mortgage-backed securities while reducing many of their perceived burdens, particularly those relating to prepayment uncertainty. The ultimate beneficiaries of CMOs and other mortgage-backed securities are residential home buyers who are able to obtain lower-cost mortgages as a result of the cheaper cost of funds to originators. As Congress has recognized, the CMO market, and the repo market for CMOs which enable Dealers in these securities, is, like the repo market in U.S. Treasury securities, important to the national economy. See generally S.Rep. No. 98–293 (1984) (noting that the Secondary Mortgage Market Enhancement Act in 1984 was enacted for the purpose of "encourag[ing] the 'broadening of the market for mortgage-backed securities by encouraging more extensive involvement of the private sector' ").

B. Characterization of the Repos

The key to the inquiry as to whether the repos in this case should be characterized as purchase and sale agreements or secured loans lies in the intention of the parties. Article 9 only applies to transactions in which the parties' intent is to create a security interest. See N.Y.U.C.C. § 9–102 (McKinney 1990); see also In re O.P.M. Leasing Servs., Inc., 23 B.R. 104, 115 (Bankr.S.D.N.Y.1982) (stating that "Article 9 applies only to a transaction which is intended to create a security interest in personal property"). To determine whether the parties to a transaction intended to create a security interest, courts look to the agreement governing the transaction. Where the parties' intention is clearly and unambiguously set forth in the agreement, effect must be given to the

Bresler & Schulman Asset Management Corp., 878 F.2d 742, 745 (3d Cir.1989).

2. As stated by the BMA, the repo market fosters important interrelationships among the different types of fixed-income securities. The market for federal agency securities, and the fixed-income markets generally, are closely linked to the market for Treasury securities: the price of an agency security is generally expressed in terms of its "spread" over Treasury securities of comparable maturity, and Dealers quickly act on arbitrages between Treasury and agency security markets. See 1992 Joint Report at D–4 to D–5. Rapid movements of securities through repos and reverse repos facilitate this process and are thus among a number of financial mechanisms that contribute to the smooth functioning of the nation's fixed-income markets.

expressed intent. See John Hancock Mutual Life Ins. Co. v. Amerford Int'l Corp., 22 F.3d 458, 461 (2d Cir.1994) (stating that where the agreement is clear, courts should look to the "terms expressed in the contract itself, rather than to 'extrinsic evidence of terms that were not expressed or judicial views on what terms might be preferable' "); In re O.P.M., 23 B.R. at 116 & n. 8 (observing that "[i]t would have been a simple matter for the parties expressly to provide * * * for the grant of a security interest," but because they did not "it is evident that no security interest was ever intended"). The objective intent of the parties "expressed or apparent in the writing controls" the agreement's interpretation, while the "undisclosed, subjective intent of the parties has no bearing" on the construction of the contract. In re Bevill, 67 B.R. at 586.

In the case at bar, the governing contracts include the PSA Agreements into which Bear Stearns and DLJ entered with each of the Funds, the PSA Agreement into which Merrill Lynch entered with Quartz, and the trade confirmations relied on by Merrill Lynch as to Granite Partners and Granite Corp.[3]

1. *The PSA Agreements*

According to the Brokers, the plain language of the PSA Agreement demonstrates that each of the Brokers was an outright purchaser of bonds from the Funds and not merely a "secured party." The Brokers assert that the intention of the Brokers and the Funds not to engage in secured transactions is made clear by paragraph 6 of the PSA Agreement, which reads, in pertinent part: "the parties intend that all Transactions hereunder be sales and purchases and not loans." Thus, under the PSA Agreement, the securities acquired by the Brokers in reverse repos were sold to the Brokers and were not collateral pledged to secure a loan. Consistent with the parties' intent to effect a transfer of ownership, paragraph 8 of the PSA Agreement states, in relevant part:

> Title to all Purchased Securities shall pass to Buyer and, unless otherwise agreed by Buyer and Seller, nothing in this Agreement shall preclude Buyer from engaging in repurchase transactions with the Purchased Securities or otherwise pledging or hypothecating the Purchased Securities.

Thus, claim the Brokers, this Court need not look beyond the four corners of the PSA Agreement to determine that the repurchase transactions at issue are purchases and sales and not secured loans.

---

3. Consideration of the agreements themselves is appropriate on the motion to dismiss because the LAB must rely on the agreements to prove contractual relations with the Brokers, the LAB had notice of them when the action was filed, and the LAB itself utilizes them in its opposition papers. See Belin, 1998 WL 391114, at *3–*4; see also San Leandro Emergency Med. Group Profit Sharing Plan v. Philip Morris Cos., 75 F.3d 801, 808–09 (2d Cir.1996) (permitting consideration of the full text of documents "integral" to plaintiff's claim on motion to dismiss); Barnum v. Millbrook Care Ltd. Partnership, 850 F.Supp. 1227, 1230 (S.D.N.Y.) (finding reference to the full text of a contract on a motion to dismiss appropriate even though the plaintiff had not formally incorporated it by reference), aff'd, 43 F.3d 1458 (2d Cir.1994).

The LAB counters that the contracts reflect the parties understanding that the Funds' repos were the functional equivalent of secured loans, extrinsic evidence will indicate that the Brokers viewed their repos as collateralized loans, and a finding that repurchase agreements are purchases and sales can only be accomplished after a careful consideration of all of the evidence on a more fully-developed record.

In the case of In re Bevill, a bankruptcy court was required to determine whether the securities underlying repo transactions were property of the debtor estates or belonged instead to repo and reverse repo participants. That issue turned on whether the repos constituted purchases and sales or collateralized loans. In determining the parties' intent, the court noted that the trade tickets of each executed repo reported them as purchases and sales, that the standard Repurchase Agreements used the language of "buyer" and "seller"—not lender and borrower—and that under these agreements the buyer could freely rehypothecate the purchased securities. The court concluded that "[t]he unequivocal language of purchase and sale in the repo and reverse repo agreements at issue * * * is strong prima facie evidence that the parties intended the transactions to be treated accordingly." In re Bevill, 67 B.R. at 597. However, despite noting that the repo agreement at issue made no reference to secured loans or to any intention to grant a security interest to the lender, because the agreements contained "terms customarily found in secured loan transactions," the court held that it had to consider extrinsic evidence of the parties' intentions before it could characterize the repos in that case as sales or loans. See id. at 590.

In its final analysis, the court in In re Bevill concluded that:

> repos and reverse repos are hybrid transactions which do not fit neatly into either a secured loan or purchase and sale classification. There is no question that repo and reverse repo transactions have functional attributes which resemble collateralized loans. The initial taking of margin (the "haircut"), the right of substitution, and the "mark-to-market" provisions are undeniably secured loan characteristics not commonly found in purchase and sale transactions. In addition, principal and/or interest paid on the underlying securities remains the property of the seller. On the other hand, the repo buyer's unrestricted right to trade the securities during the term of the agreement represents an incident of ownership which does not pass to a secured lender in a collateralized transaction. Id. at 596–97.

Indeed, as the Second Circuit stated in Drysdale, the " '[defendant] ignores a most significant difference between repos and standard collateralized loans * * *. In the latter transaction the lender holds pledged collateral for security and may not sell it in the absence of a default. In contract, repo "lenders" take title to the securities received and can trade, sell or pledge them.' " Drysdale, 785 F.2d at 41, quoted in In re Bevill, 67 B.R. at 593–94.

Furthermore, stated the court in In re Bevill:

while the risk of market fluctuations in the value of the underlying securities rests with the original seller, this truism is of no legal consequence. The seller's interest in the market value of the securities is no greater in a secured loan transaction where he retains beneficial ownership of the securities than in a purchase and sale transaction where he is contractually bound to reacquire ownership of them. Clearly, any attempt to determine whether a repo or reverse repo transaction is more like a secured loan than a purchase and sale by weighing economic factors on a finely tuned balance scale would be an essentially formalistic and ultimately unproductive exercise.

In any event, the proper characterization of repo and reverse repo agreements does not rest solely on an evaluation of the economic substance of the individual transactions. Rather, the intent of the parties viewed in the context of the entire market in which these transactions take place is the controlling consideration under * * * New York * * * law. This intent must be gleaned from the express terms employed in the transaction documents as well as relevant extrinsic evidence of intent, including trade custom and usage, market realities and the parties' course of conduct and performance. In re Bevill, 67 B.R. at 597.

The agreements in In re Bevill differ from the instant PSA Agreements in an important respect such that extrinsic evidence need not be considered: while the agreements in that case used isolated terms of purchase and sale, the PSA Agreements at issue affirmatively state the parties' intent to treat the transaction as such. Thus, claim the Brokers, the LAB cannot point to any place in the PSA Agreements that make their terms ambiguous. Moreover, they continue, the PSA contracts were created after the decision in In re Bevill and after Congress amended the Bankruptcy Code in 1984 to make clear that repos should not be considered secured transactions for bankruptcy purposes. In addition, the court in In re Bevill soundly rejected the contention that the similarities between repos and loans were a basis for construing repo transactions as secured loans. "The mere presence of secured loan characteristics in repo and reverse repo agreements is not enough to negate the parties' voluntary decision to structure the transactions as purchases and sales." Id. at 598.

Because the standard industry documentation for repo transactions prepared by the BMA and used by the Brokers in this case explicitly states that the parties "intend that all Transactions hereunder be sales and purchases and not loans," PSA Agreement ¶ 6, that intention must be honored.[4] Therefore, the repos entered into by Bears Stearns and DLJ

---

4. The operative provisions of the PSA Agreement conform to this stated intention. The parties are denominated "Buyer" and "Seller," they agree that on the "Purchase Date" for a transaction the "Purchased Securities" will be transferred to the "Buyer" or its agent against payment of the "Purchase Price." On the "Repurchase Date," this process occurs in reverse. The parties further acknowledge the difference between their repo transactions and conventional secured indebtedness by agreeing that each

with each of the Funds, as well as the PSA agreement entered into by Merrill Lynch with Quartz, are to be treated as a matter of law as purchase and sale agreements and not secured loans subject to Article 9 of the UCC.

Policy considerations and trade custom and usage support such a finding. Moreover, ignoring the affirmative intent of the parties would inject unpredictability and insecurity in the manner by which major financial institutions obtain credit. The decision by market participants to enter into a repo transaction documented using the PSA Agreement, structured as a purchase and sale, thus carries with it a wide variety of legal and regulatory consequences. Market participants who prefer to enter into secured lending transactions rather than repos may do so (with the attendant legal result that their transaction will be treated as a loan); participants who prefer to enter into a sale and wholly distinct forward purchase (with attendant legal consequences) may also do so. The determination of market participants that elect to enter into a repo transaction has been and should be respected and their settled expectations will not be overturned.

According to the BMA, repos have evolved to fulfill certain market needs and objectives that cannot be served by secured loans. Critical to the usefulness, flexibility, and liquidity of the repo market is the transfer of ownership of the repo securities to the repo buyer and the repo buyer's ability to sell, transfer, or pledge the securities purchased in a repo transaction during its term. The mobility of repo securities is what makes them a key tool of the funding markets, enabling Dealers to continuously convert their securities inventory to cash to use to finance the purchase of yet additional securities and thereby make markets. Reverse repos are often used by Dealers to obtain securities needed for deliveries when they are "short," thereby avoiding "fails" in the market and facilitating settlements and the smooth functioning of the market. The flexibility of repo buyers with respect to the repo securities also contributes to the popularity of repos s flexible cash management vehicles, thereby bringing a large supply of diverse cash investors to the repo markets.

Applying to repurchase transactions the provisions of Part 5 of UCC Article 9, asserts the BMA, which governs the disposition of collateral after default, for example, would undermine the requisite flexibility of the repo market. As many of the provisions in Part 5 are not subject to consensual predefault waiver by the parties, see U.C.C. § 9–501(3), repo counterparties would be unable to establish by contract their rights and remedies in a default situation, thereby introducing uncertainties in the repo marketplace. The health and efficiency of the repo market depends

"Transaction" is a "repurchase agreement" and a "securities contract" entitled to the benefits of special protective provisions under the Bankruptcy Code. Perhaps most telling, the parties agree that the title to the Purchased Securities passes to the Buyer, who is explicitly permitted to engage in repos with the Purchased Securities or otherwise transfer or hypothecate them. See Drysdale, 785 F.2d at 41. Under prevailing market practice, the Buyer, as owner, may sell the Purchased Securities.

on market participants' ability to transact on well-settled understandings and certainty as to the consequences of their transactions and/or failure to perform their transactions. It was this need for certainty in expectations, according to the BMA, that led the repo market participants, through the BMA, to publish the PSA Agreement as industry standard contractual documentation and provide a legal framework establishing the rights and obligations of the parties in repo transactions based on market practices.[5]

Application of Article 9 would additionally cast doubt on this efficacy of certain remedy provisions of the widely used PSA Agreement in cases of default. For example the Agreement provides that upon default of the repo seller, a repo buyer may elect, in lieu of selling the purchased securities, to engage in a "deemed sale" of the purchased securities and give the defaulting repo seller credit in an amount equal to the price obtained from a generally recognized source. See PSA Agreement § 11. The repo buyer retains its ability to seek payment from the repo seller for any remaining deficiency between the credited "deemed sale" price and the contractually agreed repurchase price (plus any other amounts owing by the defaulting party). Id. In contrast, Article 9 requires a secured party, who under certain circumstances takes in a defaulting debtor's collateral, to receive the debtor's consent and waive its deficiency claim. See U.C.C. § 9–505. The BMA proposes that the application of this provision, with its 21–day notice requirement, would nullify the "real world" swift liquidation mechanism that the repo market and its participants require. This sort of uncertainty could have adverse consequences on the repo market.

The LAB concedes that repos play a vital role in providing liquidity, thereby reducing risk and interest rates, but it attempts to distinguish the repos at issue here—which were primarily in securities issued by the government-sponsored agencies Fannie Mae and Freddie Mac by claiming that they do not play anything like the role of Treasury bills in the nation's financial infrastructure. The LAB thus urges formulation of different rules based on the type of securities involved. Yet the LAB ignores the fact that the PSA Agreement is an industry standard master repo agreement that applies generally to all repo transactions and does not distinguish between Treasuries and other types of securities. Therefore the AB requests a ruling that the same words in the very same contract should be interpreted differently depending upon the type of security at issue. Identical contracts would sometimes be subject to

---

5. The BMA also maintains that Article 9 would impinge upon repo participants' rights with respect to repo securities in the nondefault context. The BMA uses, as an example, section 9–207, which prescribes the rights and duties of a secured party holding collateral in its possession. While section 9–207(2)(e) provides that "the secured party may repledge the collateral upon terms which do not impair the debt- or's right to redeem it," it does not permit a secured party to sell or dispose of the collateral in its possession. The application of Article 9 would negate a repo buyer's contractual right to freely sell the repo securities and may hamper the repo buyer's right to rehypothecate the repo securities. These rights of the repo buyer are inherent features of repo transactions, key to their value to the capital markets.

Article 9 and sometimes not. Such a result fosters unwarranted uncertainty.

Moreover, the market for Fannie Mae and Freddie Mac securities is vitally important not only to the nation's financial markets but also to the nation's housing markets. Congress's goal in creating CMO-issuing National Mortgage Associations like Fannie Mae and Freddie Mac was to provide ongoing assistance to the secondary market for residential mortgages * * * by increasing the liquidity of mortgage investments and improving the distribution of investment capital available for residential mortgage financing; and * * * promote access to mortgage credit throughout the Nation * * * by increasing the liquidity of mortgage investments and improving the distribution of investment capital available for residential mortgage financing * * *. 12 U.S.C. § 1716. Indeed, the success of Fannie Mae and Freddie Mac and the securities they issue has helped to significantly lower the mortgage rates paid by homeowners in this country. See S.Rep. No. 102–282, at 30–31 (1992) (stating that "[m]ost mortgage interest rates are generally thought to be 1/4 to 1/2 of the percentage point lower * * * than they would otherwise be"). "Together, [Fannie Mae and Freddie Mac] now provide financing for more than a third of all home loans outstanding * * *." Id.

Furthermore, the instant ruling is consistent with case law. In contexts such as commercial law and the antifraud provisions of the federal securities law, repos generally are viewed as purchases and sales. See In re Bevill, 67 B.R. 557, and Drysdale, 785 F.2d 38. For other purposes, such as taxes, they are typically viewed as financings. See Nebraska Dep't of Revenue v. Loewenstein, 513 U.S. 123, 115 S.Ct. 557, 130 L.Ed.2d 470 (1994). For accounting purposes, they are viewed either way, depending upon particular factors. In yet other circumstances, such as under Section 559 of the Bankruptcy Code, repo transactions have been assigned a distinct legal status which acknowledges their unique attributes.

Because the PSA Agreement is not ambiguous, because it clearly provides that the parties intended the transaction to be treated as a purchase and sale, and because such a finding is consistent with the practices and expectations of the securities industry, see In re Bevill, 67 B.R. at 598, Count XI of the Complaint is dismissed as to Bear Stearns and DLJ, and as to Merrill Lynch it is dismissed only with respect to the PSA Agreement into which it entered with Quartz.[6]

2. *Trade Confirmations Upon Which Merrill Lynch Relied*

Merrill Lynch did not execute PSA Agreements with Granite Partners and Granite Corp. Instead, it relied on trade confirmations for the contract terms applicable to the repo transactions. Those confirmations state:

---

6. Additionally, the LAB's allegation that the forward contracts between the Funds and Bear Stearns resulted in secured loans is unsupported and therefore dismissed.

THE TRANSFEROR/SELLER SHALL BE DEEMED TO HAVE GRANTED THE TRANSFEREE/PURCHASER, AS OF THE PURCHASE DATE, A SECURITY INTEREST IN THE SECURITIES ("SECURITIES" PLEDGED/SOLD PURSUANT TO A TRANSACTION HEREUNDER) FOR SUCH TRANSACTION (AND IN ALL INCOME AND DISTRIBUTIONS THEREON AND PROCEEDS THEREOF) TO SECURE ITS OBLIGATION TO REPURCHASE SUCH SECURITIES, UNLESS THE SELLER IS IN DEFAULT, THE SELLER SHALL BE ENTITLED TO ALL PAYMENTS OF PRINCIPLE [sic] AND INTEREST ON THE SECURITIES, AND THE PURCHASER SHALL, UPON RECEIPT, REMIT TO THE SELLER ANY SUCH PAYMENTS RECEIVED BY IT, SUBJECT TO ITS OBLIGATION TO RESELL THE SECURITIES (OR EQUIVALENT SECURITIES) TO THE SELLER, THE PURCHASER MAY SELL, PLEDGE OR OTHERWISE TRANSFER THE SECURITIES.

Here, the language is far more ambiguous. Unlike the PSA Agreement, it does not contain an unequivocal expression of intent. In cases where the express terms of a contract or agreement are ambiguous, unclear, or conflicting, and the intended meaning and operation of the contract cannot reasonably be derived from the "four corners of the writing," courts allow the "introduction and examination of extrinsic evidence of intent as an aid in interpretation." In re Bevill, 67 B.R. at 587. Consideration of extrinsic evidence of the parties' intent is properly left to a later time, with the benefit of a fully-developed factual record. Therefore, the motion to dismiss Count XI against Merrill Lynch regarding the transactions evidenced by trade confirmations is denied.

VII. Although the Motion to Dismiss Count X Alleging Breach of Contract Due to Commercially Unreasonable Liquidations Is Denied, the Claim Is Hereby Modified

In Count X, the LAB alleges that the Brokers violated the PSA and other agreements by liquidating the Funds' securities at below-market prices. By exchanging lowball accommodation bids and conducting sham auctions that led to the sale of the Funds' portfolios at prices substantially below fair market value, the Brokers breached their obligation to liquidate at a price "obtained from a generally recognized source or the most recent closing bid quotation from such a source." (Compl. § 233.) Additionally, the LAB contends, by deliberately depressing the prices at which the Funds' CMOs were sold the Brokers breached their contractual duty to liquidate in good faith and in a commercially reasonable manner.

While DLJ does not move against this cause of action, Merrill Lynch proposes that it should be dismissed under Rule 9(b), and Bear Stearns challenges it insofar as it alleges a breach of the implied duty of "commercial reasonableness."

A. *Rule 9(b) Does Not Apply to the Contract Claim*

On its face, Rule 9(b) does not apply to contract claims, but only to "averments of fraud and mistake." Merrill Lynch's contention that Count X fails to meet the requirement of Rule 9(b) does not command solicitude because the authority it cites is inapposite to the instant case.

For example, Merrill Lynch invokes Frota v. Prudential–Bache Securities, Inc., 639 F.Supp. 1186, 1193 (S.D.N.Y.1986), in which the court applied Rule 9(b) to a claim that "merely incorporates the allegations of the securities fraud and RICO counts." By contrast, the LAB's contract claim does not "merely incorporate" the fraud allegation, nor does it depend in any way on a showing of fraud. It is based on the allegation that the Brokers' below-market liquidation of the Funds' portfolios breached specified contract provisions, as well as the Brokers' obligation to liquidate in good faith. Rule 9(b) is inapplicable to such a claim.

B. *Implied Duties of Good Faith and Commercial Reasonableness*

The Complaint alleges a breach of both the implied duties to liquidate the Funds' holdings in good faith and in a "commercially reasonable manner." (Compl. § 232.) While Bear Stearns has no quarrel with the requirement of good faith, it takes issue with that of commercial reasonableness.

"Implicit in all contracts is a covenant of good faith and fair dealing in the course of contract performance." Dalton v. Educational Testing Serv., 87 N.Y.2d 384, 389, 663 N.E.2d 289, 292, 639 N.Y.S.2d 977, 979 (1995). The covenant encompasses "any promises which a reasonable person in the position of the promisee would be justified in understanding were included," and it prohibits either party from acting in a manner "which will have the effect of destroying or injuring the right of the other party to receive the fruits of the contract." Id. (citations and internal quotations omitted); see Travellers Int'l, A.G. v. Trans World Airlines, Inc., 41 F.3d 1570, 1575 (2d Cir.1994) (stating that "the implied covenant of good faith and fair dealing inheres in every contract"). Breach of the covenant gives rise to a cognizable claim. See Chase Manhattan Bank, N.A. v. Keystone Distribs., Inc., 873 F.Supp. 808, 815 (S.D.N.Y.1994) (finding that "[a] party may be in breach of its implied duty of good faith and fair dealing even if it is not in breach of its express contractual obligations").

Indeed, the broker's "power to liquidate must be exercised in good faith under the existing facts and circumstances." Cauble v. Mabon Nugent & Co., 594 F.Supp. 985, 992 (S.D.N.Y.1984); see Modern Settings, Inc. v. Prudential–Bache Sec., Inc., 936 F.2d 640, 644 (2d Cir.1991) (stating that the "contractual power [to liquidate] must be exercised in good faith"); see also Travellers Int'l, 41 F.3d at 1575 ("Even when a contract confers decision-making power on a single party, the resulting discretion is nevertheless subject to an obligation that it be exercised in good faith.").

While an implied covenant of good faith and fair dealing is recognized in most contracts under New York law, the duty cannot be used to create independent obligations beyond those agreed upon and stated in the express language of the contract. See Warner Theatre Assoc. Ltd. Partnership v. Metropolitan Life Ins. Co., No. 97 Civ. 4914, 1997 WL 685334, at *6 (S.D.N.Y. Nov.4, 1997). Any purported duty of good faith "cannot add to, detract from, or alter the terms of the contract itself." Id.; see CIBC Bank and Trust Co., Ltd. (Cayman) v. Banco Cent. Do Brasil, 886 F.Supp. 1105, 1118 (S.D.N.Y.1995) ("[A]lthough the obligation of good faith is implied in the contract, it is the terms of the contract which govern the rights and obligations of the parties.").

The phrase "commercially reasonable manner," however, has been given special meaning under Article 9 of the UCC, and the totality of those concepts will not be imported wholesale into the PSA Agreement to which, as discussed above, Article 9 does not apply. The contract claim is to be interpreted under ordinary contract jurisprudence. Therefore, to the extent the LAB seeks to impose an implied obligation by its use of the term "commercially reasonable," Count X is to be modified such that any reference invoking the duty to liquidate "in a commercially reasonable manner" shall be deleted. If the LAB wishes, it may replace the term with the covenant of "fair dealing."

* * *

The Brokers' motion to dismiss the claim for breach of duty to liquidate in a commercially reasonable manner (Count XI) is granted as to Bear Stearns and DLJ but denied as to Merrill Lynch.

The motion to dismiss the breach of contract claim for commercial unreasonable liquidations (Count X) is hereby denied, but the claim is to be modified as directed herein.

IT IS SO ORDERED.

Problem 6–5

Bank of Illinois, a good client of yours located in Western Illinois, calls to get advice about repo transactions that it plans to enter into with a local customer. The bank visualizes several ways in which these transactions will be done. In all cases, the customer will be putting up US securities and the transactions will be established in three different ways. First in some of the cases the treasury securities will be held at Bank One in Chicago. Second in certain other cases there will be treasury securities held in various brokerage accounts of customer's around the country, some of which will be unidentified and unknown to Bank. Third in some cases customer will be willing to place the federal securities in Bank's name at Bank.

1. What documents should Bank have the customer execute and what filings or other acts should the Bank undertake in order to insure that it has first priority and the capacity to satisfy its debt upon the customer's default?

2. It is now three years later. Bank and customer entered into the transactions described above and customer has defaulted. Bank now has

liquidated the securities held in its name, has asked customer to transfer the securities that are held at different places around the country, and has asked Bank One to transfer to Bank the securities held there. The debtor's trustee in bankruptcy has challenged all of these actions. First, it claims that any attempt to get possession of or to sell securities in the possession of Bank will violate the automatic stay. Second, it claims that Bank is not perfected as to the securities held at Bank One nor to those held at different locations around the country. Bank tells you that it did file a financing statement in the client's name. What are Bank's rights vis-à-vis the trustee in this case?

3. As to the treasury bills held at Bank One, Bank One claims priority. Unbeknownst to Bank and after it had lent money to the common debtor and filed a financing statement, Bank One made a loan and took a security agreement from debtor. You are fearful that Bank will lose to Bank One. How could it avoid such a loss in the future?

Problem 6–6

Assume Bank has entered into a repo agreement (like the one below) with Debtor. Bank has control of the treasury bills it has purchased and its contract with the Seller permits it to sell the bills upon the Seller's default without notice and without advertising them. Is there anything in part 6 of Article 9 that would contradict or interfere with the Bank's right to sell according to the terms in its agreement with the Debtor?

Master Repurchase Agreement
September 1996 Version

Dated as of _____

Between _____

and _____

1. Applicability

From time to time the parties hereto may enter into transactions in which one party ("Seller") agrees to transfer to the other ("Buyer") securities or other assets ("Securities") against the transfer of funds by Buyer, with a simultaneous agreement by Buyer to transfer to Seller such Securities at a date certain or on demand, against the transfer of funds by Seller. Each such transaction shall be referred to herein as a "Transaction" and, unless otherwise agreed in writing, shall be governed by this Agreement, including any supplemental terms or conditions contained in Annex I hereto and in any other annexes identified herein or therein as applicable hereunder.

* * *

3. Initiation; Confirmation; Termination

(a) An agreement to enter into a Transaction may be made orally or in writing at the initiation of either Buyer or Seller. On the Purchase Date for the Transaction, the Purchased Securities shall be transferred to Buyer or its agent against the transfer of the Purchase Price to an account of Seller.

(b) Upon agreeing to enter into a Transaction hereunder, Buyer or Seller (or both), as shall be agreed, shall promptly deliver to the other party a written confirmation of each Transaction (a "Confirmation"). The Confirmation shall describe the Purchased Securities (including CUSIP number, if any), identify Buyer and Seller and set forth (i) the Purchase Date, (ii) the Purchase Price, (iii) the Repurchase Date, unless the Transaction is to be terminable on demand, (iv) the Pricing Rate or Repurchase Price applicable to the Transaction, and (v) any additional terms or conditions of the Transaction not inconsistent with this Agreement. The Confirmation, together with this Agreement, shall constitute conclusive evidence of the terms agreed between Buyer and Seller with respect to the Transaction to which the Confirmation relates, unless with respect to the Confirmation specific objection is made promptly after receipt thereof. In the event of any conflict between the terms of such Confirmation and this Agreement, this Agreement shall prevail.

(c) In the case of Transactions terminable upon demand, such demand shall be made by Buyer or Seller, no later than such time as is customary in accordance with market practice, by telephone or otherwise on or prior to the business day on which such termination will be effective. On the date specified in such demand, or on the date fixed for termination in the case of Transactions having a fixed term, termination of the Transaction will be effected by transfer to Seller or its agent of the Purchased Securities and any Income in respect thereof received by Buyer (and not previously credited or transferred to, or applied to the obligations of, Seller pursuant to Paragraph 5 hereof) against the transfer of the Repurchase Price to an account of Buyer.

* * *

6. Security Interest

Although the parties intend that all Transactions hereunder be sales and purchases and not loans, in the event any such Transactions are deemed to be loans, Seller shall be deemed to have pledged to Buyer as security for the performance by Seller of its obligations under each such Transaction, and shall be deemed to have granted to Buyer a security interest in, all of the Purchased Securities with respect to all Transactions hereunder and all Income thereon and other proceeds thereof.

7. Payment and Transfer

Unless otherwise mutually agreed, all transfers of funds hereunder shall be in immediately available funds. All Securities transferred by one party hereto to the other party (i) shall be in suitable form for transfer or shall be accompanied by duly executed instruments of transfer or assignment in blank and such other documentation as the party receiving possession may reasonably request, (ii) shall be transferred on the book-entry system of a Federal Reserve Bank, or (iii) shall be transferred by any other method mutually acceptable to Seller and Buyer.

8. Segregation of Purchased Securities

To the extent required by applicable law, all Purchased Securities in the possession of Seller shall be segregated from other securities in its possession and shall be identified as subject to this Agreement. Segregation may be accomplished by appropriate identification on the books and records of the holder, including a financial or securities intermediary or a clearing corporation. All of Seller's interest in the Purchased Securities shall pass to Buyer on the Purchase Date and, unless otherwise agreed by Buyer and Seller, nothing in this Agreement shall preclude Buyer from engaging in repurchase transactions with the Purchased Securities or otherwise selling, transferring, pledging or hypothecating the Purchased Securities, but no such transaction shall relieve Buyer of its obligations to transfer Purchased Securities to Seller pursuant to Paragraph 3, 4 or 11 hereof, or of Buyer's obligation to credit or pay Income to, or apply Income to the obligations of, Seller pursuant to Paragraph 5 hereof.

Required Disclosure for Transactions in Which the Seller Retains Custody of the Purchased Securities

Seller is not permitted to substitute other securities for those to this Agreement and therefore must keep Buyer's securities segregated at all times, unless in this Agreement Buyer grants Seller the right to substitute other securities. If Buyer grants the right to substitute, this means that Buyer's securities will likely be commingled with Seller's own securities during the trading day. Buyer is advised that, during any trading day that Buyer's securities are commingled with Seller's securities, they [will]* [may]** be subject to liens granted by Seller to [its clearing bank]* [third parties]** and may be used by Seller for deliveries on other securities transactions. Whenever the securities are commingled, Seller's ability to resegregate substitute securities for Buyer will be subject to Seller's ability to satisfy [the clearing]* [any]** lien or to obtain substitute securities.

* Language to be used under 17 C.F.R. § 403.4(e) if Seller is a government securities broker or Dealer other than a financial institution.

** Language to be used under 17 C.F.R. § 403.5(d) if Seller is a financial institution.

Would the use of the agreement set out above have helped Bank in problem 6–5?

Chapter Seven

BANKRUPTCY

---

§ 1. INTRODUCTION

In this chapter we consider the provisions of the bankruptcy code that apply most directly to the secured creditor. We take Chapter 11 (reorganization) as the norm. Big Chapter 11's are not short stories; they are books with many chapters, chapters that sometimes seem to have only the barest connection to one another. The opening pages in a Chapter 11 typically involve the right of the debtor in possession (DIP) to use "cash collateral" (usually the DIP's bank account and other proceeds of pre and post petition sales). Next come disputes about lifting the automatic stay (which bars almost all collection activity upon the filing of the bankruptcy petition) and about giving "adequate protection" if the stay is not lifted. To resolve these disputes the court will have to determine whether and to what extent the person who claims to be a secured creditor is truly a "secured creditor" as that term is defined in section 506.

Quick on the heels of the stay litigation may be the DIP's attempt to "avoid" the security interest. The DIP might argue that the security interest is not perfected, it is therefore vulnerable to section 544(a) or, even if perfected, may be voided by section 547. Here too there might be questions whether this security interest is really a lease and so subject to the different rules of section 365.

Finally are the rules that determine what kind of plan can be proposed and approved under section 1129. Although almost all confirmed plans result from the agreement of all of the interested parties, these agreements are bargained in the shadow of 1129 et al. To be well armed for that negotiation, the lawyer must understand what 1129 and its supporting sections give and what they withhold.

§ 2. WHO IS SECURED IN BANKRUPTCY, SECTION 506

In a Commercial Transactions course everyone who has a security interest is a "secured creditor"—even if the collateral is of little or no value. In bankruptcy one is a "secured creditor" only "to the extent of the value of such creditor's interest in the estate's interest in such property * * *." That means the parties must agree or the court must determine the *value* of the collateral that is claimed by the secured creditor. If the creditor has a $10 million claim secured by a perfected security interest on an asset worth $100,000, the creditor is an unsecured creditor for $9,900,000 and a secured creditor under section 506 only for $100,000. As we will see, sometimes it is in the creditor's interest to argue that its collateral is declining in value and has a value lower than the amount of its debt (in order to have the stay lifted), but in other times to argue that its collateral has a high value (to justify a large payment as part of a confirmed plan).

The following case illustrates the practical and strategic application of Section 506.

WINTHROP OLD FARM NURSERIES, INC. v. NEW BEDFORD INSTITUTION FOR SAVINGS

United States Court of Appeals, First Circuit, 1995.
50 F.3d 72.

STAHL, CIRCUIT JUDGE:

Chapter 11 debtor Winthrop Old Farm Nurseries, Inc. ("Winthrop"), appeals the district court order affirming the bankruptcy court's decision that, to determine the status of the claim of undersecured junior mortgagee New Bedford Institution for Savings ("NBIS") pursuant to 11 U.S.C. § 506(a), Winthrop's real property (the "Property") should be valued at its fair market value. We affirm.

I. BACKGROUND

Winthrop operates a retail garden shop and commercial landscaping business on the Property, located at 462 Winthrop Street in Rehoboth, Massachusetts. On February 2, 1993, Winthrop filed a petition for relief under Chapter 11 of the Bankruptcy Code (the "Code"). On July 16, 1993, Winthrop filed its Disclosure Statement and Plan of Reorganization (the "Plan"). The Plan provides that Winthrop will retain all of its assets except for the Property, which is to be transferred to a new entity apparently controlled by Winthrop's principal, which will in turn lease it back to Winthrop. Thus, under the Plan, Winthrop effectively retains control of the Property and its use.

The Property is encumbered by a first mortgage in the amount of $287,000 held by Northeast Savings, F.A., and by tax liens of approximately $20,000. NBIS, the holder of a junior mortgage on the Property, is owed approximately $576,000. The parties stipulated to a liquidation value for the Property of $300,000 and a fair market value of $400,000. Winthrop's Plan would transfer the Property to the new entity free and clear of all liens except for the Northeast Savings mortgage. The Plan would "strip down" the NBIS mortgage to the liquidation value of the Property, leaving NBIS's claim entirely unsecured. The Plan proposes a payout of twenty cents on the dollar over a four-year period to unsecured creditors, whose claims, including NBIS's, total approximately $756,761.

NBIS objected to the Plan, claiming that the Property should be valued at fair market value, not liquidation value. If the Property is valued at fair market value, NBIS would have a secured claim in the amount of approximately $100,000, with the remainder of its claim unsecured.

The bankruptcy court, citing a line of cases holding that fair market or going concern value is the appropriate standard in valuing collateral that a Chapter 11 debtor proposes to retain and use, granted NBIS's motion and valued the Property at $400,000. The district court affirmed, and Winthrop now appeals.

* * *

III. Discussion

Section 506(a) governs the determination of whether any portion of a creditor's claim should be classified as a secured claim:

(a) An allowed claim of a creditor secured by a lien on property in which the estate has an interest, or that is subject to setoff under section 553 of this title, is a secured claim to the extent of the value of such creditor's interest in the estate's interest in such property, or to the extent of the amount subject to setoff, as the case may be, and is an unsecured claim to the extent that the value of such creditor's interest or the amount so subject to setoff is less than the amount of such allowed claim. Such value shall be determined in light of the purpose of the valuation and of the proposed disposition or use of such property, and in conjunction with any hearing on such disposition or use or on a plan affecting such creditor's interest. 11 U.S.C. § 506(a) (emphasis added). The statute does not direct courts to choose any particular valuation standard in a given type of case. As evidenced by the emphasized language in the statute's second sentence, Congress apparently did not intend that courts would use either a liquidation or fair market value standard exclusively, envisioning instead a flexible approach by which courts would choose a standard to fit the circumstances. Relevant legislative history buttresses this notion. The House Report states:

Subsection (a) of [§ 506] separates an undersecured creditor's claim into two parts—he has a secured claim to the extent of the value of his collateral; he has an undersecured claim for the balance of his claim. "Value" does not necessarily contemplate forced sale or liquidation value of the collateral; nor does it imply a full going concern value. Courts will have to determine value on a case-by-case basis, taking into account the facts of each case and the competing interests in the case. H.R.Rep. No. 595, 95th Cong., 1st Sess. 356 (1977), reprinted in 1978 U.S.C.C.A.N. 5787, 6312 (emphasis added).

The Senate Report's commentary on 506 offers little insight, but its commentary on 361—the Code section that provides for adequate protection payments to secured creditors in some circumstances—is further evidence that Congress intended that courts would sometimes value collateral at something greater than its liquidation price:

Neither is it expected that the courts will construe the term value to mean, in every case, forced sale liquidation value or full going concern value. There is wide latitude between those two extremes although forced sale liquidation value will be a minimum.

In any particular case, especially a reorganization case, the determination of which entity should be entitled to the difference between the going concern value and the liquidation value must be based on equitable considerations arising from the facts of the case. S.Rep. No. 989, 95th Cong., 2d Sess. 54 (1978), reprinted in 1978 U.S.C.C.A.N. 5787, 5840 (emphasis added).

Although this commentary is not specifically addressed to § 506(a), it is nevertheless relevant, since a valuation for § 361 purposes necessarily looks to § 506(a) for a determination of the amount of a secured claim.[1] Indeed, since adequate protection payments immediately deplete the estate's assets—even before it is certain that a reorganization plan will be confirmed—one would expect that the valuation standard used to determine whether such payments are justified should be extremely conservative. See In re Case, 115 B.R. 666, 670 (9th Cir.BAP 1990) (stating in dictum that in a valuation for adequate protection purposes, "forced liquidation would be assumed and a deduction for selling costs would be logical"). Nevertheless, the Senate language suggests that even in a § 361 context, a court might value collateral at something more than its liquidation value.

We have not previously considered this issue. A number of courts, however, including four Circuit Courts, have adhered to this clear expression of congressional intent and declined to value collateral that a debtor proposes to retain based on a hypothetical foreclosure sale. These courts reason that because the reorganizing debtor proposes to retain and use the collateral, it should not be valued as if it were being liquidated; rather, courts should value the collateral "in light of" the debtor's proposal to retain it and ascribe to it its going-concern or fair market value with no deduction for hypothetical costs of sale.

Other courts, however, have chosen to read § 506(a) as requiring in virtually all cases a valuation of collateral limited to the net amount a secured creditor could recover if it seized or foreclosed on the collateral

---

1. See United Sav. Ass'n of Tex. v. Timbers of Inwood Forest Assoc., 484 U.S. 365, 371–72, 108 S.Ct. 626, 630–31, 98 L.Ed.2d 740 (1988) (stating that statutory construction is a "holistic endeavor" and defining value of "entity's interest in property" entitled to adequate protection under §§ 361 and 362 in light of meaning of value of "creditor's interest" in property under § 506(a)).

and disposed of it in accordance with applicable state law. These courts tie their interpretation to the first sentence of § 506(a), reasoning that even if the debtor proposes to retain and make profitable use of the collateral in the reorganized enterprise, the statute commands a valuation of the "creditor's interest" in the property—i.e., of the lien—and that value can only reflect what the creditor would be entitled to recover from the collateral under non-bankruptcy law. Thus, if the collateral is subject to the Uniform Commercial Code, the creditor's interest would reflect what it could recover from a commercially reasonable sale under the U.C.C.; if real estate, then from a foreclosure sale, perhaps with some value added if the creditor has the right and the wherewithal to bid-in, hold and resell the property on the open market. See, e.g., In re Tenney Village Co., 104 B.R. 562, 567 (Bankr.D.N.H.1989) (valuing property at fair market value because mortgage holder had ability to bid in and obtain fair market value through later private sales); In re Robbins, 119 B.R. 1, 5–6 (Bankr.D.Mass.1990) (recognizing second mortgage holder's bid-in rights but declining to ascribe any value to them where circumstances make it "unreasonable to expect" creditor to exercise them); see generally James F. Queenan, Jr., Standards for Valuation of Security Interests in Chapter 11, 92 Com.L.J. 18, 60 (1987) (real estate mortgage holder's bid-in rights "should be valued as an inherent part of his property interest").

We are persuaded that the first line of cases correctly interprets the statute. This interpretation gives meaning to both sentences of § 506(a), and enables bankruptcy courts to exercise the flexibility Congress intended. By retaining collateral, a Chapter 11 debtor is ensuring that the very event Winthrop proposes to use to value the property—a foreclosure sale—will not take place. At the same time, the debtor should not be heard to argue that, in valuing the collateral, the court should disregard the very event that, according to the debtor's plan, will take place—namely, the debtor's use of the collateral to generate an income stream. In ordinary circumstances the present value of the income stream would be equal to the collateral's fair market value. Under such circumstances, a court remains faithful to the dictates of § 506(a) by valuing the creditor's interest in the collateral in light of the proposed post-bankruptcy reality: no foreclosure sale and economic benefit for the debtor derived from the collateral equal to or greater than its fair market value. Our approach allows the bankruptcy court, using its informed discretion and applying historic principles of equity, to adopt in each case the valuation method that is fairest given the prevailing circumstances.

The interpretation championed by the second line of cases renders the second sentence of § 506(a) virtually meaningless. Moreover, it would allow a reorganizing debtor to reap a windfall by stripping down the lien to liquidation value and quickly selling the collateral at fair market value, thus pocketing equity that would have been completely beyond reach save for the filing of the bankruptcy petition. Cf. Butner v. United States, 440 U.S. 48, 55, 99 S.Ct. 914, 918, 59 L.Ed.2d 136 (1979) (bankruptcy law should "prevent a party from receiving a windfall merely by reason of the happenstance of bankruptcy") (quotation omitted). It is true that the debtor's intention to reorganize under Chapter 11 is what gives the collateral its going-concern value. And while it is also true that, absent a reorganization plan, the creditor might not recover the difference—assuming that there is in fact a difference—between the collateral's fair market value and the amount recoverable through its state law rights, we would not characterize this additional recovery as a "windfall" to the creditor, and certainly not one that will spur secured creditors to eschew their state law remedies and seek refuge in the comfortable confines of the bankruptcy courts.

We find that the bankruptcy court correctly interpreted 506(a) as according it flexibility in choosing among possible standards of valuation, and properly applied the statute to the particular facts of this case. Winthrop proposes in its Plan to retain control of the Property and continue using it in its nursery and landscaping business to generate income. In light of this proposed use, the bankruptcy court committed no error in valuing the Property at its stipulated fair market value.

For the foregoing reasons, the order of the district court is Affirmed.

Problem 7–1

What is the consequence of a finding that the collateral is worth $400,000:

1. for the purpose of 362?

2. for the purpose of 1129(a)(7)?

§ 3. THE STAY, SECTION 362

The automatic stay applies to all creditors not just to secured creditors but here we consider only secured creditors. Mostly it means no repossession, no set off, and no disposition of assets already under the secured creditor's control. Of course, the stay also stops any judicial action to collect.

In most cases the fighting issues between the debtor and the creditor will not concern the stay itself, but the creditor's request that the stay be lifted or that the creditor be given "adequate protection" of its security interest.

In practice, quarrels over the stay might come early (halting pre-bankruptcy creditor collection activity) or later (protecting the DIP's possession of business assets during the bankruptcy). During the latter stage, sections 361–363 become windows through which the court observes the DIP's use of assets, particularly when creditors seek the return or sale of those assets.

Prior to the 1978 Code, the debtor's ability to modify the rights of secured lenders under Chapter XI was limited and uncertain. Chapter 11 and the rest of the 1978 Code changed that by giving the DIP weapons to offset secured creditors' rights. But what policy is served by putting the secured lender at the mercy of the DIP and the bankruptcy judge? If the creditor loses value through delay alone, does someone else enjoy a comparable offsetting benefit? And if the stay is lifted too readily, how will a reorganization be possible? These questions lie behind decisions on lifting the stay.

Subsection 362(d)(1) orders relief from the stay "for cause, including a lack of adequate protection of the creditor's interest in property * * * ". So the creditor's first choice often is to have the stay lifted. The creditor's fallback may be to seek "adequate protection" under section 361. Examine this subsection. Relief under this provision for lack of adequate protection runs only to parties holding an "interest in property" that is inadequately safeguarded by the debtor in possession. An unsecured creditor gets no adequate protection here since it holds no interest in property.

The need for adequate protection stems in part from Fifth Amendment prohibitions on taking property without just compensation, but a more important reason is the belief that the bargain of the secured lender should be recognized in bankruptcy except where some more powerful policy overrides. Yet in bankruptcy "giving a secured creditor an absolute right to his bargain may be impossible or severely detrimental * * * , the purpose of [section 362] is to ensure that the secured creditor receives in value essentially what he bargains for". Weintraub & Resnick, *Puncturing the Equity Cushion—Adequate Protection for Secured Creditors in Reorganization Cases*, 14 UCC L.J. 284, 285 (1982).

Subsection 362(d)(1) requires adequate protection of the "value" of the creditor's interest in the property. But how is "value" defined? *Old Farm Nurseries* gives a partial answer. Does it include the value of the lost opportunity to sell promptly and reinvest? Whether section 361 value includes the right to be compensated for such lost opportunity cost was a grand bankruptcy controversy until 1988 when the Supreme Court decided United Savings Association of Texas v. Timbers of Inwood Forest Associates, Ltd., 484 U.S. 365, 108 S.Ct. 626, 98 L.Ed.2d 740 (1988).

To understand the issue, assume a creditor with a mortgage debt of $1 million secured by an asset worth $800,000. Under state law, the creditor would have been able to complete its foreclosure and sell the property on January 1, 1987. If the debtor files a petition in bankruptcy in December of 1986 and no plan was confirmed until the end of 1989, the creditor will have been deprived of interest on the value of the collateral ($800,000) for three years by comparison to results under state law. In effect, the creditor has lost the opportunity to reinvest the $800,000 and earn a return on it. Some courts regarded this lost income as part of the value to be protected under sections 361 and 362; others did not.

In *Timbers*, the Supreme Court held that its lost opportunity cost was not covered as part of the 362(d)(1) and 361 value. So, the debtor is not required to pay interest nor to protect the creditor's right to interest on the $800,000 in our case. Only the creditor's right to receive its

$800,000 is protected. (Note that section 506(b) grants lost opportunity costs to creditors who are "oversecured", i.e., to the extent that the collateral's value exceeds the amount of the debt at the filing.)

Decisions such as *Timbers* show which interests of a creditor are protected, but they leave open the issue how that protection will be provided. Section 361 states three ways adequate protection might be provided to a creditor. These three illustrations are not exhaustive; the possibilities are limitless.

First, adequate protection may be provided by periodic cash payments. This method, outlined in 361(1), is occasionally used to provide payments that offset depreciation in the value of collateral. But cash payments are not the debtor's favored method; some debtors will not have sufficient cash to make payments. Even if cash is available, every debtor would prefer to have the discretion to use whatever cash is available in other continuing business operations.

The second method, stated in subsection (2), authorizes the debtor in possession to grant security in other property in the form of a replacement lien to the extent that the stay "results in a decrease in the value of [the creditor's] interest" in the collateral. This too seems a plausible method of giving adequate protection, but in practice it also has drawbacks. Many who enter Chapter 11 will have long since granted a security interest in everything of value.

Subsection (3) of 361 is taken from an opinion of Judge Learned Hand, In re Murel Holding Corp., 75 F.2d 941 (2d Cir.1935). It provides for adequate protection through any other relief that will result "in the realization by such entity of the *indubitable equivalent* of such entity's interest in such property". The term "indubitable equivalent" was seldom used in judicial opinions or legislation until the adoption of the 1978 Code and its meaning continues to be mysterious.

The various provisions for adequate protection have one thing in common; they balance the interests of the bankrupt estate and the debtor in possession in continuing to use important property against the financial interest of the secured creditor. A fully secured creditor wants its asset; a DIP wants to use the asset to raise revenue. After *Timbers*, the secured creditor will usually suffer some uncompensated economic loss due to the delay in retaking its collateral. Adequate protection recognizes that the creditor has a protected interest in being adequately (if not completely) protected.

To understand the options actually used by debtors, one needs to make a basic distinction in treatment between an undersecured creditor and an oversecured creditor who holds an "equity cushion". An "equity cushion" exists when the collateral's appraised value exceeds the creditor's claim.

In addition to the hope that the stay will be lifted or that the court will order adequate protection, there are strategic reasons to ask for adequate protection. If the secured creditor asks for adequate protection and is turned down because it is already adequately protected or, if the additional protection given turns out *not* to be adequate, section 507(b) elevates the (now unsecured) claim to the first rank of priority claims to be paid according to the priority rules in section 507, ahead of other unsecured creditors.

ORIX CREDIT ALLIANCE, INC. v. DELTA RESOURCES, INC.

United States Court of Appeals, Eleventh Circuit, 1995.
54 F.3d 722.

EDMONDSON and CARNES, CIRCUIT JUDGES, and MOYE, SENIOR DISTRICT JUDGE:

PER CURIAM:

Delta Resources, Inc., ("Delta") appeals the district court's order requiring payment of post-petition interest as part of the adequate protection it was required to pay as debtor-in-possession to appellee, Orix Credit Alliance Inc. ("Orix"). We reverse.

I. FACTS AND PROCEDURAL BACKGROUND

On November 30, 1992, appellant Delta filed a voluntary petition under Chapter 11 of the Bankruptcy Code, 11 U.S.C. § 101 et seq., in the United States Bankruptcy Court for the Northern District of Alabama. On December 29, 1992, appellee Orix, claiming to be an oversecured creditor, moved for relief from the automatic stay, pursuant to 11 U.S.C. § 362, on the ground that, inter alia, its perfected security interest in the purchase money equipment was not adequately protected.

At the final hearing before the bankruptcy court the parties agreed that the then-value of the collateral, approximately 13 pieces of heavy equipment, was $643,500. The bankruptcy court concluded that the collateral was slightly depreciating but did not find whether Orix in fact was an oversecured creditor. Instead, the court merely assumed, as Orix had asserted, that Orix was an oversecured creditor.

The bankruptcy court determined that the equipment at issue was necessary to the effective reorganization of the debtor and thus, under 11 U.S.C. § 362(d)(2), Orix could not receive relief from the automatic stay.[1] However, the bankruptcy court did not determine whether the creditor was entitled to postpetition interest reasoning that that issue

---

1. "On request of a party in interest and after notice and a hearing, the court shall grant relief from the stay provided under subsection (a) of this section, such as by terminating, annulling, modifying, or conditioning such stay?

(1) for cause, including the lack of adequate protection of an interest in property of such party in interest; or

(2) with respect to a stay of an act against property under subsection (a) of this section, if—

(A) the debtor does not have an equity in such property; and

(B) such property is not necessary to an effective reorganization."

11 U.S.C. §§ 362(d)(1) and (2)(A) and (B) (emphasis added).

should be dealt with at the time of confirmation of the debtor's Chapter 11 plan.

The bankruptcy court also determined that Orix's secured interest in its collateral would be adequately protected by periodic cash payments in accordance with 11 U.S.C. § 361(1). The bankruptcy court granted Orix adequate protection in the amount of $9,972.41 per month to cover accruing depreciation of the equipment, but rejected Orix's contention that as an oversecured creditor it was entitled to receive postpetition interest as part of adequate protection. Accordingly, the bankruptcy court denied Orix's motion for relief from stay.

On April 26, 1993, Orix filed a notice of appeal to the district court from the bankruptcy court's order denying relief from the automatic stay. Orix also filed a motion for leave to appeal.

After Delta failed to pay the first required adequate protection payment, Orix filed a motion to compel payment which the bankruptcy court denied on April 19, 1993. Orix then filed a notice of appeal to the district court from the bankruptcy court's denial of its motion to compel payment. Once again, Orix filed a motion for leave to appeal. Thereafter, Delta filed a motion to stay the briefing schedule and objected to the appeals as premature and thus not properly before the district court.

* * *

On October 19, 1993, the district court entered a "final order" reversing the bankruptcy court. Extending the holding of United Sav. Ass'n v. Timbers of Inwood Forest Assocs., Ltd., 484 U.S. 365, 108 S.Ct. 626, 98 L.Ed.2d 740 (1988), the district court determined that an oversecured creditor is entitled to postpetition interest as part of adequate protection. The district court found that Delta should retroactively pay to Orix monthly adequate protection payments consisting of $9,972.41 for the monthly depreciation of its collateral, as well as an additional amount of $8,292.90 in postpetition interest to maintain its equity cushion. The district court remanded the case to the bankruptcy court directing that Delta pay that amount to Orix retroactive to March 17, 1993, the date of the bankruptcy court's order from the bench denying relief from stay but ordering adequate protection. Delta filed a notice of appeal challenging the district court's reversal of the bankruptcy court's orders. There is no certification under 28 U.S.C. § 1292(b).

* * *

C. Adequate Protection

The question before us is not whether an oversecured creditor whose collateral is worth more than the amount of its debt in a Chapter 11 bankruptcy case may obtain postpetition interest as part of its claim. Indeed, it seems beyond peradventure that a creditor's right to recover postpetition interest on its oversecured claim pursuant to 11 U.S.C. § 506(b) is virtually "unqualified." United States v. Ron Pair Enters., Inc., 489 U.S. 235, 241, 109 S.Ct. 1026, 1030, 103 L.Ed.2d 290, 298

(1989). Equitable Life Assurance Soc'y v. Sublett (In re Sublett), 895 F.2d 1381 (11th Cir.1990). Cf. Rake v. Wade, 508 U.S. 464, 113 S.Ct. 2187, 124 L.Ed.2d 424 (1993) (oversecured claimant entitled to preconfirmation and postconfirmation interest on arrearages in Chapter 13 cases). Rather, the narrow legal issue presented for decision is whether Orix, purportedly an oversecured creditor, was entitled to receive periodic cash payments for accruing postpetition interest as part of adequate protection, pursuant to 11 U.S.C. § 362(d)(1), in order to preserve the value of its equity cushion. Appellant Delta does not dispute that an oversecured creditor is entitled to postpetition interest on its claim, although, Delta does dispute whether Orix was, in fact, an oversecured creditor.

* * *

Appellee Orix asserts that as interest accrues on its claim the interest by the terms of its contract also becomes secured by its security interest in Delta's assets. Therefore, Orix contends, an oversecured creditor's position erodes by the accrual of postpetition interest and ultimately the adequate protection becomes inadequate. That is, unless the interest is paid, Orix's debt becomes less and less oversecured and eventually becomes undersecured. While Orix is correct that the size of the equity cushion decreases as postpetition interest accrues, the increase in the size of its secured claim resulting from the accrual of that interest is entitled to adequate protection only to the extent that the value of the collateral at the time of filing exceeded the value of Orix's original secured claim.

* * *

Similarly, we conclude that 11 U.S.C. § 506(b), providing for postpetition interest on oversecured claims, read in pari materia with 11 U.S.C. § 362(d)(1), concerning conditioning the automatic stay on adequate protection, and 11 U.S.C. § 502, regarding the allowance of claims, requires that the payment of accrued postpetition interest to an oversecured creditor await the completion of reorganization or confirmation of the bankruptcy case. The ratio decidendi enunciated by the Supreme Court in Timbers that an undersecured creditor is not entitled to receive postpetition interest on its collateral during the stay to assure adequate protection under 11 U.S.C. § 362(d)(1) applies equally well to an oversecured creditor. Such an interpretation of the Bankruptcy Code is consistent whether the secured creditor is undersecured or oversecured, otherwise "§ 506(b) would simply have said that the secured creditor [whether oversecured or undersecured] is entitled to interest 'on his allowed claim, or on the value of the property securing his allowed claim, whichever is lesser.' "Timbers, 484 U.S. at 372–73, 108 S.Ct. at 631, 98 L.Ed.2d at 749 (emphasis added). Accordingly, viewing the allowance of postpetition interest to oversecured creditors as a limited exception only,[2] we hold that an oversecured creditor's interest

2. See, Niall L. O'Toole, Adequate Protection and Postpetition Interest in Chapter 11 Proceedings, 56 Am.Bank.L.J. 251 (1982).

in property which must be adequately protected encompasses the decline in the value of the collateral only, rather than perpetuating the ratio of the collateral to the debt. The bankruptcy court accomplished that by allowing adequate protection in the amount of accruing depreciation. See In re Westchase I Assoc., 126 B.R. 692 (W.D.N.C.1991); David G. Epstein et al., Bankruptcy § 3–27, at 142–43 (1993).

We think this rule results in the appropriate balance between the conflicting interests of the oversecured creditor on the one hand and the estate, as well as other creditors, secured and unsecured, on the other hand. As one commentator points out:

> [t]here is certainly no reason intrinsic to the phenomenon of credit that entitles over-secured creditors to interest out of their collateral before junior creditors, whether secured [perhaps by the identical collateral] or unsecured, receive any of their principal. Niall L. O'Toole, Adequate Protection and Postpetition Interest in Chapter 11 Proceedings, 56 Am.Bank.L.J. 251, 253 (1982).

Here, even accepting the bankruptcy court's assumption that Orix was an oversecured creditor, although it never made such a factual finding, for the reasons stated above, Orix, as a matter of law, was not entitled to receive periodic payments for accruing postpetition interest as part of adequate protection for any period of time.

The district court's order awarding Orix monthly postpetition interest in the amount of $8,292.90 is REVERSED and this case REMANDED to the district court for further proceedings not inconsistent herewith.

Problem 7–2

In the Orix case the debtor apparently failed to pay even the first payment. That failure resulted in the suit which caused the appeal. If you are the lawyer for Orix, how would you minimize the possibility that your debtor could default and then force you to litigate with him (an expensive proposition by the time you are done appealing to the 11th circuit)?

Problem 7–3

Assume that Orix's debt was $500,000 at the outset of the bankruptcy case and the value of the collateral was then $643,500. Assume also that the debtor made five monthly payments of $9,972.41 (totaling $49,862.05) before the property was sold by the trustee.

1. If the property were sold for $700,000 what part would go to Orix?

2. If the property were sold for $500,000 what would be the answer?

FINANCIAL SECURITY ASSURANCE INC. v. T–H NEW ORLEANS LIMITED PARTNERSHIP

United States Court of Appeals, Fifth Circuit, 1997.
116 F.3d 790.

PARKER, CIRCUIT JUDGE:

This Court visits this case for a second time.[1] The Appellant, Financial Security Assurance, Inc. ("FSA"), appeals the bankruptcy court's ruling that it was not entitled to post-petition preconfirmation interest from the petition date notwithstanding FSA's over-collateralization at confirmation; the value assigned to the collateral; the appropriate confirmation interest rate; and confirmation of the bankrupt's Chapter 11 plan. On appeal, FSA asserts a myriad of errors by the bankruptcy court. T–H New Orleans Limited Partnership ("T–H NOLP") asserts two cross-issues. Finding no reversible error, we affirm.

FACTS AND PROCEDURAL HISTORY

In June of 1988, T–H NOLP acquired a Days Inn Hotel (the "Hotel") in New Orleans, Louisiana and has operated the Hotel continuously since that date. T–H NOLP is a limited partnership with a corporate general partner, Tollman–Hundley New Orleans Corp., and five individual limited partners. The day-to-day management and operations of the Hotel property are carried out by the individuals employed by T–H NOLP. T–H NOLP is also a member of the Tollman–Hundley Hotels group of companies.

In February 1989, T–H NOLP sought to restructure the under-lying mortgage debt on the Hotel through a mortgage bond financing transaction involving T–H NOLP and six other hotels owned by separate Tollman–Hundley partnerships. As part of the refinancing, T–H NOLP and the six other hotel partnerships, all controlled by Monty Hundley and Stanley Tollman, obtained separate but cross-collateralized and cross-guaranteed first mortgage loans, which were secured by the Hotel and other hotels as well as the revenues generated therefrom, in the amount of $87,000,000 from a newly created business trust (the "Issuer"). T–H NOLP executed various agreements including a Mortgage Note and Loan Agreement, and a Collateral Mortgage Note.

To raise the necessary money to make the mortgage loans to T–H NOLP and the other hotels, the Issuer issued $87,000,000 in bonds, the payment of which was guaranteed by a surety bond issued by FSA. In return, the Issuer of the bonds assigned to FSA all its rights and interest in the security agreements, and authorized FSA to be its attorney-in-fact in order to take whatever actions FSA deemed necessary to exercise its rights under the mortgage loans and related collateral.

---

1. This Court has already heard a previous appeal between the two parties to this appeal. See In re T–H New Orleans Ltd. Partnership, 10 F.3d 1099 (5th Cir.1993) ("T–H NOLP I").

By 1990, T–H NOLP and the six other partnerships were in default on the loans, and FSA stepped into the shoes of the bond Issuer. After the parties were unable to reach a settlement, FSA accelerated the mortgage note and demanded payment of all amounts due under the loan agreement and guarantee. On February 25, 1991, T–H NOLP filed for bankruptcy under Chapter 11 of the Bankruptcy Code; the other six hotel partnerships also filed for bankruptcy. At the time T–H NOLP filed bankruptcy, FSA's allowed claim was $18.424 million.

Subsequent to the bankruptcy filing, FSA filed a motion for adequate protection or segregation of hotel receipts. The bankruptcy court granted FSA's motion, finding that it had a security interest in the Hotel's prepetition and postpetition revenues from its operations, and ordered that the Hotel's business revenues be segregated. The bankruptcy court also entered a cash collateral order (dated May 1, 1992) which provided that T–H NOLP make payments from the Hotel's net revenues in order to reduce its obligation to FSA.

On appeal, this Court in In re T–H New Orleans Limited Partnership, 10 F.3d 1099 (5th Cir.1993) ("T–H NOLP I") held that T–H NOLP's postpetition Hotel revenues were "rents" under Louisiana law and, therefore, were subject to FSA's prepetition security agreement under § 552(b) of the Bankruptcy Code and must be segregated. The Court remanded the case with instructions for further proceedings consistent with its opinion.

On February 24, 1994 T–H NOLP filed its amended disclosure statement and amended plan of reorganization. The bankruptcy court approved the amended disclosure statement in June 1994. On July 15, 1994, FSA filed an objection to plan confirmation, and T–H NOLP filed an objection to FSA's claim.

The bankruptcy court, early in the case, found that the appraised value of the Hotel was $12.2 million; this valuation was based upon an appraisal report as of July 1, 1991 which was commissioned by FSA. FSA's motion for adequate protection was based upon this appraised value. Subsequently, the bankruptcy court held a hearing to determine the fair value of the Hotel and found, after considering the evidence presented by T–H NOLP and FSA, that, as of July 14, 1994, the fair value of the Hotel was $13.7 million.[2] Accordingly, the bankruptcy court found that the value of FSA's security interest in the Hotel was $13.7 million. The bankruptcy court also found that based on the uncontroverted testimony, the fair value of the Hotel would increase over the 2 year period following confirmation of T–H NOLP's proposed amended plan.

---

2. FSA provided an appraisal valuing the Hotel at a greater value. However, that appraisal did not include adjustments for a yearly corporate overhead allocation which the bankruptcy court found, based on the evidence presented, to be a necessary expense and should be accounted for in determining the fair value of the Hotel. FSA's appraiser testified that if the corporate overhead allocation charge was considered, his opinion as to the appraised value of the Hotel would decrease by the amount of the allocation and the Hotel's fair value would be $13.7 million.

The bankruptcy court also held a hearing on FSA's allowed claim. FSA stipulated for purposes of the confirmation hearing that its allowed claim as of the petition date was $18,424,000. T–H NOLP presented evidence showing that it had made postpetition cash collateral payments of $4,675,945 through the end of September, 1994.[3] Thus, the bankruptcy court, after accounting for the postpetition rent payments (pursuant to the May 1, 1992 cash collateral order) on FSA's claim and not including any potential entitlement to postpetition preconfirmation interest, found that FSA's claim amounted to $13,748,055 as of September 30, 1994.[4]

The bankruptcy court therefore found that because FSA's claim of $13,748,055 was greater than the fair value of the Hotel ($13.7 million), thus making FSA's claim undersecured, FSA was not entitled to postpetition, preconfirmation interest on its claim under § 506(b) of the Bankruptcy Code until the time when the value of its collateral exceeded the amount of its claim. At that point, FSA would be entitled to interest at the contract rate on its claim to the extent that the value of the collateral exceeds its allowed claim, i.e. the equity cushion, and that any postpetition interest was limited to the equity cushion created by the monthly accrual of net rents generated by the Hotel.

Finally, with respect to T–H NOLP's amended plan of reorganization (the "Plan"), FSA was the only creditor to object to confirmation of the Plan and to vote to reject the amended Plan.[5] FSA argued against Plan confirmation on several grounds which are addressed in each of its issues on appeal. All other classes of creditors either voted affirmatively to accept the amended Plan or were deemed to have accepted the amended Plan. Thus, T–H NOLP sought confirmation of its amended Plan under the "cramdown" provisions of Chapter 11 of the Bankruptcy Code. Following three days of confirmation hearings, the bankruptcy court on March 27, 1995, entered an order denying Plan confirmation.[6]

3. A representative of FSA testified that FSA had received cash collateral from T–H NOLP in the amount of $4,770,666 as of September 23, 1994; however, FSA's representative failed to present any supporting evidence to support FSA's position.

4. The bankruptcy court applied the cash collateral payments against the unsecured portion of FSA's claim, following the bankruptcy court in In re 354 East 66th Street Realty Corp., 177 B.R. 776 (Bankr. E.D.N.Y.1995). In reaching its decision, the bankruptcy court analyzed the two line of cases that have addressed this issue, i.e., the addition cases and the subtraction cases. See, e.g. In re Union Meeting Partners, 178 B.R. 664 (Bankr.E.D.Pa.1995). However, we do not answer today the question of whether the bankruptcy court's reduction of the unsecured portion of FSA's claim was proper, as that issue was not raised on appeal.

5. FSA's claim was a Class 4 claim in the amended plan which was to be treated as follows: (a) reduction of FSA's claim from the prepetition amount of $18.242 million by application of postpetition, preconfirmation payments made to FSA under the bankruptcy court's May 1, 1992 cash collateral order; (b) payment of the remaining amount of the FSA claim through twenty-four monthly payments of principal and post-confirmation interest, based on a twenty-year principal amortization at 8% interest or such other cramdown rate approved by the bankruptcy court, with a balloon payment of all remaining principal and interest at the end of two years; and (c) payment of the remaining balance, after application of all prior payments, in one of three ways (1) refinancing with another lender; (2) sale of the Hotel; or (3) a dation en paiement transferring ownership of the Hotel.

6. The bankruptcy court denied plan confirmation based on language in Section

On March 30, 1995, the bankruptcy court entered an order confirming T–H NOLP's amended Plan under the cramdown provisions of Chapter 11. The bankruptcy court also determined that the proper postconfirmation interest rate was 11.5 percent. On June 27, 1995, the bankruptcy court denied FSA's motion for reconsideration or new trial.

Both FSA and T–H NOLP appealed to the district court for a review of the bankruptcy court's decisions. The district court affirmed. This appeal ensued. We now address FSA's and T–H NOLP's arguments raised before this Court.

DISCUSSION

1. FSA's Entitlement to Postpetition Interest

FSA asserts that the value of the Hotel was increasing during the bankruptcy proceedings, and that its claim was decreasing due to the monthly cash collateral payments. Thus, at some point between September 1994 and the March 30, 1995 confirmation order the value of the property became greater than its claim. Therefore, FSA argues that since the collateral's value exceeded its claim on the day the Chapter 11 plan was confirmed or became effective, it was entitled to postpetition interest under § 506(b) to the extent of its contract rate for the entire postpetition period. FSA also argues that it should have been paid the postpetition interest monthly instead of at confirmation. In response, T–H NOLP relies on the bankruptcy court's conclusion, and objects to the allowance of any postpetition preconfirmation interest on FSA's claim until that point in time when the Hotel's value was greater than FSA's claim. T–H NOLP also asserts on cross-appeal that the bankruptcy court erred by requiring it to make postpetition preconfirmation interest payments while FSA appealed the bankruptcy court's order confirming T–H NOLP's Plan.

The parties' arguments raise the following questions for our consideration. First, where a secured creditor is receiving cash collateral payments which reduce the creditor's allowed claim such that at some point in time prior to plan confirmation the creditor may become oversecured, is that creditor entitled to accrue interest under § 506(b)? Second, when, under § 506(b), does interest begin to accrue, and the extent to which a creditor is entitled to postpetition interest?

There is no question that a creditor's entitlement to postpetition interest on its claim is determined under § 506(b) of the Bankruptcy Code. Section 506(b) states in relevant part that "[t]o the extent that an allowed secured claim is secured by property, the value of which * * * is greater than the amount of such claim, there shall be allowed to the holder of such claim interest on such claim * * *." 11 U.S.C. § 506(b). The United States Supreme Court in United States v. Ron Pair Enter., Inc., 489 U.S. 235, 109 S.Ct. 1026, 103 L.Ed.2d 290 (1989) made clear

X.2 of the plan which it considered overly   delete this language.
broad and ambiguous. T–H NOLP agreed to

that under § 506(b) a creditor is unqualifiedly entitled to postpetition interest on its oversecured claim. Id. at 241, 109 S.Ct. at 1030; see In re Pointer, 952 F.2d 82 (5th Cir.1992); In re Sublett, 895 F.2d 1381 (11th Cir.1990). However, § 506(b) applies only from the date of filing through the confirmation date.

Under § 506(b), the creditor's entitlement to postpetition interest is clearly predicated on the threshold establishment of the two values to be compared, that of the property and the claim. Thus, the first inquiry under § 506(b) is usually a finding of whether the creditor is oversecured and thus entitled to accrue postpetition interest on its claim. In arguing that at some point between the time the petition was filed and confirmation of the Plan, the value of the Hotel became greater than the value of FSA's claim thus entitling FSA to postpetition interest, FSA invites us to consider when valuation should occur for purposes of determining a creditor's entitlement to postpetition interest.

With respect to the first question, the parties in their argument cite this Court to United Sav. Ass'n. of Texas v. Timbers of Inwood Forest Assoc., Ltd. (In re Timbers of Inwood Forest Assoc., Ltd.), 793 F.2d 1380 (5th Cir.1986), on reh'g, 808 F.2d 363 (5th Cir.1987) (en banc court reinstating panel opinion), aff'd, 484 U.S. 365, 108 S.Ct. 626, 98 L.Ed.2d 740 (1988). In Timbers, an undersecured creditor sought postpetition interest representing lost "opportunity costs" on the amount of its secured claim under § 362(d) of the Bankruptcy Code. This Court declined the creditor's request and held that an undersecured creditor was not entitled to postpetition interest on the value of its collateral as an element of adequate protection. In reaching its ruling, the Timbers court examined other Bankruptcy Code provisions that bore "indirectly" on the question considered. In considering § 506(b) and (c), the Court noted that:

> [t]he timing of the payment of accrued interest to an oversecured creditor (at the conclusion of the proceeding) is doubtless based on the fact that it is not possible to compute the amount of § 506(c) recovery (and, accordingly the net allowed secured claim on which interest is computed) until the termination of the proceeding. Timbers, 793 F.2d at 1407. (emphasis added).

Although beneficial, this language does not answer the question we are presented with in the instant case. In addition, the Timbers Court was not confronted with the question we are presented today. We note that the creditor in Timbers was undersecured at the time of the adequate protection hearing and its appeal to this Court, and the value of the collateral was not increasing and there was no evidence that future appreciation would provide for post-petition interest.[7]

7. We also note that In re Delta Resources, Inc., 54 F.3d 722 (11th Cir.), cert. denied, sub nom. Orix Credit Alliance, Inc. v. Delta Resources, Inc., 516 U.S. 980, 116 S.Ct. 488, 133 L.Ed.2d 415 (1995), addressed the narrow issue of whether a purportedly oversecured creditor was entitled to receive periodic cash payments for accruing postpetition interest as part of adequate protection in order to preserve the value of

Under § 506, valuations are to be made in light of the purpose of the valuation. In re Landing Assoc., Ltd. 122 B.R. 288 (Bankr.W.D.Tex. 1990). We recognize that the value of a debtor's collateral and the amount of a creditor's claim are among the most important issues between the debtor and the secured claimholder. Valuation issues can arise in various contexts throughout the entire bankruptcy case. See In re Stanley, 185 B.R. 417 (Bankr.D.Conn.1995). Establishing equity, allowing claims, adequate protection, and plan confirmation are only a few examples of when the issue of valuation can be raised. Id. at 423. Neither Bankruptcy Code § 506(b) nor the Bankruptcy Rules define or establish the time for determining valuation of collateral for purposes of § 506(b). In re Fox, 142 B.R. 206 (Bankr.S.D.Ohio 1992). The legislative history to § 506(b) is also silent on this point. This Court's research has not disclosed any circuit authority which has discussed the question before us today, although we note that the lower courts that have faced this circumstance have selected a single valuation date. See, e.g., In re Hulen Park Place, Ltd., 130 B.R. 39, 43 (N.D.Tex.1991) (determining whether creditor's claim is oversecured must be determined as of the petition date); In re Landing Assoc., Ltd., 122 B.R. 288, 297 (Bankr. W.D.Tex.1990) (measurement date is confirmation date).

We decline to follow such a narrow path. Therefore, we conclude that for purposes of determining whether a creditor is entitled to accrue interest under § 506(b) in the circumstance where the collateral's value is increasing and/or the creditor's allowed claim has been or is being reduced by cash collateral payments, such that at some point in time prior to confirmation of the debtor's plan the creditor may become oversecured, valuation of the collateral and the creditor's claim should be flexible and not limited to a single point in time, such as the petition date or confirmation date. We further hold that, notwithstanding the bankruptcy court's determination of a creditor's secured status as of the petition date (if such a finding is made), the party who contends that there is a dispute as to whether a creditor is entitled to interest under § 506(b) must motion the bankruptcy court to make such a determination. The creditor though bears the ultimate burden to prove by a preponderance of evidence its entitlement to postpetition interest, that is, that its claim was oversecured, to what extent, and for what period of time. In re Grabill Corp., 121 B.R. 983, 991–92 (Bankr.N.D.Ill.1990). This ruling recognizes the discretionary nature of bankruptcy courts as courts of equity. However, bankruptcy courts are not precluded from fashioning remedies to prevent unwarranted multiple redeterminations.

its equity cushion. We are not confronted with this question.

In comparing when adequate protection is measured versus interest under § 506(b), the Delta Resources court held that a creditor's claim is measured as it existed at the time of the petition date because postpetition interest is limited to the amount by which the claim was oversecured at that time. We agree with this general proposition in the ordinary "underwater" asset case; however, in the context where the collateral is rising and the creditor's claim is decreasing (as in the present case), we find this ruling to be inappropriately narrow.

A flexible approach recognizes the fact that a creditor's allowed claim, which is being reduced over time, may become entitled to accrue postpetition interest, and that under the plain language of § 506(b) there is nothing limiting that right. See United States v. Ron Pair Enter., Inc., 489 U.S. 235, 109 S.Ct. 1026, 103 L.Ed.2d 290 (1989) (employing a plain meaning reading of § 506(b)). A flexible approach also recognizes that any increase over the judicially determined valuation during bankruptcy rightly accrues to the benefit of the creditor, and not to the debtor. Moreover, as the bankruptcy court in In re Addison Properties noted, the single valuation approach generally balances the bankruptcy process in favor of the debtor. In re Addison Properties Ltd. Partnership, 185 B.R. 766, 772 (Bankr.N.D.Ill.1995). Because of the equitable nature of bankruptcy in seeking a balance between debtors and creditors (debtor's right to a fresh start versus the creditor's right to the value of its claim), we reject the single valuation approach under the particular facts of this case.

Thus, applying this ruling to the instant case, if FSA believed that under § 506(b) it was entitled to accrue postpetition interest on its claim during the period following the confirmation hearing, then absent agreement between the parties as to the point in time when FSA's claim became oversecured, FSA was required to motion the bankruptcy court for a redetermination of its secured status. The bankruptcy court in this case was presented with the unusual fact situation where FSA's claim was being reduced and the Hotel's value was appreciating during the time from the petition date to the confirmation hearing. However, the bankruptcy court found that, for the period from the confirmation hearings to Plan confirmation, FSA's claim went from being undersecured to being oversecured and that this would probably occur in October 1994. Because the bankruptcy court made the factual finding as to when FSA would become oversecured, under the particular facts of this case we cannot say that the bankruptcy court was clearly erroneous in its decision.[8]

We next address the accrual of interest under § 506(b) and the extent to which a creditor is entitled to interest under § 506(b). We find this question to be relatively straightforward. The measuring date on which the status of a creditor's collateral and claim are compared is determinative of a creditor's right to accrue interest under § 506(b). Thus, a secured creditor's entitlement to accrue interest under § 506(b) matures at that point in time where the creditor's claim becomes oversecured.[9] However, as Timbers dictates, accrued interest under § 506(b) is not paid to an oversecured creditor until the plan's confirmation or its effective date, whichever is later. United Sav. Ass'n of Texas

---

8. We note that the bankruptcy court found that FSA "probably" would become oversecured sometime in October 1994. Although we find it to be a close question, we are persuaded that the bankruptcy court's finding is supported by the evidence in this case.

9. In the instant case, the parties agreed that FSA could accrue interest under § 506(b) when its claim became oversecured. Thus, the parties agreement comports with our reading of the law under § 506(b).

v. Timbers of Inwood Forest Assoc., Ltd. (In re Timbers of Inwood Forest Assoc., Ltd.), 793 F.2d 1380, 1381, 1407 (5th Cir.1986), on reh'g, 808 F.2d 363 (5th Cir.1987 (en banc court reinstating panel opinion)), aff'd, 484 U.S. 365, 108 S.Ct. 626, 98 L.Ed.2d 740 (1988). Thus, to the extent that the bankruptcy court's order does violence to the teachings of Timbers by ordering the payment of interest pending confirmation as opposed to ordering interest to accrue, it was error. However, because of the particular facts of this case, we are not inclined to set aside the bankruptcy court's ruling. On the effective date of the Plan's confirmation T–H NOLP would be receiving a credit for the interest paid during this time.

FSA also asserts that it was entitled to the postpetition interest that would have accrued during the entire postpetition preconfirmation period on its claim since the petition date. We disagree. The Supreme Court has made it clear that an oversecured creditor is entitled to postpetition interest on its claim only "to the extent that such interest, when added to the principal amount of the claim, [does not] exceed the value of the collateral." Timbers, 484 U.S. at 372, 108 S.Ct. at 631; see also Landmark Financial Serv. v. Hall, 918 F.2d 1150, 1155 (4th Cir.1990) (an oversecured creditor's claim may include interest up to the value of the collateral). Thus, the amount of interest allowed under § 506(b) is limited to that amount of interest which, when added to the amount of FSA's allowed claim, will not exceed the value of its collateral.

Finally, we address FSA's assertion that the bankruptcy court erred in valuing the Hotel at $13.7 million at the confirmation hearing. The Bankruptcy Code does not prescribe any particular method of valuing collateral, but instead leaves valuation questions to judges on a case-by-case basis. See House Rep. No 95–595, 95th Cong. 1st Sess. 216, 356 (1977), reprinted in 1978 U.S.S.C.A.N. 5963, 6176, 6312. Valuation is a mixed question of law and fact, the factual premises being subject to review on a clearly erroneous standard, and the legal conclusion being subject to de novo review. In re Clark Pipe & Supply Co., Inc., 893 F.2d 693, 697–98 (5th Cir.1990). Value under § 506 is to be determined in light of the purpose of the valuation and of the proposed disposition or use of the property. Associates Commercial Corp. v. Rash, 520 U.S. 953, 117 S.Ct. 1879, 1884–85, 138 L.Ed.2d 148 (1997); In re Sandy Ridge Dev. Corp., 881 F.2d 1346 (5th Cir.1989). In this particular case, valuation was made for the purpose of plan confirmation. We note that FSA's appraisal expert agreed with T–H NOLP's expert regarding the Hotel's value once FSA's appraisal incorporated the overhead allocation charge, which the bankruptcy court found to be a necessary expense. Therefore, based on our review of the record, we concluded that the bankruptcy court did not err in its valuation of the Hotel. We find FSA's remaining arguments to be without merit. * * *

§ 4. DEBTOR'S USE OF COLLATERAL, SECTION 363

Section 363 gives the DIP the right to continue to run the business the day after the bankruptcy filing in essentially the same way as it did the day before. The DIP may buy, sell, manufacture, pay salaries and do most of the other things that businesses do without a court order and under the protection of the automatic stay.

There are two important limitations. First, subsection 363(b) bars non-ordinary course uses, sales or leases without a hearing; it so forestalls unilateral business transactions that are out of the ordinary course. Second, subsection (c)(2) prohibits the use of "cash collateral" unless there is either an agreement with everyone who has an interest in the collateral or an order of the court. Subsection (a) defines cash collateral. In most cases a deposit account held with a creditor bank will be cash collateral, so the first order of business (even before the filing) will be to negotiate a cash collateral agreement with the bank that can be entered as a court order.

This of course means that a secured creditor's inventory can be sold, that a secured creditor's equipment can be damaged or otherwise reduced in value by use and that with the court's approval even non-ordinary course sales of subsidiaries and divisions may be made. So a Chapter 11 proceeding is treacherous for the secured creditor. Generally the secured creditor must watch out for its own interests by negotiating with the DIP or by asking the court for prohibitions or protection.

Problem 7–4

Kahn Craft, a manufacturer of commemorative plates, is contemplating bankruptcy. It comes to you for advice. Kahn wonders whether section 363(c)(2) will bar use of its bank accounts.

1. Kahn owed Bollinger Bank $2 million borrowed for operating expenses. Kahn's account at Bollinger Bank has a balance of $500,000. This is cash collateral even if Bollinger is unsecured. Do you see why? Kahn could avoid the restrictions of section 363(c)(2) by moving its account to a bank to whom it does not owe a debt prior to the filing, true?

2. If Kauper Bank has a security interest in proceeds from the sale of plate inventory, this would be cash collateral even if it were not deposited in an account at a non-creditor bank, true?

––––––––

Because after acquired property clauses are snuffed out by section 552, a secured creditor that is relying on a changing mass of inventory must make a deal with the DIP or get a court order. If the DIP sells the inventory and uses untraceable cash to buy new inventory or other assets, the secured creditor may find itself unsecured because of section 552(a) (unless it can trace its collateral into the new assets as "proceeds" of the old, see 552(b)). So both the DIP and the secured creditor need a "cash collateral" agreement, the former to escape the prohibition of 363(c)(2) and the latter to revive its after-acquired clause in the face of 552(a).

Look carefully at the agreement set out below. Who got what? Note well: the DIP and its principal secured creditor will not be bashful about conspiring to favor themselves at the expense of less agile creditors. Paragraphs #4 and #7 might diminish the rights of competing creditors. Look at them and think about how that might happen.

UNITED STATES BANKRUPTCY COURT, EASTERN DISTRICT OF MICHIGAN SOUTHERN DIVISION—FLINT

In the Matter of:

ACTION AUTO STORES, INC., a/k/a Action Auto, Inc.

a/k/a Sabo Corp.,

a/k/a JED Co., Lansing Lewis Services, Inc.

Debtor.

Chapter 11
Case No. 90–11710–S.

Judge Arthur J. Spector

CONSENT ORDER AUTHORIZING DEBTOR'S USE OF CASH COLLATERAL AND OTHER RELIEF PENDING FINAL HEARING

At a session of said Court held in the Federal Building, Bay City, Michigan on June 22, 1990
Present: Hon. Arthur J. Spector
United States Bankruptcy Judge

Action Auto Stores, Inc. ("Debtor"), having filed a motion (the "Motion") for authority to use the cash collateral of Michigan National Bank (hereinafter the "Bank") and Travelers Insurance Company ("Travelers"), the Court having examined the Motion, and upon completion of a preliminary hearing as provided for under Bankruptcy Rule 4001(b);

THE COURT FINDS AS FOLLOWS:

A.   On June 15, 1990 (the "Filing Date"), Debtor filed a petition under Chapter 11 of the Bankruptcy Code ("Code"). Since that time, Debtor has remained in possession of its assets and has continued to operate and manage its business as a debtor in possession pursuant to 11 U.S.C. sections 1107 and 1108.

B.   No committee of creditors holding unsecured claims (the "Committee") or any other committee has been appointed, as provided by section 1102 of the Code.

C. Prior to the Filing Date, the Bank entered into certain financing arrangements with Debtor, evidenced by, among other things, notes, loan agreements, security agreements, mortgages and other documents and writings (collectively hereinafter referred to as the "Prepetition Loan Documents").

D. According to the Bank's books as of the Filing Date, the Debtor was indebted to the Bank in the approximate amount of $24,800,000 plus interest, costs and expenses (the "Indebtedness").

E. The Bank maintains that the Prepetition Debt is secured by cash collateral pursuant to the Prepetition Loan Documents.

F. All cash, checks, refunds (including tax refunds), negotiable instruments, documents of title, deposit accounts, securities, and other cash equivalents which are now or may hereafter come into the possession, custody or control of the Debtor, constitute and will continue to constitute cash collateral of the Bank, must be segregated and accounted for, pursuant to section 363(c)(4) of the Code, and cannot be used by the Debtor in operating its business or managing its affairs, necessitating the immediate authorization of its use of cash collateral to avoid immediate and irreparable harm to the estate pending the final hearing provided for in this Order (the "Final Hearing").

G. Debtor has provided notice of this preliminary hearing and the terms of the Motion to all creditors holding secured claims of record, creditors holding the twenty largest unsecured claims (according to Debtor's Bankruptcy Rule 1007(d) filing), and the United States Trustee as set forth in a proof of service filed herein and such notice, together with the Notice procedure set forth in paragraph 9 hereof, constitutes sufficient "notice and a hearing" under 11 U.S.C. sections 102 and 363 and Bankruptcy Rules 2002, 4001 and 6007.

H. The entry of this Order is in the best interest of the estate and its creditors.

     1. Until the Final Hearing, these findings of fact shall be binding upon the Debtor only and shall not bind any other creditor or other party in interest.

Accordingly, IT IS HEREBY ORDERED as follows:

     1. Debtor is hereby authorized to use cash collateral only as described herein.

     2. Debtor may use cash collateral only to the extent that the same is necessary to avoid immediate and irreparable harm. The use of cash collateral shall be limited to those categories of items and in the amounts set forth in Schedule A. Cash collateral may not be used to pay or cure any prepetition obligations of the Debtor, including any arrearages under any lease, equipment or executory contract.

     3. To secure the Debtor's use of the Bank's cash collateral, the Debtor is, by entry of this Order, authorized to, and by virtue hereof

does hereby, grant Bank a lien in all of the Debtor's right, title and interest in all of the Debtor's property acquired on or after the Filing Date to the same extent that the same is a substitution for that existing prior to the Filing Date as set forth in the Prepetition Loan Documents.

4. To the extent that the Debtor has provided the Bank with adequate protection of the Bank's interest in the Debtor's property and the Bank's interest, notwithstanding such adequate protection, in such property is diminished, then to the extent that the same is diminished, the Bank shall be and is given by virtue of this Order an 11 USC § 507(b) BR claim to all of the property of the estate and the proceeds thereof including but not limited to, all causes of action and proceeds of causes of action of the Debtor granted to the Debtor under Chapter 5 of the Code, from which the amount of diminution shall be paid.

5. Upon entry of this Order, Bank shall receive copies of all insurance policies presently in effect showing Debtor's coverage of the Bank's interest in all of the Debtor's property.

6. Until repayment of all Indebtedness, Debtor will:

(a) Deliver to the Bank, Travelers, and Sun Refining copies of all reports and other financial information filed with the Bankruptcy Court concurrently with the filing thereof, permit the Bank to audit the books and records of Debtor at all times reasonably requested by the Bank and to make copies thereof or extracts therefrom, and permit the Bank access to the Debtor's premises at any time during normal business hours.

(b) Promptly give to the Bank, Travelers, and Sun prior written notice of:

(i) the sale or execution of a contract for sale of any property other than in the ordinary course of business as presently being conducted, which notice shall be sufficient advance notice to permit the Bank reasonable inquiry concerning the transaction; and

(ii) the occurrence of any event or any matter which has resulted or will result in a material adverse change in its business, assets, operations or financial condition.

(c) Deliver to the Bank and counsel, Travelers and counsel, and Sun Refining and its counsel concurrently with their filing copies of each pleading or report heretofore or hereafter filed with the Bankruptcy Court by the Debtor, and shall notify counsel for the Bank of any pleading received, save and except for proofs of claim, including, but not limited to, any application or motion to the Bankruptcy Court by any party in interest for the appointment of a trustee or dismissal of the Bankruptcy Case, or for a change of venue.

(d) Provide the Bank (to the attention of John June) and counsel, Travelers and counsel, Sun and its counsel with: (i) weekly statements of actual cash receipts and disbursements by the Tuesday of each week for the prior week and weekly copies of Debtor's check register by Tuesday of each week for the prior week; (ii) a profit and loss statement for the proceeding week by the Tuesday of the subsequent week (beginning June 26); (iii) inventory reports required by the Bank on a weekly basis commencing Tuesday, June 26 and by the next Tuesday for each subsequent week thereafter, (if the report is not satisfactory to the Bank, Debtor shall provide such additional information as the Bank shall reasonably request); (iv) all other documentation reasonably required by the Bank; and (v) a weekly status report in writing on efforts to sell the Debtor and its property and the prospects for any sale.

(e) Debtor shall immediately obtain and maintain during the term hereof, insurance covering all property subject to the Bank's liens to its full replacement value without deduction for depreciation. All insurance policies required pursuant to this paragraph shall be written on forms which provide no less coverage than the so-called all risk property form and shall be carried in sufficient amount so as to avoid the imposition of any co-insurance penalty in the event of a loss. All such policies of insurance shall be further endorsed to name the Bank as an additional named insured and provide a mortgagee clause in favor of the Bank.

(f) At all times comply with all laws, statutes, rules, regulations, orders and directions of any governmental authority having jurisdiction over the Debtor or its business, the violation of which would have a material adverse effect upon the Debtor.

7. Upon entry of this Order, the liens granted to the Bank by virtue of this Order shall be valid and perfected as against all third parties, without regard to applicable federal, state or local filing and recording statutes, provided, that the Bank may, but need not, take such steps as it deems appropriate to comply with such federal, state or local statutes.

8. If any or all of the provisions of this Order are hereafter modified, vacated or stayed by subsequent order of this or any other Court, such stay, modification or vacation shall not affect the validity of this Order or the validity and enforceability of any lien or priority authorized and granted hereby to the Bank, and notwithstanding such stay, modification or vacation, any authorized use of cash collateral pursuant to this Order prior to the effective date of any modification, stay or vacation, to or for the benefit of the Debtor shall be governed in all respects by the original provisions of this Order and the Bank shall be entitled to all the rights and benefits granted herein.

9.   Within two (2) business days from the date of the entry of this Order, Debtor shall serve (or cause to be served) (a) a copy of this Order on each creditor holding a secured claim of record and (b) creditors identified on the lists filed pursuant to Bankruptcy Rule 1007(d). A final hearing shall be held in Bankruptcy Court, 102A Federal Building, 600 Church Street, Flint, Michigan 48502, on July 3, 1990 at 2:30 p.m. (the "Final Hearing") to determine whether this Order shall become a final order.

10.   It is further ordered that the Debtor shall immediately supply to the Bank copies of all records and/or materials necessary to establish the amount and cost of all inventory of the Debtor as of the Filing Date which shall be completed, to the extent possible, prior to the Final Hearing.

11.   Absent an earlier termination, the Debtor is authorized to use the Bank's cash collateral, subject to the terms and conditions set forth herein, until the Final Hearing.

_____

United States Bankruptcy Judge

Counsel for Action Auto Stores, Inc.:
Robert H. Skilton
Warner, Norcross & Judd
900 Old Kent Building
111 Lyon Street, N.W.
Grand Rapids, MI 49503–2489

Counsel for Michigan National Bank:
Lawrence K. Snider/Jeffrey Chimovitz
Jaffe, Snider, Raitt & Heuer
Professional Corporation
One Woodward Ave., Suite 2400
Detroit, MI 48226

§ 5. AVOIDANCE POWERS, SECTION 544

Subsection 544(a) of the Bankruptcy Act is the DIP's "strong-arm clause". This clause gives the trustee in Chapter 7 and the DIP in Chapter 11 the rights of a lien creditor as of the date the petition is filed in a voluntary case. Review it to understand how it fits hand-in-glove with the lien creditor's rights to strike down unperfected security interests under 9–317.

Section 544(b) is more obscure. It is a direct descendant of section 70e, the section involved in the case of _In re Plonta_ infra. By reading _In re Plonta_ and applying to it the UCC and the Bankruptcy Code of 1978, see why 544(b) no longer threatens secured creditors.

The other avoidance section that merits detailed study is section 547 on preferences. It allows a trustee in bankruptcy to recapture payments and other assets that have been transferred by the debtor to a creditor prior to the filing of the petition. Two "transfers" that will concern us in this course are the grant of a security interest and the payment of a debt.

Sections 549 through 552 are adjuncts to the more significant avoidance rights of sections 544 and 547. In addition we will consider section 548, a mini-fraudulent conveyance act, and section 558 which gives to the trustee the defenses that would have been available to the debtor.

To get a grip on the basics examine the lawyer's opinion in the following problem. The lawyer is not always correct.

Problem 7–5

Assume that Gene Ovelli owns a small lumber mill that has been in financial difficulty for some months. During the current year, Ovelli has engaged in the transactions listed below.

1. January 8: Adams finances Ovelli's purchase of a $10,000 piece of equipment from Jones, charges a usurious rate of interest and acquires a security interest duly created and perfected pursuant to Article 9 and which gives Adams a veto power over all of Ovelli's future dealings with others on credit.

2. January 10: First National Bank lent Ovelli $40,000 and took Article 9 security in Ovelli's two cement mixers, but because of a slip-up, no financing statement was ever executed or filed.

3. June 11: Holt, who had lent $30,000 to Ovelli a year previous pursuant to an unsecured note, became panicky and demanded that Ovelli give him security in a caterpillar tractor that Ovelli owned free and clear. Ovelli and Holt duly executed a valid financing statement that referred to the caterpillar as "collateral" and Holt then filed it.

4. June 12: Stein who had lent $40,000 to Ovelli pursuant to a secured obligation 2 years previously, but who had never filed a financing statement, filed a financing statement on June 12.

5. April 19: Brown, who had sold several power saws to Ovelli on unsecured credit, got a judgment against Ovelli and levied on the saws which the sheriff now has in his possession pending a scheduled judicial sale.

6. January 16: Ovelli transferred title to his new and unencumbered Cadillac sedan to his wife. At different times he has described this transfer as a gift out of love and affection for his wife or as a payment for her service without pay at the lumbermill as a bookkeeper. Over the years she has done office work at the mill; she was never paid a formal salary for that work.

7. May 30: Costa, a cousin of Ovelli, lent Ovelli $50,000 pursuant to an Article 9 security interest in lumber worth $53,000 on Ovelli's premises. Costa did not, however, perfect this interest until June 7. Meanwhile, on June 5, Martin, an unsecured creditor of Ovelli (with a $20,000 claim) armed with a judgment, levied on the lumber with knowledge of Costa's interest.

8. June 28: Adams lent Ovelli $5000 pursuant to a valid and contemporaneously perfected security interest in Ovelli's only remaining unencumbered personalty, a compressor worth $7500.

Against the foregoing background, Ovelli went to his lawyer, Drake, stated that his situation seemed hopeless, and that he wanted to "take bankruptcy" and start over.

Ovelli filed a petition in bankruptcy on July 3rd. The trustee in bankruptcy for Ovelli's estate has asked a lawyer, Fraser, to serve as his attorney during the course of the proceeding. The trustee has given Fraser a memorandum recording the eight transactions described above and asked what rights the trustee has, if any, in respect to each. Fraser's comments, gratuitous and otherwise, on some of the transactions follow:

1. *Trustee v. Adams.* Under section 558 the estate has the defenses of the debtor. Among those would be a claim in this case that the contract was usurious and arguably unconscionable.

2. *Trustee v. First National Bank.* This one we will challenge under section 544(a). It is a classic non-perfection lien creditor situation in which the trustee beats the unperfected secured creditor by asserting the rights of a lien creditor under sections 9–317 and 544.

3. *Trustee v. Holt.* This is a classic section 547 case.

4. *Trustee v. Adams and Stein.* This too is a preference; or did the "transfer" occur before the 90 day term?

5. *Trustee v. Brown.* This one could have been challenged under the old section 67(a) that struck down almost all judicial liens that arose within four months of bankruptcy. I don't see a provision identical to that one in the 1978 Code; there must be one though.

6. *Trustee v. Mrs. Ovelli.* We should consider the use of section 548, but we may have difficulty in proving a case under section 548 since she gave value by working. I think I will ask my associate if there are other bases upon which we could attack this transfer. What do you think?

7. *Trustee v. Costa and Martin.* We have lots of possibilities here it would seem. First I think we could strike Martin's claim down under section 547. Section 547 does not seem to help us against Costa because he perfected within 10 days. What about the possibility of subrogating ourselves to Martin's claim under section 544(b) directly? I wonder if the reference in section 544(b) to subrogation only to a creditor "holding an unsecured claim" deprives us of that right? Conceivably we can reassert Martin's claim under section 551, having struck it down, but does that mean we can unseat Ovelli only to the extent of $20,000?

8. *Trustee v. Adams.* I am tired, I will let the students work this one out.

Consider section 544(b) in connection with the following case.

IN RE PLONTA

United States Court of Appeals, Sixth Circuit, 1962.
311 F.2d 44.

CECIL, CHIEF JUDGE:

This is an appeal from the United States District Court for the Western District of Michigan, Southern Division. The controversy grows out of the bankruptcy of Eugene (Dean) W. Plonta. Sears, Roebuck and Co., the appellant, claims to be a secured creditor of the bankrupt

Plonta. Wadsworth Bissell, trustee in bankruptcy, is the appellee. The parties will be referred to as the Bankrupt, Sears and Trustee, respectively.

The pertinent facts are not in dispute and may be stated as follows: The Bankrupt purchased a 22–foot cabin cruiser from Sears on a conditional sales contract April 30, 1956. The cruiser was in kit form and by agreement between the purchaser and seller, the boat hull, engine, parts and equipment were to be shipped for assembly to North Shore Marina, Incorporated, at Grand Haven, Ottawa County, Michigan. The various parts and equipment arrived at the marina about the middle of May, 1956. The boat was completed and given a trial run on July 3rd or 4th.

After the trial run, the boat remained at the marina for the installation of some additional items of equipment purchased by the Bankrupt and for which he paid the marina. On June 13, 1956, the Bankrupt executed and delivered a promissory note to Sears, for the balance of the purchase price and gave a chattel mortgage to Sears covering the boat and equipment as security for the payment of the note. The chattel mortgage was filed in the office of the Register of Deeds of Muskegon county, Michigan, June 21, 1956. The mortgage was not filed with the Register of Deeds of Ottawa county, the county in which North Shore Marina was located. At all times pertinent to this litigation, the Bankrupt was a resident of Muskegon county.

The installation of the additional equipment was completed about the middle of August. At this time, the Bankrupt took the boat to the Muskegon Yacht Club, in Muskegon county, docked it there one night and then returned it to North Shore Marina, in Grand Haven. It was then taken to a marina in Bear Lake channel, in Muskegon county, and left there two or three nights and again returned to Grand Haven. The Bankrupt traveled back and forth between North Shore Marina and Bear Lake channel until the latter part of August. At this time he was able to rent docking facilities in the channel. The boat remained here until October, when it was returned to the marina in Grand Haven and stored for the winter.

During the following year 1957, although the Bankrupt sometimes used the boat, it was continuously kept at the marina in Grand Haven for repairs and storage. On December 16, 1957, Sears repossessed the boat in foreclosure of its chattel mortgage and paid North Shore Marina its accumulated storage, repair and upkeep charges against the Bankrupt. About two hours after the repossession, the Bankrupt filed his petition in bankruptcy. The time relation between these two events was coincidental and not a race for priority. Subsequent to the repossession, Sears sold the boat for $2300, which was considered to be its fair and reasonable value.

The history of the litigation is as follows: On January 13, 1959, the Trustee filed a petition to require Sears to turn the $2300 over to the bankrupt estate. There was a hearing on this petition and the referee found from the facts above stated that the location of the boat for the purpose of filing a chattel mortgage, under Michigan Statutes Annotated 26.929, M.C.L.A. § 566.140, was Ottawa county, Michigan. He further found that the mortgage was invalid as to the Trustee for failure to file with the Register of Deeds of Ottawa county, and ordered Sears to turn over $2300 to the estate. There was a petition for review of this order and on review the District Judge adopted the referee's findings of fact and conclusions of law and sustained his order.

Later counsel for Sears moved to set aside this order and for reconsideration of its petition for review. In the meantime, the Supreme Court of Michigan had decided the case of Schueler v. Weintrob, 360 Mich. 621, 105 N.W.2d 42, in which it was held that repossession by a mortgagee prior to the time of filing a petition in bankruptcy was in legal effect equivalent to filing in the county of location (M.S.A. 26.929) and deprived the Trustee in Bankruptcy of any rights under section 70, sub. c of the Bankruptcy Act. (Sec. 110, sub. c, Title 11, U.S.C.A.)

A motion was then filed on behalf of the Trustee for the court to receive additional testimony or remand the matter to the referee to take testimony concerning the extension of credit to the Bankrupt between the date of the execution of the mortgage on June 13, 1956, and the repossession of the property on December 16, 1957. The court sustained the motion and remanded the case to the referee for the purpose of taking further evidence. Upon hearing the referee found that within the interim period involved, Albert B. Doherty extended credit to the Bankrupt in the amount of $10, without knowledge of the mortgage and it was unpaid. The referee concluded that the existence of this interim creditor invalidated the mortgage as a security document pursuant to section 70, sub. e (Sec. 110, sub. e(1), Title 11 U.S.C.A.) of the Bankruptcy Act and that the benefits of the invalidity inured to all the general creditors of the Bankrupt. The turnover order of $2300 was again entered. On petition for review, the District Judge affirmed the order of the referee. In a subsequent order, the motion of Sears to vacate the original order of the court, dated October 20, 1960, was denied.

The first question presented for our consideration is whether, under the law of Michigan, the chattel mortgage should have been filed in Ottawa county, as well as Muskegon county. The Michigan Statute (M.S.A. 26.929) provides: "Every mortgage or conveyance intended to operate as a mortgage of goods and chattels which shall hereafter be made which shall not be accompanied by an immediate delivery and followed by an actual and continued change of possession of the things mortgaged, shall be absolutely void as against the creditors of the mortgagor, and as against subsequent purchasers or mortgagees in good faith, unless the mortgage or a true copy thereof shall be filed in the office of the register of deeds of the county where the goods or chattels are located, and also where the mortgagor resides * * *."

The referee found and concluded, from the facts as stated herein, that Ottawa county was the county of location and under the Michigan statute the mortgage should have been filed there.

* * *

We are bound by the finding of the referee and the District Judge that under the law of Michigan the mortgage was required to be filed in Ottawa county, unless such finding is clearly erroneous. * * *

The conclusion of the referee, affirmed by the trial judge, is amply supported by the evidence. His interpretation of the facts and the inference drawn therefrom as to the location of the boat was warranted and certainly not clearly erroneous.

The mortgage then was invalid, under the Michigan statute (M.S.A. 26.929) as to creditors of the Bankrupt. After the opinion of the court on the question of the necessity of filing the mortgage in Ottawa county, it seemed that Sears' security might be salvaged by the decision of the Supreme Court of Michigan, in Schueler v. Weintrob, 360 Mich. 621, 105 N.W.2d 42, to which reference is heretofore made.

Counsel for the appellant objected to having the case remanded to the referee for further consideration and a determination of the Trustee's rights under section 70, sub. e of the Bankruptcy Act. We find no merit to the appellant's claim that the court erred in remanding the case to the referee for further hearing. It was the duty of the District Judge to see that there was a full and complete discovery of all available evidence pertinent to any issues presented by the facts and law involved.

Section 70, sub. e(1) of the Bankruptcy Act (110, sub. e(1), Title 11, U.S.C.A.) provides: "A transfer made or suffered or obligation incurred by a debtor adjudged a bankrupt under this title which, under any Federal or State law applicable thereto, is fraudulent as against or voidable for any other reason by any creditor of the debtor, having a claim provable under this title, shall be null and void as against the trustee of such debtor."

The following facts, as found by the referee, are substantiated by the evidence: The mortgage was not filed in Ottawa county as required by the Michigan statute. Albert B. Doherty became a creditor in the amount of ten dollars July 20, 1957, when the mortgage was off record and his claim was provable against the Bankrupt under the Bankruptcy Act. The conclusion of the referee, sustained by the District Judge, that the mortgage being invalid under the Michigan statute as to interim creditor Doherty, was null and void as against the Trustee, is a correct application of the law. * * * Moore v. Bay, 284 U.S. 4, 52 S.Ct. 3, 76 L.Ed. 133.

So far as we have been able to ascertain, the amount of the credit extended is immaterial and the validity or invalidity of the chattel mortgage is not affected by the size of the creditor's claim. Neither is it material that the debt was not scheduled or that the creditor did not know of the existence of the chattel; nor is it necessary to prove that the creditor would not have extended the credit if he had known of the mortgage. Counsel for the appellant have cited no authorities in support of these claims.

Finding no error in the record, the judgment of the District Court is AFFIRMED.

Notes

1. The adoption of the UCC in Michigan reversed Plonta. To see why, review 9–201.

2. By far the most common use of section 544(b) are cases where a trustee seeks to use an unsecured creditor's rights under the applicable state fraudulent conveyance law. The trustee might use this route (rather than the more direct route through section 548) because the transfer occurred more than one year before the filing or because the local law is more favorable for other reasons. Local fraudulent conveyance laws fall into one of three classes, the Uniform Fraudulent Conveyance Act, the later Uniform Fraudulent Transfer Act or some homegrown variation of English or other law on fraudulent conveyances.

Where 544(b) applies, it "avoids" the entire transfer—and so is more threatening than a section like 551 that merely "subordinates". Thus Doherty's $10 could have upset a $300 million loan in its entirety under 544(b) whereas Doherty's claim under 551 is hardly a fly speck—the right to the first $10, leaving everyone else in place. Note the specific provision in 544(b) that denies its use to subrogate the trustee to the rights of a secured creditor. If the trustee could assume the rights of every senior creditor over every junior creditor under 544(b), the world would be turned upside down.

§ 6. PREFERENCES, SECTION 547

We have touched on section 547 above. Because preferences offer interesting and intricate intellectual problems, they probably command more law school time than they deserve. But part of lawyers' fun is playing with such puzzles.

The principal goal of the preference rule is to prevent a debtor from favoring one creditor over others similarly situated through a transaction occurring within a short period prior to bankruptcy. Evidently Congress believed that one who sees bankruptcy on the horizon, and who is already insolvent, should not be free to favor one creditor over another, but should be required to treat all alike. Congress also wished to preserve the debtor's going concern value by diminishing the creditors' incentive to dismember the debtor. Thus, the classic preference is the simple payment on the eve of bankruptcy of one creditor's debt when comparable payments are not being made to others, or the seizure of an asset by one creditor's judicial process. Such a transfer or seizure might disable the debtor, so destroying its going concern value.

A second common form of preference is to give property to a creditor, not in the form of money but in the form of a grant of a security interest to secure an earlier loan—"after thought" security. The granting of an unavoidable security interest to a creditor has the same consequence—at least for competing creditors—as the payment of that creditor's debt, true?

Still different is a preference given by means of the *perfection* of a previously created security interest within 90 days. One might think that the "transfer" between the creditor and the debtor should be considered to have occurred when the security agreement was executed and a property interest conveyed to the creditor. That creditor could argue that he was not an "after-thought" creditor for he had received the grant of a security interest well before the 90–day period. Here we assume a case in which a security agreement was signed and the loan made long before the 90 days, but where perfection occurred within 90 days of bankruptcy.

Section 547 condemns this transaction (though for different reasons) just as much as the one in which the security transfer, and its perfection, occurs after the loan and within the 90 days. True, the creditor here is not an after-thought creditor; he bargained for his transfer at a time when bankruptcy was not imminent. This creditor may be guilty of another kind of crime, namely that of holding an undisclosed security interest. If we uphold a security agreement that is executed long before the 90 days but perfected by a public filing for the first time on the eve of bankruptcy, we make it easier for the debtor and a conspiring creditor to keep that transfer secret, to mislead other creditors into lending in the belief that the debtor has not granted a security interest, and thus ultimately to distort the distribution in bankruptcy. In this case the preference legislation can be justified as an attack on "secret liens." By putting the creditor at risk for 90 days *after* he perfects, the bankruptcy law makes the granting of such a secret lien more risky than it would otherwise be.

There are variations on these themes: What if a secured creditor's pot is filled by after-acquired property, property acquired for the first time within the 90 days? Before 1978 the secured creditor could argue that such a "transfer" of after-acquired property occurred at the time of perfection, outside the preference period, but the 1978 Code nixes that argument. So a DIP will be able to avoid some security interests to the extent that they attach to collateral acquired within 90 days of bankruptcy. A second variation is the preference that occurs not by an intentional late filing, but by a mistaken one. This is the creditor who makes the loan and intends to perfect at once but perfects later, when, for example, he learns that his first financing statement was not filed in the right place.

Read section 547(b):

Except as provided in subsection (c) of this section, the trustee may avoid any transfer of an interest of the debtor in property—

     (1) to or for the benefit of a creditor;

     (2) for or on account of an antecedent debt owed by the debtor before such transfer was made;

     (3) made while the debtor was insolvent;

     (4) made—

         (A) on or within 90 days before the date of the filing of the petition; or

(B) between ninety days and one year before the date of the filing of the petition, if such creditor at the time of such transfer was an insider;

(5) that enables such creditor to receive more than such creditor would receive if—

(A) the case were a case under chapter 7 of this title;

(B) the transfer had not been made; and

(C) such creditor received payment of such debt to the extent provided by the provisions of this title.

The trustee or DIP must satisfy all five of (b)'s conditions to void a transfer. If it fails on one, the transfer is not voidable. Several will seldom be disputed. First, the debtor is presumed to be insolvent within the 90 days; thus the trustee will invariably satisfy subsection (b)(3). Second, the transfer will almost always be "to or for the benefit of the creditor", so subsection (b)(1) will seldom be an issue. The same factors that control subsection (b)(2) are likely to control subsection (b)(4) and vice versa. Thus, for example, if the creditor can convince the court that the transfer occurred outside the 90 days, he may be simultaneously convincing the court that the transfer occurred at the same time as the giving of value and therefore that subsection (b)(2) is not violated. Invariably when a security interest is at stake, the time of the transfer will be critical.

The time of transfer is a technical matter governed for the purposes of 547 by 547(e):

(e)(1) For the purposes of this section—

(A) a transfer of real property other than fixtures, but including the interest of a seller or purchaser under a contract for the sale of real property, is perfected when a bona fide purchaser of such property from the debtor against whom applicable law permits such transfer to be perfected cannot acquire an interest that is superior to the interest of the transferee; and

(B) a transfer of a fixture or property other than real property is perfected when a creditor on a simple contract cannot acquire a judicial lien that is superior to the interest of the transferee.

(2) For the purposes of this section, except as provided in paragraph (3) of this subsection, a transfer is made—

(A) at the time such transfer takes effect between the transferor and the transferee, if such transfer is perfected at, or within 10 days after, such time, except at provided in subsection (c)(3)(B);

(B) at the time such transfer is perfected, if such transfer is perfected after such 10 days; or

(C) immediately before the date of the filing of the petition, if such transfer is not perfected at the later of—

(i) the commencement of the case; or

(ii) 10 days after such transfer takes effect between the transferor and the transferee.

(3) For the purposes of this section, a transfer is not made until the debtor has acquired rights in the property transferred.

Generally, the subsection gives a secured creditor a 10 day grace period in which to perfect. If it perfects within that time, the "transfer" is deemed to have occurred at the earlier point when the security agreement was signed or the loan made. This relation back causes the transfer to occur simultaneously with the giving of value and thus to make the transfer *not* for an antecedent debt. Note that the tests for perfection with respect to real estate and personal property are different.

The final condition, subsection (b)(5), finds its principal importance with respect to payments to secured creditors. The very idea of a preference is that the transfer enables one creditor to get more than it would have gotten if there had been liquidation immediately prior to the transfer. If a creditor has a security interest that is perfected and that gives it a claim to collateral equal to the value of its debt, no payment to that creditor will enable it to receive more than it would have received under Chapter 7 (i.e., on liquidation) without the transfer. That is because the creditor would take 100 cents on the dollar on liquidation, namely the amount for which its collateral could be sold, and not more. To the extent that it receives a payment prior to liquidation, its claim would be reduced and it would be entitled to only 100 cents on the remaining debt. The payment frees collateral for others. Thus, a secured creditor with a $100,000 claim and collateral worth $120,000, will receive $100,000 on liquidation. A pre-bankruptcy payment up to $100,000 will not improve its position or injure others. Even though the payment comes out of the estate, the estate is not diminished because that payment frees $100,000 of collateral for the other creditors. Hence no preference, 547(b)(5).

After mastering the substantive provisions in section 547(b), turn to the exceptions in subsection 547(c). With the 1984 amendments, the exceptions have become so expansive that they may be more important than subsection (b) itself. Subsection (c)(1) might be looked upon as a loosening of the restraints imposed by subsection (b)(2). For example, it would cover the case in which a creditor transferred goods to a debtor, the debtor paid by check, and the check cleared only a week or ten days later. On a strict reading of subsection 547(b) the transaction might constitute a voidable preference because the payment coming ten days after the creditor's transfer of goods might be regarded as for an antecedent debt under (b)(2). Presumably (c)(1) would stretch the antecedence requirement at least this far and would take the transaction out of section 547.

A more difficult question is whether subsection (c)(1) ever applies to extend the ten-day relation back rule for filing that is embodied in subsection 547(e)(2)(B). It seems doubtful that Congress intended subsection (c)(1) to change the specific requirement of ten days in subsection 547(e).

Many payments both to secured and unsecured creditors that would otherwise be voidable preferences will now be saved by subsection (c)(2). Study the subsection to see which payments within the 90–day period might not qualify under subsection (c)(2). Surely it cannot be intended to save all payments. Prior to the 1984 amendments, subsection (c)(2) was much more limited. As it existed prior to 1984, subsection (c)(2) applied only to payments made "not later than 45 days after the debt was incurred." Under that version only short-term obligations such as trade credit or utility obligations could conceivably be covered and payments to commercial lenders rarely fit within the 45–day rule. With removal of the 45–day limit in 1984, it is open season on payments of debt irrespective of when the debt was incurred.

Subsection (c)(3) protects purchase money interests that might otherwise fall afoul of (b), and subsection (c)(4) is to cover the case where the creditor receives a preference but later makes a loan to the same debtor.

Subsection (c)(5) is intricate and interesting but of limited significance. It deals with after-acquired property and we will see it in problem 7–10.

The following analysis, in steps, is useful in applying section 547:

1. Did the debtor make a transfer "of an interest of the debtor in property?" See subsections 101(48) and 547(b).

2. When was the transfer made? See subsection 547(e). Note that if the transfer was a payment, it was made at the time it took effect between the parties. See subsection 547(e)(2)(A). If, however, the transfer was the grant of a security interest, it may have been made later than the time it was effective between the parties. Thus, if a security interest attached on July 1 but was perfected by filing on July 15, the transfer was made—at the earliest—on July 15. Read subsection 547(e) carefully.

3. Was the transfer voidable because all five conditions in 547(b) were satisfied?

4. If the answer is yes, was the transfer saved by any of the five exceptions in subsection 547(c)?

Problem 7–6

Debtor, a small business, borrowed $200,000 from Creditor 1 on July 1 and $400,000 from Creditor 2 on July 15. The loans were unsecured. Debtor issued Creditor 1 a note payable in six months and issued Creditor 2 a note payable on demand. Debtor filed a petition on December 1.

Can either of the following transfers be avoided under subsection 547? The DIP asserts that they are all "unfair" grabs within the 90 day period and should be avoided.

1. On September 15, Creditor 1 "coerced" Debtor into granting a security interest in certain collateral in consideration of the existing $200,000 debt. Creditor 1 perfected the security interest by filing on September 17.

2. On October 20, Creditor 2 demanded payment of the note. Debtor paid Creditor 2 $175,000 by check on October 25.

Problem 7–7

In the ninety days before bankruptcy Debtor makes payments in four situations. Which of these payments is protected by 547(c)(2)?

1. Debtor makes payments to various utilities for electricity, phone and water.

2. Debtor makes a $2 million payment of a loan that is amortized at $2 million per month. Assume alternatively that (i) Debtor made payments regularly until six months ago and this is the only payment in the last six months, or (ii) Debtor has never missed a payment.

3. Debtor makes a $2 million payment on a loan where its practice has been to make large payments at irregular intervals. This is the only payment this year and that Debtor made two payments last year—one in January and one in December.

4. Debtor makes a $2 million payment. This is the only payment the Debtor has ever made on the $10 million line of credit that has been outstanding for six months.

Problem 7–8

Unsecured Creditor comes to Debtor and demands payment of its $5 million claim on which Debtor is in default. Creditor offers alternatively to take security or to take a letter of credit.

1. Eighty days before bankruptcy Bank issues a $5 million letter of credit to Creditor with Debtor as applicant. Debtor grants Bank no security. Preference?

2. The letter in 1. is called by Creditor and Bank pays Creditor ten days before the bankruptcy. Preference?

3. Debtor gives Bank a perfected security interest (to secure its promise of reimbursement) at the time the letter is written. Preference? Here Bank argues no preference because it gave new value in the form of its new promise. Surely there is new value, but surely there is a preference here somewhere, not so? Consider the language of 547 "for the benefit of a creditor" and the language of 550 that allows recovery either from the one benefited or from the initial transferee.

The Special Case of the "Floating Lien" in Bankruptcy
Sections 552 and 547(c)(5)

Recall that Article 9 permits a secured party to create a security interest in existing and after-acquired collateral and proceeds in a single, written security agreement and to perfect that security interest by filing a single financing statement. If the financing statement is filed first, the security interest attaches to and is perfected in the after-acquired collateral when the debtor has "rights in the collateral", 9–203(1). Under Article 9 that creditor has priority over almost all later creditors, see 9–317 and 322.

An initial problem for the secured creditor with an after-acquired property clause in a Chapter 11 debtor's assets is posed by section 552(a) which reads as follows:

> Except as provided in subsection (b) of this section, property acquired by the estate or by the debtor after the commencement of the case is not subject to any lien resulting from any security agreement entered into by the debtor before the commencement of the case.

> Subsection (b) of 552 gives back some of what is taken away under 552(a). Subsection (b) allows the security interest to attach to "proceeds, products, offspring, rents, or profits." Thus if new inventory is proceeds of old inventory and if the secured creditor's claim does not depend exclusively on an after-acquired property clause, the security interest will attach. However, even the modest concession with respect to proceeds and products given by 552(b) is subject to the discretion of the court and does not apply if the court, "based on the equities" of the case, orders otherwise.

Property that was acquired within 90 days of the date of the petition in bankruptcy and so first came within the grasp of the after-acquired property clause will be claimed by the DIP on the ground that the attaching of the security interest to that property was preferential. Outside of bankruptcy, priority against other secured creditors is determined by the time of the filing (9–322), yet it is clear that the security interest is effective between the debtor and secured creditor at the time of attachment. If attachment occurs within the 90 days before bankruptcy, 547(e)(3) treats that as the time of transfer. Thus, in bankruptcy at least, the transfer in after-acquired property is for an antecedent debt.

Grain Merchants of Indiana, Inc. v. Union Bank and Savings Co., 408 F.2d 209 (7th Cir.1969) decided under the UCC but prior to the Bankruptcy Reform Act of 1978, held that a secured creditor had an unassailable security interest in after-acquired collateral. In that case the trustee challenged secured creditor's right to after acquired accounts receivable that had arisen within the preference period preceding the debtor's filing. The trustee reasoned that no transfer could occur until the asset transferred came into existence and at that time the creditor was not making contemporaneous loan advances, so the after-acquired accounts receivable constituted preferential transfers.

The secured creditor's most powerful response was that no other creditor had been injured or misled by the "turnover" of collateral, whether that collateral constituted inventory, accounts receivable, or something else. In *Grain Merchants* the secured creditor put forward several other arguments. The central textual argument was that the transfer as defined in section 60 (the predecessor to section 547) had occurred at the time the security interest became so far perfected that no lien creditor could have priority over it. Under Article 9 the secured creditor maintained that this event occurred upon filing, an act that occurred well outside of the preference period. The court accepted that argument, but this left critics uncomfortable. For example, the argument would have validated the acquisition of after-acquired property where the creditor coerced the debtor into building up its accounts receivable or inventory immediately prior to bankruptcy and so arguably preferred the secured creditor over others. Since the transfer would have been deemed to have occurred when the financing statement was filed, long before the preference period, there would be no preference even in that case. In response to these concerns, Congress passed 547(e)(3) which destroys the creditor's textual argument used in *Grain Merchants*. In addition Congress added subsection 547(c)(5) which protects after-acquired property claims where there is no "buildup."

Grain Merchants' accepted several other creditor arguments that section 547 does not address. One is that the accounts receivable should themselves be looked at as a "single entity" that is transferred at the outset even though individual accounts come and go. If one regards the "property" as some metaphysical group of accounts and not as single accounts, then 547(e)(3) does not necessarily invalidate a transfer. But surely it rejects this argument. It contemplates the possibility that each item of inventory, each account receivable—commonly recognized as having an individual identity—is to be treated separately for the purpose of bankruptcy.

Another argument appearing in the *Grain Merchants'* decision that has continued vitality is the "substitution of collateral doctrine." Presumably no preference occurs when a secured creditor within the preference period agrees to allow its debtor to substitute one asset as collateral for another. In that case, contemporaneous value is given by the creditor's release of the original collateral in return for acquiring new collateral. In *Grain Merchants,* the court indicated:

> As existing accounts receivable were collected by Grain Merchants and deposited to its accounts at the bank, the funds from previously collected accounts were made available to the debtor, enabling it to continue in business and obtain new accounts receivable. * * * Here the newly arising accounts receivable may be considered as having been taken in exchange for the release of rights in the earlier accounts and for present consideration. 408 F.2d at 217.

Nothing in section 547 rejects the substitution theory; presumably it too has continuing vitality.

Problem 7–9

On July 1, Seller sold Debtor equipment on credit. Seller created and perfected a security interest in Debtor's "equipment, existing and after-acquired," and Debtor agreed to pay the balance of the contract price on January 2. On September 1, Debtor owed Seller $25,000 and the value of Debtor's equipment was $25,000. On October 1, Debtor sold the equipment to Buyer for $25,000 and used the proceeds to purchase new equipment from another seller. On December 1, the date of bankruptcy, Debtor owed Seller $25,000 and the value of the new equipment was $27,500.

1. The transfer of the security interest in the new equipment is not protected by (c)(5); do you see why?

2. Do any of the other safe harbor provisions apply?

Problem 7–10

On July 1, Debtor granted Secured Party a written security interest in "inventory, accounts and proceeds, existing and after-acquired." Secured Party made a first advance of $5 million and agreed to make additional advances over the next 12 months of no more than $95 million "in its sole discretion." A financing statement was filed on July 1.

On September 1, Debtor owed Secured Party $30 million and the collateral was valued at $25 million. On December 1, the date of bankruptcy, Debtor owed Secured Party $25 million and the value of the collateral (which had completely turned over) was $23 million.

1. Is the transfer of the inventory (clearly a preference to some extent under subsection 547(b)) saved by subsection 547(c)(5)?

2. On October 1 Debtor pays $10 million to Secured Party. Is this a preference? See subsection 547(c)(2). If so, and if Secured Party must return the payment, how should this affect the application of subsection 547(c)(5)?

3. On September 5 Secured Party advances an additional $10 million so the debt stands at $40 million and the collateral has a value of $25 million. Before the bankruptcy on December 1 the inventory turns over completely and now totals $35 million. DIP argues that there is a $35 million preference under 547(b) and only $25 million is saved under (c)(5). The Secured Party argues that (c)(5) saves the entire $35 million since the "gap" at the end is no smaller than it was 90 days earlier. Read 547(c) carefully and think about the implications of the arguments; the DIP should win. Do you see why? Do you see why the new advance on September 5 does not immunize other transfers under 547(c)(4)?

§ 7. LEASES, SECTION 365

Section 365 of the Code is so unclear in purpose and so filled with exceptions that it is nearly incomprehensible. Most of it deals with real estate leases and with executory contracts; in this course we ignore those issues. Here we are concerned only with personal property leases that are not security agreements. Review the materials in Section 6 of Chapter 1.

It is easy to summarize the application of section 365 to personal property leases. In general the DIP has the choice of returning the leased goods or of complying with the lease. To continue to use the goods, the DIP must normally cure past defaults and may have to give assurance of faithful future performance. But the significance of Section 365 is that it denies the power to keep the leased asset by paying its current value.

To understand consider an example. In the case of In re Lykes Bros. Steamship (p. 44) assume that over 20 years Debtor was obliged to pay a present value of $40 million for one of the ships. Assume the market value of the ship was only $30 million. If the DIP was a debtor who had granted a security interest in the ship, it could eventually "strip the lien" and force the unwilling creditor to accept $30 million in the plan of reorganization (and treat the remaining $10 million as unsecured debt entitled to a small payment that might be made to the unsecured). If on the other hand, the DIP had signed a lease (as that term is defined in 1–201(37)), the DIP would have to give up the ship or pay the $40 million value according to the terms of the lease.

For this difference between a lease and a security agreement to be important, the DIP must somehow value the ship at more than its $30 million "market value". If the DIP could buy a new ship on the market for a present value of $30 million, it would be foolish to lease one for a present value of $40 million. There are several reasons why a DIP might reaffirm an apparently uneconomic lease (or to enter a bargain at a price higher than $30 million). First the claim of a market at $30 million may be false; there may be a courtroom market at $30 million but no real market at that level. Second the market may not be open to the DIP (who by hypothesis is bankrupt), yet the DIP's current creditors are bound to it by agreement and may be made to stay with it against their will under section 365 if the DIP assumes the lease or crams down a plan. Third there may be other idiosyncratic qualities (like a large potential tax liability that would arise from cancellation of the lease) that tie the DIP to this lease or exclude it from the market. If any of these circumstances apply, the DIP's current lease may be more favorable than a market with an apparently lower price. Review In re Lykes Bros. Steamship at p. 44; the difference in the treatment of a security interest under 1129 and of a lease under 365 may have been the reason for the complicated arguments in that case.

§ 8. SECURED CREDITORS & THE PLAN OF REORGANIZATION, SECTION 1129

Most successful plans are negotiated, not imposed on unwilling creditors, but the law that grants the right to impose a plan is still important because all of the bargaining among the creditors and the DIP takes place in the shadow of that law. When the law is modified by Congress or clarified by the courts, the negotiations under it also change. Since this course deals principally with secured creditors, we ignore many of the provisions of 1129 and its fellow travelers. So beware, you are looking at Chapter 11 through a narrow lens here, much is omitted and some is distorted.

Before looking at 1129, one must review section 506 and visit section 1122. Because unsecured creditors are put into different classes than secured creditors, one must determine whether and to what extent a creditor's claim is secured for the purposes of 1129. Recall that a creditor with a perfected and unassailable security interest will nevertheless be unsecured for the purposes of Chapter 11 if that creditor's collateral is worth less than the amount of the claim. So a creditor with a $200 million claim on an Eastern Airlines aircraft worth $75 million will be treated in the plan as a secured creditor for $75 million and as an unsecured creditor for $125 million. Section 506 says so.

Under section 1122 only claims that are "substantially similar" can be put into the same class. Generally no secured creditor's claim is considered to be substantially similar to any other; therefore each secured creditor will have its own class. The same is not true of unsecured claims, and parties often fight over the inclusion or exclusion of a particular unsecured claim in or from a class. That issue may become particularly heated where a secured creditor also has a large unsecured claim that the secured creditor would like to include with other unsecured claims so the secured creditor (now voting its unsecured portion) can insure that no class votes for a plan.

Section 1126(c) provides that a class accepts only upon the affirmative vote of "two-thirds in amount" and "more than one-half in number". So a single holder of 34% of the value of the claims in a class can veto an approval by the others no matter what their number and even if they are unanimously in favor. To get the favorable vote of a friendly class of unsecured, the DIP may propose to exclude the secured creditor's overpowering unsecured claim from that class. The case that follows involves such a proposal.

BOSTON POST ROAD LIMITED PARTNERSHIP v. FEDERAL DEPOSIT INSURANCE CORPORATION

United States Court of Appeals, Second Circuit, 1994.
21 F.3d 477.

POLLACK, SENIOR DISTRICT JUDGE:

Debtor seeks confirmation of a Plan of Reorganization filed under Chapter 11 of the Bankruptcy Code. The Bankruptcy Court denied confirmation, holding that the Plan impermissibly (i) separately classified similar claims solely to create an impaired assenting class; and (ii) classified as "impaired" a class of residential security depositors whose interests were in fact benefited by the Plan. The District Court affirmed the Bankruptcy Court's rulings on both issues. Debtor challenges both holdings.

BACKGROUND

Plaintiff–Appellant, Boston Post Road Limited Partnership ("BPR"), is a limited partnership formed pursuant to the Connecticut Uniform Limited Partnership Act, Conn.Gen.Stat. §§ 34–9 to –82 (1993), consisting of a single individual general partner, George Boyer, and a single limited partner, George Myers. BPR was formed in 1984 to acquire and manage a residential and office complex located in Waterford, Connecticut. In March of 1988, BPR mortgaged the complex to Connecticut Bank and Trust Company ("the Bank") to secure a loan of approximately $1.6 million. BPR thereafter defaulted on the mortgage payments, and on July 20, 1990, the Bank instituted a mortgage foreclosure action in Connecticut state court. In January 1991, the Bank became insolvent, its assets were seized by the U.S. Comptroller of Currency, and the Federal Deposit Insurance Corporation ("FDIC") became the holder of BPR's mortgage.

The FDIC continued to pursue foreclosure of the mortgaged property and on August 1, 1991, the Connecticut Superior Court entered a judgment of strict foreclosure against BPR and set October 28, 1991 as BPR's last day for redemption. On that date, BPR filed a voluntary pro se petition for relief under Chapter 11 of the Bankruptcy Code in the United States Bankruptcy Court for the District of Connecticut, thereby staying foreclosure. Approximately six months later, on March 16, 1992, the FDIC filed its proof of claim in BPR's bankruptcy.

On June 18, 1992, BPR filed its Second Amended Plan of Reorganization (the "Plan") in the Bankruptcy Court. The Plan proposed the following seven classes of creditors:

Class 1—unsecured claims of residential tenants to security deposits entitled to priority under Section 507(a)(7) of the Bankruptcy Code;

Class 2—secured claims held by creditors with liens and/or security interests on or in the real estate asset of the debtor (i.e., the secured portion of the FDIC's mortgage);

Class 3—secured interests of residential tenants whose security deposits are being held by the Debtor in interest-bearing bank accounts;

Class 4—unsecured claims of trade creditors;

Class 5—unsecured deficiency claims of creditors who have some security for their debt but not enough to cover the full amount owed (i.e., the unsecured portion of the FDIC's mortgage);

Class 6—interests of the limited partner; and

Class 7—interests of the general partner.

In relevant part, the Plan proposed to pay the FDIC's secured claim (Class 2), estimated at $1.445 million, over a fifteen-year term, utilizing negative amortization with a balloon payment at the end of the fifteenth year following confirmation of the Plan; to pay the trade creditors' unsecured claims (Class 4), totaling approximately $5000, over a six-year term without interest; to pay the FDIC's unsecured mortgage deficiency claim (Class 5), estimated at $500,000, without interest following the earlier of a sale of the property or the fifteenth year following Plan confirmation;[1] and to pay the residential security deposit holders (Class 3) a rate of interest on their residential security deposits higher than that statutorily mandated. In essence, the Plan was fashioned to permit a possible "cramdown" under 11 U.S.C. § 1129(b), over the anticipated objections of the FDIC, by far BPR's largest unsecured creditor. Ultimately, Class 1 turned out to be non-existent; Classes 2 and 5 voted to reject the Plan; and Classes 3, 4, 6 and 7 voted to accept the Plan.

On August 12, 1992, the Bankruptcy Court (Robert L. Krechevsky, Chief B.J.) held a hearing on the Plan's confirmation. At the hearing, the FDIC challenged the Plan on several grounds. In particular, it faulted the Plan for (i) segregating the Class 4 unsecured trade debts from the unsecured mortgage deficiency claim of the FDIC solely to gerrymander an impaired class which would approve the Plan; and (ii) classifying as "impaired" the Class 3 residential tenants with security deposits who would receive a higher interest rate on their security deposits than the statutorily mandated rate.

After hearing initial arguments, the Bankruptcy Court requested briefs and thereafter rendered a decision denying confirmation of the Plan on October 2, 1992. In its decision, the Bankruptcy Court held that (i) the FDIC's unsecured claim should have been placed in the same class with other unsecured creditors; and (ii) the residential security deposits were not "impaired" within the meaning of Bankruptcy Code § 1124(1). In light of these two rulings, the Code requirements for Plan confirmation were not satisfied because the Plan failed to obtain an affirmative vote of a legitimately impaired class of non-insider creditors. The District Court affirmed on June 23, 1993, and the Debtor has appealed to this Court.

Discussion

A plan of reorganization under the Bankruptcy Code may be confirmed if either of two voting requirements is met: (i) each class of impaired claims has accepted the Plan, 11 U.S.C. § 1129(a)(8); or (ii) "at least one class of claims that is impaired under the plan has accepted the plan, determined without including any acceptance of the plan by any insider." 11 U.S.C. § 1129(a)(10). The latter makes available a "cramdown" procedure. If the debtor chooses to utilize the cramdown procedure (having failed to secure the vote of all the impaired classes), the plan must meet all of the statutory requirements enumerated in § 1129(b) (essentially that the plan is fair and equitable and does not discriminate unfairly against any impaired claims), in addition to the prerequisites of § 1129(a) which are imposed on every plan.

The voting structure set forth in the Bankruptcy Code for approval of a reorganization plan mandates that claims be placed in classes and that votes be counted on a class basis. Acceptance by a particular class of

---

1. During the hearing on approval of the debtor's disclosure statement, the FDIC chose to have the deficiency (excess of debt over the value of the property) treated as a separate unsecured claim. See 11 U.S.C. § 1111(b)(2).

creditors occurs when "at least two-thirds in amount and more than one-half in number of allowed claims of such class * * * have accepted * * * such plan." 11 U.S.C. § 1126(c).

Cramdown of a plan of reorganization involving claims secured by real property owned by the debtor also often implicates Sections 506(a) and 1111(b) of the Bankruptcy Code. Section 506(a) provides that a claim secured by a lien on property is considered secured up to the value of such property and unsecured for the remainder. In this case, the FDIC's claim, totaling $1,945,000, is secured by the Debtor's sole asset, a residential and office complex. The value of the property, as agreed to by Debtor and the FDIC, is $1,445,000. Thus the FDIC has a secured claim in the amount of $1,445,000 and is entitled to an unsecured deficiency claim for the remaining $500,000. Under Section 1111(b)(2), a secured creditor may elect to have its entire mortgage claim treated as secured notwithstanding Section 506(a), thereby waiving its entitlement to an unsecured deficiency claim and increasing the amount of its secured claim. Here, however, the FDIC did not make such an election and the time to do so has expired.

In a typical single asset real estate case such as this, the mortgagee creditor often objects to the proposed plan, thereby requiring the debtor to seek cramdown of the Plan over the mortgagee creditor's objection. Here the Debtor took two approaches in an attempt to obtain a consenting class of "impaired" creditors. First, Debtor classified the FDIC's unsecured mortgage deficiency claim of $500,000 separately from unsecured trade claims, which total only $5,000. If the deficiency claim were classified together with the other unsecured claims, the FDIC's vote against the Plan would preclude acceptance by that class. This is so because the amount of the FDIC's deficiency claim is one hundred times the amount of all other unsecured claims, making it impossible for Debtor to obtain the affirmative vote of two-thirds in amount of such class as required by Section 1126(c) of the Bankruptcy Code. Debtor's second approach to obtaining a consenting class of "impaired" creditors was to create a purportedly impaired class of residential tenants who placed security deposits with Debtor (Class 3). The Plan provided that holders of such claims would receive interest on their security deposits at a rate of 8% rather than the 5¼% mandated by Connecticut state law. Debtor asserted that this "enhancement" of that class' claims constituted "impairment" within the meaning of Section 1124.

Debtor contended that the approval of each of classes 3 and 4 satisfied the requirement of consent of an impaired class. (The consent of classes 6 and 7, the general and limited partners, could not be counted because these were insider classes.) Both the Bankruptcy Court and the District Court held (i) classifying the FDIC's unsecured mortgage deficiency claim separately from the unsecured claims of trade creditors solely to create an assenting allegedly impaired class was impermissible; and (ii) the class of claims comprising residential tenants with security deposits was not properly classified as impaired, because the value of such claims was enhanced—not impaired—under Debtor's Plan. These rulings precluded Debtor from obtaining acceptance of its Plan by an impaired class of claims, and thereby precluded cramdown. Debtor challenges both holdings on appeal.

A. Separate classification of the several unsecured claims was without a legitimate reason.

Section 1122 of the Bankruptcy Code generally governs classification of claims:

§ 1122. Classification Of Claims Or Interests.

(a) Except as provided in subsection (b) of this section, a plan may place a claim or an interest in a particular class only if such claim or interest is substantially similar to the other claims or interests of such class.

(b) A plan may designate a separate class of claims consisting only of every unsecured claim that is less than or reduced to an amount that the court approves as reasonable and necessary for administrative convenience.

While the section bars aggregating dissimilar claims in the same class, it does not explicitly address whether similar claims must be placed in the same class. This issue of the permissibility of separate classification of similar types of claims is one that has yet to be addressed by the Second Circuit, and it remains a "hot topic" both among practitioners and in the academic community. See Peter E. Meltzer, Disenfranchising the Dissenting Creditor Through Artificial Classification or Artificial Impairment, 66 Am.Bankr.L.J. 281 (1992).

In addressing this question, the Bankruptcy and District Courts in the instant action were guided by the holdings of several other circuits, in decisions cited infra, that similar claims could not be placed in different classes solely to gerrymander a class that will assent to the plan. See In re Boston Post Road Ltd. Partnership, 145 B.R. 745, 748 (Bankr.D.Conn.1992) ("The courts * * * have uniformly prohibited a debtor from classifying similar claims differently in order to gerrymander an affirmative vote in favor of a reorganization plan."); In re Boston Post Road Ltd. Partnership, 154 B.R. 617, 621 (D.Conn.1993) ("classes may not be manipulated so as to gerrymander the voting process and circumvent the § 1129 requirements"). The other circuits have generally held that separate classification of similar claims is permissible only upon proof of a legitimate reason for separate classification, and that separate classification to gerrymander an affirmative vote is impermissible. See, e.g., Phoenix Mut. Life Ins. Co. v. Greystone III Joint Venture (In re Greystone III), 995 F.2d 1274, 1279 (5th Cir.1991), cert. denied, 506 U.S. 821, 113 S.Ct. 72, 121 L.Ed.2d 37 (1992) ("[T]hou shalt not classify similar claims differently in order to gerrymander an affirmative vote on a reorganization plan.").

Debtor contends that the Second Circuit should decline to follow the leads of the other circuits. It urges that Section 1122 be interpreted to permit far more liberal separate classification of similar claims. Debtor attempts to support its contentions with reference to recent judicial interpretations of Section 1122, legislative intent, and policy considerations.

Debtor first cites two recent opinions by bankruptcy judges holding that separate classification of similar claims is in fact mandated. See In re D & W Realty Corp., 156 B.R. 140, 141 & n. 3 (Bankr.S.D.N.Y.1993) (holding that "separate classification is not only appropriate, it is in fact mandated by the Bankruptcy Code and Rules," but acknowledging that it "has not found [this opinion] articulated anywhere else"), rev'd, 165 B.R. 127 (S.D.N.Y. 1994); In re SM 104, Ltd., 160 B.R. 202, 218–19 (Bankr.S.D.Fla.1993) (holding that unsecured deficiency claims created by § 1111(b) are not substantially similar to other unsecured claims, while asserting that the "circuit courts and the majority of district and bankruptcy courts have missed the forests for the trees").

Debtor then notes that the wording of Section 1122 does not require that all unsecured claims be classified together, but merely states that only claims that are substantially similar may be placed together. Debtor contends that this wording, especially when compared with the less flexible wording of the Bankruptcy Act of 1898, reflects Congress' intent to dispense with the requirement that similar claims be classified together.

Finally, Debtor contends that prohibiting separate classification effectively bars the debtor in single-asset cases from utilizing the cramdown provisions of the Code. In single-asset bankruptcy cases, the creditor-mortgagee usually has an unsecured deficiency claim, which, if placed in the class containing other unsecured claims (usually trade debt), will often overwhelm the class. Consequently, the mortgagee will control the vote of the class and the debtor will be unable to present an impaired class to approve the plan. Debtor suggests that such an outcome creates a "conflict of interest": the mortgage creditor will vote its deficiency claim primarily to protect its interests as a secured creditor, whereas only those creditors who have truly unsecured claims should be the spokespeople of the unsecured class.

Debtor's arguments in support of its suggested interpretation of § 1122 are unavailing. First, the ruling in In re D & W Realty Corp., 156 B.R. 140 (Bankr.S.D.N.Y.1993) was reversed on appeal. In re D & W Realty Corp., 165 B.R. 127 (S.D.N.Y. 1994). The ruling in In re SM 104, Ltd., 160 B.R. 202 (Bankr.S.D.Fla.1993), runs counter to the overwhelming weight of judicial authority. All the circuit courts that have heretofore visited the question of when similar claims may be classified separately have held that similar claims may not be separately classified solely to engineer an assenting impaired class:

> [I]f § 1122(a) permits classification of "substantially similar" claims in different classes, such classification may only be undertaken for reasons independent of the debtor's motivation to secure the vote of an impaired, assenting class of claims. Greystone III, 995 F.2d 1274,

1279 (5th Cir.1991), cert. denied, 506 U.S. 821, 113 S.Ct. 72, 121 L.Ed.2d 37 (1992);

[A]lthough separate classification of similar claims may not be prohibited, it "may only be undertaken for reasons independent of the debtor's motivation to secure the vote of an impaired, assenting class of claims." Travelers Ins. Co. v. Bryson Properties, XVIII (In re Bryson Properties, XVIII), 961 F.2d 496, 502 (4th Cir.) (quoting Greystone III, 995 F.2d at 1279), cert. denied, 506 U.S. 866, 113 S.Ct. 191, 121 L.Ed.2d 134 (1992);

[I]f the classifications are designed to manipulate class voting * * *, the plan cannot be confirmed. Olympia & York Florida Equity Corp. v. Bank of New York (In re Holywell Corp.), 913 F.2d 873, 880 (11th Cir.1990);

The debtor's discretion to place similar claims in different classes is not unlimited, however. Classifications designed to manipulate class voting must be carefully scrutinized. There is potential for abuse when the debtor has the power to classify creditors in a manner to assure that at least one class of impaired creditors will vote for the plan, thereby making it eligible for the cram down provisions. Hanson v. First Bank of South Dakota, N.A., 828 F.2d 1310, 1313 (8th Cir.1987);

Unless there is some requirement of keeping similar claims together, nothing would stand in the way of a debtor seeking out a few impaired creditors (or even one such creditor) who will vote for the plan and placing them in their own class. Teamsters Nat'l Freight Industry Negotiating Comm. v. U.S. Truck Co. (In re U.S. Truck Co.), 800 F.2d 581, 586 (6th Cir.1986).

Indeed, some courts have gone even further, holding that a plan must classify all substantially similar claims together, regardless of the debtor's intent. See Granada Wines, Inc. v. New England Teamsters and Trucking Indus. Pension Fund, 748 F.2d 42, 46 (1st Cir.1984).

The preeminent case on the question is Greystone III, a case whose facts are quite similar to those in the instant case before the court. In Greystone III, the Court of Appeals for the Fifth Circuit observed that although similar claims may be placed in different classes, a wholly permissive reading of the statute would render subsection (b) of § 1122, which specifically allows separate classification of small claims, superfluous. In widely quoted language, the Fifth Circuit concluded:

[There is] one clear rule that emerges from otherwise muddled case law on § 1122 claims classification: thou shalt not classify similar claims differently in order to gerrymander an affirmative vote on a reorganization plan. Greystone III, 995 F.2d at 1279.

Furthermore, contrary to Debtor's position, several courts have concluded that an analysis of legislative history in fact sheds little light onto the meaning of Section 1122. See U.S. Truck, 800 F.2d at 585–86 (concluding, after careful analysis of the classification sections of the former Bankruptcy Act and legislative history of Section 1122, that "Congress has sent mixed signals on the issue"); In re Jersey City Medical Center, 817 F.2d 1055, 1060 (3d Cir.1987) (noting that "the legislative history behind § 1122 is inconclusive" regarding the significance of the wording of the section). Moreover, a reading of Section 1122 in the context of the rest of the Code suggests that discretionary separate classification of similar claims would undermine the Section 1111(b) election. As explained above, Section 1111(b) of the Bankruptcy Code permits an undersecured creditor to choose whether (i) its claim should be divided into a secured claim equal to the court-determined value of the collateral and an unsecured claim for the deficiency, or (ii) its entire claim should be considered secured. The purpose of the Section 1111(b) election is to allow the undersecured creditor to weigh in its vote with the votes of the other unsecured creditors. Allowing the unsecured trade creditors to constitute their own class would effectively nullify the option that Congress provided to undersecured creditors to vote their deficiency as unsecured debt.

Finally, approving a plan that aims to disenfranchise the overwhelmingly largest creditor through artificial classification is simply inconsistent with the principles underlying the Bankruptcy Code. A key premise of the Code is that creditors holding greater debt should have a comparably greater voice in reorganization. Thus, although Debtor protests that prohibiting it from separating the unsecured claims of the FDIC from those of its trade creditors will effectively bar single asset debtors from utilizing the Code's cramdown provisions, Debtor fails to persuade that a single-asset debtor should be able to cramdown a plan that is designed to disadvantage its overwhelmingly largest creditor. Chapter 11 is far better served by allowing those creditors with the largest unsecured claims to have a significant degree of input and participation in the reorganization process, since they stand to gain or lose the most from the reorganization of the debtor. This Court thus holds that separate classification of unsecured claims solely to create an impaired assenting class will not be permitted; the debtor must adduce credible proof of a legitimate reason for separate classification of similar claims.

In the instant case, Debtor was unable and failed to adduce credible proof of any legitimate reason for segregating the FDIC's unsecured claim from the unsecured claims of BPR's trade creditors. Debtor's reasons for why it should have been permitted to separately classify the FDIC's unsecured claim were: (1) the FDIC's and the trade creditors' unsecured claims were created from different circumstances and arise under different Bankruptcy Code sections; and (2) BPR's future viability as a business depends on treating its trade creditors more favorably than the FDIC. Neither is availing. The different origins of the FDIC's unsecured deficiency claim and general unsecured trade claims, claims which enjoy similar rights and privileges within the Bankruptcy Code, do not alone justify separate segregation. See Meltzer, supra at 299. More importantly, BPR has failed to present any evidence of a legitimate business reason for the separate classification of similarly situated unsecured creditor claimants. The trade creditors in Class 4 were few and consisted of a landscaper, property appraisers, rubbish removers, and accountants. None were essential to BPR's future. Both lower courts accordingly found an absence of a valid justification for the isolation of the FDIC deficiency claim. No evidence to the contrary was adduced.

B. The residential security holders are not a class entitled to vote on the Plan

Debtor classified the residential tenants whose security deposits it was holding as a separate and "impaired" class for the purposes of a cramdown under § 1129(a). In fact those interests were not harmed at all by the Plan, but are better off under the Plan. Under Connecticut law, residential security holders are entitled to interest on their security deposits at a rate of 5¼%. Conn.Gen.Stat. § 47a–21 (1993). Under the proposed Plan, the interest payable on security deposits held by the landlord was increased beyond the statutory rate to 8%.

Debtor urges that the word "impaired" in § 1124 be interpreted merely as "altered" or "changed" and contends that the Class 3 creditors' rights were certainly altered by the Plan. In support of its interpretation of § 1124, Debtor points first to the language of the statute, legislative history, and a recent Ninth Circuit opinion, In re L & J Anaheim Assoc., 995 F.2d 940 (9th Cir.1993), which allegedly adopted Debtor's interpretation of Section 1124.

This Court need not even reach the issue of whether an "altered" claim may qualify as "impaired." In this case, the Class 3 tenant security depositors could not constitute a voting class of creditors for purposes of effecting cramdown. Any claim for return of tenant security deposits would arise from the lease between the debtor and the tenant. Under the Bankruptcy Code, unexpired leases must be assumed or rejected by the Debtor. 11 U.S.C. § 365. When, as in the instant case, the Debtor does neither, the leases continue in effect and the lessees have no provable claim against the bankruptcy estate. Greystone III, 995 F.2d at 1281. The obligations assumed by the debtor under the continued leases constitute post-petition administrative claims. See 11 U.S.C. § 503(b)(1)(A). Such administrative claims are defined as priority claims under 11 U.S.C. § 507(a)(1), and must be paid in full in cash pursuant to 11 U.S.C. § 1129(a)(9)(A); their holders are not entitled to vote on a plan of reorganization. As the Fifth Circuit held in Greystone III:

> A debtor in Chapter 11 must either assume or reject its leases with third parties. 11 U.S.C. § 365. If the debtor does neither, the leases continue in effect and the lessees have no provable claim against the bankruptcy estate. See Matter of Whitcomb & Keller Mortgage Co., 715 F.2d 375, 378–79 (7th Cir.1983); In re Cochise College Park, Inc., 703 F.2d 1339, 1352 (9th Cir.1983). Under the Code, only creditors are entitled to vote on a plan of reorganization. See 11 U.S.C. § 1126(c). A party to a lease is considered a "creditor" who is allowed to vote, 11 U.S.C. § 1126(c), only when the party has a

claim against the estate that arises from rejection of a lease. In re Perdido Motel Group, Inc., 101 B.R. 289, 293–94 (Bankr.N.D.Ala. 1989). If, however, the debtor expressly assumes a lease, the lessee has no "claim" against the debtor under § 1126(a). See 11 U.S.C. §§ 365(g), 502(g). The rights created by assumption of the lease constitute a post-petition administrative claim under section 503(b)(1)(A) of the Code. LJC Corp. v. Boyle, 768 F.2d 1489, 1494 n. 6 (D.C.Cir.1985). The holder of such a claim is not entitled to vote on a plan of reorganization. 11 U.S.C. § 1126(a); In re Distrigas Corp., 66 B.R. 382, 385–86 (Bankr.D.Mass.1986). Greystone III, 995 F.2d at 1281. See also In re Cantonwood Assocs. Ltd. Partnership, 138 B.R. 648, 656 (Bankr.D.Mass.1992) (where Debtor neither assumes nor rejects leases, tenants' claims are post-petition administrative claims). Thus the Class 3 creditors' approval of the Plan was of no effect because its members were not entitled to vote on the Plan.

CONCLUSION

To summarize: Debtor's Plan of Reorganization was properly denied confirmation for lack of the assent of an impaired non-insider class of creditors. The unsecured trade creditors do not qualify as such a class; they were segregated without any demonstrated legitimate reason from like unsecured creditors, who rejected the Plan and whose claims predominated in amount over those of the trade creditors. Nor do residential security deposit holders qualify as such a class; as holders of administrative claims, they were not entitled to vote on the Plan of Reorganization.

AFFIRMED.

Turn now to section 1129. It has many conditions; we will bother with only a few. Note that the plan must give each non-accepting claimant (not just each non-accepting class) as much as that claimant would have received in a Chapter 7 liquidation, ((a)(7)(A)(ii)). At least one class must vote for the plan, ((a)(10)) and, the plan must be likely to succeed (be "feasible"), ((a)(11)).

The most critical subsections for our purposes are 1129(a)(8) and 1129(b). Since most classes will be "impaired" (some of their rights will be altered by the plan), either every *class* must accept or the plan must comply with subsection (b). That, of course, means that every disgruntled secured creditor by a single negative vote has the power to force the DIP to satisfy subsection (b) with respect to that creditor. To force a plan on a non consenting class (in this case on a single secured creditor who is the only member of its class) is to "cram down" the plan; subsection (b) is the cram down provision.

To cramdown on a secured creditor, the DIP must satisfy 1129(b)(2)(A); read it carefully and consider its meaning and significance:

With respect to a class of secured claims, the plan provides—

(i)(I) that the holders of such claims retain the liens securing such claims, whether the property subject to such liens is retained by the debtor or transferred to another entity, to the extent of the allowed amount of such claims; and

(II) that each holder of a claim of such class receive on account of such claim deferred cash payments totaling at least the allowed amount of such claim, of a value, as of the effective date of the plan, of at least the value of such holder's interest in the estate's interest in such property;

(ii) for the sale, subject to section 363(k) of this title, of any property that is subject to the liens securing such claims, free and clear of such liens, with such liens to attach to the proceeds of such sale, and the treatment of such liens on proceeds under clause (i) or (iii) of this subparagraph; or

(iii) for the realization by such holders of the indubitable equivalent of such claims.

Problem 7–11

Assume Bank holds a perfected security interest in twenty 737s of bankrupt Airline. The 737s are worth between $10 million and $15 million each; Bank's debt is $500 million. Which of the following plans could be approved under 1129(b) over the objection of Bank?

1. A plan that continues the Bank's security in the twenty aircraft which will be used by the reorganized airline. As part of the plan the new airline will promise to pay Bank $200 million over 10 years with interest at 10%. (It would be relevant whether the prime rate was 7% or 12%. Why?)

2. A plan to sell the 737s over a two month period and remit the proceeds to the Bank (assume that such a sale would probably bring $9–$10 million per plane).

3. A plan to give the Bank 49% of the stock of the new company (assume the DIP's investment bankers will testify that half of the reorganized company will be worth at least $300 million).

†